Go Big

ED MILIBAND

Go Big

How To Fix Our World

THE BODLEY HEAD
LONDON

1 3 5 7 9 10 8 6 4 2

The Bodley Head, an imprint of Vintage, is part of the
Penguin Random House group of companies whose addresses
can be found at global.penguinrandomhouse.com

Penguin
Random House
UK

First published in the UK by The Bodley Head in 2021

www.vintage-books.co.uk

A CIP catalogue record for this book is available from
the British Library

Hardback ISBN 9781847926241

Typeset in 11.5/15 pt Sabon LT Std
by Integra Software Services Pvt. Ltd, Pondicherry

Printed and bound in Great Britain by Clays Ltd, Elcograf S.p.A.

The authorised representative in the EEA is Penguin Random House Ireland,
Morrison Chambers, 32 Nassau Street, Dublin D02 YH68

Penguin Random House is committed to a sustainable future for
our business, our readers and our planet. This book is made from
Forest Stewardship Council® certified paper.

FSC
www.fsc.org
MIX
Paper from
responsible sources
FSC® C018179

For Justine, Daniel and Sam

And with profound thanks to Joel

Contents

Introduction   1

Part I A New Social Contract   13
    1. The End of the World   22
    2. A Housing Revolution   35
    3. Free to Choose   45
    4. Family Values   59
    5. Everybody's Business   70

Part II Life Beyond the Market   83
    6. That Which Makes Life Worthwhile   89
    7. Jobs of the Future   98
    8. The Time of Our Lives   109
    9. Lina and Goliath   119
    10. On Your Bike – and Your Feet   131

Part III Take Back Control   145
    11. Jury Service   150
    12. The Kids Are All Right   162

13. Westminster Doesn't Know Best   173

14. Constant Gardeners   184

15. The Wrong Trousers   196

Part IV Changemakers   207

16. You Only Get the Justice You Have the
Power to Compel   212

17. Twenty-First-Century Trade Unions   224

18. Follow the Money   236

19. The Preston Story   248

20. It Takes a Movement   257

Conclusion   271

Acknowledgements   275

Notes   279

Index   327

INTRODUCTION

Like many modern love stories, it began on the internet. The date was 17 March 2017. Radio presenter Geoff Lloyd – now my 'late in life' friend as his wife Sara calls him – wrote to someone who used to work for me. 'I've had an idea kicking around in my head for a few months, and for my own sanity I thought I'd ask the question, however ludicrous.' The email went on: 'Would Ed be interested in working on a podcast with me? I want to explore the new, big ideas from around the world. I'd love to play the everyman and have Ed explain accessibly what's coming out of the think tanks, academia and policy units ... I suspect this is preposterous, but if not, I'd love to talk.'

The truth is that I was immediately interested. I was a recovering ex-leader. Nobody can quite understand the impact of losing an election unless you've experienced it yourself, although I wouldn't recommend it. One minute you're discussing the phone call you would need to have with Barack Obama the day after your election, the next you're grateful for a call about your PPI.

As Geoff brilliantly saw, lots of people felt incredibly down. By March 2017 we had had Trump as well as Brexit, and the Labour Party was facing one or two issues of its own. We were all drawing inward. As he put it in the email, there was a 'huge potential audience of frustrated, progressive realists' and much of the debate on TV and radio was in a short bite-sized format, favouring a 'for and against' slugfest. What about a podcast format that just pitched ideas to make the world a better place? He also came up with a great name – *Reasons to be Cheerful*.

I was sceptical about whether it would work. When you have been in the front line of politics and then you retreat – enforced retreat in my case – you lose confidence, you start to get comfortable with your irrelevance. From being someone who delivered hour-long speeches without a note (sometimes successfully and sometimes not) I was now cautious and worried about venturing out into the public square. Let's be frank, this was a pretty ugly place. Broken bottles, old mattresses and pools of vitriol. In the period after I lost the election I did occasionally venture out into the ugliest corner of that square – Twitter – and people were encouraged, surprised, not to say flabbergasted, that I appeared to have a personality. By the way, if you're one of the people who tweeted, 'Where was this personality in 2015?' I know who you are and where you live.

This is all a long way round of saying the podcast idea came at the right moment. I was frustrated, I wanted a way to get big ideas across, to learn at the same time; and maybe it was a chance not to be too po-faced about it. So I said yes, and in the nearly four years *Reasons to be Cheerful* has been going we've spoken to academics, activists, campaigners, business people as well as mayors and prime ministers. It's not the big-name guests who have most often moved our listeners, but people new to us all who have had amazing insights and ideas for changing our world.

We have heard hundreds of ideas, from how to tackle inequality and renew our democracy, to ways of addressing the climate crisis, reining in the power of Big Tech and improving life in the workplace. Some ideas have been at the stage of conception, others are already being put into practice around the world. It turns out that if you lift your eyes you can discover solutions to so many of the problems we face. We have gone looking on behalf of our listeners and discovered that the answers are almost always out there somewhere. What I have learned is that the greatest challenge is not devising solutions but finding the imagination and political will to make them happen.

This book is inspired by the podcast but goes beyond it. Both draw on my profound belief that we need big changes to fix the problems we see in our society. But the aim of the book is to do something more than just gather twenty of the best or most radical ideas for change. It aims to ground these ideas in a broader analysis of the condition of our country, and what about it most needs to change. It seeks to paint a wider picture of the kind of society we need. In writing at length about these ideas, the book also offers a more thorough examination of their origins, why they have become a reality in some places and the challenges we face in making them happen.

Why do we need to 'go big'? We need only look at our recent history. In the last decade or so we have seen the biggest financial crash for eighty years, the biggest political crisis since the Second World War – Brexit and its aftermath – and, as I write, the worst public health crisis for a hundred years, resulting in the worst economic crisis for three hundred years. All three sets of events demonstrate the need for wide-ranging change.

The financial crisis marked a repudiation of a model of economics that bets everything on ever-greater faith in markets – not just in finance – as a one-way route to success. That model turned out to be a recipe not just for roaring inequality but also a massive economic crash, a crash which ordinary people – who had no responsibility for it – paid for with their jobs and the austerity that followed. While some reforms have been made to the banking system, we cannot honestly claim to have acted on the lessons of the crisis. Inequality continues to go unrestrained, assumptions about markets and their power still hold sway, and the squeeze on wages and living standards of most people has yet to be addressed. Acting on the deep implications of the financial crisis remains, more than a decade on, unfinished business.

Then there is Brexit. Wherever you stand on the issue itself, I think that vote – and the discontent it signified – tells us something profoundly important. The discontent was partly grounded in people's view about our relationship with the EU, but I am convinced it goes deeper. I learned this from many conversations in my constituency in Doncaster, which voted Leave by one of the largest margins in the country. So many people who voted for Brexit said similar things to me. 'I'm voting for a better future for my children.' 'Things need to change.' 'Things can't get any worse.' This discontent cannot be divorced from the aftermath of the financial crash – austerity and stagnant wages – but nor can it be separated from longer-term trends: the ongoing economic and social shock of deindustrialisation, the deeply exploitative world of work that many people face and fears about prospects for the next generation. Meeting this deep-seated wish for change, for something better, is certainly not going to happen without a significant transformation.

Of course, no sooner had the Brexit argument been settled by the result of the 2019 election than we had the awful visitation of coronavirus. We had read about pandemics in history books, but few believed one would happen in our lifetimes, and nobody has been immune. The death toll has been grim, the restrictions on normal life severe, and the long-term health and economic effects will be profound.

The pandemic has also done something else. It is as if the tide has gone out on our economy and society, exposing what lay hidden beneath the water – the best and the worst. The best is the British people, who have been stoical, communal, caring, compassionate, pulling together. That best has been extraordinary and we should not gloss over it. Think of all those who have put themselves in harm's way on behalf of us all: the carers, doctors, nurses, delivery drivers, supermarket workers, teachers, postmen and -women, those who work in the emergency services. While many of us have stayed comparatively safe they have been in the eye of the storm. Think too of the teams of scientists who developed vaccines in record time and the Nightingale hospitals built almost overnight. It is remarkable what people and government can do when the urgency and will are there.

We have also shown a degree of solidarity the like of which I don't think I have seen at any other point in my lifetime. One story of this crisis is the emergence of local mutual aid groups to help the elderly, vulnerable and those in need: a staggering 2,061 groups from Aberdeenshire to St Austell.[1] The evidence also suggests that our perceptions of society and one another have changed markedly in response to the pandemic. Before it, the predominant view was that ours is a country where people simply look after themselves, whereas now many more believe it's one where we look after each other.[2]

The best has made us proud, the worst – the inequalities and injustices in our society and economy, which we have allowed to exist under our noses – should make us ashamed. Those very same key workers, the people who really matter the most, who keep us safe, are so often paid the least and protected the worst. It may have become apparent who really matters when it comes to keeping our society going, but this is not recognised in the way they are treated.

Our society is so riven by inequalities in income and wealth that these differences have also shaped profoundly how we have been affected by the pandemic, from the quality of life under lockdown to matters of life and death. The country has been divided between those who can continue to earn a living from home and those who have no choice but to go out to work, sometimes with no assurance of safety. Meanwhile, our benefits system doesn't provide those in need with enough to subsist, even those who have been sick with Covid. Our public realm – underfunded, outsourced and devalued over at least a decade – was ill prepared for the pandemic.

In response to what we have experienced, we need to come to a realisation and make a choice. The realisation is that there is a yawning disconnection between the best in us – who we really are and the values we hold – and the society and the economy we have. It is time to reconnect our society with our values. The choice must be that when the tide comes back in, we cannot forget, we cannot ignore what was previously and may once again be hidden.

Each of these three crises is a manifestation of the underlying political, social and economic crisis that has been brewing across the developed world over the last forty years. Despite the promises, our political and economic system has failed to produce fairness and wealth for all, and instead has created deep inequalities, divisions and pain for many. Look ahead at what the future holds and the case for big change is further reinforced. The climate emergency threatens to render our planet uninhabitable for hundreds of millions of people, and we have been fiddling while the world burns. Meanwhile, the tech revolution, in particular automation, which has enormous liberating and democratic potential, will upend many of the assumptions about the jobs we do and threatens to reinforce inequality, not diminish it.

The Italian philosopher Antonio Gramsci wrote, 'The crisis consists precisely in the fact that the old is dying and the new cannot be born; in this interregnum a great variety of morbid symptoms appear.'[3] The reason this has been quoted a lot in the last decade is that it's true. We are in a strange kind of ideological interregnum. We are a long way away from 'the end of history' – the triumph of a particular ideology – which some people believed occurred at the end of the 1980s, but still trying to work out what comes next.

Logically, the financial crisis should have marked the end of an era, but we have struggled to come to terms with what a new settlement should look like. Deep injustices remain unaddressed, and it is high time we did something about them. If we do not, other, pernicious forces will fill the gap. Unless progressive change is not just promised but delivered, the appeal of the strongman, of false, simplistic solutions, will grow ever stronger and more dangerous. Donald Trump was indeed a morbid symptom. One apparent answer to these challenges is to defend the status quo more vigorously, another is to make modest changes to calm things down. But these responses mis-understand the soil in which these toxic political weeds grow. It is the conviction that our economy and society are failing people which helps these forces gain support. My case is that small changes cannot address the discontent and therefore will not deal with the roots of these dangerous movements.

The outcomes we have seen cannot be divorced from the dominant political ideology of the era. This can be summarised as follows. What is good for the richest is good for everyone else. Our economic system should prioritise them, then hope their wealth trickles down to everyone else. The best way for an economy to succeed is for governments to give the freest possible rein to the decisions and actions of individuals in the market. This ideology has played an outsized role in recent British history. Meanwhile, part of the challenge that demo-cratic politics faces is that the implicit message of the last few decades has been that some big problems – like the scale of inequality and injustice – are just too big to surmount, leaving the narrative about solutions to the dangerous politics of the Right. Both mainstream Left and mainstream Right bought into a language and approach to the forces of markets and globalisation which accepted that some of their results were unfortunate but inevitable and therefore beyond political reach.

So in saying we need to 'go big' I am advocating not just the consideration of ideas that promise significant change but for politics to rediscover its sense of agency. You may like my solutions – I hope so – or you may dislike them, but I am ask-ing that we believe again that politics can rise to the biggest challenges we face. We should never shrink from the injustices of our world and say they are simply too big to conquer.

If this sounds ambitious, it is meant to be. In truth, we have ignored a whole set of social and economic problems, and their accompanying political disaffection, for too long. For years we have had the wealth, the power, the know-how to create a different and fairer world. The real question has always been whether we have the inclination to do so. My sense is that more people than ever are open to persuasion on that score, and my hope is that this book might speak to that. There is cause for hope. In the wake of previous upheavals, society was remade. After the Second World War we saw major social and economic reform worldwide. In the UK this included the creation of the NHS and the modern welfare state. After the First World War and the 1918 pandemic the franchise was extended, for the first time children were required to stay in school until the age of fourteen, and women were given their first protection against employment discrimination.[4]

I cite these examples partly because they were a response not simply to the immediate catastrophe of the wars but to long-standing injustices and inequalities that hadn't been confronted. William Beveridge's famous report in the midst of the Second World War identified the 'five giants' of want, disease, ignorance, squalor and idleness.[5] These had long been seen as problems, but it was the experience of the war years which supercharged the belief that eradicating them was a priority. It is my view that the injustices and inequalities that have been building since before the events of the last decade require an equivalent remaking – and that is what this book is about.

Covid will obviously make improvement harder to achieve, as we struggle to deal with both public health challenges and the crises faced by businesses, workers and government. But this must be a moment of reckoning in which we look at our society and learn from the collective experience we have been through. That is what previous generations did, and we owe it to all those who have suffered in this crisis to do so again. If not now, when?

Of course, we should be sober about the scale of the task and the time it will take. Our problems are both broad and deep. If the issues we face have been brewing for a generation or more, turning them round will take at least a generation.

That informs the character of the ideas in this book. They are not designed with an electoral cycle in mind or for the next Labour manifesto and are definitely not a statement of Labour Party policy. Indeed, while I make no attempt to disguise where I am coming from politically, part of what I am trying to do is ensure that, like the podcast, this book isn't party political or at least not yah-boo-sucks party political. (One of the gratifying things about the podcast is that often an email from a listener will begin, 'Hi, Ed and Geoff. I am a Conservative but ...' And that is another interesting thing about this moment: people across the spectrum are looking for answers to our current predicament.) So this is not a party platform; hopefully some of the ideas will appeal to supporters of all parties and none. What I also hope to do is tackle the failure to think long term, beyond the limits of the electoral cycle, that has led to a lot of the problems we face being swept under the carpet to fester.

The nineteenth-century German politician Otto von Bismarck said, 'Politics is the art of the possible.' This has become a cliché used to make the case for compromise and pragmatism, and of course it is what a lot of everyday politics is about, including mine. Pragmatism and compromise can change people's lives for the better; in no sense do I diminish their importance. But I have come to believe that Bismarck was only partially right. In fact, the politics that matters as much, if not more, to people's lives in the long run is something else – it is that which makes the seemingly impossible possible. Think of some of the great changes that mark our political history, and have changed lives fundamentally: the universal franchise, trade union rights, the National Health Service, LGBT rights, a national minimum wage. All of them at one point seemed impossible, but became possible.

This need to champion big and irreversible change equal to the moment is something of which I have become more convinced in the last six years. This is a different book to the one I would have written in 2015, and it seems to me there are two ways that the impossible can become possible – two ways to go big.

Sometimes making the case for incremental change – the art of the possible – can be part of a vision which leads eventually to a set of more profound changes down the line. Margaret Thatcher realised this when she set about transforming the British economy in the early 1980s. She eventually privatised telecoms, water, electricity and gas. But what did she propose in her 1979 manifesto? None of these things. She later recalled that they seemed 'all but unthinkable' at the time.[6] So that manifesto merely proposed to sell off the nationalised aerospace and ship-building industries. In her first term she presented privatisation as the sale of a small number of publicly owned companies – a pragmatic choice to raise revenue for the government.[7] Even after the first set of privatisations of the 1980s, the idea that a national institution like Royal Mail should be in private hands would have been absurd. But those early moves sowed the seeds for what became a comprehensive programme to transform the economy, and when the Coalition government privatised Royal Mail thirty years later, the previously unthinkable occurred.

But there is also a different route forward – making the case for more profound change, even when it can seem out of reach. The case for a National Health Service was made in a minority report on the Poor Law in 1909.[8] At the time this seemed outlandish and unattainable. Only in 1948, four decades later, would it come to pass. If those seeking big change had lowered their sights to the art of the possible, that change might never have happened, but after struggle and difficulty, over decades, eventually they won.

There are moments in history when there is a recognition that things just cannot just go on as they did before – the case after World War Two. At these times big change can seem not only necessary but possible. As we seek to rebuild our country after coronavirus, as we contemplate the crises of the last decade, as we confront future threats, this is the moment to make the case for big change.

Making the case for radical change can also shift the terms of what is possible or acceptable in political debate – what is known as the Overton window – and in that way paves the way for much bigger change than seems conceivable at the time.[9] After I lost the general election in 2015, I approached David Cameron, George Osborne and others to suggest that the UK legislate for the principle of net zero greenhouse gas emissions – without demanding a specific date. Lots of people I talked to in the green movement were very sceptical I would get anywhere. After some discussion and the enshrining of net zero in the Paris Agreement, the government agreed to the principle, although they were reluctant to move quickly. Four years later, net zero by 2050 is seen as the least ambitious position in this debate. Of course, it is mainly scientific evidence about the pace of global warming that has driven this, but those who might be seen as impossibilists – like the people demanding net zero by 2025 – have also shifted the terms of the debate.

Debates often do not shift as quickly as this. But if we believe that our economy and society need big change, then both ways of getting there – making the case for incremental changes which point the way to a different vision of the country, and making the case for bigger ideas – are valid. You will find both types of ideas in this book. We can find a different and better way of living together. There are positive, optimistic ideas out there which can change the country. I hope you come away feeling uplifted, inspired, hopeful. That's obviously a big ask. At the very least, I want you to feel there *are* solutions. I would also like you to think that you can be part of building them.

What follows is divided into four parts, each of which speaks to a central problem I believe we face. The boundaries between the sections are not hard and fast. The solutions to the problems I outline overlap. You may well read a chapter in one part of the book and think it also has broader relevance to other themes in the book, and you would be right.

Part I starts with how the social contract – what we can expect from being members of society and what we owe to each other – has broken down in multiple ways. I set out what a renewed social contract might involve and some ideas about how to get there. Part II is about the role of markets in our country and the need for us to act collectively to protect the things we value, which markets alone cannot guarantee and may well actively undermine. Part III is about power – who has it and who doesn't – how we make collective choices about our society and how we rebuild a broken politics. It looks at how we can genuinely give people back control, from the way politics is run to the provision of public services to the voice of employees at work. Part IV is about how change happens, who can make it happen and what tools we have at our disposal to bring it about. Making the case for big ideas is one thing, but this final section is about how you can be part of making them a reality.

Contrary to what many people believe, I think it is possible to find a broad majority to support at least some of the ideas in this book. If ever a country needed a project of national renewal it is Britain in the years ahead. When I began in politics in the mid-1990s the parameters of how things might change were pretty clear. Today, everything is much more up for grabs. The next ten or twenty years could be bleak. Indeed the world is already pretty scary. But we can bring about profound and positive change. The future is not yet written. It's our job to write it. So let's do it.

PART I
A New Social Contract

Our (unwritten) social contract defines what we can expect from being members of society and the responsibilities we owe one another to make that possible. This is the invisible glue that binds our country together. When people feel that they don't have a stake in society, then the social contract breaks down, including our sense of obligation to each other. But while the particulars may change over time, there is one thing on which the contract relies above all: the shared sense that it is fair. This is what gives us the assurance that, whatever the challenges we face, we are all in it together.

The social contract familiar to the grandparents and great-grandparents of today was born out of the series of changes that were made in the aftermath of the Second World War. These involved the creation of a platform of decent public services, including the foundation of the NHS, a post-war housing boom, much of it council housing, and stable employment for men, much of it industrial. In theory, whoever you were, whatever your background, you were able to find a stable job that paid enough to feed and house your family, gave you a pension and guaranteed that your children would have better opportunities than you had. For a time there was full employment for men. We must not romanticise this era. The jobs were often hard and dangerous. Class stratification was deeply entrenched. Women had second-class status in the employment market (few worked, and even fewer in top jobs), and few people went into higher education. If you were LGBT or a person of colour there was enormous prejudice. Life was grindingly hard for many people.

As a result, there is a tendency to dismiss as pure nostalgia any hankering for these bygone days. Rationality says that people are miles better off today than they were back then, and most people are. But this profoundly misses the point. There is more to life than earning and owning, and the social contract and the collective institutions that supported it in post-war Britain offered some important things – not for all but for many. There was a degree of security about housing and employment prospects for people's children; a place in society which – as far as industrial jobs were concerned – conferred status and respect; a set of mutual support mechanisms through institutions from the church to trade unions. People felt they had a stake in society and that society valued them in return.

Modern life could not be more different. Its much greater fluidity is accompanied by a sense of opportunity and possibility for some. But with that, for others, comes a sense of being unmoored, an absence of control, a danger of being left out of prosperity. Sometimes politics is inhospitable to paradoxes, but in real life they exist. When I talk to older people in my constituency in Doncaster, where tens of thousands used to be miners, they don't clamour for those hard, dangerous jobs to come back, but they do believe something important has been lost. When we gather in November – as we have every year apart from 2020 – in the village of Bentley to commemorate the two pit disasters of 1931 and 1978, which killed forty-five and seven men respectively, we pay our respects to those victims and their relatives. We mark how dangerous mining was but also its important national role and the community that was built around each of the pit villages I represent.

The social contract of the post-war period blew up during the economic crises of the 1970s and was dismantled in the 1980s. The closure of the pits happened very quickly from the 1980s onwards but casts a long shadow, including in the communities I represent, generations later. In its place came a second social contract. This can be said to represent the settlement of Margaret Thatcher, later modified by Tony Blair. This was a much more atomised, less collective vision. Yet for a time it commanded a significant degree of support.

In this social contract, the argument went, the 'shackles' of high taxation and state regulation were thrown off. People were encouraged to work hard by being allowed to keep more of what they made, and working-class people were helped to own their own homes and pass them on to their kids. Just as we might romanticise the first social contract, so it is easy to demonise the second. But it appealed to something important. There may be more to life than earning and owning, but home ownership had hitherto been mainly the preserve of the middle class. The selling of council homes turned out to be in so many respects deeply damaging – most notably because they weren't replaced – but owning their own home gave some people an asset and security they had not had before.

By the 1990s, however, it was clear that this settlement was not at all what it seemed. Wealth did not trickle down as had been promised; most of it stayed with the rich and made them richer. Private affluence was combined with public squalor. That is where New Labour came in, investing significantly in public services and bringing greater fairness, including through the minimum wage and tax credits, which substantially cut child poverty, as well as social reforms, including big strides in the area of LGBT rights. These changes transformed people's lives for the better. At the same time, much of the economic framework of the Thatcher era was left in place. Privatisation was not reversed; trade unions remained weak and the labour market relatively unregulated; income and wealth inequality were not fundamentally altered. So we can identify a further, modified version of the second post-war social contract: a mix of Thatcher and Blair, still economically liberal but socially inclusive and with a strong belief in the public realm.

For a time this seemed a good combination, but it imploded in the financial crisis of 2007–8. In the decade that followed, those inequalities which had been tolerable when most people's incomes were improving became intolerable. It became apparent that the regional imbalances in the country, accentuated by the boom in financial services, had not been properly addressed. The jobs that were on offer to those who hadn't been to university entailed huge insecurity and gave little of the identity or security that industrial work had offered.

Today, in the midst of a pandemic, it's hard to assess the state of the social contract in Britain. By and large, people have sought to obey the laws and keep each other safe. It has been a time of social solidarity, as I noted in the Introduction. Our bonds with each other and our communities are stronger than before. But the issues that became increasingly apparent after the financial crisis have not gone away. Young people have been hit hardest by job losses in the Covid recession – on top of the student debt, unaffordable housing and job insecurity they faced anyway. As if that wasn't enough, the climate crisis will change the way they and their children live their lives. But older people too face a tough time. Many of the old certainties are gone. Some feel that a sense of community and belonging has been lost, and many worry about isolation.

The sense of a broken contract cuts across categories of age. Economic opportunity is concentrated in cities rather than towns, and there is a widespread belief that resources are concentrated in London. Inequality is a defining feature of life not only between parts of the UK, but also within them; consider for example the gulf between rich and poor that exists within cities. The gap between the richest and the rest is key here. The top 1 per cent, especially the top 0.1 per cent, have sailed off into the sunset compared to everyone else. Increasingly we are a country where money and opportunity go hand in hand: if you have the first, you will enjoy the second and can pass it on to your children, but if you don't, life is much more of a struggle.[1] Social mobility is at best stalled. We are not, in the resonant words of former prime minister John Major in the 1990s, 'a nation at ease with itself' and certainly not the 'classless society' to which he said he aspired.

Partly in consequence, those who govern us are trusted less by those who are governed. Given the wider breakdown in the social contract, it is hardly surprising that this bond is so much in question. For many people, the country simply fails to deliver for them. The deep story of the Brexit referendum is partly that of a repudiation of the second social contract, driven by a sense of loss of some aspects of the first. And yet there is no going back to the post-war social contract. It belonged to a totally different era, nor should we want to bring back many aspects of it. The second contract, meanwhile, was as profoundly discredited in the aftermath of the 2008 financial crisis as the first one was in the 1970s.

This is why we need to redraw the social contract for our time. The ultimate aim of any social contract should be to ensure everyone feels they have a stake in the society in which they live, a belief that the economic and social settlement offers something to them. But what does that actually mean? There are three building blocks which ensure everyone has a stake in society, each level providing a foundation for the next.

First and most fundamentally, having a stake means being able to meet basic needs. The social contract should guarantee a minimum standard of living below which people should not be allowed to fall. It is both appalling and shameful that in the fifth-richest country in the world we have hundreds of thousands of people reliant on food banks and millions of children growing up in poverty.[2] The starting point of any renewal must be to address poverty, but the sense of not having a stake goes beyond the poorest. Work must pay for people; jobs should carry status and recognition. Affordable, decent homes must be available to rent or buy. Some of these were elements of the first social contract. For our own time, they need to be reinvented.

Second, meeting the basics isn't enough if fear and insecurity about losing everything stalks the land. Under the post-war contract there was a sense that individual risk was shared with the state and business. The welfare-state safety net was designed to catch those who fell; there was much greater security of employment, and many were guaranteed a decent occupational pension. Today, by contrast, the state and private sector have loaded risk onto the individual – from the weakening of the welfare-state safety net to the loss of employment rights like workplace pensions or job security. This creates insecurity and the sense that we're each facing the world on our own.

The whole point of a social contract is to share rights and obligations, but lots of rights have been lost and lots of obligations conferred. It's no wonder people feel a sense of discontent and loss of control. There can of course be no return to the past – the 'job for life' of the post-war era is probably gone for ever – but economic fear is both corrosive and real, and the state and business need to step up in new and different ways to share the burden of risk. For the state, new approaches to social housing, parental leave, childcare, social care and social security can help rebalance risk away from individuals. For businesses it is about recognising, as many do but some do not, their obligations to workers and wider stakeholders rather than just the bottom line.

Third, a real stake means everyone having the opportunity to pursue their own idea of a good life. A minimum standard of living and protection against risk are important, but given all the technology and wealth at our disposal we can aim for something much more ambitious. This is about the ability to go where your talents and interests take you, what has been called the 'power to create'.[3] This is something that those with money, assets and opportunity can almost take for granted: real freedom. Everyone should have the platform to shape their own lives, regardless of the situation they are born into. This self-realisation goes beyond the material and is about, for example, time with loved ones, and control of that time, something explored later in the book.

A renewed social contract isn't just about everyone having a stake in society, about what we each individually have, but how we relate to each other. Think back to the phrase 'We're all in it together.' It can sound absurd because it has become a political cliché so far from the world that we inhabit, but it is the right aspiration because it speaks to a sense of social solidarity, of looking after each other. However, social solidarity will never be achieved if it feels like we're all signed up on different terms. In the post-war era, some people were of course paid more than others, but the gap now between those at the top and everyone else is of a completely different order.

Evidence from around the world is that more egalitarian societies have greater social solidarity, while the more unequal we are, the more people lead parallel, separate lives.[4] It is also the case that enabling everyone to achieve a meaningful stake in society is very difficult in the context of huge levels of inequality. Where one generation ends up is where the next generation sets out from. The further apart the rungs on the ladder, the harder it is to climb. For these reasons, a new social contract must address the enormous inequalities we face as a society.

This means addressing inequality in all its dimensions, including all those ignored previously. Racial injustice continues to shape people's life chances and their experiences. Fifty years on from the Equal Pay Act, we remain deeply unequal in our gender relationships. And then there is the injustice of climate breakdown, which at its heart is an intergenerational issue. All the chapters that follow are founded in the belief that we have an absolute obligation to restore the social contract for the young, that we owe it to them, and future generations, to live in a different way and not to act as if nobody is coming after us. As we face the task of renewing the social contract, this is the right place to start.

CHAPTER 1

The End of the World

It's 19 December 2009. I am standing in a hotel room in Copenhagen in my pants getting ready to go to bed for the first time in forty-eight hours. Those who know a little about me may not be surprised to learn that I haven't been on a two-day Nordic bender but am attending the UN climate talks as the UK climate change secretary. My phone rings as I am about to finally get some sleep. It is Pete Betts, the lead negotiator for my department: 'The agreement is going down the pan. Too many countries are objecting. You better come and try and do something.'

I reacted with horror. The high-profile summit was already a fiasco, dogged by arguments between developing and developed countries about who should bear the burden of tackling the climate crisis, whether the world's ambition was remotely adequate and whether countries could be legally bound to act. But the one thing that seemed to have been salvaged was a short, three-page agreement with some basic commitments including, for the first time in an international agreement, a commitment to seek to keep global warming below 2°C.[1]

This was in no small part due to the determination, cajoling and sheer bloody-mindedness of the UK prime minister Gordon Brown, who in the chaos of bitter recriminations that had begun before the summit was even over, had effectively taken control of it and stayed up all night to get the basic agreement, negotiating with a ragbag of heads of state and perplexed junior ministers from assorted countries. His parting words to me as he left for London the next morning were something like: 'OK, at least we've got this – don't screw it up now.'

His words rang in my ears as I got dressed and raced out of the hotel back to the conference centre in a blind panic. Many poorer countries were objecting to the inadequacy of the agreement. The chair of the powerful G77 bloc of developing countries, a Sudanese diplomat called Lumumba Di-Aping, had even compared the draft summit conclusions to the Holocaust: '[This] asks Africa to sign a suicide pact, an incineration pact in order to maintain the economic dominance of a few countries. It is a solution based on values . . . that funnelled six million people in Europe into furnaces.'[2]

My grandfather and other family members died at the hands of the Nazis. I was sleepless and outraged. Speaking from the United States microphone because the UK's was on the blink, I attacked the 'disgusting comparison' and the idea that because the summit hadn't done enough – which I admitted it hadn't – we shouldn't agree anything at all. I appealed to the delegates not to leave empty-handed. After more haggling the agreement was rescued, sort of, but it didn't really change the impression that the world had comprehensively failed to grasp the scale and nature of the climate crisis.

As people reflected on the outcome of the summit in the weeks and months afterwards, they looked for different explanations – blame the Danish hosts, blame the US for not having done enough to tackle the problem or, as I did at the time, blame the Chinese government, who had their own objections to the agreement. But the more I reflected on it, the more I concluded that the failure was a symptom of a much deeper problem: the shadow of global injustice in which the negotiations were conducted. The poorer countries were outraged that the rich nations had essentially grown rich by using up the carbon resources of the world, creating a world with massive disparities of income and wealth, and were now denying the same opportunity to them.

Much has changed since the Copenhagen summit in terms of the world's willingness to act, but we are still not doing nearly enough. Just before Covid-19 hit, I met up with a friend of mine, Todd Stern, who represented the United States at that summit. As we discussed what the world needed to do, he put the point graphically to me: 'Imagine if we knew a meteorite was heading towards earth to wipe out parts of our land and disrupt our way of life. We would mobilise all the resources at our disposal to stop it.' The problem is we aren't. The climate crisis can no longer be mistaken for a future threat. The world has warmed by 1°C since 1880, and the result has been unprecedented wildfires from Australia to California even to the Arctic Circle, heatwaves in India and continental Europe, and flooding across the world.[3] We know that climate change is making these events far more devastating and frequent than they would otherwise be.[4]

The bad news is that there will be lots more of this in Britain and across the world if we don't get our act together fast. The Paris Climate Accord of 2015 represented a great step forward from Copenhagen, establishing a global target to limit warming to 1.5°C rather than 2.[5] But there is a problem. When you look at the pledges made at Paris, they actually amount to something approaching 3°C.[6] If that were to happen, the best evidence suggests that coastal cities will be threatened, hundreds of millions more people may face food and water stress, 99 per cent of coral reefs will disappear, and dangerous heatwaves are likely for much of the world's population.[7]

The Intergovernmental Panel on Climate Change, which provides expert advice to governments on these matters, tells us that we now have less than ten years to attack the problem in a way that no country anywhere in the world has yet truly managed. To have a chance of keeping global warming to no more than 1.5°C, we have to cut emissions by around half in the next decade.[8] So the decisions we make in the next ten years will have the most profound implications for generations to come about the world we inhabit, our quality of life and indeed our chances of renewing the social contract.

If you want to know why this is the first chapter of this book, the preceding paragraph pretty much sums it up. And the reason for telling the story of Copenhagen is that it goes to the heart of the argument of this chapter. I believe there is a particular character to the solutions we need. If we treat the climate crisis as a technical or technological problem to be solved and think we can do so while leaving other injustices in place – without renewing the social contract in its broadest sense – we will fail. That is true globally, and it is true at home.

First of all, it is just wrong to believe that we should undertake this massive economic and social transformation, reconstructing the way we live, and yet reproduce the deep injustices and inequality that scar our country and our world. It would amount to remaking the high-carbon, unjust world as the zero-carbon, unjust world. Second, as I will explain, we won't bring people with us if we try to tackle the climate crisis without addressing these structural injustices.

Every time I hear the facts about the climate threat, I ask myself why, in non-pandemic times, averting this disaster wasn't the number-one issue on everyone's agenda every day of every week of every month in every country of the world? What has been holding us back? The answer is that the climate threat – which until recent years has felt pretty distant in countries like the UK – clashes directly with the normal rhythm of politics and the more immediate injustices so many people face in their lives: low wages, insecure work, uncertain prospects for their children, a rickety NHS, the housing crisis. If you are worried about getting to the end of the week, the end of the world seems a distant prospect. That's why the climate disaster is the ultimate challenge for politics. Even now, the full effects of actions we take in mitigating global warming won't be felt for a generation or two or three or more. And yet the time horizon of politicians – and the public – is the here and now.

There is also the danger that meeting concerns about the end of the world is seen to actually conflict with meeting concerns about the end of the week – pursued by people who can afford to do so at the expense of those who can't. Indeed, there are people who deny the climate crisis and portray it this way. When President Trump presented his plan to pull out of the Paris Agreement in 2017, he framed the action as a defence of America's industrial workers in the face of global elites: 'I was elected to represent the citizens of Pittsburgh, not Paris.'[9]

Other forces that stand in the way of the change we need are also a product of our unequal world. Ever since the Industrial Revolution, economies such as the UK's have grown thanks to a model that relies on fossil fuels – coal, oil and gas. The climate challenge asks us to abandon this 300-year model of economic growth. This is an immense transition in itself but it also faces a set of hugely powerful vested interests. Just 100 oil, gas and other fossil-fuel firms are ultimately responsible for an astonishing 71 per cent of industrial emissions over the last three decades, and many are fighting tooth and nail to carry on with business as usual.[10] But it is not just the fossil-fuel companies. We have built a whole financial and economic structure based on investment in these companies, and the forces stopping us breaking out of that cycle are perhaps even stronger. In Chapter 18 we will look at ways to take these forces on, and there are reasons to be hopeful, but we should be under no illusions about the scale of the task.

People in positions of power need also to look at themselves. The way we have campaigned for action has not helped. For those concerned about climate issues, economic and social concerns have too often been seen as separate, or taken for granted. If it's green it must be fair, or so it has seemed. This is partly what has made the climate argument vulnerable to the Trumpian attack. For those working in the fossil-fuel industries or in manufacturing reliant on those fuels, from the automotive to the steel sector, the threat of dislocation and change is real.

Unless we put justice for these workers at the centre of our vision, the climate case will lose support – and for good reason.

On the other hand, those who prioritise jobs and fairness have tended to tack the climate emergency on as an afterthought to political manifestos focused on the here and now, as if it can be tackled separately, missing the existential threat that climate change poses. In fact, if we are serious about tackling the economic and social injustices we face, we cannot ignore the climate crisis. There is no route to a renewed social contract that does not involve putting the climate threat front and centre because it threatens most those who have least, and that is as true in Britain as it is anywhere else. If we fail on climate, we will make inequality and unfairness worse.

I know this first hand from the floods that hit Doncaster in late 2019 which led to thousands of families being evacuated from their homes.[11] Some of the same families had been flooded just twelve years earlier in 2007. What was once thought to be a one-in-a-hundred-year event has happened twice in barely a decade.[12] Each of these family's stories is one of heartache, loss, fear and continuing anxiety, but it was the most vulnerable people, often living in homes in flood plains, some of whom didn't have insurance, who were hardest hit, and frequently had nowhere else to go.

As I said in the introduction to this section, the climate crisis is also the biggest intergenerational betrayal. On current estimates, a baby born today will need to have a 'carbon budget' of just one eighth of someone born in 1950 if we are to avoid climate disaster.[13] Future generations will look back at us as drunken revellers at the carbon party who smashed up the joint and left them with a mess of epic proportions to clear up.

When you stop and think about it, the way forward is rather obvious, at least in theory: if we tackle the climate crisis in a way that also tackles the other deep injustices we face, we are asking people to act not just for the sake of the future but for the sake of now. We are speaking to their immediate concerns, uniting those worried about the end of the world with those worried about the end of the week. The good news is that there is already a big idea that seeks to do exactly this. It was conceived in the UK at the time of the financial crisis of 2007 by a group of economists and activists. Like a lot of people, they had the simple insight that we could match the urgency of the economic crisis with the demands of the environmental crisis by creating well paid, worthwhile jobs to tackle both. They called it the Green New Deal.[14]

The genius of the Green New Deal idea is its recognition that the scale of the transformation we need – from how we heat our homes to the way we get around our towns and cities to how we use our land and generate power – also demands we rethink and remake our societies. We do not try to solve the climate problem while leaving existing injustices in place; we do so by prioritising the creation of well paid, decent jobs, by tackling poor-quality housing, inadequate public transport systems, the silent killer of air pollution and the absence of green spaces. In other words, we rebuild and renew the social contract.

The name and the notion hark back to US president Franklin Delano Roosevelt and his New Deal of the 1930s. He came to office on the back of the Great Depression. As one historian put it: 'A quarter of the labour force was unemployed … people had lost farms, homes and small businesses, thousands of banks had collapsed, taking with them the deposits and savings of millions of people … Starving people wandered the streets. Food riots broke out. The future of capitalism, indeed of democracy itself, appeared grim.'[15] What FDR realised was that an effective response to the crisis required breathtaking boldness and new thinking. It needed not just a change in this policy or that but a mobilisation of all the powers of government to win what he likened to a war as 'if we were in fact invaded by a foreign foe'.[16] FDR certainly knew how to go big. Eight million people who would otherwise have faced the desolation of unemployment were put back to work with government investment. Those workers constructed hundreds of thousands of miles of roads, more than 100,000 public buildings and thousands of parks across the country.[17] He even had an initiative called the Civilian Conservation Corps, which utilised 3 million men to plant 3 billion trees.[18]

This much is well known about Roosevelt's New Deal, but there was something more to it, which is spoken about less. It did not just represent an emergency programme to put America back to work; FDR rewrote the social contract of America, not just giving workers a stake in the future but also setting America on a more equal course, giving greater rights to working people and restraining the power of finance. As he put it, his aim was to supplant the old order of 'special privilege' with a 'new order of things designed to benefit the great mass of our farmers, workers and business men'.[19]

The Green New Deal had some impact in the late 2000s, but as we saw from Copenhagen the world was not yet ready to act, and it played only a modest role in economic recovery plans after the financial crisis. In the last couple of years, however, this idea, born more than a decade ago in London, has become the dominating climate policy theme in American politics, supported by a grassroots movement and much of the Democratic Party. The concept has become central to the US debate thanks in large part to the efforts of Congresswoman Alexandria Ocasio-Cortez, an insurgent Democratic politician elected in 2018.[20] You may have heard of her – she has a gazillion Twitter followers and is a bona fide political rock star. But I want to tell you about someone else, whom you probably won't have heard of but who has played a pivotal role in fleshing out what the Green New Deal idea should mean in practice.

Rhiana Gunn-Wright is an African American, born on the South Side of Chicago. She came to climate not through a traditional environmental route; in fact, as a health policy analyst working with marginalised communities, her attitude towards the climate crisis was initially dismissive. 'I just felt like other people are already doing that work,' she said. 'They don't need me.'[21] But then she started seeing the vulnerability of the poor to the climate threat. She discovered that 70 per cent of African Americans live near coal-fired power plants, and recalled her own experience of asthma growing up near one herself. She realised that the climate threat was a social justice issue and that the profound changes our societies will have to undergo means confronting the way they are run now and considering how they could be run in a more just way.[22]

At this point, a critic might ask, why make the climate crisis even harder to tackle by loading onto its shoulders all the injustices and inequalities of our world? Won't that make it harder to win allies and more difficult to advance? The resounding answer is that the opposite is true. Polling done in 2020 in the UK shows that climate can transcend political boundaries and unite us in hope. The vast majority of people across all political persuasions agree that climate is a real and present danger, and believe that the changes required are an opportunity to create meaningful work. Concern is not confined to those on the Left or the better-off, it goes deep and wide across our country. But the same polling tells us that if the burden of change falls disproportionately on particular groups of people, including those least able to afford it, then it will become a source of division not unity.[23] We also cannot tell people that the deep injustices they face in their lives will have to wait for decades because the climate challenge takes precedence. That would be wrong and, just as important, it won't work. We can only build the necessary coalition if we tackle both the climate crisis and inequality together.

The transformation required in the UK, as in every country, is huge: we must change the way we heat nearly thirty million homes, take tens of millions of petrol and diesel cars off the road, alter the way we use our land and the manner in which we power our country. Alongside this massive and complex task we also face the economic fallout from Covid. Either on its own demands Roosevelt-scale ambition, but together the case for a bold response is even clearer. If this became a national mission, backed with appropriate government resources, it could create fulfilling work for hundreds of thousands of people.

For example, about 15 per cent of total greenhouse gas emissions in the UK come from the way we heat our homes.[24] We have made little progress in changing things over the last decade, so there is a huge job to be done here – first insulating and upgrading the buildings so we stop wasting so much energy, and then overseeing the transition from natural gas or oil to zero-carbon sources of power. To do this will require at least 200,000 additional jobs over the next three decades.[25] This is something to get really excited about. Imagine a 'zero-carbon army' going from house to house, street by street, neighbourhood by neighbourhood, to insulate homes and help people change the way they heat them. Just as with FDR's programme, people would have the sense of being part of a shared mission for the country, giving us the greenest homes in the world.

An inspiring example of this on a small scale is Retrofit Get-in, a cooperative in Manchester owned and run by its workers, which is employing stagehands, technicians and joiners who have lost their jobs in theatre during the pandemic to insulate homes. It turns out their skills are eminently transferrable.[26] Of course, we want these workers to be able to get their jobs back in the theatre, but this illustrates the principle and points the way to what could be done with an equivalent scheme on a national scale.

As we face this transition, those who run the fossil-fuel industry do not merit our support, but those who work in it – and all other industries that underpin our high-carbon economy – deserve all the support we can possibly muster. There are an estimated 300,000 jobs in the UK dependent on the oil and gas sector alone, concentrated in particular areas of the country.[27] And these jobs tend to be decently paid, with good pensions and unionised workforces. Unless we handle the change well, we will let down entire communities and fail to bring people with us. The problem is that in the UK we haven't been doing enough to create equivalent jobs even in areas where we appear to be doing well on green issues, like offshore wind.

Over the last two decades, successive governments have made great strides in turning the UK into a global leader in offshore wind generation. By first mandating energy suppliers to renewables and, more recently, by guaranteeing the offshore wind industry a price for the power it produces, the government has played a crucial role in this success. But that success has been a narrow one.[28] BiFab is a company based in Fife in Scotland, barely ten miles from what will be Scotland's largest offshore wind farm, which will supply power to hundreds of thousands of Scottish homes. Bifab has spent most of its history building oil and gas platforms, but more recently has been pitching to build platforms for the wind turbines planned off Scotland's coasts. But those wind farms will not be built by BiFab because in 2020 it went into administration. In April 2021, a deal was struck to use its facilities to manufacture eight platforms, but that leaves the vast majority to be manufactured in Indonesia, the UAE and China, and shipped thousands of miles to reach us. BiFab is a parable for a failure to build a domestic wind industry. It needn't be this way. Just across the North Sea, Denmark has shown that with a proper industrial policy that uses the power of government for investment, alongside the private sector, you can compete on the basis of high standards with good wages and still create green jobs. I return to the issue of industrial policy in Chapter 5.

A planned transition means creating alternative employment and also giving the best help to people at risk of unemployment. In 2012 coal miners in Spain undertook a 457-kilometre *Marcha Negra* (Black March), protesting against the reduction of subsidies by the national government. In 2018 a new government negotiated a 'just transition agreement' to invest €250 million in mining communities. This involves funding early retirement for older workers, retraining schemes for younger employees and, crucially, developing renewable energy, improving energy efficiency, and investing in and developing new industries.[29] The government and unions have recently struck a similar deal for regions and workers affected by the closure of thermal power plants.[30]

We need to ensure the transition is fair not just for workers but for all citizens. As a country the UK is now committed to phasing out new petrol and diesel cars by 2030, but at the moment electric cars are still relatively expensive. If those on lower incomes lose out, a backlash will occur. Electric cars will soon be cheaper than petrol and diesel cars over their lifetimes, but the upfront costs will remain higher. We need to work out how we make them affordable – some have suggested zero-interest government loans, for example – and not just for those on the highest incomes.

But transport also offers an example of how replacing a current system with a lower-carbon alternative is not enough. The carbon cost of producing electric cars means we cannot simply replace every petrol and diesel car with an electric one, so public transport will assume greater importance. But from the point of view of our social contract, there are deep inequalities that will need to be addressed if we are to unite around the transition. There is a long-standing problem with our privately run rail system, characterised by its tendency to privatise profits when times are good and socialise its losses to the taxpayer when the going gets tough, as has happened once again during the pandemic.[31] Bus services outside London are often infrequent, expensive and unreliable. To go over to a lower-carbon transport system while leaving these inadequate services in place and not re-imagining our transport system so that people have proper alternatives to car use (a subject I return to in Chapter 10) would be both unjust and doomed to fail.

What is true of transport is true more generally. We must take the opportunity to think what a renewed social contract should offer people in the round – access to green spaces, clean air, a safe, warm home (the subject of the next chapter) and affordable energy bills. There are big issues to consider, including the important role of democratic public ownership in energy and how we distribute fairly the benefits and burdens of the transition. This is just a small preview of the action required, but the principle that unites it all is that every policy and every decision aimed at going green must tackle the deep inequalities and injustices of our country too.

If you are wondering how much all this would cost, the answer is far less than you might think. The government's independent climate advisers at the Climate Change Committee (CCC) estimate the net costs at less than 1 per cent of our national income each year (about £20 billion in today's money).[32] That's partly because going green may cost us at the outset but it leads to savings in the longer term. As mentioned, the cost of an electric car over its lifetime will soon be less than those of a petrol and diesel car, and onshore wind is now the cheapest fuel at our disposal.[33] In any case, 1 per cent of national income seems a small price to pay to prevent climate disaster and create a better life for people.

Moreover, creating a better life for people isn't just the right and necessary thing to do, it is what will inspire people to act. In his famous speech at the March on Washington in 1963 Martin Luther King declared, 'I have a dream.' He didn't say, 'I have a nightmare.' King understood the motivation of hope and the coalition it could build around a positive vision of an integrated, tolerant, equal America. Those who care about the climate emergency, me included, have been good at talking about the nightmare. But we have a dream too. The promise of the Green New Deal is not just to tackle the climate crisis; it is also to create better lives – good jobs, high-quality public transport, affordable energy and a decent home. That is a cause worth fighting for in the here and now.

CHAPTER 2

A Housing Revolution

You can live in a great way in every city in the world when you are well off. The great thing about this city is that you can live there, love it there, work there and have an affordable rent when you are a worker and when you are not the winner of social bingo.

Jürgen Czernohorszky, city councillor[1]

Which city has for ten years in a row been rated the best place to live in the world, beating everywhere from Copenhagen to New York to Zurich? It's a capital city where even low-paid workers can afford to live right in the centre. One of the most affordable major cities in the world, a rare example of a conurbation where population growth hasn't been accompanied by a housing crisis. It's not on most people's bucket list to visit, unless you love opera and schnitzel, but it should be for policymakers. The city is – maybe you've guessed – Vienna.

Austria's capital shows that it's possible to live in a modern, desirable town or city whether you are wealthy or not. That even in a prosperous capital there can be mixed communities, rich and poor, all enjoying secure and affordable homes. Britons have become so used to a dysfunctional housing market characterised by scarcity, insecurity and eye-watering costs that we could be forgiven for believing it's just a feature of modern life. That there is no alternative. And yet what could be more basic than having a roof over one's head and a home fit for the twenty-first century?

Any project to renew the social contract worthy of consideration must tackle the housing crisis we face, and our starting point has to be understanding that if we keep doing things as we have been for four decades, we will keep failing. But before we look at where we're going wrong, let's examine the secret of Vienna's success.

If you live in Vienna, chances are you're living in some form of social housing, alongside nearly two thirds of the city's population.[2] Renters spend an average of just 25 per cent of their income on accommodation.[3] Vienna has achieved this by maintaining a large stock of high-quality social housing. The city owns 220,000 homes directly and subsidises a further 200,000 housing association homes.[4] In these homes residents are charged a 'cost-rent', covering the cost of building and maintaining housing, rather than a price set by the market. This prevents rents spiralling. Low-income households receive subsidies to make their rents cheaper still.

The city is constantly building new social homes so that supply keeps up with the city's growing population. Rather than spending public money on subsidising the cost of renting in the private sector (more on the problems of that below), Vienna focuses on investing in new homes. Enough new homes are built each year to avoid long waiting lists for social housing and to prevent housing costs rising in the private sector.[5] And what is significant is that social housing is not simply for the poorest. The vast majority of the population is eligible for these homes, and developments are built with different types of housing – public, housing association, private – side by side.

Vienna has spent almost a century building this vision, and today's residents are reaping the benefits, but the city isn't an outlier. There are abundant examples of other cities where they do things better than us, with a much bigger role for social housing: from Rotterdam to Bilbao to, perhaps surprisingly,

Singapore, where 80 per cent of the population live in public housing that they can own on 99-year leases.[6]

What about us? Over the last few decades we have seen a revolution in housing in the UK, but not the revolution in home ownership we were promised. In fact, home ownership rates are back down to broadly the same level as forty years ago and now below the European average.[7] No, the revolution we have seen is a huge growth in the private rental market. Private renting has more than doubled in the last twenty years alone. Gone are the days when it was largely confined to people in their twenties. Eleven million people in 4.4 million families in England now rent privately, including people at all stages of their lives: the average private renter is now forty years old, and about one in three are households with children.[8]

As a private renter you pay more for housing than any other group – more than a third of your income on average.[9] Worse, many literally cannot afford to pay the spiralling costs of private renting on the money they earn. One in five renters cuts back on food to pay their rent.[10] During the Covid crisis, four in ten private renters became reliant on housing benefits to cover their housing costs.[11] But this isn't just about afford-ability. Renters have little security in the UK. At the mercy of their landlords, many are forced to move regularly and plagued by the knowledge they might have to move again, unsure from one year to the next whether, for example, their children will have to change schools. In 2020, nearly seven in ten private renters reported serious problems with their homes including mould, damp, leaks, electrical hazards and infestations.[12] Many renters face the very real risk of being kicked out of their home if they complain.[13]

No one would choose these conditions, but often private renting is the only option. For many, home ownership is out of reach, having fallen from 70 per cent of those under the age of 65 in the 1990s to just 57 per cent today.[14] And if you want to live in social housing, you'll have to join a waiting list of 1.2 million people.[15] Just as many who rent did not choose to do so, as a society we have not chosen this situation. It was not promised in a manifesto. This is a silent revolution, which has taken place with little public discussion or political debate. As we will see, it is the consequence of failures of policy by governments of both parties.

The core of the housing crisis is very simple: we don't have enough affordable homes. This is what has led to the private renter reliant on housing benefit, the family stuck on a council house waiting list for years and the homeless person forced to sleep on a friend's sofa. How has it come to this?

For a time there was a consensus across both Labour and Conservative Parties that building social housing was the right thing to do. That by maintaining a stock of publicly owned housing with reasonable rents not set by the market you could ensure there were enough affordable homes. Starting in earnest in the inter-war period, at pretty much the same time as in Vienna, British governments started to clear privately owned slum housing. Building new homes became a national mission. More than a million council homes were built between the wars, with local authorities leading the way.[16] Yet it was after the war that the golden age of social housing construction really happened in the UK. The Labour government of 1945–51 built 800,000 homes in addition to those constructed by the private sector. It built 190,000 in the single year of 1948 – a number only bettered by the Conservative government in 1953, when 229,000 were built. Indeed, the parties desperately competed as to who could build more.[17] In all, in the thirty years after the Second World War governments of both parties built on average 128,000 social homes (mainly council houses) in England *each and every year*.[18]

Then in the late 1970s something changed. Margaret Thatcher swept to power and with her came an ideology that was deeply sceptical not just of building social homes but of their very existence. On this view, social housing bred reliance on the state and should only be a last resort for those who had nowhere else to go.[19] The government slashed the money spent on building social housing, believing that left to its own devices the market was the most efficient way to provide the homes required. Any public money spent on housing would not go towards providing social housing at low rents but towards paying housing benefit to those renting in the private sector. Her famous Right to Buy scheme offered council tenants the opportunity to buy their homes at a below-market price.

In the last thirty years or so, an average of just 24,000 social homes have been built in England each year – over 100,000 fewer houses each year than the post-war period.[20] Taken together, that's three million fewer homes built over the thirty-year period. Meanwhile, two million social homes have been sold off since Right to Buy was introduced.[21] Put the two figures together and our social housing stock has dwindled drastically. So the Thatcher model has certainly succeeded in making council housing a last resort – mainly because there is so little of it. It has also succeeded in demolishing public investment in housing. Eighty pence in every pound spent on housing used to be invested in bricks and mortar; now more than eighty pence in every pound going into housing is spent on housing benefit (£23 billion in total).[22] What we as a society get for this money, apart from subsidising private landlords – as well as some councils and housing associations – is unclear.

A growing population and stubbornly low wages mean that while the stock of social housing has dwindled, the need for affordable housing has not, so, what about the other promise of the new approach? Has the market provided instead? Unfortunately, it's a resounding no. In the period 1946 to 1980 the average number of houses built by the private sector was 121,000 homes per year, and in the period since 1981 it is 124,000 homes per year.[23] In other words, we can say with certainty that the private sector has not filled the gap. In England alone it has left us with somewhere between three and four million fewer homes than we need.[24]

But the truth is, it's not just that the market has not provided enough affordable housing; the model of property development that prevails in the UK *will never* provide it, either on the scale or at the speed that is necessary. At the moment house-builders compete to buy land on which to build houses that they later sell, and the developer who plans to build the most expensive homes will usually outbid the competition. There is also little incentive for developers to build quickly because to do so would flood the market, thereby reducing the price of what they're selling. So there is a lot of hoarding of land with planning permission but no development. This also means that housebuilding dries up in times of recession as developers wait for prices to recover.[25]

Markets, properly regulated, work well for restaurants and retail and a whole range of other things, but on their own cannot deliver on the objectives we have as a country for housing. At the time of writing the government has the laudable target of 300,000 new houses being built across the public and private sector every year to meet demand. However, there is no earthly way we are going to get to that level unless there is a decisive shift towards social housing. In 2018/19 a measly 6,000 social homes were built.[26] But given they're still being sold off, this has actually led to a net loss of 17,000 social homes.[27]

Governments have tried specifying the proportion of affordable housing in private developments, reforming the way councils deliver the houses they do have, changing the way housing associations work and subsidising home ownership in multiple ways. You name it, and it has been tried – apart from building social homes on a substantial scale. However, the Viennese experience teaches us that that is exactly what we need to do again. This could mean a mix of housing owned by councils, housing associations or other non-profit organisations. The provider matters less than the distinguishing feature of social housing: rents linked to local incomes and what people can actually afford to pay rather than market rates. Social homes will not solve all of our housing problems – for example, we also need to think about greater security for those who rent privately – but they are a good place to start.

In the wake of the Grenfell Tower disaster, the housing charity Shelter brought together a group of housing experts, tenants and a cross-party group of politicians – Baroness Sayeeda Warsi, Lord Jim O'Neill (both of whom served in David Cameron's government as Conservative ministers) and myself – in a commission. Sayeeda and I in particular were, on the face of it, unlikely allies. While I was Labour leader, she had spent a couple of years as chair of the Conservative Party issuing press releases attacking me. However, despite our differing histories and ideological backgrounds, we agreed: the government needs to build social housing, and build at scale.

We also agreed that it was important not to romanticise social housing. We now know that the housing of Grenfell residents was unsafe and they felt their concerns were ignored.[28] The Shelter commission found that those living in social housing commonly lack any real voice or power. More than half of social renters in England have experienced problems such as electrical hazards, gas leaks or faulty lifts in the last three years.[29] Many value the stability of social renting and feel close to their neighbours but also think estates are often poorly designed, unattractive and unsafe, with complaints including impersonal tower blocks and a lack of decent public space. A quarter think they would live in a better neighbourhood if they rented privately.[30] Social renters do tend to say they have good relationships with their landlords (usually a council or housing association) but are in fact more likely than people renting privately to feel their problems and complaints are left unresolved. The Shelter commission also found that some tenants are embarrassed to admit they live in social housing.[31]

This range of problems might make you wonder whether social housing can really be an answer, but all of them are solvable – indeed *have* to be solvable if we are going to fix the mess that we are in. In Chapter 14 I write about how the state needs to work better and differently with its citizens – definitely true in relation to social housing – and there is evidence that social housing landlords have recognised that the Grenfell catastrophe holds fundamental lessons for the whole sector.

There are also some outstanding examples of social housing that belie the poor reputation of its past – and to some extent its present – and can be a blueprint for the future. In 2019, Goldsmith Street, a development of 105 new social houses in Norwich, became the first ever social housing development to win the prestigious RIBA Stirling Prize for architecture, previously won by the Gateshead Millennium Bridge, the Scottish Parliament and London's Gherkin building. The judges described it as 'a modest masterpiece ... high-quality architecture in its purest, most environmentally and socially conscious form'.[32] Goldsmith Street proves that there is no reason social housing cannot be beautiful. The houses have big windows, front and back gardens, as well as communal outdoor spaces with tables and benches. They're all designed to the Passivhaus standard of energy efficiency, meaning they are incredibly well insulated so cheap to heat, and have low carbon emissions. All of this at an affordable rent. It shows what can be done with imagination and political will.

And here's something else that might surprise you. Building social homes will be good for the millions who *don't* live in them. Indeed it is the backbone of a functioning housing market. Our failure to build social homes has increased demand for private rental property at a much faster rate than it is becoming available, driving up rents and leaving renters with weak bargaining power with landlords.[33] Other things being equal, building more social homes will make the overall housing supply more able to meet demand. If renters have the option of decent low-cost social housing then private landlords will have to compete on quality and price to attract them.

All this is why the Shelter commission recommended that government invest in housing once again. We should move away from a vision of council housing as a last resort for the poorest and view housing in general as a part of our economic and social infrastructure, just like transport. Far from simply being a cost, housing would become an investment with a crucial economic and social return for government. The commission recommended we build an average of 150,000 social homes – council and housing association – each year over the next twenty years. While we reckoned the initial cost of this at about £10 billion a year, factoring in tax revenues from those working in construction and eventual savings in housing benefit the ultimate cost would be far less – somewhere between £3.8 and £6 billion depending on the precise assumptions.[34] That puts the maximum net cost over twenty years somewhere around that of HS2, and it would have a direct impact on the lives of millions of families. Instead of paying massive subsidies to private landlords via housing benefit, we would be creating an economic and social asset.

This housebuilding project would be a crucial component of the Green New Deal I explored in Chapter 1. The new generation of social homes should be built to the highest possible environmental standards – well insulated, energy efficient and with low-carbon heating to reduce the energy bills for those living in them. And located with public transport, walking and cycling links in mind, and with ample access to green space. Developments like Goldsmith Street show this can be done.

After the Second World War the London County Council had the largest architects' department in the world.[35] Town planners and architects were celebrated.[36] In the post-war years they thought big despite the straitened circumstances of the time. On the passage of the 1949 Housing Bill, which specifically removed the previous stipulation that council housing was only for the 'working class', Aneurin Bevan, NHS founder and housing minister in the 1945 Labour government, said, 'If we are to enable citizens to lead a full life, if they are each to be aware of the problems of their neighbours, then they should all be drawn from different sections of the community and we should try to introduce what was always the lovely feature of English and Welsh villages, where the doctor, the grocer, the butcher and the farm labourer all lived in the same street.'[37]

Bevan's picture of mixed communities may sound nostalgic
to some, but we do not need to romanticise the past to applaud
its ambition – and seek to emulate it for our generation. A
social contract is about more than what each individual gets;
it includes how we live together. Recent trends in housing have
increasingly segregated us according to class and income.[38] For
people other than the richest, living – and certainly buying a
home – in many of our cities is simply out of reach. We are
not about to become Vienna in our levels of home ownership
(theirs are much lower than ours) – nor should we want that.
People value and want the chance to own their homes and
pass them on to their children. But shifting towards providing
social housing at scale does not conflict with that aspiration.
Indeed, the Shelter commission saw it as one way for people to
build up savings on their way to home ownership. Interestingly,
there is no party political or other divide on this issue among
voters. Polling done for the commission showed that whether
you were Leave or Remain, Conservative or Labour, building
social housing was seen as the right choice for the country.[39]
More broadly, it is a way to share the burden of risk between
individual and state more fairly, so that people are not at the
mercy of insecure private tenancies.

If you want to know why this matters, listen to Alex and
her son Tommy, who live in prize-winning Goldsmith Street. In
their previous home Alex would often turn on the oven or put
on extra layers rather than switch on the heating because she
couldn't afford the bills. Her new Passivhaus has substantially
cut her fuel costs. The communal space of Goldsmith Street
means her son Tommy can play outside. 'Tommy's level of
exploring is just so much better. Last night when it was tipping
down with rain, he just ran outside and was living his best life
playing in the puddles. Whereas before he was so limited.'[40]

Being able to afford to heat your home and having a safe
place for your child to play should be the very basis of a
twenty-first-century social contract. So too should a financial
platform on which to stand.

CHAPTER 3

Free to Choose

In lieu of the natural inheritance which, as a right, belongs to everyman, over and above the property he may have created, or inherited from those who did ... there shall be paid to every person, when arrived at twenty-one years, the sum of fifteen pounds sterling, as a compensation ...

Thomas Paine[1]

As Alaska's governor, I believe the historic PFD [Permanent Fund Dividend] program represents a share of our natural resource wealth. It allows every Alaskan to share in our natural resource wealth, which ultimately belongs to the people, and ensures that government is accountable to the people.

Michael J. Dunleavy, governor of Alaska[2]

At first sight, radical pamphleteer Thomas Paine, British-born son of an eighteenth-century tenant farmer and champion of the French Revolution, might not have much in common with the current Republican governor of Alaska, Michael Dunleavy. Yet they are bound together by a shared belief: that every citizen has a right to a share of the wealth of the nation.

The Alaska Permanent Fund Dividend (PFD) came into being in 1982. It is a dividend paid out from the returns on investment of the tens of billions of dollars' worth of oil revenues accumulated over previous decades. Every year since, the state has sent a cheque of up to $2,000 to every resident, regardless of income, subject only to the conditions that they have lived in Alaska for at least a year, intend to continue doing so, and haven't been imprisoned in the last twelve months. On average, each Alaskan household receives around $4,000 per year.[3]

The Permanent Fund was established after the construction of the Trans-Alaska Pipeline in the late 1970s provided a windfall for the state. It was argued that putting this money into a fund would prevent it being squandered in the short term and ensure that future generations could benefit from the state's oil wealth even after the initial revenue had dried up.[4] The PFD is now untouchable. Think of Britain's attachment to the NHS and you get a sense of how Alaskans feel about it. In a state where 42 per cent of voters identify as ideologically conservative (compared to just 24 per cent liberal), it gets the kind of poll ratings that, believe me, a politician would die for: 78 per cent of Alaskans feel positive about it, 84 per cent support it being paid to all residents and 62 per cent say the fund should never be touched by the government for other purposes, even in a crisis.[5] No wonder the successor to the governor who introduced it, having toyed with abolition, concluded that getting rid of it would be 'political suicide'.[6]

Thomas Paine would, I think, have approved of the Alaska fund. He called for a similar principle in *Agrarian Justice* nearly 250 years ago. His proposal has since become known as a social inheritance – giving everyone a lump sum of cash as they reach adulthood in order to provide a financial foundation for their lives. Or as he put it, 'to enable him or her to begin the world'.[7] Alaska and Thomas Paine point to another way to renew the social contract: giving everyone a guaranteed financial stake in society. They do so in different ways – an annual income versus a one-off lump sum – but while these mechanisms are often discussed as two separate ideas, they are underpinned by a similar motivation.

At their heart, the case for both is about expanding freedom. The most profound inequality in our society is between those who have freedom over their own lives because they have money and those who do not. Freedom at its most basic is freedom from destitution. But it is also the power to choose a course for one's life – the freedom to care, to volunteer, to look after our children, to start a business, to take risks. Think back to the building blocks of the social contract that I set out in the introduction to this part of the book. Giving everyone real freedom requires a bedrock of economic security.

In case this all sounds rather theoretical, consider the following. A report by the Joseph Rowntree Foundation at the end of 2020 found that more than two million people in the UK suffered from destitution – defined as lacking two basic essentials such as shelter, food, heating, lighting, clothing or basic toiletries – even before coronavirus.[8] There is something fundamentally wrong about any society in which millions of people cannot afford to eat. The pandemic has made things worse as workers have been laid off or forced to reduce their hours. Millions, including many self-employed, have fallen through the cracks and been ineligible for government support schemes.[9] The number of families using foodbanks doubled in the first month of the Covid lockdown.[10] And millions of people in Britain have no savings to fall back on in an emergency. Before the pandemic, nearly half of households had less than £1,500 of savings or no savings at all.[11] A quarter of families say they would be unable to make ends meet for more than a month without their main source of income.[12] They are literally a payslip away from poverty.

The reasons for destitution are not mysterious – they are high housing costs, low wages, insecure work and the meanness of our benefits system.[13] A five-week waiting time for the first payment of Universal Credit is one of its more egregious failings. As we emerge from the pandemic, there is an absolutely essential and immediate job to be done in tackling the inadequacy of our welfare state, which expects an adult without a job or other means of support to live on seventy-four pounds a week, less than half the amount needed to reach the poverty threshold.[14] But this chapter seeks to look further ahead, beyond essential and hopefully possible changes, to improbable, even seemingly impossible ones. What can we learn from experiments like Alaska about ways to distribute income and crucially, wealth, in our country, so that we give people not just a guarantee of freedom from destitution, but something more? A genuine financial stake for everyone, whoever they are, whatever background they are from.

Alaska's guaranteed annual payment is perhaps the most extensive manifestation of an idea that has been gaining ground in recent years. In the 2020 Democratic presidential primaries Andrew Yang called it 'the freedom dividend', but it's also known as the universal basic income (UBI). The concept is a flat-rate payment to all citizens regardless of income which, unlike the Alaska PFD, is enough to live on.[15] The idea is not actually that new. Perhaps the most interesting aspect of its history is how it has straddled traditional ideological lines. Over the decades it's been supported by a group of the strangest bedfellows including former US president Richard Nixon, civil rights leader Martin Luther King, right-wing economist Milton Friedman and tech billionaire Elon Musk.[16] President Obama expressed an interest and so too did Hillary Clinton during her presidential campaign: 'I was fascinated by this idea, as was my husband, and we spent weeks working with our policy team to see if it could be viable enough to include in my campaign. We would call it Alaska for America. Unfortunately, we couldn't make the numbers work.'[17]

Clinton is right. The numbers are daunting – and we'll get to that – but this is a book not about next year or even necessarily the next five years, but about the world we want to create well beyond that. So what is its point and what is its appeal?

The freedom dividend has two important features: it is universal – everyone is entitled to receive it – and unconditional – you do not have to do anything in exchange. The difference from our current welfare state is immediately apparent. Universal Credit, which is the main social security payment in the UK is means tested, meaning that claimants must declare any other income or savings they have. If they move into work, they lose a substantial proportion of their benefit, and the more they earn, the lower the benefit. It is also highly intrusive and conditional – claimants must account for their time and show they are searching for a job or they risk losing their benefit. In practice, there have turned out to be some real flaws in the way the system works, for example, the 'poverty trap' caused by the withdrawal of benefit for every pound extra earned.[18]

This problem was highlighted, believe it or not, by the success of the vegan sausage roll. After Greggs, the high street bakery, introduced its wildly successful new vegan range in January 2020 it saw a surge in profits, and Greggs announced that every staff member would get a £300 bonus. Yet it soon emerged that some on Universal Credit would only keep 25p in every pound of that bonus.[19] Explaining the problem in an article entitled 'Why bakers are taxed more than bankers', *The Economist* wrote, 'The government is rightly keen that poorer people should work rather than sponge off the welfare system. An implicit marginal tax rate of 75 per cent does not encourage them to do so.'[20] By the time National Insurance and tax is taken into account, some people on Universal Credit lose something like 75p in every extra pound they earn.[21] The UK used to have this level of marginal tax for the very rich and got rid of it in the 1970s, but it's essentially still in place for some of the country's lowest paid workers.[22] This is an inevitable feature of a means-tested system. The precise rate at which you withdraw the benefit can be changed, but wherever you draw the line the trap persists to some extent.

The way sanctions have been applied in the UK benefits system in recent years has also been appalling in many cases. Sanctions are applied when claimants are judged not to have complied with certain requirements. A comprehensive analysis of the sanctions regime in 2018 concluded they are 'largely ineffective' in getting people to work, 'do little' to improve motivation, 'routinely trigger profoundly negative personal, financial, health and behavioural outcomes' and 'for a substantial minority [lead to] … increased poverty, and on occasions, destitution'.[23]

So Universal Credit is means tested and conditional. Means testing is based on the idea that benefits received should only go to those who need them. Meanwhile, conditionality is based on the intuition that if benefits are unconditional, people will not work. The problem with the approach as manifested in the current system is that it is disempowering and alienating. It creates an unequal and disrespectful relationship between the state and its citizens (a problem I return to more fully in Chapter 14) because it assumes that the claimant is dishonest, will try to manipulate the system and cannot be trusted.

It is against this backdrop that the advocates of the freedom dividend make their case. It upends the unequal relationship by giving people autonomy over how they use the resources they are given to live on. Rather than catching them when they fall, a regular source of income provides a foundation on which to stand and a choice about whether to care, work or learn. People will, it is argued, be freed from welfare bureaucracy. It addresses the issue of economic insecurity in an era when few are guaranteed a job for life, and the economic cushion it provides means people can afford to take risks. It also gives them the ability to say no to a boss who wants to underpay or exploit them, rebalancing power at work.

There will always be the worry that people will simply fritter the money away, but the logic behind the freedom dividend is that people are basically decent, and it is the self-fulfilling prophecies of an untrusting state that make them more likely to behave otherwise. This is a bet on human beings. It says that if we give people freedom, they will use it wisely. What is more, the argument goes, if we are entering an era when computers and robots are likely to replace even more of our jobs, the freedom dividend is a way to protect people as the technological storm rolls in.

All of this sounds very attractive, but the big question is whether in practice it would actually work. Let's start with the supposed Achilles heel of the freedom dividend: if you give people money with no strings attached, won't everyone just stop working? Well no, actually. A recent study examining various experiments that have been conducted over the years concluded, 'The evidence does not suggest an average worker will drop out of the labour force when provided with unconditional cash, even when the transfer is large.'[24] A recent, albeit fairly limited Finnish trial of UBI found little impact on employment either way – neither encouraging nor disincentivising work.[25] This is supported by decades of evidence from Alaska. Even though the payments there are insufficient to live on, we might expect that if a full freedom dividend is likely to disincentivise people from working altogether, then there might be at least some reduction in people's appetite for work. Just 1 per cent of Alaskans say the PFD has had such an effect on their work habits. Indeed, more people say it has increased their incentive to work.[26] So the notion that people will simply give up working as a result of a freedom dividend has not – on the evidence so far – been seen on anything like a level which should cause concern.

These results shouldn't surprise us. The freedom dividend provides a foundation, but only that. Most people want to earn more than a basic minimum, and earning money is not their only reason to work – it can give meaning to our lives. So the freedom dividend should be seen as complementary to, rather than a replacement for, work. At the same time, one of the arguments made for the freedom dividend is that it would enable those with children to work less in order to spend more time caring for them. If the freedom dividend allowed some people to spend a bit more time looking after their children or caring for elderly relatives, would that really be a bad thing?

While fears about the freedom dividend haven't been borne out by trials, some hopes have been realised. In US experiments in the 1970s there were positive impacts on nutrition, high school attendance, grades and test scores for children.[27] In Alaska the PFD has helped it buck the trend towards greater income inequality. Between the 1980s and 2000s Alaska was the only state in the US where the incomes of the bottom 20 per cent grew faster than those of the top 20 per cent.[28] Meanwhile, the recent Finnish trial found positive effects on mental wellbeing, alleviating depression and improving happiness and satisfaction with life.[29] As one participant said, 'the most significant effect of basic income is psychological'. It eased the stress and fear related to her financial struggles every month.[30]

You might now see why these ideas appeal to both Left and Right. They diminish the role of the state in one way, while expanding it in another. They prioritise autonomy and freedom, values often championed by the Right, but aim to ensure a more equal society, something valued by the Left. Most fundamentally they cross ideological lines in addressing what we really value in our society: family, care, compassion and, above all, people being the authors of their own lives.

However, before we get too excited, two rather big obstacles stand in the way of introducing a freedom dividend. First, the question of ethos. While in practice it appears not to have discouraged work, some people worry about the principle of giving people 'money for nothing'. In other words, the freedom dividend might have the paradoxical characteristic that it works in practice but not in theory. Some left-wing thinkers agree. André Gorz, a famous thinker of the 1960s and 70s who was partly responsible for reviving the idea of the shorter working week, wrote, 'Excusing people from working by securing them an income anyway is not a way of giving them full membership of their society. You cannot become a member of any community if you have no obligation whatsoever towards it. Being a member of a group means that you can rely on the others, but also that they can rely on you. There can be no inclusion without reciprocal obligations.'[31]

The second problem is money. As one academic has summarised it, 'An affordable UBI is inadequate, and an adequate UBI is unaffordable.'[32] In the particular circumstances of Alaska's windfall, the Permanent Fund Dividend is a nice thing to have but not enough to live on. On the other hand, providing one that is enough to live on would be prohibitively expensive. This was Hillary Clinton's conclusion.

It certainly feels that way when you look at the numbers. There are a range of estimates, but one analysis suggests that a freedom dividend even set at existing benefit levels would cost £76 billion annually (around 4 per cent of national income), including savings on means-tested benefits, which really is an eye-watering sum.[33] Separate payments for housing costs would continue under this model, and if payments for disability are protected, which is essential, the cost rises significantly further. One of the problems of a universal payment is that we do not have universal needs. The freedom dividend could not replace all of the targeted benefits of our current welfare system without people with specific needs missing out.

The question we must ask is under what circumstances the freedom dividend could ever be the number one priority for spending such a large amount of money. In other words, why would you spend money on financing a freedom dividend which will be paid to all irrespective of income, when we face poverty, the climate crisis, underfunded public services and dozens of other pressing issues? Governments always have a limited amount of money to spend and an endless number of problems they need to address. The rationale for means testing is that it enables governments to target the money they have on those who need it most.

There is merit in this argument, but while it is true that means testing concentrates benefits on a smaller population, much depends on the levels at which benefits are set, and that in turn depends on the political support for the benefits in question. In fact, there are good reasons for thinking that targeted systems enjoy *less* overall public support, so that targeting benefits on the poor might lead to the effect of reducing what poor people receive. As the social scientist Richard Titmuss famously put it, 'services for poor people have always tended to be poor quality services'.[34] What are the untouchable things in British politics? The NHS and pensions. Both are universal, not targeted or means tested. In contrast, those on means-tested social security benefits have, until recently, attracted little public sympathy. This may have changed in the light of some of the catastrophic problems of Universal Credit, but the general point still holds. Services and benefits that go to more people enjoy more support. Titmuss was right.

You could argue we have seen this principle in practice during the pandemic with the furlough scheme, under which people have been paid a proportion of their lost wages. It has been incredibly popular. Lots of other countries have this kind of system in place permanently for sickness or maternity pay, and people who lose their jobs get a fixed proportion of their previous income for at least the initial period of unemployment.[35] We used to have something like this in the UK, and there are remnants of the practice, such as mothers receiving 90 per cent of their previous earnings in statutory maternity pay for the first six weeks (a subject we return to in the next chapter).

For me, the freedom dividend has one big selling point: the promise of a foundation on which people can stand which would give them real freedom over their own lives. For that reason the idea deserves to be kept under consideration, but realistically, even going big, I can't see it happening any time soon. Apart from anything else, with all the other problems and challenges we face, there are higher priorities. Nonetheless, the *principle* of guaranteeing everyone a share of the nation's wealth remains relevant, and there is another way of making this happen, one that could sit alongside a more conventional social security system. It draws on Paine's idea for a universal social inheritance, the lump sum payment on reaching adulthood.

In one sense, Paine's *Agrarian Justice* speaks very much to the era that he was living through – he suggested, for example, that a prudent twenty-one-year-old might use the fifteen pounds given to them on reaching adulthood to invest in a cow. But in another sense his idea has proved timeless. In fact, believe it or not, a generation of British young people is beginning to benefit from a policy directly inspired by Paine's legacy.

Back in the mid-2000s the Labour government introduced the Child Trust Fund – putting £250 into a savings account for every baby born after September 2002, with an additional £250 for children from low-income families and a commitment to top it up with a further sum at age seven. The children would be able to access the money once they turned eighteen, although family members could add to the amount in the meantime. In September 2020 the first recipients gained access to their accounts.[36] Admittedly only some cohorts of young people will benefit from Child Trust Funds, as they were abolished by the Coalition government after 2010, yet six million eighteen-year-olds will eventually benefit from an average of £1,200 each.[37]

In a limited way this helps address the fact noted earlier that around half of households have less than £1,500 in savings, and it should have a very direct effect on many people's lives. There is strong evidence that having assets has an impact on people's wellbeing; significantly, having assets in early adulthood is found to improve employment prospects, wages and health later in life.[38] Indeed, it was these wide-ranging impacts of wealth, or rather the lack of it, that underpinned the case for Child Trust Funds more than a decade ago.

Maybe to some readers £1,200 doesn't sound like very much, but even a relatively modest amount of wealth can make a meaningful difference.[39] As Gavin Kelly, who helped conceive the programme, argues, 'Some people say, "Well what's the point in doing something which might only give someone £1,000 or £2,000, or whatever it is." I've never heard a person without much money make that point, never. I only ever hear people who've got comfortable bank accounts make that point.'[40] When we discussed Child Trust Funds on *Reasons to be Cheerful*, a listener emailed in to say that £1,000 had opened up a world of opportunity for her. Although she was born before Child Trust Funds were established, her parents and grandparents had put £1,000 in a savings accounts that she could access on turning eighteen. She used it to buy a laptop and told us, 'That laptop carried me through my undergraduate degree. I used it to apply to my dream MSc programme in Germany, to help me learn two languages, learn to code, and keep in touch with friends and family ... and then to work remotely in [my] job for three months during lockdown ... it made the absolute world of difference in terms of access to higher education and jobs.'

All of the evidence suggests this applies more widely: according to the research, 'assets do not need to be large to have a positive significant effect' on wages, employment and physical and mental health.[41] So, in principle, there is a case to be made for reviving something similar to the Child Trust Fund. Of course the larger the sum, the greater the impact; an ambitious version of the plan involves all young adults being given a sum of £10,000.[42]

As things stand, we face a staggering wealth inequality problem. Inequality is measured using something called the Gini coefficient, which uses a scale from 0 – perfect equality – to 1, where a single person owns all the income or wealth in a society. Family income inequality in the UK scores 0.34. That's high by international standards and remains stubbornly so, but inequality of wealth – what a person owns, rather than what they earn –in our country is far worse. Using the Gini coefficient, wealth inequality is 0.66, inequality in value of property owned is 0.71, pensions 0.75 and financial wealth – measuring bank accounts, savings, shares and unsecured debt – is an extraordinary 0.93, reflecting the debts that so many lower- and middle-income people have.[43] There is a massive racial wealth gap too. For every £1 that white British families have in the UK, Pakistani families have 50p, Black Caribbean families have just 20p and Black African and Bangladeshi households a mere 10p.[44] Child Trust Funds or a similar scheme aren't going to solve the problem of wealth inequality on their own, but they could begin to ensure wealth was more widely held.

It's worth saying that the UK's Child Trust Fund cost a fraction of the freedom dividend – when it was abolished, £500 million a year.[45] That's less than 0.1 per cent of total government spending in 2019. To finance a more ambitious version of such a scheme, obviously general public expenditure is one option, but there is also another way to think about this. In Alaska the PFD came about as a way to prevent oil revenues from being squandered. Norway has similarly benefited from oil revenue and, having invested the money, now has a $1 trillion sovereign wealth fund and is one of the richest countries in the world.[46]

The UK has also benefited from North Sea oil revenues since the 1980s. By one estimate, if we had created a similar fund to Norway's it could be worth £500 billion today, but we spent the money instead.[47] It might not have been enough to afford even an Alaskan PFD but we could certainly have afforded a very generous version of the Child Trust Fund. There is unfortunately no sign of further windfalls on the scale of North Sea oil coming our way, although the Treasury may get a decent sum from the selling of offshore wind licences.[48] And the public finances in the UK will take some time to recover after the economic crisis of coronavirus. But the lost opportunity of North Sea oil revenues should make us at least take seriously the principle of putting money aside and using it to give every citizen a financial stake.

The freedom dividend and social inheritance come from different places and address different issues. The first would likely involve a fundamental overhaul of our welfare system, the second would give people some additional protection while sitting alongside the system. But they are united by the principle of sharing the nation's resources to promote economic security and freedom. Each offers a clear example of how a new social contract could guarantee everyone a material stake in our economy. The one-off sum of social inheritance would do less to promote security and, unless set at a high level, do less to fundamentally reorder the way our society works, but it would still be a world away from where we are today, and is far more likely to come about. As we see a generation of young people benefiting from Child Trust Funds over the next few years, we will be able to gauge their effects, and it may become easier to imagine something similar being introduced. Some form of social inheritance could profoundly change our society by establishing the principle that each person is entitled to a share of the nation's wealth in order to provide them with real freedom, which only the better-off have today.

What I am certain about is that in the light of the pandemic and all it has revealed –inequality in incomes and wealth, the inadequacy of our welfare system and benefits, the precariousness of people's finances, the real risks and insecurity many are having to cope with as a result – we cannot carry on as we are. However we choose to change, we cannot allow these deep injustices to disappear beneath the waves as we return to normal life.

CHAPTER 4

Family Values

Women are waking up. They know that men have ruled the
world since time immemorial. And how has that world been?
Aðalheiður Bjarnfreðsdóttir, representative of Sókn,
a trade union for low-paid women workers[1]

One Friday at the end of October, Iceland came to a standstill. Schools closed, theatres shut, flights were cancelled. Bank
bosses had to staff the tills because their cashiers were not in
work. One in ten Icelanders gathered at a mass rally in the capital Reykjavik, demanding a shift in how the country was run.
Remarkably, in homes across the nation one half of the population stopped doing all housework, cooking and childcare.

The year was 1975. The protesters were all women. Ninety
per cent of Icelandic women went on strike that day in protest at
their subordinate role in society.[2] The immediate consequences
made their point for them: the country couldn't run without
women's labour, so it was time to value it properly.

Within five years Iceland would pass anti-pay-discrimination
laws and elect the first female head of state in Europe. Shortly
afterwards, the Women's Alliance Party was formed, and women
were elected to 15 per cent of the seats in parliament.[3] Fast-
forward to today, and Iceland has one of the highest percentages
of women in work at 85 per cent, has legislation in place to

mandate equal pay in all firms with over twenty-five employees, has a law stipulating that 40 per cent of positions on company boards are to be filled by women and provides childcare for almost all one-to-five-year-olds. It also currently has a woman prime minister. No wonder the country has topped the global Gender Equality Index for more than ten years in a row.[4]

Perhaps the most forward-thinking and transformative aspect of Iceland's policies when it comes to the roles of women and men – and which provides the inspiration for this chapter – is that it is now the European and arguably the world's leader in equal parental leave. On the birth of a child, each parent in Iceland is entitled to five months away from work, paid at 80 per cent of their salary. The parents share a further two months that can be divided between them as they wish. Fathers in Iceland take a higher proportion of total parental leave than anywhere else in the world.[5] Importantly, same-sex couples have the same entitlement as mixed-sex couples.

I said at the start of Part I that our two previous social contracts are not coming back and nor, for various reasons, would we want them to. One of the reasons for this is that both had deep gender discrimination baked into their expectations of the way most people would and should lead their lives. Any new social contract has to have gender equality at its heart. Paid parental leave is a crucial part of the social contract because it determines how we as a society support those who want to have a family and how we share the 'risk' – in the sense of cushioning the impact – of having children on parents' ability to work and earn an income. The right kind of parental leave can therefore help build a world where mothers are better able to balance work and family, and ultimately where women and men have equal freedoms and opportunities.

Yet too often gender equality is framed as only being about how to extend to women the chance to compete on the same terms as men but in a society defined in the traditional image of men's lives – centred around work. Our ambition should be to build a world where men engage equally in the caring that has historically been done by women, and in so doing reorder the values of work, family and love so that work does not always come first.

At the risk of Nordic fatigue, these issues were explained very well by a former Swedish prime minister, Olof Palme. In 1970 he gave a far-sighted speech entitled 'The Emancipation of Man'. 'We have talked long enough about the emancipation of women, of the problem of women's role in society. But in order that women shall be emancipated from their antiquated role the men must also be emancipated ... We say that the aim over the long run must be that men and women should be given the same rights, obligations and work assignments in society.'[6] If a Swedish leader could be talking about this fifty years ago, surely we can reach for something better as a country today.

Having had this dose of optimism, let us now consider the cold reality of where Britain currently stands on these issues, which has been made starkly apparent during the pandemic. One of the uncomfortable truths about our society is that, when it comes to juggling work and family, it is mothers who have often shouldered the lion's share of the responsibility. Parents have faced stress as never before during Covid-19, with many combining working from home with looking after children and home-schooling. Detailed research in the UK during the first lockdown showed that under pressure traditional gender roles reinforced themselves. Fathers working at home managed double the amount of uninterrupted work time on average compared to mothers in the same situation.[7] You might wonder if this is a consequence of fathers' earnings generally being higher, and therefore the family making an economic decision about whose work to prioritise. But even in families where the mother was the higher earner, they undertook an average of one and a half hours more childcare each day. The pandemic has revealed that we have a long way to go – a very long way – in the pursuit of gender equality.

It won't surprise you to learn, however, that there has been a revolution in attitudes and expectations in recent decades. As recently as the 1980s, the British Social Attitudes survey tells us, half the public agreed that 'a man's job is to earn money' and 'a woman's job is to look after the home and family'. Today it is down to nearer one in ten.[8] Fathers today spend seven times more quality time with their kids than they did forty years ago.[9] So although under Covid-19 fathers weren't sharing the burden equally, they were doing proportionately more childcare than they had ever done before.[10] There has been a wholesale change in cultural attitudes and norms – not to complete equality, but a big change.

What is so interesting is that our institutions are miles behind our attitudes – and I think that explains lots of our problems. This is most apparent when it comes to employment. Fathers' requests for flexible working (such as part-time employment) are refused at almost twice the rate of mothers'. Dads who ask to work part time are judged by potential employers to be less committed to their jobs than mothers who make the same request. Unsurprisingly, dads are therefore twice as likely to fear that asking for flexible working will damage their careers.[11]

I can speak to this from personal experience. Two months after I became leader of the Labour Party in 2010, my wife Justine had our second child, Sam. I took less than a measly two weeks off and already there was muttering. Of course being the leader of a political party is an unusual job, and you might think the muttering had more to do with my leadership (probably true). But clearly it's not just me.

Indeed, it's when a baby is born that the gender pay gap between men and women really takes off, and, given the support available, that's not surprising. There is a yawning disparity between what is available to mothers and fathers. In the UK mothers are entitled to 90 per cent of their salary for six weeks, then a flat-rate payment of £150 a week for thirty-three weeks, and subsequently thirteen weeks' unpaid leave.[12] In practice, some but by no means all employers offer better arrangements to mothers.[13] This is an extremely ungenerous system by international standards particularly in monetary terms, but the support for fathers is even less generous: a miserable two weeks' paternity leave paid at a flat rate of £150 a week.[14] That's it for dedicated father's leave. Just two weeks. One survey found that more than nine out of ten British fathers say they would do 'whatever it takes' to be involved in the early weeks of their child's life. But fathers in the UK were among the most likely to cite financial constraints as the biggest barrier to taking more leave with their newly born or adopted child.[15] The state support available to new British fathers clearly implies that they are expected to take a brief paternal pit stop, often at financial cost to the family, and then speed off back to work as if nothing has changed.

This situation holds us back and reinforces gendered roles, rather than challenges them. UK parental leave provision is designed for the twentieth-century economy of men at work and women at home. A wholesale reordering is required.

As we contemplate what that reordering should look like, it is worth considering why previous efforts to remedy the problem have failed. In 2015 the government introduced arrangements whereby the nine months of maternity pay and the three months of unpaid leave could be shared between mothers and fathers. When it was introduced Deputy Prime Minister Nick Clegg heralded it thus: 'For too long, mums have been told their place is at home with their child, while dads return to work. I want parents to choose for themselves how to balance work and family.'[16] Unfortunately, and despite undoubted good intentions, this is not the way it has worked out. When the government introduced the policy, it anticipated that between 2 and 8 per cent of eligible fathers would use the new option of sharing leave. While official figures are opaque, take-up is thought to be running very much at the lower end of that.[17]

Why is this? First of all, various qualification requirements render as many as half of households ineligible.[18] But even for those who do qualify, the £150 flat-rate payment represents less than twenty hours per week of work at the current statutory living wage of £8.72. For the vast majority of families, that means a substantial drop in earnings. The pressure is therefore on the lower-paid parent to give up work. Here, the reality of the gender pay gap delivers a double whammy: in couple families with at least one working parent, only one mother in five earns the same as or more than her partner.[19] Given that fathers are so much more likely to be earning more, it often simply doesn't make financial sense for the man to take substantial leave.

This situation brings to mind the philosopher R. H. Tawney's famous lines about dining at the Ritz: 'the right of all who can afford it to dine at the Ritz ... must be accompanied by conditions which ensure that ... [it] can in fact be exercised'.[20] For many fathers, the freedom to choose to give up work is about as attainable as dining at the Ritz. The right of fathers to take parental leave has got to be accompanied by policies that enable them to do so.

What's more, as experts warned at the time, there is something inherently problematic with the design, even the concept, of shared leave. The wearying thing is that if we had looked at the Nordic countries, we would have seen that they went through exactly the same failed experiment almost *fifty* years ago – about the time Nick Clegg and I were toddlers. In 1974, in the spirit of Olof Palme's speech that I cited earlier, Sweden became the first country in the world to introduce not just maternity leave and pay but shared parental leave – to be taken by the father or the mother. But twenty years after the 1974 reforms, fathers were only taking 10 per cent of the total leave – the remaining 90 per cent taken by mothers. Half of men took absolutely no leave at all.[21] 'Men did what they had always done: work,' according to the deputy prime minister of the time, Bengt Westerberg. 'Women were much better at breaking into the men's world than the other way round. We had done only half the revolution.'[22]

Offering shared leave removes none of the pressures we have described, neither the cultural ones, which would have been strong in 1974 and remain so in many environments today, nor the financial ones – on men to keep working and women to be the primary care-givers. It is the equivalent of granting a mother the right to give up some of her leave to her partner (at a financial loss) rather than actually providing couples with a real choice.

It was the absence of men from what has become known as the second shift (unpaid work in the home) that powered a further movement for change, beginning in the 1990s in places like Sweden and Iceland. This resulted in a crucial adjustment: the father's months of leave would be provided on a use-it-or-lose-it basis, paid at a generous level, as a high proportion of previous income. The effects of use-it-or-lose-it have been dramatic. The proportion of total leave taken by fathers in Sweden has risen to 29 per cent.[23] If anything, it's been even more striking in Iceland. In 1995, with no paid paternity leave, men took just 0.1 per cent of leave. In the year 2000, after fathers became entitled to two weeks' paid leave, as in Britain today, they took 3 per cent of total leave.[24] Today, on the latest figures available, men are taking 30 per cent of the total.[25]

The benefits of this policy go beyond mitigating the immediate effects of childbirth on women's careers or giving fathers more time with their new-born children. All the evidence suggests that it has long-term effects on the division of labour in the home. According to a recent study, when scrutinising what could make a difference to this, 'Only one specific family policy stood out: non-transferable paid paternal leave – also known as a father's quota. When use-it-or-lose-it paid leave was offered, men participated more at home.'[26] Another study confirmed this, showing that fathers who took leave around childbirth were still doing more childcare when their children were two and three years old.[27] There is even evidence that nine years after a baby's birth paternity leave has had long-term effects on the quality of father–child relationships.[28]

The case for adopting use-it-or-lose-it paternity leave at a level that provides a proper choice is overwhelming. But this is just the start. Making our aspirations for gender equality

a reality will take much more than this. In the Nordic countries the commitment to paternity leave is embedded in a
much wider network of policies, including generously paid
maternity leave, comprehensive childcare arrangements and
a commitment to flexible working hours. Again, here the UK
finds itself well behind the pack, coming twenty-eighth out of
thirty-one of the world's richest countries in a recent ranking
of family-friendly policies by UNICEF. Our highest ranking is
for childcare enrolment for under-threes, yet even here we lag
miles behind the Nordic countries.[29] The average British family
with a two-year-old child spends 34 per cent of its income on
childcare compared to 5 per cent for a Swedish family.[30] It's
worth underlining that British parents face some of the highest childcare costs in the world because of the relative lack of
government support.[31] That further reduces the employment
rate of women in particular because these costs frequently
outweigh the financial benefit from earning. (We will return
to these issues in Chapter 7.)

The results of the Nordic countries' approach are plain to
see. They have significantly lower gender gaps in both employment and pay.[32] Estimates suggest that the rise in women's
employment is also responsible for a significant proportion of
their economic growth. And some argue that greater gender
equality even leads to greater happiness among both girls and
boys as it leads to societies with greater social and emotional
support.[33] By now you are probably convinced that the Nordics
are a great place to live when it comes to gender equality, even
if they still have some way yet to go, but the interesting question is not just what good looks like but how they got there.
More to the point, how can we make it happen here?

If you want gender equality, you've got to think about who
is in the room making decisions. Equal political representation
matters. After the 2019 general election in the UK, we patted
ourselves on the back about the record number of female MPs
elected. Women made up 34 per cent of MPs, albeit just 25
per cent of the governing Conservative Party.[34] But leaving

aside the fact that that is still only a third of MPs, even this put us well behind the Nordics. Denmark, Finland, Norway and Sweden were all above 34 per cent female representation more than twenty years ago.[35] It's no wonder we seem decades behind them in our family policies when we are decades behind in political representation. Dig into the history and the connection between the two is absolutely crucial.

By the late 1960s, 15 per cent of Swedish MPs were women (compared to only 4 per cent in the UK).[36] They challenged the male breadwinner model – the notion that men were the workers and women should stay at home. Their arguments were given impetus by a shortage of labour and the resulting need for women to go out to work, but it is surely no coincidence that it was women who made them. More recently, a German study showed that when a woman beat a man in local council elections, childcare provision in the relevant area increased on average by 40 per cent. Having women in positions of political power changes the political conversation and changes policy.[37]

Of course, the Nordic countries also have very strong social democratic traditions emphasising equality – unlike the UK, where our first woman Prime Minister, Margaret Thatcher, stood for a much more individualised, market-based politics. Indeed, it is that context that helps explain how women got into positions of political power earlier in these countries, and thus were able to advocate for the relatively advanced state of gender relations and family policy now enjoyed in them. The demand for women's equality drew on a wider prevailing political philosophy – in Iceland, as we saw, women were willing to go on strike for the cause – establishing a virtuous circle of relative gender equality, women's participation in work and generous childcare and leave arrangements.

We in the UK feel a long way from this virtuous circle. Indeed, we seem at times to be in a vicious circle – a labour market still divided by gender, lower employment for women than in Scandinavia, weak childcare arrangements and poor parental leave – in which the lives of men, dominated by work rather than family, tend to define what we mean by success and shape the world of work in their image.

Changing this work culture is something that employers can and increasingly will have to play a part in (as we discuss further in Chapter 8). Sensing that public policy lags behind the values they espouse, British multinational insurer Aviva decided in 2017 to give equal paid time off to fathers and mothers – six months each. As they said in explaining their decision, 'We believe that unconscious hiring and promotional bias is inevitable in any system that treats men and women differently when they become parents. We also know that parenting is seen as equally important no matter people's gender.'[38] Has it worked? Undoubtedly yes. After a year, 500 Aviva employees had taken advantage of the policy, almost half of whom were men.[39]

Aviva concluded that it helped their business too, improving the working environment for parents at the company and in particular giving men new insights into the pressures that mothers face in balancing work and family life.[40] Of course, even funded by government, as opposed to a company making the decision itself, use-it-or-lose-it parental leave could place additional pressures on businesses. But this shows that there are definitely benefits too. Sam White, director of public policy at Aviva, was one of those who benefited:

> What I've gained from it is feeling very bonded with my kids. I got to do a lot of that stuff that many dads don't have the opportunity to do, for good or for ill, scraping porridge off the floor, but great stuff, like parks and feeding ducks and toddler groups. I don't think I'd have had the time to memorise every lyric in *Frozen* ... It's becoming a cultural norm within the organisation, in part, because people are going out of their way to talk about it and say this is not a career limiting thing, that we know people value their family life and we want you to.[41]

This demonstrates something very significant: when given a real choice, fathers will take up paid leave as much as mothers.

There is no iron rule that says it will always be mothers. The opportunities available shape the culture, custom and practice. The flip side of this is that if we *do* manage to change expectations, then those expectations can themselves become a powerful force for change in policy. Imagine if it was expected that men should spend more time with their children, to the extent that not to allow it was considered outdated or even sexist. What more would we be demanding from government? How would employers act?

The direction of the Nordic countries continues to be illuminating. Iceland has steadily increased the number of months of leave reserved for fathers.[42] Finland is planning to extend its parental leave to nearly seven months for each parent, albeit with the option to transfer about half of this to the other. As with Iceland, this will take a gender-neutral approach, meaning same-sex couples will have the same entitlement as others.[43] Once we're on the path to change, policy and social attitudes can reinforce one another.

Think what more equal parental leave would do for parents, children, our society and economy as a whole. This matters because it would set us on a different path – the possible, opening up what currently might seem impossible. We would start to break free from a culture which loads so much onto women, penalises them for having children, constrains them in a particular stereotype, and, as Palme said, constrains men culturally too. If we get this right, everyone can contribute to economic success and acquire more choice about how they balance work and family life. It would also make a statement about what really matters in our society. Work would not dominate our existence. It could be the start of a remaking of the social contract between women and men and between work and family life. This chapter has also shown there is a crucial role for business in how the social contract can be renewed. That takes us to a much wider discussion about its role in our society.

CHAPTER 5

Everybody's Business

The businessmen [who] believe that they are defending free
enterprise when they declaim that business is not concerned
'merely' with profit but also with promoting desirable 'social'
ends ... [are] preaching pure and unadulterated socialism ...
unwitting puppets of the intellectual forces that have been
undermining the basis of a free society these past decades.

Milton Friedman, 13 September 1970[1]

The US outdoor clothing company Patagonia would offend
Milton Friedman, one of the most consequential right-wing
economists of the last hundred years. Patagonia prides itself on
its environmental and social record. It has given out $90 million
in grants in the last three decades to environmental causes. It
has funded campaigns to stop mining pollution in Alaska, save
grizzly bears in Yellowstone National Park and protect forests
in Poland. It even sued the US government when the Trump
administration tried to remove protection from large parts of
a national park. Patagonia pioneered childcare for its employees when it wasn't fashionable, pays the living wage to all in
the company and tells people not to buy its products on Black
Friday, giving away 100 per cent of its Black Friday profits.[2]
Patagonia is one of the most famous examples of a type
of company known as a B Corporation (or B Corp), whose

enshrined purpose is to be accountable not simply to its share-holders – a corporation's normal fiduciary duty – but also to its employees, the community and the planet. Other famous B Corps include Ben and Jerry's (ice cream), the Body Shop (cosmetics retailer), Danone (global food brand) and around 3,700 other firms across the world.[3] An example of a British B Corp is Cook, the high-end frozen-meal delivery company. Cook pays its employees the real living wage (independently set at a level to provide an acceptable standard of living, currently £10.85 an hour in London and £9.50 elsewhere),[4] limits the salary ratio between its highest- and lowest-paid employee to 15:1, has bought a vacation cabin for workers struggling to afford to pay for holidays, and recruits people facing barriers to employment, including mental health, homelessness or a prison record.[5]

In different ways, these companies are reaching for a new way of doing business because they feel the old model is bust. Explaining their approach, the co-chair of Cook James Perry, who loves business but hates the current model of capitalism, sounds like a left-wing politician, though maybe more radical than most: 'It is now clear that the current operating system, which drives relentless profit maximisation, is harming us all in its single-minded conversion of social and natural capital into financial capital. It is a failed and broken system in urgent need of an upgrade.'[6] And it's not just B Corps. For decades, social enterprises including household names such as Café Direct, Belu water and Divine Chocolate have been pioneering a similar approach.[7] Beyond these companies, increasing num-bers of businesses recognise that their future is not in simply maximising profits but something bigger: the triple bottom line of people, profits and planet. As a leading thinker Colin Mayer describes it, we need purpose-driven businesses that 'produce profitable solutions to the problems of people and planet, and not profit from producing problems for people or planet'.[8]

This feels a long way from the quotation at the start of this chapter, which has shaped many of the institutions and practices that we live with today. Milton Friedman was the intellectual guru of politicians like Ronald Reagan and Margaret Thatcher, and his ideas cast a long shadow. The essay quoted, published at the dawn of the 1970s in the *New York Times*, was not just a provocative intervention but foreshadowed the spirit of an age, a classic exposition of the pursuit of what is known as shareholder value. The kernel of this philosophy is that the job of firms is simply to get on with maximising profits and not to dabble in 'social purposes'. (The flip side of this is that the best thing governments can do to help them prosper is get out of the way – an assumption we will return to towards the end of the chapter.)

As Friedman put it, the responsibility of an executive 'is to conduct the business in accordance with [the shareholders'] desires, which generally will be to make as much money as possible while conforming to the basic rules of the society, both those embodied in law and those embodied in ethical custom'. If a company executive acts to 'reduc[e] pollution beyond the amount that is in the best interests of the corporation or that is required by law ... Or hire[s] "hardcore" unemployed instead of better qualified available workmen to contribute to the social objective of reducing poverty' then the executive is taking over the proper functions of government and acting as 'simultaneously legislator, executive and jurist'.[9] In other words, not doing their job.

In the introduction to Part I, I argued that to succeed a social contract has to guarantee everyone a stake in society. Today, businesses are so powerful in shaping our world that we cannot renew the social contract without discussing their role. And for many people – particularly those working in the private sector – their stake in society is intimately connected to their relationship with business. It is companies that help them meet their basic needs by providing their jobs and paying their salaries. At their best, employers share the burden of life's inherent risks by offering sick pay, decent pensions and job security to their workers. And yet, over the last forty years or so we have seen too many businesses step back from this role. Indeed, the Friedman essay is a manifesto for them to do so. In the Friedman world a pension for a worker is a burden for the firm that it should eliminate if it can. A contract of guaranteed employment is an annoyance if it can get away with a zero-hours contract instead. Doing right by the planet, beyond the minimum required by law, is a waste of money. In the world where the shareholder is king, everything and everyone else is a dispensable pawn.

However, in recent years we have learned that we need business to think more broadly about its role. Environmental pollution, low wages and workers' insecurity have real effects on society which the market, left to its devices, does little or nothing to mitigate and are hard for governments to clear up. Yet, at the same time, firms rely absolutely on taxpayer-funded infrastructure and services – from education to the NHS to the transport network – for their success. Business as a whole cannot operate in isolation but has wider obligations to the societies in which it functions and prospers. At the same time, we also need to recognise the power of business to do good. The ingenuity, imagination and inspiration of the private sector is essential for us to be able to overcome so many of the world's most complex and knotty problems. The idea of the social contract is a recognition that ultimately the fate of businesses, their workers and wider society are intertwined. We rise and fall together.

It is too simplistic to ascribe the problems we have seen simply to the motives of those running businesses. The truth is that most businesses want to create profits and function with social purpose, as do the people who work for them. Just think of the companies that have stepped up in response to the coronavirus crisis, providing free school meals for children, manufacturing ventilators, and looking after their workers. This is true of millions of small and medium-sized businesses in our country, but larger businesses too, which, for example, put climate at the heart of their mission or champion the living wage. It is the rules of the game that make it harder not easier for businesses to do the right thing.

In the 1980s there was massive deregulation of finance in the US and UK. As a result – in contrast to the more staid and stable financial regime of forty years ago – the stock markets are now dominated by hedge funds and other financial institutions chasing short-term returns. As recently as 1990, 50 per cent of shares in Britain's publicly listed companies (whose shares are quoted on the Stock Exchange) were held by UK pension funds and insurance companies, institutions that traditionally like to invest for the long term. Today that figure is less than 10 per cent. Around 10 per cent of shares are held directly by individuals, who are also for the most part longer-term investors, against 50 per cent in the 1960s. The majority of shares are now held by investment funds with a shorter-term focus on high returns. On average, shares are now held for less than six months, compared to six years in 1950.[10] The UK is bottom of the international league when it comes to committed shareholders.[11] To put it in the jargon, patient capital has been replaced by impatient capital.

This means that the pressure on companies to earn a fast buck is much more intense than before, which in turn accounts for the fact that in the UK dividend payouts to shareholders are consistently much higher than the average across the world.[12] The pressure companies face to keep their share price up has also led to an unprecedented surge in share buybacks – where companies use their profits not to invest in themselves or develop new lines of business but to buy their shares *back* from their shareholders, thus reducing the number of shares in circulation and so raising, temporarily at least, the price of each remaining share. In the US $6 trillion was spent on share buybacks between 2010 and 2019.[13] In the same period in the UK, FTSE 100 companies gave back an eye-watering £136 billion more to shareholders through buybacks than they raised from them by issuing new shares.[14] It's no wonder the Bank of England estimates that only one in four businesses prioritises investment as a use of internal funds.[15]

Today, more than a decade on from the financial crisis, there are strong signs that the Friedman model is in disrepute. A recent poll showed that more than seven out of ten people believe 'Capitalism isn't working well or is harmful to the UK economy' and a similar number think that 'Business should have a legal responsibility to the planet and people, alongside maximising profits.'[16] If the public as a whole has lost faith with the kind of capitalism we have, younger generations are even more sceptical. A large majority of millennials (those born between 1983 and 1994) across thirty-six countries believe that business leaders 'have no ambition beyond wanting to make money', and the opinion of them held by Gen Z – the generation born in 1995 and after – is if anything even lower.[17]

The corporate world has also changed its tune. In 2019 the Business Roundtable, an association of the CEOs of the largest multinationals in the US, formally abandoned its belief, held for the previous two decades, in shareholder primacy, favouring instead 'a commitment to all stakeholders' – although there are reasons to be sceptical about how serious this commitment really is.[18] This is where B Corps and others come in. The B Corp movement provides a standard by which to assess and certify that commitment. It measures a company on a number of metrics: governance, workers, community, environment and consumers. To achieve certification as a B Corp, the firm must also make a legal change, replacing its primary duty to shareholders with legally enshrined duties to multiple stakeholders.

How stringent are the B Corp criteria and how well does the movement address the problems of shareholder value? It's possible to argue this both ways. On the one hand, one in ten B Corps in the US don't pay the living wage and some companies in the highly controversial US prison business have managed to get themselves registered as B Corps.[19] On the other hand, there is reason to believe that becoming a B Corp is more than just corporate whitewash. After Etsy, the online marketplace for handmade goods, got B Corp certification, its shareholders became unhappy with the constraints and it eventually deregistered.[20] So the change must have counted for something.

What's also remarkable is that the B Corp idea, started by three friends in the 2000s, has now spawned legislation in thirty-eight US states that allows companies to officially incorporate with a wider social purpose of creating public benefit – for say society or the environment – alongside benefit to shareholders. Some 10,000 companies have used this to become 'public benefit corporations'.[21] And it's not just states run by Democrats. B Corp legislation was even signed by Donald Trump's vice president, Mike Pence, when governor of Indiana, as well as many other Republican governors.

I can understand the suspicion. If supporters of Donald Trump are happy with the idea, just how radical can it be? The key thing to understand about the legislation is that it provides a mechanism for companies to *choose* how to run themselves. It does not force them to do so in a particular way. In that sense, it gives business greater freedom, not less. That's partly why it got the support of Republicans as well as Democrats. But there is another, more intriguing reason for the support. In the US, the country that modelled Milton Friedman's form of capitalism, there is now a bipartisan recognition that it isn't working. In the words of Marco Rubio, former Republican presidential candidate, 'Nothing about [shareholder primacy] guarantees that capital will be deployed to the [most] productive ends ... [It] has tilted business decision-making towards delivering returns quickly and predictably to investors, rather than building long-term capabilities through investment and production ... and [it] has resulted in a diminished understanding of the role workers play and the risk they undertake in the value creation process.'[22]

The freedom to choose is what has helped gain the B Corps support, but it is also likely to be insufficient for the kind of change we need. Even if the B-Corp movement grew exponentially, what about those firms that either have no interest in moving away from the shareholder-value model or are incapable of doing so? We cannot simply rely on the good intentions of the many well-motivated businesses – welcome though they

are. It is the legal system – and dry as it might sound, company law specifically – that has always shaped the rights and
responsibilities of firms and those who run them.

In the UK the crux of the issue is the disputed meaning of
Section 172 of the 2006 UK Companies Act – passed by a
Labour government. This states that a company director should
'have regard' to the interests of employees, suppliers, customers
and the environment, but their primary duty must be to act in
a way to 'promote the success of the company for the benefit of
its members [shareholders] as a whole'.[23] Some people interpret
this as an affirmation of the primacy of shareholder value, others that the law clearly points to a wide array of other interests
and should be described as 'enlightened shareholder value'.
In reality, whenever there is a conflict between the interests
of shareholders and other stakeholders, it is the shareholder
who is likely to win out – as the current law requires that. As
Andy Haldane, chief economist of the Bank of England, says of
the act, 'for the first time in history, shareholder primacy had
been hard-wired into companies' statutory purposes'.[24] Since
then, changes in 2018 to the Corporate Governance Code do
mean that companies over a certain size are expected, for the
first time, to explain their fundamental purpose, values and
strategy and to show how they are engaging with stakeholders.[25] However, the code is voluntary and subordinate to the
2006 legislation.

That's why in the UK the B Corp movement and others want
to see a fundamental rewriting of Section 172 in order, in their
words, to 'reset capitalism'.[26] Under the new model the core
purpose of every business would be to produce benefit not simply for its shareholders but wider society, including its workers
and the environment. This would reshape the duties of every
company director and force boards to develop strategies and
business plans that benefit all stakeholders. By rewriting a key
part of company law it would enshrine a different approach.
Shareholders would retain a central role, but other stakeholders
would have parity, and there would be no way any business

or director could contract out of these requirements. It would also help shield those running companies against short-term shareholder pressure and help protect the best businesses from being undercut by the less scrupulous.

All very well, you might think, but don't shareholders bear the risk of things going wrong and therefore deserve their top spot in the pecking order? Actually, it's more complicated than that. If a company goes bust, shareholders' liability is strictly limited by law, and while most shareholders today own stock in many different companies, most employees rely exclusively on one company – the one that employs them – for their income, so it is they who arguably bear most risk from it going under.[27] More to the point, it's at best dubious that the pursuit of shareholder value at the cost of other stakeholders has served the country well, economically or socially. Over the last thirty years, while the proportion of company cash going to shareholders has increased, the proportion being reinvested in companies has fallen.[28] Increasingly, when it comes to business investment, our economy lags behind other major countries. And while we have great, world-class companies, we also lag behind many of our competitors in productivity.[29]

While it is difficult to establish causality, it is notable that many of the countries ahead of us in productivity do not have this shareholder primacy model. Indeed, it's only in the English-speaking world that it's the predominant one. Japan, Germany, France and Scandinavia follow much more of a stakeholder model. This means employees in particular take their rightful place as a priority alongside, and not secondary to, shareholders. German corporate law, for example, defines the role of a company's board as governing the corporation for the 'good of the enterprise, its multiple stakeholders, and society at large'.[30]

Those advocating the reform of Section 172 maintain that it would not sacrifice profitability and success in order to treat other stakeholders better; they believe it can produce more successful companies. They argue that the short-term,

dividend-maximising approach tends to discourage the investment essential for long-term success. Employees and customers
care about values, so purpose-driven companies may also be
in a better position to attract the right workforce and build
customer loyalty.

Of course, one new clause in the companies act would not
be enough on its own to solve the problems of UK capitalism
but it could be the linchpin of a different future. There are an
array of other reforms that could also make a difference. In
Chapter 15 I look at ownership models, including cooperatives and employee-owned firms, which lead firms to prioritise
other stakeholders, particularly workers. Another need that it
is absolutely vital to address is the availability of patient capital, and one solution is reform that encourages asset owners
to become long-term 'stewards' of companies. The other is to
find new sources of such capital. And here we return to the
assumption that I touched on briefly towards the start of the
chapter about the nature of the relationship between business
and government.

Just as we need a new relationship between businesses and
society, so too a new bargain must be forged between business
and the state, one in which government does not just get out
of the way but actively supports business instead. The term
'industrial strategy' refers to how government uses the various
levers at its disposal (subsidies, tax breaks, research grants,
infrastructure support, regulation, competition policy) to create
the conditions in which businesses can thrive. In this way of
thinking, the state defines the big challenges facing society and
effectively says to businesses, 'These are our priorities. We'll
support you to help us solve them together.' One of the most
remarkable successes over the last decade is the fall in the cost
of renewable energy like onshore wind that I mentioned in
Chapter 1, but this only happened because governments around
the world found ways of subsidising its take-up – it was only
as more wind turbines and solar panels were produced that
their prices fell to commercially attractive levels.

The corollary is that for those businesses that tackle government priorities, the state becomes a source of finance – in other words, patient capital. Industrial policy that supports businesses with both loans and investment is quite normal in other countries, including France, Germany and even the United States, whose governments recognise that markets on their own may be too impatient to fund certain kinds of industries that are important to the economy over the long term, particularly emerging technologies. Such support is provided in the form of loans from public investment banks and, in some cases, by public institutions taking a stake in a company.

Some companies which are now household names started out with government support, including in the US, where there is an ironic contrast between the country's rhetorical commitment to the swashbuckling corporate entrepreneur succeeding on their own and the reality of state and private sector succeeding together. Apple, now a trillion-dollar company, started out with public investment funding from the state of Illinois in 1980.[31] Elon Musk doesn't boast about it, but Tesla got a $465 million loan at a crucial moment in 2009 from the US government.[32] Indeed, examples abound all round the world. In Chapter 19 we will hear the story of a Danish fossil-fuel company that has transformed itself into a renewable energy company in just a decade. That was only made possible by being 80 per cent state-owned and through patient long-term government finance.

Governments can also make a difference by contributing to the research and development which underpins private-sector success. As a leading scholar in this area, Mariana Mazzucato, points out, the iPhone is an extraordinary invention, but it depends on the internet, whose predecessor was funded by the US Department of Defense, on GPS technology, which began as a US military programme, and on touchscreen technology, which was funded by grants from the National Science Foundation. Even Siri was a spin-off of a US Defense Department project.[33]

Constructing this partnership between the state and private enterprise in such a way that the taxpayer doesn't take on an unfair share of risk is complex. In the 1970s state involvement in industry got a bad name in the UK as it became synonymous with bailing out failing companies. There is also the danger that public-sector support is not rewarded with a fair return when companies or products succeed. But there is rightly now a growing consensus across most of the political spectrum that we have been prisoners of that history for too long. As a country, if we are to succeed, we need to learn from other nations which have been implementing successful industrial strategies for decades, while we in Britain have been sitting on the sidelines.

The experience of tackling Covid, in which government and business have had to work hand in hand, and the potentially even greater challenge of fostering a long-term economic recovery from it, only reinforces this imperative. The truth is that we face such serious challenges, the state cannot abdicate its crucial role in being an active partner with business in creating economic success, and business cannot ignore its responsibilities to society. In other words, we need a new social contract between government and business. Meanwhile, up and down the country many businesses are showing that they can generate jobs, innovation and wealth without subscribing to a Friedmanite view of the world. Many, many businesses want to contribute to our society, and at the moment we have institutions that stand in their way.

Indeed, there are people in every sector of society – from business to government to civil society – who want to be part of building something better, but too often their values are at odds with the way our country is run. In Part II I move on from how to rebuild the social contract to the question of how those values can guide the institutions of our economy and society.

PART II

Life Beyond the Market

To allow the market mechanism to be the sole director of the fate of human beings and their natural environment ... would result in the demolition of society.

Karl Polanyi, *The Great Transformation*[1]

Economics are the method; the object is to change the heart and soul.

Margaret Thatcher, 1981[2]

At its core a market is simply a mechanism for people to exchange goods or services – food or houses, holidays or haircuts – for money. The market mechanism has become one of the most powerful tools in our society and a vital part of our large, complex and ever-changing modern economies. It has huge creative potential. In classical economics the promise of markets is that they translate the self-interest and free choices of individuals into unintended benefits for society. One of the most famous quotes in economics comes from Adam Smith: 'It is not from the benevolence of the butcher, the brewer, or the baker that we expect our dinner, but from their regard to their own self-interest.'[3]

Yet it won't have escaped your attention that so many of the problems we discussed in Part I are rooted in markets.

Fossil-fuel companies have a market incentive to continue to find new ways to drill for oil and gas despite the existential threat of the climate crisis. The private sector has failed to build enough affordable houses because developers can profit from choking the housing supply. Some businesses fail to provide job security, decent wages or sufficient flexibility for their workers, figuring they can profit from driving down the costs of employment, regardless of the impact on workers' wellbeing. In each of these cases, it is clear that there is no guarantee that the outcomes of exchanges in the market are the best outcomes for society.

Over the last thirty or forty years market mechanisms have come to dominate the way our society is run. We have seen weaker constraints on the operation of the market – diluted employment protections for workers and less regulation of institutions like banks and financial markets. We have seen fewer islands of protection from the market – a diminishing of the welfare safety net. And we have seen greater levels of inequality translated into the increased ability of a wealthy few to exercise power in the market. In the words of philosopher Michael Sandel, 'without quite realizing it ... we drifted from having a market economy to being a market society ... A market economy is a tool – a valuable and effective tool – for organizing productive activity. A market society is a way of life in which market values seep into every aspect of human endeavour. It's a place where social relations are made over in the image of the market.'[4]

Should the market be our servant or our master? Most economists today would accept that there exist what are known as market failures, when for whatever reason the mechanism of free exchange in the service of self-interest fails to distribute goods and services in the most efficient way. So, for example, if a firm gets so large as to become a monopoly this can prevent the competition on which markets rely. Sometimes markets fail to account for externalities – things that are not incorporated into the price of a transaction – such as the pollution of the

environment. When buyers and sellers lack sufficient information to make informed choices about exchange, this also leads to
market failures. It is widely accepted that in such circumstances
governments may need to step in to ensure the market works.

But there is a deeper reason, which incorporates but goes
beyond these factors, why we do not want the market to be
the sole director of our fate. In the market everything is treated
as a commodity – an item to be bought and sold at market
prices – but what if the thing for sale was not designed to be a
commodity? This is true of both people and natural resources.
If people are treated purely as commodities, we ignore some
of their most important needs – for time with their families,
for example, which requires limiting the hours they work.
This isn't an efficiency argument but a moral one. The price
of commodities can go up and down, but people need a decent
standard of living regardless of the current market value of
their labour. If natural resources are exploited without restraint
then our environment will face depletion and those resources
will eventually run out.

Karl Polanyi wrote a famous book at the end of the Second
World War, warning of the dangers of leaving markets to
their own devices. He argued that society cannot withstand
the impact of treating people and natural resources as mere
commodities: 'Robbed of the protective covering of cultural
institutions, human beings would perish from the effects of
social exposure ... Nature would be reduced to its elements,
neighbourhoods and landscapes defiled, rivers polluted, military
safety jeopardized, the power to produce food and raw materi-
als destroyed.'[5] Polanyi introduced the idea that markets need
to be 'embedded' in social and democratic choices. In other
words, they can serve us well, but as a society we need to
keep markets in their place so we can protect what we value.

Margaret Thatcher has been a recurring character in this
book. Decisions taken during her time in office underpin much
of the political and economic settlement discussed in Part I,
including the current dominance of markets. In 1981, two years

into her first term, she set out her view of the ethos of British society and how she meant to change it: 'What's irritated me about the whole direction of politics in the last thirty years is that it's always been towards the collectivist society ... If you change the approach you really are after the heart and soul of the nation. Economics are the method; the object is to change the heart and soul.'[6]

She certainly changed our economics, but did she change our soul? I don't think so. There is now a massive gap between who we really are and the institutions of our society. Those institutions now do less to protect people from the harsh judgements of the market, but the spirit of solidarity and empathy has lived on. The task facing us is to match that spirit with the way we run our country, to recast the institutions of our society so that they truly reflect who we are and how we want to live our lives. We are not just consumers, owners and workers, but parents, friends, neighbours and citizens. The market economy is a good tool for organising the sale and purchase of goods, but it must be kept in its place, subject to the values of society.

An unrestrained market society is not only deeply destructive but fatalistic. It believes that market forces are so much more powerful and wise than we are that it is a fantasy to think we have the power to shape our world more effectively and fairly than they can. This part of the book is about jerking us out of that fatalism and showing that we can and must make collective choices about the things that matter to us. Above all, it asks two questions. What are the things that markets cannot protect but need protection? And how do we go about protecting them?

CHAPTER 6

That Which Makes Life Worthwhile

Gross national product counts air pollution and cigarette advertising, and ambulances to clear our highways of carnage ...
special locks for our doors and the jails for the people who
break them ... the destruction of the redwood and the loss of
our natural wonder in chaotic sprawl ... napalm and ... nuclear
warheads and armoured cars for the police to fight the riots
in our cities ...

Yet the gross national product does not allow for the health
of our children, the quality of their education or the joy of their
play ... the beauty of our poetry or the strength of our mar-
riages, the intelligence of our public debate or the integrity of
our public officials. It measures neither our wit nor our courage,
neither our wisdom nor our learning, neither our compassion
nor our devotion to our country, it measures everything, in
short, except that which makes life worthwhile.

Robert Fitzgerald Kennedy, 18 March 1968[1]

I love these words. I can hear Kennedy saying them in his distinc-
tive lilt as I read them. They represent the definitive destruction
of gross domestic product (GDP) as *the* way to measure human
progress.[2] They are also still profoundly relevant today. Our
chief measure of success is out of step with our values. Since

how we act as a society is shaped by what we measure, using GDP in this way risks leading us in the wrong direction.

GDP is the poster child for 'the market is king' philosophy, and as I hope to show in this chapter its cult damages our society. If we are to properly put our values at the centre of the way we run our country, we need to change our measurement of success. In fact, GDP is a recent invention. In 1934 economist Simon Kuznets presented a report to the US Congress in which he proposed a statistical gauge of how the economy – at that point stuck in the Great Depression – was performing. He did this essentially by adding up the total value of all goods and services produced in a country over a set period of time. This new measure streamlined and gave coherence to the ragtag national accounts that had existed up to that point.

GDP provides a measure of national output, and for example during the pandemic, as we have seen much of our economy close down, it has been useful in providing one measure of the scale of loss of production in our country and others. By providing a gauge of how much an economy is producing, it also gives us an idea of productivity per worker, which in turn provides a measure of technological progress. For some specific purposes then, GDP has something going for it.

Yet a cursory look at this metric tells us how partial and misleading it is as the overriding measure of economic success that it has become. The Bank of England tells us on its website, 'Gross domestic product is a measure of the size and health of a country's economy.'[3] Size? Sort of, although it excludes quite a lot, as we will see shortly. But economic health? GDP tells us nothing about who enjoys the benefits of economic growth. Poverty can be rampant, inequality soaring and GDP still rising. If you're an average private-sector worker in America, your living standards have flat-lined over the last forty-five years: average hourly earnings, adjusted for inflation, were $23.68 in 1973; in 2018 they were $22.65.[4] Yet in that same period US GDP has risen from $5.7 trillion to $18.7 trillion.[5] So in terms of GDP America is doing three times better than in 1973, but the average private-sector worker is worse off. Is the US economy really three times healthier?

We see a similar problem in the UK. If you lined everyone in the country up in order, from those earning most to least, the person in the very middle would have what is called median earnings. GDP growth used to rise and fall more or less in proportion to median earnings, but not in recent years. Median pay in 2018 remained lower than in 2008 while GDP had increased.[6] Indeed in 2017, despite rising growth, the Resolution Foundation think tank declared that the UK was in the midst of the 'weakest decade for wage growth since the Napoleonic wars'.[7]

This disconnect has consequences. If politicians in the US had fully realised and been forced to acknowledge that many citizens had endured nearly fifty years of wage stagnation, perhaps they might have woken up more quickly to the discontent and rage that helped Donald Trump win power. If we have the wrong metrics, we draw the wrong conclusions. We miss the warning signs. Think of the Remain argument during the referendum campaign – it was partly about the potentially negative economic impacts of Brexit and, according to George Osborne and David Cameron, the need to protect economic success. But success by what measure? True, GDP was up, but the reality for many families was profoundly different – incomes stagnating or falling. The way we measured our progress as a country obscured rather than revealed the truth.

The problems of GDP don't stop at who gets what. GDP, as Kennedy explained, only looks at the value of things that have a price. So even if providing your goods or services involves destroying public goods, you still get points on the board for GDP. Cut down a pristine forest and offer the wood for sale and it's a GDP bonanza. Close down libraries so people are forced to buy their own books – you've done your bit for GDP. Conversely, put in a free water fountain so people don't buy single-use plastic bottles and you're damaging GDP. Open outdoor gyms in parks so people don't have to pay to exercise, and GDP goes down. The amazing free parkrun movement, which organises communal runs on a Saturday morning? Good for the health of your community, bad for GDP.

If GDP alone was a flawed measure of societal progress for the twentieth century, it is catastrophic for the twenty-first. We know without doubt that we are living way beyond our environmental means, yet in the world of GDP we get credit for doing that. Producing the plastic with which we pollute the ocean, burning the fossil fuels which are choking our atmosphere and heating our planet, reducing our biodiversity; it all counts as a positive. As Herman Daly, one of the founders of environmental economics, has said, 'the current national accounting system treats the earth as a business in liquidation'.[8] Everything is for sale ... while stocks last.

Putting a premium on monetary value above all else is deeply destructive in other ways. British GDP went up by £10 billion a few years ago when activities such as the trade in illegal drugs were factored into the calculation for the first time.[9] No politician I know would celebrate the growth of trade in illicit narcotics, but this supposed measure of economic health does. On the other hand, unpaid care work in the UK is currently valued at £1.2 trillion, equivalent to more than 60 per cent of what is measured by GDP, and yet it is left out.[10] Of course, if this care was actually paid for, GDP would rise, but because it isn't, the prime measure of our national economy excludes something as fundamental as the care we provide for our children and elderly relatives. It is no coincidence that women mainly do this work, and by effectively hiding it from view, we discount its importance and ignore the unequal burden it imposes, as we will see in the next chapter.

GDP is like a very powerful but very focused set of binoculars. By targeting a narrow measure of economic value, GDP blinds us to the rest of the picture, yet listen to government or turn on the news and it reigns supreme. As someone who worked in government, I can tell you that GDP drives the decisions that are made. Figures are produced monthly and guide policy.

The definition of a recession, the ultimate economic failure, is two quarters of falling GDP. Median wages and incomes get more attention than they did, partly because so many people have been drawing attention to the squeeze on them, but rarely beat GDP in news coverage. We know that what makes life worthwhile cannot be boiled down to one number, so why allow GDP to have such power over our society? There is no better way to guarantee the dominance of market thinking.

The good news is that there are signs of change. In 1990 the UN devised the Human Development Index, which takes into account life expectancy, education and per capita income to measure the progress of countries. It started after Nobel-Prize-winning economist Amartya Sen and a colleague discussed the flaws of GDP and concluded that even if developing countries substantially increased their GDP, it would still not necessarily represent the development they wanted to see in health, education and life expectancy.[11] In 2009 a commission of economists assembled at the behest of President Sarkozy of France reported on how to move beyond GDP. As he put it at the launch of the commission's report, 'The world over, citizens think we are lying to them, that the figures are wrong, that they are manipulated. And they have reasons to think like that. Behind the cult of figures, behind all these statistical and accounting structures, there is also the cult of the market that is always right.'[12]

The trend towards looking beyond GDP to alternative scales of progress and success often turns to measures grouped loosely under the category 'subjective wellbeing' – asking people how they feel about their own circumstances. Since 2012, following a resolution at the UN, the 'World Happiness Report' has been produced, ranking countries by the self-declared life satisfaction of their populations. Intriguingly, the results reflect much of what we see in the more objective measures of the Human Development Index: Finland, Denmark, Iceland and Norway take four of the five top places, while the UK and US are thirteenth and eighteenth respectively.[13]

A further milestone came in 2019 when New Zealand became the first country in the world to unveil a 'wellbeing' budget. Just a few years earlier the country had famously been described as having a 'rockstar' economy, with GDP growth outpacing many of its peers.[14] And yet finance minister Grant Robertson recognised that this wasn't being felt by many people: 'How could we be a rockstar, they asked, with homelessness, child poverty and inequality on the rise?'[15] So prime minister Jacinda Ardern's government devised an assessment of living standards using sixty-one indicators, including the economy, environment, culture, mental and physical health, wellbeing and much more. This led to it concluding that all new spending decisions should be assessed according to how they contribute to five goals: improving mental health, reducing child poverty, supporting indigenous people, moving to a low-carbon economy and succeeding in the digital age. In line with these priorities, New Zealand has boosted spending significantly in certain areas such as mental health and tackling domestic violence.[16] Iceland's prime minister Katrín Jakobsdóttir is pursuing a similar agenda based on thirty-nine indicators of wellbeing.[17]

Progress has also been made closer to home. In 2015 the Welsh government introduced the Wellbeing of Future Generations Act, which requires all public bodies across Wales to take seven wellbeing goals into account when making decisions. The act is notable for focusing on citizens not just now but also in the future and has put Wales on the path to replacing GDP as the defining measure of economic success.[18] Thinking about progress differently has changed decisions. For example, Wales's future generations commissioner, Sophie Howe, was influential in scrapping plans for the M4 relief road, which would probably have been approved on GDP grounds, but was rejected in the light of issues like climate change and biodiversity.[19]

So the door is open for change, yet we must be realistic about the scale of the challenge. In the UK David Cameron deserves credit for having opened up this debate nearly fifteen years ago as leader of the opposition and then carrying it through into government, instituting the production by the Office of National Statistics of a new set of metrics that measures national wellbeing. These indicators have revealed things that GDP could not have. For example, that anxiety has been steadily increasing in the UK since the start of 2018. Or that happiness was on a downward trajectory even before the Covid-19 crisis, which unsurprisingly has led most measures of subjective wellbeing to deteriorate.[20] Yet, for all these new metrics, it would be hard to claim that UK government policy and practice in the last decade have been significantly reoriented away from GDP and towards wellbeing. There is certainly greater awareness of, for example, the importance of mental health, but by and large the supertanker of government continues to sail in the same direction. Outside the UK, in a recent follow-up to the Sarkozy commission, some of its authors concluded that there has been 'a change in the question that we face, from "how to develop credible metrics of people's lives?" to "how to use these metrics in the policy process once you have developed them?"'[21]

A singular advantage of GDP that we would do well to bear in mind as we think of alternatives is that it can be expressed in a single number so is easy to understand. In David Cameron's national statistics on wellbeing in the UK, forty-three different indicators are listed.[22] Each one has a lot going for it, but as a whole they don't provide much clarity. If we really want to drive change, governments probably need to crunch things down into about half a dozen indicators that matter most. Of course, different governments will have different priorities, but at least there will be clarity.

So what should we include on our dashboard of success? First, there does need to be a measure of people's incomes. As we have seen, a key problem with GDP is that it is an aggregate measure, added up at a national level, telling us very little about economic reality as experienced by the average person. So, to take distribution into account, we would do far better to look, for example, at median incomes or income inequality.

Second, there is more to life than how much income you receive; we need other measures, but which to choose? There are objective metrics like life expectancy, and subjective measures like wellbeing. Whichever we select, it is essential to remember that we do not live our lives in aggregate. Overall life expectancy in the UK is going up, but the gap between the richest and poorest is now more than nine years for men and more than seven years for women – and is growing.[23] Again, we must focus on distribution – and inequalities – to get a true picture.

We should also remember that any set of measurements, even ones more in tune with our values, may help us identify problems in our society, but in isolation cannot give us all the solutions. As we have seen, wellbeing measures in the UK show that anxiety is on the rise and that should lead us to spend more on mental health services, which in the past haven't been given anything like the priority they deserve. But we should also be asking what is causing that rise in anxiety. For example, how might it be linked to the poverty, inequality and insecurity that many face?[24]

Third, we absolutely need to measure whether we are living within the environmental boundaries of the planet. In her book *Doughnut Economics* economist Kate Raworth includes a diagram: the 'one doughnut that might actually turn out to be good for us'.[25] Think of it as two rings, one inside the other. The inner ring represents the 'social foundation', without which people lack the basics needed to live a decent life – not just food, water and housing but things like education, a political voice and gender equality. The outer ring depicts the 'ecological ceiling', beyond which we are overreaching the natural boundaries of the planet as indicated by things like climate change, ocean acidification and biodiversity loss. Between these two rings lies the 'sweet spot' where society can meet the needs of all within the means of the planet.[26] Any dashboard of measurements needs to include an indicator of our relationship to planetary boundaries, including carbon emissions and biodiversity. Imagine if there were the kind of focus on carbon emissions that there currently is on GDP. Why shouldn't carbon footprint figures be produced every quarter, or even every month?

As you can see, even in my limited dashboard there are choices to be made. So who gets to decide? In Chapter 11 we will consider a way in which randomly selected members of the population can be brought together in citizens' assemblies to deliberate on issues of precisely this sort. Just having a debate across society about how we should measure our social and economic progress would itself be a huge step forward. Imagine a national debate facilitated by assemblies across the country every few years about what really matters to us as a nation. As we start to recover from the pandemic, it would be an ideal time to have that conversation.

The absolutely crucial final step in this process is to make sure that whatever indicators we choose actually influence the work of government. New Zealand has managed to put wellbeing at the heart of government policy not through its departments of health or education or justice but through its ministry of finance. For as long as GDP continues to be the primary focus of chancellors and central banks and ministries of finance, all of the other metrics will seem like fluffy stuff in comparison and GDP will retain its hold. By assessing the work of the finance ministry against a measure of wellbeing, New Zealand gets to the very heart of the problem.

Creating a different kind of society means creating a different kind of economy – one that revolves around the things that really matter to us and serves our needs within the limits of the planet. As we go about building the future, we should not be imprisoned by a national accounting system devised early in the last century. But GDP is not just a cause of the way our society operates; it is also a result. What we measure shapes our goals, but of course our goals also shape what we choose to measure. So we need to go back to the drawing board when it comes to our deeper conception of what a successful economy looks like.

CHAPTER 7

Jobs of the Future

Chika works in a job of the future, in a pioneering industry that could create hundreds of thousands of jobs all across the country, an industry that provides some of the basic infrastructure that allows the rest of the economy to operate. Our society will undergo profound changes in the next few decades but, if anything, Chika's work will only get more important. It will continue to play a vital role during the transition to a zero-carbon economy. But Chika's job isn't manufacturing electric cars, building high-speed trains, rolling out fibre-optic broadband or fitting solar panels. Those are all important jobs, but no – Chika Reuben is a social care worker.

Care might not be top of the list when you think about the future of work, but this chapter is about why it should be. It is time to properly value the workers looking after our elderly and other adults who need care, as well as those looking after our children. The bad news is that they're a long way from the top of our list of priorities at the moment. Chika started working in social care in London about ten years ago because she wanted to look after other people and because she wanted to make a difference. Chika is paid exactly the minimum wage and she's not the only one. One and a half million people work in social care in England – looking after adults in residential care or in their own homes.[1] Nearly two thirds are paid less than the real living wage. In fact, up to 160,000 are paid less than the legal minimum wage, and up to a quarter of the workforce are on precarious zero-hours contracts.[2]

If things were bad already, they got even worse during the pandemic. Like millions of families, ours had a sign in our window: THANK YOU, KEY WORKERS with the rainbow symbol. In those first months we went outside at 8 p.m. on Thursday nights to clap for the essential workers we relied on, but as time wore on, it became increasingly apparent that this gesture of gratitude and support was entirely at odds with how we actually treated them. Many social care workers didn't have the personal protective equipment to minimise the risk of infection. Those who showed symptoms were often expected to self-isolate with the bare minimum of sick pay. As Chika told me, 'Working during that crisis time it was actually very frightening. At first nobody actually knew what was going on. People kept on dying, the elderly kept on dying. So a lot of people were frightened … But at the same time, because of the duty of care we are meant to actually stay and look after these residents.'[3] Social care workers were twice as likely to die from Covid as the general population.[4] We labelled these workers essential but as a society that is not the way we operated.

We also undervalue childcare workers. The average wage in the early-years workforce in England is £7.42 an hour – well below the living wage. This is partly due to a reliance on young apprentices, who do not have to be paid the standard minimum wage. A staggering 13 per cent are paid under £5 an hour.[5] Almost half of childcare workers rely on benefits or tax credits to make ends meet.[6] Our failure to support childcare providers in the first few months of Covid left up to a quarter of them on the brink of collapse and thousands of workers facing the risk of redundancy.[7] A recent report by the government's own Social Mobility Commission described the problem of childcare wages as 'startling' and asked, 'Are the 280,000 people who look after and educate our children becoming our forgotten key workers?'[8]

This neglect has very real consequences. Both childcare and social care in England suffer from rapid staff turnover. About a quarter of workers in early-years care and 30 per cent in social care were leaving their jobs each year even before the additional pressures of the Covid crisis.[9] There are more than 100,000 vacancies for social care workers alone. Childcare and social care providers struggle to pay wages competitive with other low-paid sectors like retail, leading staff to leave in search of better pay elsewhere.[10] This makes it difficult to build up a stable, qualified and experienced workforce. Low pay and high turnover has been found to affect staff morale and the quality of the service that those in their care receive.[11]

Nurturing the young and giving dignity to the old – can we think of anything more important? Apparently we can. Judging by the pay, professional support and security that our society offers them, childcare and social care workers would seem to be doing something we regard as of little value. Both sectors are largely made up of private providers and individuals privately funding the childcare or social care they need. The government subsidises childcare and funds some social care, recognising that the market undervalues these services, but there remains a profound gap between the way these markets work and the interests of those who use the services, those who work in them and our society more widely. We have recognised as a country that the state needs to intervene, but we still deeply undervalue care. Now we need to make a collective choice as a society to elevate its importance.

The shortcomings in these sectors – low pay, poor working conditions, unmet care needs, providers on the brink of collapse – also reflect a deeper problem with how we think about the economy. The truth is, we rarely think about care as really being a part of the economy at all. Or at least not a part of the economy that governments should have any interest in. Think back to Chapter 5 and the argument I made there for the state supporting those businesses on which our future relies, encapsulated by the term 'industrial strategy'. What does that phrase conjure up to you? Workers in car plants, heavy industry, making aerospace engines? These are absolutely vital jobs, central to many communities, crucial to exports, and lead to many more jobs through their supply chains, and we need a much more effective industrial policy in these areas. But when we think about industrial strategy, how often is it about the care worker as well as the car worker? Almost never, I would say. Former chancellor George Osborne started a fashion, believe it or not. It was for politicians to pose in high-vis and hard hats. I might have done it myself once or twice. How often have you seen politicians promote an economic strategy in a residential care home or a nursery?

The economy is, essentially, the system that allows us to produce and distribute the things we need to live our lives. Care is at the heart of that for a number of reasons. First, care work clearly matters for the millions of people who do it. Second, care work is a necessary foundation for the rest of the economy to operate. As we have seen so powerfully during the pandemic, no parent is able to work without someone else caring for their children, whether or not they pay them to do so. And third, care work matters because it is essential to those who depend on it – which at some point is all of us. Care is the work that sustains life. We cannot discuss the economy in any meaningful sense without acknowledging the importance of the care economy.

From the perspective of the economy, the social infrastructure of education, childcare and social care ought to be at least on a par with the physical infrastructure of roads and buildings. And yet, as Katrín Jakobsdóttir says,

By focusing on physical infrastructure to the exclusion of social infrastructure, economists and policymakers ignore an obvious truth: we need both in order for our societies to thrive and develop ... This dualism classifies money spent on physical infrastructure as an investment and, therefore, worthy of public monies. On the other hand, social infrastructure is branded as expenses or operating costs, preferably the first in line to be cut. Yet these are the structures that sustain us from birth to death and create the conditions that make life worthwhile.[12]

This point is fundamental. Social infrastructure is vital for sustaining us and is only going to get more important in the future.

Given our ageing society, it has been forecast that the English social care workforce will have to increase by a further half a million people by 2035 to keep up with demand.[13] Think also about the zero-carbon economy of the future. Many jobs will change but care work will be as necessary as ever – by its nature, it is low-carbon work already. We need to transform our economy so that our social needs are met within the means of the planet, and social infrastructure will be vital to that. The UK already lags far behind the Nordic countries on employment in the care economy. In Sweden and Denmark about 10 per cent of people work in childcare or social care. We are not going to get to those levels of employment any time soon, but they show the potential for hundreds of thousands of care jobs to be created in the UK.[14]

The government's 2017 industrial strategy aims to 'help businesses to create high quality, well paid jobs right across the country'.[15] But according to one estimate, the government's multi-billion-pound Industrial Strategy Challenge fund targets sectors employing just 1 per cent of the population.[16] Clearly, the government expect these sectors to grow and to support jobs in other parts of the economy, but their strategy still reflects what one policy paper has described as the 'fetish of the frontier'.[17] In the meantime, our failure to properly value care work has a more immediate impact – on those who need it. One and a half million older people in England are not getting the support they need with essential day-to-day activities such as washing or getting dressed. Workers often do not have the time, training or resources to deliver proper care or build proper relationships with their clients.[18]

If care work provides a vital service, then why is it so over-looked in policy discussions? This partly relates to the subject of the previous chapter: the way we think about economic value and how we measure it. Our old friend GDP has had notorious and long-standing problems trying to account for public services. It's not difficult to see how you measure the economic value of a car because it is captured well in a market-determined price, but it's a lot harder with a care visit or a nursery place. GDP used to estimate this by how much is *spent* on public services. In recent years it has tried to measure the 'outputs' of those services – hospital operations, pupils taught and so on.[19] But the fact is that GDP is profoundly ill suited to providing a true measure of their contribution. GDP finds it very hard to tell us anything about the caring touch of the worker looking after someone with Alzheimer's, the risks taken by the nurse when tending to someone with a severe illness, or the comfort provided to a crying toddler by a nursery worker. These actions make a difference that is literally immeasurable. The more GDP is used to judge what matters in an economy, the more these services will be overlooked.

But there is a deeper reason care work is undervalued across our society: historically and traditionally, it has been done by women for free, as we saw in the last chapter. The family model in which men go out to work has always relied on women being at home to cook, clean and look after the children. It is hard to overstate how far conventional economic thinking has overlooked unpaid work done by women. In the introduction to this section I quoted one of the most famous passages from Adam Smith's *The Wealth of Nations* about the role of the butcher, the brewer, and the baker in providing our dinner.[20] But Katrine Marçal points out that Adam Smith lived with his mother for most of his life. She cooked for him while he wrote the book. Smith shouldn't just have thanked the butcher, brewer and baker for his dinner – but also his mum.[21]

In the last few decades care work has increasingly become paid work, but it is still largely done by women. Eighty-two per cent of social care workers and more than 95 per cent of childcare workers are women.[22] It is worth noting that they are also disproportionately women of colour: the proportion of social care workers who are Black is significantly higher than the population as a whole.[23] The history – and the gendered and racial division of care work today – leads us to continue to undervalue this work, even when it is paid.[24] We have created an unspoken hierarchy of work according to what we think really matters, and care work is towards the bottom of the pile. When it comes to discussions of the productive economy, it is so often thought of in terms of jobs mainly done by men – care work is at best ignored and at worst seen as a burden.

If the big idea of this chapter is that we need to value care work properly, what would that look like in reality? We can look to the NHS for inspiration, which is underfunded but enjoys a completely different status from the care work we have been discussing. It was created out of the rubble of the Second World War with ambition and vision, and is our most popular institution: the public see it as 'a symbol of what is great about Britain and [believe] we must do everything we can to maintain it'.[25] It should give us hope that institutions designed according to our deeper values, not those of the market, can be popular and endure.

The ambition of the NHS parallels what the Nordic countries did in the 1960s and 70s for childcare. Sweden pioneered the idea of investing in a system of universal childcare provision for the sake of children, their parents and gender equality.[26] Today Swedish municipalities provide childcare between the ages of one and five. Costs are highly subsidised by the state and capped based on parents' income, with the lowest-income families paying nothing and the wealthiest paying the equivalent of about £130 per month.[27] The skills required of childcare workers are also taken much more seriously. In Sweden 39 per cent of the profession are university graduates, eight times more than in the UK. Add those who have three-year vocational training, and the proportion rises to 60 per cent.[28] Furthermore, the average childcare worker earns about 290,000 Swedish krona per year, equivalent to about £25,000 – far above childcare workers in the UK.[29]

This contrasts with an incredibly complex system in England, where parents of children between two and four are entitled to limited free nursery education and childcare, some of which is dependent on whether and how much they work.[30] The result of this system is that the average cost of twenty-five hours of care for children under two is £130 a week – about the same as the highest-earning Swedish parents would pay in a month.[31] But the problem with our system goes beyond the cost to parents. Childcare providers have long argued that the funding they receive from the government is insufficient to cover their bills and pay adequate salaries, resulting in the instability we see in the sector.[32]

Truly universal childcare would be a shining social and economic achievement for any government that took on the task, forming a crucial cornerstone of a renewed social contract. It is also probably the best investment that we can make as a society in realising equality. The early years, from birth to age five, have a greater impact on cognitive development than any other period in life. Wealthier parents are more likely to have the financial resources to support their child's development during these years. This contributes to the disparity in educational outcomes between children from disadvantaged families and their peers that continues throughout their school years.[33] The provision of high-quality childcare in the early years would help close the gap.[34] Indeed, research has found that receiving quality childcare has an impact on people's educational outcomes all the way up to GCSE level.[35]

All the evidence is that this is also one of the best investments we can make in the economy. Investing in childcare has been estimated to produce a 7–13 per cent per year economic return based on increased school and career achievement as well as reduced costs in remedial education, health and criminal justice system expenditures. That's higher than the return on

job training or investment in schools.[36] Truly valuing childcare
– investing in the sector, paying workers properly and supporting providers – could pay dividends.

But what about social care? The question of how to fund
social care properly is one of the defining political challenges
of our time. Ultimately, it is the question from which all else
flows, and we will not truly address the structural problems in
the sector without answering it. In England we are still dealing
with the legacy of social care being left out of the NHS in the
1940s. The divide between comprehensive, free healthcare and
patchy, largely privately funded social care has remained ever
since.[37] A number of ideas have been proposed to correct this.
Scotland has offered the over-65s personal and nursing care,
free at the point of need, since 2002. This means those that
need it can get support with eating, personal hygiene, mobility
problems and certain other needs, so extending the principles
of the NHS to parts of social care.[38] However, individuals fund
their own accommodation and other needs, while younger
adults with care needs are not covered by the system. More
than a decade ago, the government commissioned a report
into social care funding in England that recommended a 'lifetime cap' for how much individuals would have to contribute
towards their care needs (the report proposed £35,000), with
the state funding the rest.[39] A social care system held in the
same esteem as our NHS – where the pay and treatment of
workers and service users matched the gratitude we showed
in those first few months of the pandemic – would be another
defining legacy for any government.

The reason the funding question is such a challenge is
because, whatever the balance of individual and government
spending, people's social care needs can be incredibly expensive.
But while we have yet to come to an agreement as a society
about how to solve this challenge comprehensively, there is
surely no excuse for allowing all the problems we see in the sector to continue in the meantime. At a bare minimum we should
ensure all social care workers are paid at least the real living

wage, with clear routes to higher rates of pay. As a society we should not accept the present reliance on low-wage and insecure work. We should develop good-quality jobs in the sector, with decent training and career development opportunities.[40] Staff should be able to specialise, for example training as specialists in care for people with dementia or learning disabilities.[41] This could improve the quality of service while giving workers the opportunity to progress.

Properly valuing social care should also lead us to look at the business models and types of practice that are appropriate to the sector. If I told you about a company that had changed hands multiple times in recent years, whose control had shifted from Germany to Qatar to the USA and had recently gone bust because it couldn't afford the interest payments on its debt, you might think this was some high-risk, financial services venture. But this is exactly how one of our biggest care-home providers has been run. Four Seasons looks after 6,538 elderly people and by 2019 was effectively controlled by a hedge fund based in Connecticut.[42] We surely can't be content with a system where the care homes looking after our elderly relatives are flipped like a commodity from one private owner to another with no guarantee of financial viability.

Regardless of the exact mix of public and private provision, we should have clear expectations of providers. Conditions could also be attached to public-sector contracts to promote our wider vision for the sector, ensuring it is run in the interests of workers and service users.[43] I return to this issue of public sector procurement in Chapter 19.

The biggest lesson of this chapter is that we have to take the care economy seriously. It comes down to the choices we make as a society: how much we are willing to pay for the care of our children, disabled, sick, elderly – and whether we think it is in principle up to the individual to take the strain, or we recognise the practical advantages of pooling our risks and resources. Also, how seriously do we take the needs of those working in care and those who are reliant on it, which ultimately is all of us? The Covid crisis has shone the starkest spotlight on how our society has for decades failed to value this most essential part of our economy and society. It shouldn't have taken a pandemic to get here. But now we have to decide what we really value as a society.

Moving care work from the bottom to the top of our list of priorities is part of rethinking what economic success looks like. But there is also a wider question here to do with the nature of work itself: whether our lives should be about serving the economy or whether the economy should serve us. That is the question to which I now turn.

CHAPTER 8

The Time of Our Lives

The first official Football League season began on the 8th of September 1888 ... West Bromwich Albion beat Stoke 2–0, Preston defeated Burnley by five goals to two, Derby won 6–3 at Bolton and Everton beat Accrington 2–1 ...[1]

Three o'clock on a Saturday afternoon has a sacred place in English football. For the last 130 years, it has been the standard kick-off time for matches in the English football leagues and, until Covid at least, the only time that live games could not be broadcast on TV.[2] What has been largely forgotten is the reason for this time.

Until halfway through the nineteenth century those who worked in mills and factories tended to work as much as twelve hours a day, six days a week. But in 1850 the Factory Act was passed, mandating that all textile mills and factories must close at 2 p.m. on Saturdays.[3] It was out of this change in the law that the first football clubs formed, encouraged by churches and factory owners who believed the healthy distraction of football would keep workers out of trouble during their new-found leisure time – and in particular curb excessive drinking. In fact, the purpose of the Saturday-afternoon shutdown was to end workers' long-standing tradition of bunking off on a Monday to get in some much-needed rest, drinking and, by all accounts, debauchery before the start of another exhausting week. This phenomenon was referred to as Saint Monday, in an ironic nod to the calendar of saints' days.[4]

What has happened since then shows how working lives can change. In 1868 the average working week was 62 hours. Today, including part-time work, it is 36 hours, and for full-time workers around 42 hours.[5] But these changes didn't come without a fight. It was fully two hundred years ago that the social reformer Robert Owen came up with the slogan 'Eight hours labour, eight hours recreation, eight hours rest.'[6] This objective was adopted by the trade union movement, which spent decades campaigning for change. Major legislation to actually limit the working day for adults in the UK (as opposed to the 2 p.m. shutdown) came with the Factory Act of 1874, which prescribed a ten-hour maximum.[7] Gradually, the ten hours became eight – in coal mines in 1908 and across industry more generally in 1919. Collective agreements between trade unions and bosses secured the eight-hour day for many workers.[8] After the Second World War, with unemployment low and unions strong, further significant reductions in working hours were secured.[9]

There is a crucial lesson here. The big idea of this chapter is that how much we work, when we work, even where we work should be determined by us as a society and cannot simply be left to the market. The laws and regulations that have been introduced by governments are an assertion of this idea. They are society's way of installing safeguards to protect people from being treated like commodities without rights, to be bought and sold. Before government got involved, people's hours of work were under the control of market forces and, by extension, employers. In so many ways we are a long way from those days, but, as we will see, in other ways we are not. The struggle to control our working hours – whether they fit into our family life or give us enough time to see our friends – remains as important today. How much control over when and how long we work is a measure of our progress as a society. The evidence is that many people would work fewer hours if they could, but progress in this direction has stalled. So too has flexibility over the timing and nature of our work. There is nothing necessary or inevitable about this state of affairs, and the quality of the lives we lead depends on us fighting to change it. That means putting the market in its place.

I should make a confession at this point. I feel this issue of working time keenly. My boss for ten years was Gordon Brown including when he was chancellor of the exchequer. As you may guess, he had a strong work ethic. So strong, in fact, that in the days before ubiquitous mobile phones, he would often call me at home on my landline. Things got so intense that for a period I would unplug the phone from the wall on Saturday and Sunday mornings to avoid an early-morning call. But I can't just blame Gordon; I suffer from the tendency too. I spent five years as leader of the opposition feeling like I hardly saw my two young children, Daniel and Sam. Even when I was present, I tended to be absent. Even now my tendency is too often to put work first. Including this book …

At least I have a choice. Many do not. British full-time workers put in some of the longest hours in Europe.[10] In 2018 over 3 million employees in our country worked over forty-eight hours a week and 1.4 million people worked on all seven days of the week.[11] Two thirds of people say they work longer hours than they would like and one in four an excess of ten hours or more.[12] Eighteen million working days are lost each year as a result of work-related stress, depression or anxiety, and the predominant cause of this is workload pressures.[13] What's more, the forward march of leisure has been halted. The year 2014 marked the first since the middle of the Second World War that average working hours in the UK were higher than they were a decade earlier. Even between the 1970s and the 2000s there was only a very slow decline compared to most previous periods.[14] If the post-war trend towards shorter hours had continued after 1980 at the same rate, we would be stopping work today at lunchtime on a Friday.[15]

We don't just face a crisis of overwork but also of control. It starts with those people on zero-hours contracts, an agreement to employ a worker but with no guarantees of hours of work or pay. One million people are on these contracts, sometimes not knowing until the day itself whether they will work and be paid.[16] The problems go beyond these workers. Before the pandemic hit, two thirds of UK workers said they would like to work more flexibly than they were able to – to have a choice over when their working day starts and ends, to work part or full time, to perhaps work at least partly from home.[17] The Chartered Institute of Personnel and Development says progress in the last fifteen years has been 'glacial' and rates the UK twenty-fourth out of twenty-five countries with comparable economies in work–life balance.[18] If we care about families, community, stress, we should aspire to do better.

The good news is that there are some examples out there to inspire us. Andrew Barnes runs a company called Perpetual Guardian in New Zealand, employing 240 people to deal with trusts, wills and estate planning. In 2018 he worked out that if his employees did another forty minutes of productive work each day, they could work the equivalent of four days not five. He duly emailed his head of human resources who thought he must be joking and deleted the email. Barnes went ahead and announced the plan on breakfast TV. It started as a two-month, academically analysed trial and is now Perpetual Guardian's permanent way of doing things. The results are outstanding: revenue and productivity have improved, stress levels have declined, and the perceptions of the company's employees about their ability to balance work and family life have soared.[19]

Just as certain companies are showing that it is possible to have shorter working hours, so certain countries are showing that greater flexibility is possible too. Finland is the world leader here. Since 1996 most Finnish workers have been able to vary their start and finish times by three hours to fit in with their family or other requirements.[20] But the Finns have recently concluded that isn't good enough and have now legislated to go further. Henceforth, workers will be able to vary their start and finish times by four hours and will for the first time in most professions be able to decide when and *where* they do 50 per cent of their work – home, office or elsewhere. Finally, if this doesn't sound idyllic enough, workers will be able to 'bank' hours worked to take extended holidays.[21] You might assume that this has been done in the teeth of employer opposition, but you would be wrong. Flexible working is seen as a vital tool of recruitment by employers, a staggering 92 per cent of whom offer it to their workers.[22]

All this feels a long way from where we are as a country. But before we work out how shorter hours and greater flexibility might be possible, we need to take a step back and ask what drove the progress in reducing working hours we made in Britain in the nineteenth and twentieth centuries and why has it recently stopped? The answer lies in the three Ps: productivity, power and pay.

Since 1930 the UK has seen an eight-fold rise in national income.[23] This is largely because the productivity of the average UK worker (the value of what each produces in a given time) has risen dramatically during this period, in turn a result of new technology, infrastructure and methods of production. That trend is what has allowed workers to be on the job much less than in the 1860s and yet for employers to be able to pay them significantly more. Each individual is producing so much more (in terms of value) for every hour they work – in the context of many of the goods we produce having changed a lot. In simple terms, higher productivity produces a much bigger cake, meaning employers can pass on a bigger slice to their employees. The problem is that in recent years the cake has stopped growing nearly as fast. Productivity grew at an average annual rate of 3.1 per cent between 1950 and 1973, 2.3 per cent between 1979 and 2007 and has gone up just 0.4 per cent annually since 2008.[24]

Of course, it's not just the size of the cake that matters but how it is divided up. That's where unions and worker organisation comes in. It is striking that when we look at working hours across the world, it is those countries with strong unions where workers tend to work fewer hours – so, for example, the US has the longest hours among richer countries, Germany has some of the shortest.[25] In the UK we have seen a steep decline in union membership, from thirteen million at its peak in the 1970s to six and a half million today.[26] This is because we have moved away from large-scale manufacturing industries – 40 per cent of the workforce were employed in manufacturing in 1961 compared to just 10 per cent fifty years later – and because of laws passed in the last few decades. Both have made unions much harder to organise.[27]

As a result of these changes in productivity and power, not only has the cake stopped growing nearly as fast but less of it has gone to ordinary workers and more elsewhere, including to shareholders and the highest income earners. The UK is now more than twelve years into the longest squeeze on wages in two centuries: during this period 70 per cent of employees have seen the value of their pay fall.[28] This fall in wages is crucial to bear in mind when thinking about reducing working hours. One in four low-paid workers say they would like to work fewer hours, *but only if their pay doesn't fall*. Fewer than one in ten are in favour of fewer hours if that means lower pay, while one in seven say they want to work *more* hours.[29] It is higher-paid workers who tend to work the longest hours, but we cannot let their desire for shorter hours blind us to the needs of lower-paid workers to earn more.[30]

Even the notion of what 'working less' looks like is more complex than you might think. When asked, 45 per cent of workers express a preference for a four-day week, while 25 per cent would prefer a three-day week and only 10 per cent prefer the five-day week.[31] Among younger workers, fully 67 per cent say the offer of a four-day week would influence their choice of work.[32] And yet today half of women and nearly one third of men don't actually do a five-day week and even fewer do a traditional nine to five, forty-hour week.[33] A four-day week might be shorthand for working less, but the reality must be tailored to people's circumstances and is as much about hours as days, and the crucial issue of control.

So how do we crack the hard nuts of productivity and power if they are the gateway to shorter hours? Britain's productivity puzzle is very complex, and it would take a whole book in itself to unpack it, but there is an increasingly vocal school of thought that says it isn't simply that higher productivity enables higher wages. In fact, the converse is also true: higher wages might enable higher productivity.[34] According to this line of thinking, the UK is currently stuck in a low pay, low productivity equilibrium: it is precisely because labour is cheap that employers are not incentivised to invest in the plant and machinery – and now automation – that enhance productivity. And it is true that in all these areas we lag behind many other countries.[35] So productivity remains low, which in turn means pay stays low, perpetuating a vicious cycle. For this reason, a higher minimum wage may well be part of the solution, as increasing the cost of labour – accompanied by a wider set of changes, including more conventional solutions like investing in infrastructure and education – might help to drive productivity higher and reverse the cycle in the desired direction.

A similar argument can be made about working hours. Just as we can't wait for higher productivity to deliver higher wages so the same might be true about waiting for improved productivity to deliver shorter hours. What if the long hours culture is itself making workers more unproductive? Back to Andrew Barnes from New Zealand. He was clear about one thing above all – what he called the 100–80-100 rule: 100 per cent of the pay, 80 per cent of the time but, crucially, delivering 100 per cent of the productivity. Barnes's key point is that this works not just for employees, who get the same pay for fewer hours, but for employers: they get the same output, but with happier workers, who are less stressed and more creative, and there is less staff turnover

This is echoed in a report by the Henley Business School, which recently surveyed 500 businesses in the UK and found that half had allowed at least some of their employees to switch to a four-day week at a full-time salary. Nearly two thirds of the businesses that allowed the switch reported increases in productivity, quality of work and reduced sickness absence, while 70 per cent said there was less stress at work. Crucially, 63 per cent of these businesses said that offering flexible working helped them to attract the right talent.[36] In Japan, one of the highest-intensity work cultures in the world, Microsoft experimented with a four-day week in August 2019, and productivity went up by 40 per cent, outstripping the 20 per cent reduction in hours.[37] This approach might seem much more challenging in other sectors, like care for example, where there are limits to productivity gains, but there have been experiments around the world which suggest otherwise. A nursing home in Gothenburg, Sweden, experimented with six-hour working days, instead of eight. Productivity and quality of service went up and staff turnover went down. True, these gains did not appear to completely offset the overall rise in costs, but some argue that the long-term savings of the scheme weren't taken into account.[38]

All this suggests there might be ways to get to shorter working hours and higher productivity. Businesses might also be tempted to head in this direction in order to attract the best employee talent. But to make progress we cannot ignore the third P – power. In Chapter 17 we will return to the question of the role of trade unions in our society, but for now the point that needs making is simply this: if we want a fairer distribution of wages in our society, enabling people to have higher standards of living and shorter hours, all of the evidence suggests that trade unions have a crucial role to play.

What else can government do? A mandated shorter working week looks unlikely – both in terms of whether it could work economically any time soon or whether it is what most workers want. Even Finnish flexibility looks a bit improbable from the UK standpoint. But the Covid pandemic has perhaps shifted what is possible and pointed to a different future. In truth, for all the difficulties, strains and tensions at home, these awful circumstances have stimulated new ways of working. Many people don't want simply to go back to the way things were before. Many workers who either couldn't or didn't work flexibly have done so by necessity. We should not sugarcoat the fact that, as we saw in Chapter 4, the experience of juggling work and childcare has led to massive stresses for many parents. Nor should we forget those who have not been able to work from home. Yet of those who have worked flexibly during lockdown having not done so before, a staggering 94 per cent want to work more flexibly in the future.[39] As one father put it during lockdown, 'I was previously working a nine-day fortnight. During the outbreak I have reduced my hours to six per day but have been working every day. [I] have been able to see the benefits of eating with [the] children [and] being around more in [the] morning/early evening ...'[40]

You might think it is just employees who want change, but there is evidence that bosses are persuaded that greater flexibility can work. Before the pandemic 15 per cent of employers said that more than half their workforce were working at least one day a week at home. Now, fully 40 per cent of employers believe this will be the case post-pandemic.[41] The role of the office in our society looks set to change, so surely working hours can evolve too. The potential for change here is very real. As we grasp it, we will need to be alert to the new inequalities that might arise, especially those faced by people unable to work from home, either because of the nature of their job or because of their home circumstances. These workers tend to be in lower-paid sectors.

In the meantime, there are some immediate and obvious fixes to be made. It was a decade ago that we first started talking about solving the problem of zero-hours contracts, but we are no closer to getting rid of them. The solutions are not rocket science. People deserve to know their schedule in advance and should have the right to regular hours and pay once their working pattern is established.[42] Likewise, we need to strengthen the right to work flexibly. Your boss can wait three months before responding to a request for flexible working, and you don't get the right even to make that request until you've been in your post for six months. One in three requests for flexible working are turned down. There is also currently no requirement to state in a job advert whether it can be done flexibly, or to justify why it cannot. All these issues need addressing.[43]

But this is just the start. Out of the darkness of what we have been through in the pandemic, we have a duty to find something better – and to think big not small about what is possible. Why shouldn't we aspire to have flexible working like the world's best, Finland, building a coalition of employers and workers for change? Why shouldn't we aspire as a society to shorter working hours as a goal of public policy, earned through productivity and the better sharing of that productivity through a stronger voice for workers? Let's ensure the changes that can be made more quickly point the way if not to the impossible then at least to the improbable.

For now, the most important lesson of this chapter is that the amount we work is a political question. It is decided by power in the workplace and who wields it; by productivity, yes, but also by how we choose to drive productivity, which is in turn an expression of our working culture and whether it reflects our values as a society. The hours and days we work are not predetermined by some natural order but determined by us and what we can agree.

We should remember what really matters in life. Work is part of it, but so are many other things. We are not just workers, but parents, children and friends. These parts of our lives need protection from the market. Labour markets, like all markets, have incredible creative power, but unrestrained they have destructive power too. That is also true in relation to technology, the issue to which I now turn.

CHAPTER 9

Lina and Goliath

If markets are leading us in directions that we, as a democratic society, decide are not compatible with our vision of liberty or democracy, it is incumbent upon government to do something.

Lina Khan, Columbia Law School[1]

When you give everyone a voice and give people power, the system usually ends up in a really good place. So, what we view our role as, is giving people that power.

Mark Zuckerberg, founder of Facebook[2]

It's not very often that an academic paper by a graduate law student goes viral. But at the start of 2017 Lina Khan's ninety-six-page treatise 'Amazon's Antitrust Paradox' was published in the *Yale Law Journal* and became an immediate hit. Khan made a devastating case against Amazon, arguing the company had 'marched towards monopoly' and was amassing power that could be used to the detriment of users, other businesses and society as a whole.[3] Meanwhile, governments were systematically failing to recognise the threat posed by the growth of Amazon and its fellow tech giants. Rather than making the world a better place for all, as they claim, Khan argued that so-called Big Tech (a term usually used to denote Amazon, Apple,

Microsoft, Google and Facebook) was concentrating power in the hands of a few. It was time to take action.[4] The paper was picked up by media outlets across the world. In September 2018 the *New York Times* proclaimed the article had 'reframed decades of monopoly law'.[5] Critics said Lina Khan was at the vanguard of a 'hipster anti-trust' movement ('hipster' appeared to be a term of abuse in this context).[6]

The Covid crisis has brought home how far our lives have been transformed by digital technology. During the lockdowns around the world the internet has kept us in touch with loved ones and provided a world of entertainment. It has allowed us to stay up to date on the latest public health advice and buy food without trips to the shop. It has enabled many to continue their work or education from the safety of their homes. Consider how it would have been if the pandemic had hit twenty years ago, when most of us didn't have access to the internet in our homes at all.[7]

Ultimately, we have become dependent on digital technology because it hugely benefits our lives. Three quarters of people in the UK use a search engine almost every day and half of us use social networking sites every day.[8] Most jobs involve tech in one way or another, while the number of people in the UK who work for digital technology companies or in allied jobs, such as software development, now stands at 3 million. At the rate we're going, this will only rise and rise.[9]

Each of us has our own personal relationship with the tech revolution. Mine began in the early 1980s, when I was, I believed, at the cutting edge. I played a game called Manic Miner on the ZX Spectrum, obsessively, on our family TV. I got to Level 20 – the end of the game – not bettered by any of my mates. I was not so proficient at its mildly disappointing sequel, Jet Set Willy. The next twenty years in tech more or less passed me by until 2003, when I was teaching politics at Harvard University around the time that an undergraduate there named Mark Zuckerberg was founding Facebook. 'Zuck' was not in my class but I taught a very nice young undergraduate called Joe Green, who was his room-mate, I discovered later.[10] I remember Joe telling me excitedly about something called Friendster, a social networking site that predated Facebook, and trying to impress upon me that this was going to change the world and politics in particular beyond recognition. I was, in retrospect, more dismissive than I should have been, nodded absently and asked him where his essay was. Joe, you were right and I was wrong.

I absolutely believe that technology can be – indeed often *is* – a force for good in our society. I see this with my kids, who can't imagine a world without the ability to find out facts, connect with friends and do all the other things tech enables you to do. Tech firms offer the promise of advance and solutions for an extraordinary range of problems, but we're going to have to rein in the power of a few of the biggest players in the market to ensure technology works in the interests of society.

A particular aspect of the tech revolution has become apparent during the pandemic, which illustrates what happens when markets are left to spiral out of control. While essential workers have faced insecurity, low pay and very real risks to their lives, a small group of businesses (and their owners) have been doing staggeringly well. At the start of 2020, before the pandemic, five of the six most valuable companies in the world were US-based tech firms: Apple, Microsoft, Alphabet (Google's owner), Amazon and Facebook.[11] The top two of these were valued at more than $1 trillion each. During Covid, as people became increasingly dependent on their services, the value of these and many other tech firms skyrocketed.[12]

Amazon was the biggest winner of all. Its founder and CEO Jeff Bezos – already the richest person in the world – saw his personal fortune shoot up by more than $70 billion in the six months after the first lockdowns began.[13] When this was discovered, it was estimated that Bezos could give every Amazon worker $105,000 and still be as rich as he was before Covid hit.[14] This must have sounded like a bad joke to Amazon warehouse employees, given the well documented problems with how they are treated.[15] (At the time of writing, Jeff Bezos is yet to announce this generous bonus for his hard-working staff.)

Jeff Bezos's fortune is clearly a problem if we care about inequality, but there's something else going on here too. This stupendous accumulation of wealth, and indeed the enormous value of these companies, reflects their market dominance.[16] In the UK 93 per cent of internet searches are done on Google.[17] Facebook and Google together take eighty pence of every pound spent on digital advertising spending in the UK.[18] A third of all of our online shopping is done on Amazon.[19] More than 99 per cent of smartphones in the UK use either Apple or Google software.[20] None of these are absolute monopolies – a situation where there is only a single supplier – but they are clearly very concentrated markets.

If a few companies are dominant, isn't that just a sign that they're getting something right? These companies have great products but there is a lot more going on here. It's not that these companies haven't faced potential competitors, but that they've gobbled them up. Between them, the five largest Big Tech firms have purchased more than 400 smaller companies over the last decade.[21] When Facebook snapped up Instagram back in 2012, it bought out a fast-growing app on its way to becoming a serious competitor. When Google bought route-mapping app Waze in 2013, it similarly took over a successful product challenging its own Maps software. When Amazon bought Whole Foods in 2017, it extended its dominance of retail to include the US food market.[22] There are concerns that tech entrepreneurs starting companies are now more focused on being bought by a Big Tech firm than competing with them.[23]

Acquisitions aren't the only way Big Tech firms have entrenched their dominance. Amazon, for example, has been accused of keeping its e-book prices artificially low to squeeze out other e-book services.[24] In 2017 Google was fined €2.4 billion by the European Union for prioritising Google Shopping in search results at the expense of other shopping comparison websites.[25] In other words, Google used its power to promote its own product on its search engine and shut competitors out. If the tech giants are able to either buy up or shut out any potential competitor then no one has a hope of challenging their position, now or in the future.

Why should this bother us? The promise of markets is that competition between multiple firms ensures that consumers get what they want at the best price, but this only works if new providers are able to enter the market and consumers have real choices. As a result, monopoly is a classic case of the market failure I mentioned in the introduction to this part of the book, where intervention is needed to ensure that markets work properly. More fundamentally, Part II is about protecting the things that matter from the destruction that markets left to their own devices can bring. If the undoubted concentration of power in the tech sector is doing us harm, then it is time for society to step in.

On the surface, there might seem little to worry about with firms such as Google or Facebook; after all, they offer free services that make our lives easier. But look deeper and things aren't so rosy. To get to the heart of it, we've got to understand that the business model of many of these firms is about extracting and selling our personal data – a model dubbed surveillance capitalism.[26] Each time we message a friend, search for a product or share a link to an article, we are tracked. This builds a powerful picture of our actions, views and preferences, which can then be used to refine services, market products to us directly or sell targeted advertising opportunities to third parties. In a sense, we're not really the consumer but the product. Or rather, our attention is the product, sold by the tech platform to the companies that wish to advertise to us.

The UK's Competition and Markets Authority (CMA) recently came to an important conclusion: 'weak competition in search and social media leads to reduced innovation and choice and to consumers giving up more data than they would like'.[27] In other words, the extent of intrusion into our lives is connected to the market dominance of Big Tech. We have nowhere else to go, so the dominant firms prioritise their bottom line over the interests of users. A recent report commissioned by the UK government similarly concluded that, with greater competition between services, platforms would have to do more to attract users – show fewer adverts, for example, or collect less of our data, or even pay us for it.[28]

Meanwhile, more than a million UK advertisers, many of them small businesses, now depend on Facebook and Google to market their products and services.[29] Google has more than a 90 per cent share of the £7.3 billion search advertising market in the UK, while Facebook has over 50 per cent of the £5.5 billion display advertising market. In a competitive market we might expect prices to be driven down over time, but the CMA found that Facebook's revenue per user has gone up ten-fold over the last decade and the amount Google charges is 30 per cent to 40 per cent higher comparing like-for-like search terms to a rival platform.[30] This is bad for those businesses that have to pay higher prices and for consumers too. As the CMA put it, 'Weak competition in digital advertising increases the prices of goods and services across the economy.'[31]

We should be particularly worried about the effect of this on one specific type of business: media organisations. The dominance of Facebook and Google in online advertising threatens the funding stream of high-quality journalism, which the Competition and Markets Authority has warned could 'have detrimental effects on the functioning of our democracy and the accountability of those in positions of power'.[32] Online publishers such as newspapers are reliant on the platforms for traffic. Changes to the design or algorithms of tech services can have a huge impact on the traffic, and therefore revenue, that news publishers receive. The concentration of power in the tech industry means publishers have little bargaining power and are at the mercy of decisions made by Big Tech.[33] Furthermore, Google owns many of the tools and services in the digital advertising market, meaning it is involved in selling adverts on news publishers' websites. So publishers are even more dependent on Google for advertising revenue. The weak bargaining position of news publishers risks translating to less ad revenue, which in turn means less money to invest in the news that is our primary means of holding the powerful to account.

The potential harm caused by the dominance of a business such as Amazon is slightly different. The accusations that I mentioned about e-book prices matter because if a firm can squeeze out competitors, it puts them in a position to raise prices down the line when customers have fewer alternatives. Indeed, Amazon now controls 65 per cent of the e-book market in the US. This market dominance could also be used to put pressure on book publishers to accept less favourable terms, in turn weakening the publishing industry.[34] So, by gaining dominance in an industry, a firm such as Amazon risks causing harm to businesses, consumers and society more widely.

As if all this isn't enough, the rapidly growing economic power of the tech giants has allowed them to acquire influence in the political arena, and that influence has been used to lobby against more regulation of their activities. In the US, Big Tech has become the second-largest lobbying industry (after pharmaceuticals), with Facebook, Amazon and Google among the most powerful corporate lobbyists.[35] In fact, the office block that is home to Google's lobbyists in Washington is the same size as the White House.[36] Now they are turning their attention to Europe.[37]

The truth is, the very nature of these services means they have a tendency to become monopolies. Many tech services are platforms – they connect their users to information or other users. But the thing about a platform is that the more people use it, the more useful it gets. This is known in economics as a network effect. Facebook is good for keeping in touch because all of our friends and family are on it. Uber allows us to get home quickly because so many drivers are signed up to it. Network effects mean that once a platform is successful, it will attract more and more users. Furthermore, this tendency for success to breed success is exacerbated by the value of data to tech services. The more data a company has, the better able it is to refine its services for users or offer targeting tools for advertisers. Part of the reason Google is such a useful search engine is because it has developed its algorithms over billions of searches, and part of the reason Facebook is so valuable to advertisers is because it has built up data that allows them to precisely target users. Network effects and the value of data favour existing firms, suggesting that market dominance is in the DNA of Big Tech.

If all of this is true, why haven't governments acted? Part of the explanation is that the internet was born with, and still has, brilliant liberating tendencies. Breaking the control of media gatekeepers gives everyone access to a mass audience as a YouTuber, blogger, even a podcaster. But the liberating appeal of this technology has been used as an excuse for libertarianism – making information free from gatekeepers has been conflated with making the tech giants free of government regulation. The message from Silicon Valley has been, 'Trust us. We know what the future is more clearly than you, so leave us alone.' And tech moves at warp speed. The philosophy of Facebook is 'Move fast and break things'; the approach of government tends to be 'Move slowly and analyse things.' As Big Tech innovates, policymakers have been left behind scratching their heads.

Governments around the world have failed to step up to their duty to protect society from market dominance. They have largely taken the view that because the Big Tech firms don't appear to be using their dominance to drive up prices for consumers, their monopoly power isn't harmful. The core of Lina Khan's paper was that governments had been too focused on this kind of narrow price-based interpretation of what's known as 'consumer welfare'.[38] Such an approach dictates that if, for example, one company tries to buy another, governments should only intervene if this will lead directly to customers paying higher prices.[39] It's worth pointing out this doesn't even work on its own terms: anti-competitive practices may have no effect on prices in the short term but empower a company to jack up prices once it becomes dominant. In the meantime, a narrow price-based approach does not take into account the erosion of our privacy, the undermining of quality journalism or the other threats to society and democracy that Big Tech poses.

Some argue that we don't need to abandon the consumer welfare approach entirely because, in the UK at least, regulators are able to take factors beyond prices into account. So consumer welfare can be interpreted in a broader sense to include things like innovation and the quality of services.[40] But Lina Khan's overriding point is one of principle: we shouldn't allow our interests as consumers to crowd out everything else we value. After all, she argues, we don't just interact with tech firms as consumers, but also 'as workers, producers, entrepreneurs, and citizens'.[41] Interestingly, the Competition and Markets Authority has argued that the UK needs a tech regulator with a duty 'to further the interests of consumers and citizens'.[42]

The good news is that we can change course, and whatever approach we choose, there is increasing momentum for change. There's nothing inevitable about the continued lack of accountability of Big Tech. Without oversight, many markets over the years have tended towards monopoly, and governments have successfully stepped in. Back in the early twentieth century, US president Theodore Roosevelt broke up monopolies in the oil industry and railroads, earning a reputation as a 'trust buster'.[43] Telecoms giant AT&T was split by the US government into eight different companies in the 1980s.[44]

Lina Khan represents a growing movement calling for trust busting to be brought into the twenty-first century, and in recent years governments around the world have begun to heed the calls. In the US, state governments and federal agencies began a string of lawsuits at the end of 2020 accusing Google and Facebook of exploiting their market dominance.[45] Around the same time, the EU began developing new laws to prevent the largest online gatekeepers from acting unfairly.[46] To give credit where it's due, the UK government has also backed proposals for a new Digital Market Unit within the Competition and Markets Authority. If and when it is created, we will have a dedicated regulator to look at tech competition for the first time.[47] But change depends on making sure a regulator has the right powers – and uses them when it is appropriate.

Getting to grips with Big Tech is going to take a well equipped toolbox, and by now we should be past the point of fumbling around inside. There are three tools we should be using in particular. First, we need to prevent Big Tech firms exploiting their dominance. Some tech companies both run platforms and compete on them. Think of Amazon selling own-brand products on its Marketplace platform or Google Maps or Google Shopping coming up as results on Google Search. We should have clear rules in place to stop them squeezing out other businesses through for example deprioritising competitors in search results or copying their products.

Second, and related to the above, we have to address the problem of anti-competitive takeovers. As we've seen, globally in the last decade there have been hundreds of takeovers by Amazon, Apple, Facebook, Google and Microsoft. Competition regulators haven't blocked a single one.[48] Whether a specific takeover is a problem is a matter for in-depth scrutiny and debate, but it's reasonable to think we could do more here. How much influence can we in the UK have over companies based thousands of miles away in Silicon Valley? The answer is more than you might think. Tech platforms are subject to the laws of each country they operate in, regardless of where they are headquartered. It is not quite clear what would happen if a tech merger was blocked in one country but not another. However, a high-profile inquiry into digital competition carried out for the UK government in 2019 concluded that any decision to block a merger in the UK might well be adopted by other countries around the world. Remarkably, a number of companies involved in mergers told the inquiry they would have abandoned them completely if they had been blocked in the UK.[49] This suggests the UK could influence the global practices of Big Tech. Already the CMA has proposed that the most powerful digital platforms should be subject to more stringent rules when it comes to takeovers.[50]

Third, regulators should address the root causes of concentrated markets, one of which is the inherent advantage of size conferred by network effects. Let's try an extremely fanciful thought experiment. Imagine I wanted to set up Edbook as a competitor to Facebook – don't worry, I get that Silicon Valley has enough former British politicians as it is, and I missed my chance with Joe Green. However good it was, and even if it offered all sorts of services that Facebook does not, perhaps the biggest obstacle I'd face would be persuading people to start a new profile from scratch, kissing goodbye to the years of contacts, images, conversations and followers they'd built up.

But now imagine if that wasn't a problem: you could take your photos, messages, list of friends from one social network over to another.[51] This would require the tech firms to adopt common standards and file formats but is perfectly possible from a technical point of view; indeed, data mobility and interoperability are common elsewhere.[52] Just think about how easy it now is to transfer a mobile number to a different phone network or move money, direct debits and standing orders to a new bank account.[53] Why shouldn't the same be true of tech services? By making it significantly easier to switch to an alternative, we could begin to erode the network advantages of the existing firms. There are many more applications. Think of being able to transfer your viewing history to a new streaming app so it can recommend TV programmes or films relevant to you. Or newsfeed apps that bring together updates from your friends regardless of which social network they use.[54] Of course, we would have to consider the implications of each of these innovations for data privacy, but if well designed and secure, regulators could even be given the power to mandate them in circumstances where there is little competition.

The solutions discussed so far assume that a combination of regulation and structural reform can mitigate the tech industry's tendency towards monopolisation. If they fail, some believe we may be forced to conclude that tech platforms are in fact *natural* monopolies, where incumbents have such an advantage that competition just isn't possible. In the past this has led to water, electricity, telecoms and broadband companies being regulated as 'utilities' because of the essential services they provide. Some critics of Big Tech advocate for a fourth tool which would be to regulate them as utilities, limiting what they can do and the profits they are allowed to make.[55]

However, given how little has been done so far to rein in Big Tech, it is not at all clear that they are natural monopolies, so this seems a step too far. Finally, while the UK could go it alone, an internationally coordinated approach would be far more likely to succeed, which means cooperating with the US and EU in particular.

The extraordinary technological developments of the last few decades have changed our lives in innumerable and positive ways, but when it comes to the dangers of tech dominance, we have been asleep at the wheel, our most basic assumptions stuck in the past. The new reality of free services and valuable data requires a new approach to competition policy, one that looks beyond a narrow focus on short-term market prices. The lesson here is that when technological change happens, markets change too, and public policy must adapt if innovation is to benefit society as a whole.

CHAPTER 10

On Your Bike – and Your Feet

Wander around a big city like London or New York at the end of the nineteenth century and you'd see horses. Lots of them. Horses were the backbone of urban transport, pulling carts, buses and trams. The problem with horses is they produce a rather unfortunate waste product. Horses can relieve themselves of twenty pounds of excrement or more each day.[1] Multiply that by the tens of thousands of animals on the streets of a city like London and, as I'm sure you can imagine, we're talking about a weighty problem. By the 1890s, people were in a panic about what to do about the rising mounds. One New Yorker predicted that in a few decades the build-up of waste would reach the third floor of Manhattan's windows.[2] City leaders are said to have struggled to come up with solutions to what has since become known as the Great Manure Crisis.[3]

Looking back now, of course, we all know what happened next. While city planners were fretting about horses, engineers were inventing the motorcar. Within decades, cars were being mass-produced at an affordable price and quickly became the mode of transport of choice, leaving any worries about horses and their waste far behind. While some people argue the extent of the crisis has been exaggerated in hindsight, the story may still offer lessons for us today (beyond the obvious about horses and excrement).[4] Depending on who you ask, it is a parable about our tendency to assume the future will resemble the past, or it proves the power of technology to find solutions to our most overwhelming problems. Or even, less optimistically, it is a warning that just as technological progress has replaced animals with machines, it could do the same to us.[5] But here's another thought: maybe it should lead us to think about how we get around today.

A key reason for the rise of the car is that it has been absolutely emancipatory for our lives. It's easy to take the car for granted now, but its widespread use from the mid-twentieth century onwards radically opened up where people could go and what they could do. Cars made it easier to commute, enabling workers to live further away from their jobs. Shopping was no longer limited to the local area. People could travel across the country to see friends, family or go on holiday whenever they wanted, unconstrained by the routes and timetables of the railways.[6] We shouldn't lose sight of the multitude of benefits that cars have brought.

But while we've got rid of the manure, that doesn't mean we're out of the doo-doo. Our changing transport habits have been liberating but at the same time thrown up new problems. The Great Pollution Crisis. The Great Road Safety Crisis. The Great Inactivity Crisis. The Great Public Space Crisis. Not to mention the Great Climate Crisis. Lots of people rely on cars, particularly in more rural areas, and cars will continue to be necessary for many and play a vital role in getting us where we want to go. Lots of people also depend on driving for work and income. But alongside the role of the car and public transport, this chapter is about how we provide better alternatives. In particular, the extraordinary potential of two other ingenious ways of getting around. Both are cheap, convenient and already widely available. When it comes to tackling the really big challenges of our world, you might not immediately think of them. But it's time to recognise the potential of the humble bicycle and our own two feet

First, though, I have a confession. You know how most children learn to ride a bike around five or six? Well, I learned late – about eleven or twelve – and have always been a very, very nervous rider. What's more, having learned, I left it more than three decades before doing anything more than a few minutes of uncomfortable wobbling. We went through six prime ministers, drainpipe trousers, Duran Duran, the invention of the internet, email, Twitter, Facebook, the bacon sandwich – and still I resisted two wheels.

When the first lockdown began and people were discouraged from using public transport, I had to work out how I could get to work in an environmentally friendly way. This led to a brief flirtation with an adult tricycle – as in, I test-drove one (nervously). But somehow it didn't seem for me. I was a bit worried about the stigma (and the photos) and I had a vision of myself blocking the cycle lanes. Then, aged fifty, thanks to my podcast co-host Geoff and a holiday accidentally taken in Europe's mountain-biking capital – the French resort of Châtel – I had an epiphany. Geoff kept telling me that he had taken up cycling and it was brilliant. He told me not to worry because he wasn't very coordinated either. And now, here I was with my family in Châtel, where the main thing to do was cycle. So I hired an electric bike.

This was the eureka moment. I realised I could ride better than I thought, save for once toppling over into what you might loosely call a cabbage patch, and electric bikes were fun. Then back in London I started venturing out on local journeys and have now even made it to work. Apart from causing a major hold-up on the Embankment cycleway (sorry to that lady and her grandchild), it went smoothly, even if it took me some time. I also got a Conservative MP who was standing at the entrance to my office in Westminster to take a picture to show I had done it. I now have the zeal of a convert.

In all seriousness, though, we've seen throughout this part of the book how policymaking is often out of step with the things we really value in our lives, and yet it shapes them so profoundly that we can lose sight of the fact that even the most apparently immutable things – the way we travel every day, the design of our cities, even my fear of cycling – all could be different. One of the more subtle impacts of the dominance of markets is the erosion of the idea that as a society we can make decisions about the future we want to build. There is an ingrained assumption that market forces merely enact the inevitable, and government's role is therefore to facilitate that. This assumption is wrong, and we should ask ourselves, if we were thinking from scratch about how we wanted to travel around our towns and cities, what would we prioritise?

I would put safety and speed at the top of my list. I would also want transport that was affordable and accessible for everyone, that didn't take up more public space than it had to and had a minimal impact on both the local environment and our planet as a whole. Ultimately, if town and city planning reflected the lives we want to live, I think walking and cycling would be taken far more seriously.

For a start, they can make us healthier and happier. At the moment one in three of us in the UK fails to do the 150 minutes of weekly exercise recommended by health professionals.[7] Physical inactivity causes one in six deaths.[8] The impact on our mental health is just as stark, given that physical activity is associated with lower levels of depression and anxiety.[9] Of course, we all know that exercise is good for us, but the problem is that building it into our lives is easier said than done. Here we can learn from the so-called blue zones. These include the island of Sardinia, Okinawa in Japan and Nicoya in Costa Rica, described as 'rare longevity hotspots around the world where people are thriving into their 100s'.[10] Their secret? It's not that they have lots of branches of PureGym. People in these places exercise as they go about their daily lives – walking and gardening, for example – without really thinking about it.[11] If your go-to ways of getting around involve exercising, you no longer have to find the time or energy to fit it in at the end of a busy day. Exercise just happens.

Inactivity isn't the only deadly consequence of our current transport habits. Every year around 25,000 people are killed or seriously injured on our roads.[12] Air pollution, meanwhile, is associated with a whole range of health problems and is thought to be responsible for approximately 40,000 deaths in the UK each year.[13] Poor air quality has a disproportionate impact on particular groups. Research in London has found that deprived communities and communities with a high proportion of Black residents are more likely to be exposed to harmful levels of air pollution than other neighbourhoods.[14] Giving people decent alternatives so we reduce the number and length of car journeys will make our air cleaner and streets safer. As for the streets themselves, designing our lives purely around the car just isn't an efficient use of public space. One study found cycle lanes can carry 2.5 times as many people as car lanes, despite taking up half the space.[15] And if you added up the square metreage taken up by parking spaces across the country, you'd get an area larger than Birmingham.[16]

These issues bring to mind a cartoon someone once showed me of an audience at a conference listening to a speaker list all the benefits of taking action on the climate crisis – from cleaner air to healthier children. Someone in the crowd interrupts: 'What if it's a big hoax and we create a better world for nothing?'[17] Even before we get to thinking about tackling the climate crisis, more walking and cycling could help build a better world. That said, the most urgent case for change is that road transport currently contributes around a fifth of carbon emissions in the UK, and most of that that comes from cars.[18] Emissions from public transport are negligible in comparison.

As I said in the first chapter of this book, electric cars are without a doubt key to getting emissions down. They offer a really important part of our transport future, but just replacing every conventional car journey with an electric car journey isn't going to be enough. The government's climate change advisers say we need to reduce our car use overall. They propose a reduction in car miles of at least 9 per cent by 2035, 17 per cent by 2050.[19] There are a number of reasons this is necessary. These include the fact that changing the UK's entire fleet of cars from petrol and diesel to electric is going to take a while. Just think of how long people tend to own cars, and then add to that how long second-hand cars stay in circulation after their first owner has passed them on. The average car stays in use for fourteen years, meaning that even if every brand-new car sold is fully electric by 2030, the transition will continue for years after that.[20] Additionally, manufacturing and powering electric cars still results in carbon emissions. We are making progress on decarbonising the production process and electricity supply but cannot ignore the emissions in the meantime.[21]

Of course, walking and cycling aren't the only answers here. There are going to have to be far more journeys on buses, trains and trams. That will require proper investment in all forms of public transport. (In Chapter 12 I will discuss how local communities should have more powers to improve transport.) But there is one final advantage of walking and cycling over alternatives. The average UK household spends nearly sixty pounds a week on owning and running a car, about 10 per cent of its household budget, and a further fifteen pounds on other forms of transport including bus and rail fares.[22] The beauty of walking and cycling is that they cost next to nothing and so have the potential to make a serious dent in the cost of everyday travel.

Yet in Britain just 2 per cent of journeys are made by bike. That compares to 12 per cent in Germany, 16 per cent in Denmark and a staggering 27 per cent in the Netherlands.[23] When it comes to walking, we're closer to the European average with about a quarter of trips taken on foot, but there is still enormous potential for us to spend less time in the car. A quarter of our current car journeys are under two miles, and more than half of car journeys are under five miles.[24] We can't walk and cycle everywhere, but these kinds of distances are short enough to be covered on foot or bike if we made it easier to do so.

So why don't we cycle more? History matters here. For Britain, as for many other countries, the twentieth century was the century of the car. From a standing start at the turn of the century, cars quickly became the mode of transport of choice. There were 3 million motor vehicles on the roads in 1939, 4.5 million in 1950 and more than 9 million in 1960.[25] In the middle of the century politicians talked up Britain's promising future as a 'car-owning democracy' and, for obvious and understandable reasons, the car came to symbolise the independence and aspiration of the age.[26]

By the late 1950s and early 60s, however, congestion and road safety were becoming real issues. In 1961, for example, 7,000 people were killed and 350,000 people injured on British roads.[27] The government commissioned civil servant Colin Buchanan to come up with a solution. The 1963 Buchanan Report concluded that while traffic could be limited in some areas, many towns and cities would have to be wholly reconstructed around cars.[28] While never adopted in full, the report shaped development for decades. Car parks, flyovers and urban motorways were considered the infrastructure of the future, and road spending increased rapidly.[29] Other ways of getting around were neglected: cycling declined from 10 per cent of all travel by distance in the 1950s to just 1 per cent in the 1970s, while car journeys increased from less than 30 per cent to around 75 per cent of total distance travelled.[30]

Contrary to what you might expect, a similar thing happened in the bike utopia of the Netherlands. From the early twentieth century, the Dutch had been ahead of other European nations on cycling, perhaps a result of their famously flat landscape.[31] But they weren't immune to the draw of the car. Just as in the UK, the post-war years saw a boom in car ownership and urban planning centred around automobiles rather than bikes. Cycling fell rapidly in the 1960s and 1970s and journeys became increasingly hazardous for those who kept on their bikes.[32]

But then something changed. In October 1971 six-year-old Simone Langenhoff was killed by a speeding car which hit her as she was cycling on a narrow road to school. She became one of more than 3,000 people, including 450 children, killed on Dutch roads that year.[33] Simone's father, Vic Langenhoff, was a journalist on a national newspaper and used his platform to campaign for road safety. This helped set off *Stop de Kindermoord* (Stop the Child Murders), which grew into a huge social movement across the country. With activists stopping traffic and unilaterally pedestrianising entire roads, *Stop de Kindermoord* caught the national mood and Dutch politicians began to take notice. Alongside the impact of the 1973 oil crisis on fuel prices, it led the Netherlands to abandon the car-first planning model.[34] Over the following decades, the government invested in cycling infrastructure and built the segregated bike lanes that the country is now famous for, which went from 9,000 kilometres in the mid-70s to more than 30,000 kilometres today. Bike use rose again.[35]

Cyclists are now far from an afterthought in the Netherlands. Rather than them having to rely on helmets to lessen the consequences of collisions, streets are designed to prevent accidents involving cycles happening in the first place. When they share road space with bicycles, drivers are restricted to low speeds and reminded to look out for other road users. Wherever possible, cyclists are given separate lanes, protected by barriers and bollards.[36] Cycling lessons are widespread in schools – something that would have really helped me. It works. In cities such as Amsterdam around two thirds of all trips are by bike or on foot, compared to less than a third (28 per cent) in London.[37]

The Dutch experience shows that if you want people to cycle, you've got to make people of all ages and abilities feel safe and comfortable. As a late convert to cycling, I feel this really strongly. Cycle lanes, for example, slow my pulse and make me feel much more comfortable. On my first trip to Westminster, I discovered some byways that were cyclists only, as well as the more formal cycle lanes. They were such a relief.

There is another important lesson here too: if you build it, they will come. This relates to the point I made earlier about markets, government and how we shape the future. Through much of the twentieth century, British transport planning operated on the principle of 'predict and provide'.[38] In other words, if you expect car use to increase, then you've got to build the roads to accommodate it. This treats the demand for any type of transport as predetermined and inevitable. But transport choices aren't inevitable; they are influenced by the environment that we build. Invest in good-quality walking and cycling routes so people have good alternatives and they will use them. If the only easy and safe way to get around is by car then it's no surprise we are so dependent on them. We shape our streets and then our streets shape us. Let's decide what kind of transport system we want, give people the widest possible choice and then design our towns and cities to facilitate it.[39]

The tale of two Spanish cities shows how rapidly change can happen. Pontevedra and Seville are very different places. One is a small municipality in the north-west of the country, the other a southern city more than ten times its size. But they have both revolutionised their use of public space.

Back in 2000, Pontevedra was like a lot of places in Spain – and indeed the UK. Thousands of cars passed through the city each day, and traffic congestion was ruining the place. As Miguel Anxo Fernández Lores, mayor of Pontevedra since 1999, says, 'The historical centre was dead ... There were a lot of drugs, it was full of cars – it was a marginal zone. It was a city in decline, polluted, and there were a lot of traffic accidents. It was stagnant. Most people who had a chance to leave did so.'[40] Mayor Lores decided to do something different. He pedestrianised 300,000 square metres of the centre, making it only accessible to walkers and cyclists. Parking spaces have been removed from the inner city and replaced with an out-of-town car park.[41] The result is that traffic has reduced by 90 per cent in the centre and 50 per cent across the city as a whole.[42]

Pontevedra's fortunes have been transformed. Three quarters of previous car journeys are now made on foot or by bike; carbon emissions are down by nearly three quarters, and traffic collisions are down too. People are now clamouring to move into the municipality rather than out of it; Pontevedra is the fastest growing-city in the region, with 12,000 more residents than it had two decades ago.[43] Most important is the effect the changes have had on residents' quality of life. You can walk right down the middle of most streets with no fear of being knocked over. Polluted roads have been replaced with tree-lined plazas. Unsurprisingly, Pontevedra has won a string of awards around the world.[44]

It is far harder to pedestrianise somewhere the size of Seville (population 1 million), but this city has also learned to imagine life with fewer cars. In the mid-2000s Seville's new city council leadership decided to take cycling seriously. Back then only between 1 and 2 per cent of journeys in Seville were made by bike.[45] However, a group of cycling enthusiasts had been lobbying for decades for things to change, and they won. Over five years from 2006, Seville built a huge network of 120 kilometres of segregated Dutch-style cycle lanes.[46] The city built fast so the potential of the new system could be demonstrated as quickly as possible, and the effects are now clear to see. Wander down a street in Seville today and you'll see everyone from children to people in their seventies using the new lanes. Between 2006 and 2011, when the network was completed, the number of bike trips in Seville increased five-fold.[47] They're still a long way off Dutch levels of cycling, but getting five times as many cyclists on the road in just a few years is significant progress. Seville is proof that change can happen quickly and at scale.

Pontevedra and Seville show the impact that imaginative local leaders can have, and from Manchester to London to Paris to New York, lots of the most exciting action on urban transport has come from local and regional governments.

Nothing demonstrates this better than the Bee Network being constructed in Greater Manchester. When Andy Burnham was elected the first mayor of the region in 2017, he immediately appointed Olympic gold medallist Chris Boardman as his walking and cycling commissioner. Passionate about figuring out how to get Greater Manchester cycling, Chris went to each of the area's ten local authorities and asked them to think about how their roads could be redesigned. Within a few months, they had a plan for a thousand-mile network of walking and cycling routes across the city region. If completed it will be the largest network in the UK. It includes seventy-five miles of fully segregated cycle lanes, 1,400 safe road crossings and dozens of low-traffic neighbourhoods.[48] An online consultation with members of the public generated 4,000 comments. According to Chris, the most negative response was: 'Where's ours?'[49]

The genius of the Greater Manchester approach was to bring together a bottom-up process and a grand overall vision. To build consensus for change and reassure people they weren't going to lose out, Andy Burnham and Chris Boardman got local authorities and residents involved in the process. And while it would have been hard to build excitement about a single bike junction, a region-wide project offers something really to get behind. As they build the network bit by bit, residents can go online and see how local changes fit into the big picture. The plan has now grown to a proposed network of 1,800 miles and is at the heart of Greater Manchester's plan for its post-Covid recovery.[50]

Inspiring as these examples are, we may need even more imaginative thinking about our cities and towns. Many are designed around zones for different purposes – residential areas, business districts, out-of-town retail, industrial parks – meaning that many of the everyday trips we make are too long to walk or cycle.[51] And while in bigger cities people may have decent public transport options for these journeys, in many towns and smaller urban areas far too many do not.

Mayor of Paris Anne Hidalgo is so convinced there is a better way of doing things that in 2020 she made turning Paris into a *ville du quart d'heure* (fifteen-minute city) the centrepiece of her re-election campaign. This is the idea that you should be able to meet all of your daily needs within fifteen minutes' walk or cycle of where you live.[52] Melbourne has been pioneering something similar, aiming for twenty minutes by 2050.[53] To achieve these aims would require thinking way beyond changes to transport infrastructure and also to the location of schools, hospitals, shops and workplaces. Instead of living in one area, working in another and spending your weekends somewhere else, you would spend far more time in your own neighbourhood, giving you the most valuable thing of all – more time. All those hours wasted commuting or stuck in traffic jams would be a thing of the past.[54]

A couple of years ago work might have been one of the biggest barriers to this, particularly for those commuting to offices, but, as we saw in the chapter on working time, the need for many to work at home during the Covid crisis has opened up our ability to imagine something different. In Paris there is talk of ensuring there are offices and co-working spaces in every neighbourhood so people can work closer to home.[55]

Of course there are obvious challenges to achieving this. It would require us to think differently about where we build our housing, not to mention reimagining the character of entire neighbourhoods and districts where thousands if not millions of people live. This kind of change really would be a long process of evolution. A recent study found that new housing developments are overwhelmingly designed around car use without good alternatives, so residents are dependent on out-of-town retail and leisure complexes. The report noted that housing is often cut off from walking and cycling routes, with 'astonishing' amounts of space given up to roads and parking.[56] So it may take decades to realise the vision of fifteen-minute towns and cities, although we can hope the principles behind the idea will increasingly influence the location and design of new housing.

The response to the Covid crisis has reminded us that there is nothing inevitable about how we use our public space. In the worst of times and for the worst of reasons, the first few weeks of the lockdown in March and April 2020 saw road traffic fall by nearly three quarters to its lowest level since the 1950s.[57] Towns and cities around the world experimented with giving more space to walkers and cyclists. From Manchester to Mexico City, from Bogota to Budapest, cities opened pop-up bike lanes and widened pavements. London announced the biggest car-free zone of any city in the world. Milan brought forward its 2030 plan to reduce car use by a whole decade.[58] On some days that spring, cycling reached double, or even triple, its pre-Covid levels in the UK.[59] Following temporary changes across the country, more than three quarters of British people said they supported permanent measures to encourage more walking and cycling.[60]

Ultimately, the big idea of this chapter isn't actually about transport; it's about building a better life for people: ensuring everyone can live in a clean and attractive neighbourhood and giving them more choice about how to get around. And the big idea of Part II has been that when it comes to our choices as a society, we cannot leave it to the market to decide. We need to make those choices ourselves, collectively, putting the market in its place. But the question we haven't yet answered is *how* we do that. How do we really take back control?

PART III
Take Back Control

The promise of democracy – government by the people – is that power ultimately rests in all of our hands. This section asks whether we are currently living up to that promise.

The signs that we might not be are plain to see. The fight for representative democracy was the defining political struggle of the nineteenth and twentieth centuries. It was and is a magical, revolutionary idea: that all of us should count equally when it comes to electing our governments. It had to be fought for in the teeth of opposition from the rich and powerful who said that property or gender should continue to be qualifications to vote. Yet less than a century from the triumph of universal suffrage, our model of democracy is creaking. The turnout at every one of the last six general elections in the UK has been lower than at the previous eighteen conducted when all adults could vote.[1] Satisfaction with our democracy is at a historic low.[2]

The question of why people are turning off is a complex one. Some of it is down to vanishing folk memories of the days when the vote was restricted to a tiny elite; an awareness of people having fought and died for the right to vote makes it more valued. We can see this declining awareness in the fact that older generations are much more likely to regard voting as a civic duty.[3] But we also can't avoid the issue of declining faith in the ability of the present model of politics to deliver. I have met many committed non-voters, but not one has ever said, 'I think you're all great and whoever is elected will do a tremendous job, so really I'm fine with whoever gets in.' Persistent abstention speaks to dissatisfaction, even despair, not contentment. That is why it should trouble us. And there is a striking link between inequality and the degree of discontent, suggesting that the more people are left out of the social contract the greater the tendency to give up on democratic institutions.[4] Denmark and Norway, characterised by high levels of equality, are rare examples bucking the trend towards greater voter distrust.[5]

If we put down dissatisfaction, at least in part, to the failure of our democracy to deliver for a lot of people, this suggests one solution to the problem of voter abstention is the kind of changes I've advanced in the first half of this book. By showing people that politics can make a difference, maybe we can reduce discontent. But Part III is about why rebooting our democracy should go beyond those changes. There are reasons that 'Take back control' was the most successful political slogan of at least the last decade. The remoteness of European institutions? Definitely. But it was about much more. It spoke to the wider experience of our lives – the sense that so much that matters is out of our control. When discussing how to change our country, we need to focus on issues like inequalities of income and wealth, but inequalities of power matter as much. If we care about the right of each of us to pursue our conception of a good life, then power matters. Not just the power we have as individuals, but the power to shape our street, our neighbourhood, our town, our country.

A Labour minister, Douglas Jay, famously said in the 1930s, 'The gentleman in Whitehall really does know better what is good for people than the people know themselves.'[6] That is still the heart of the problem. We live in a country where the deference of Douglas Jay's time has largely gone, and people expect more control over their lives, but power remains beyond our reach. As we will see, we lack the ability to exert influence over everything from local public services to what happens at our place of work. This needs to change. If people are to reconnect with democracy, they need to be able to exert power over their lives at every possible opportunity.

The case for rebooting our democracy is not just that our current system is failing to deliver for people or that there is a principled case for more control, it is also that the system *cannot* deliver against the complex challenges of the modern age. Think about any issue we face today, and the knowledge and involvement of ordinary people are essential to tackling it. From climate change to loneliness in our communities, these are not problems that lend themselves to government simply pulling levers in Whitehall – or indeed the town hall. The state can't do it on its own; people need to be at the heart of designing the solutions.

All this leads me to believe that while improving the institutions of representative democracy matters a lot, we need to go further and give people more of a voice than they get from voting in an election every few years. What is really exciting is that there are lessons to be learned from all round the world about how to achieve this. There is so much democratic experimentation on which we can draw to *truly* take back control.

CHAPTER 11

Jury Service

What innovation helped overwhelmingly Catholic Ireland become the first country to legalise same-sex marriage through a referendum? How did Texas, the leading oil and gas state in America, become its leader in renewable power? What does the contemporary Mongolian constitution have in common with ancient Greece? These may sound like questions from the nerdiest pub quiz of all time, but the answer to all three, and the subject of this chapter, is an intriguing and increasingly fashionable tool for revitalising democracy.

On 22 May 2015 an amendment to the Irish constitution that extended marriage rights to same-sex couples was approved in a referendum with 62 per cent support.[1] It followed the deliberations of a citizens' assembly: a gathering of sixty-six randomly selected members of the public and thirty-three legislators, brought together over a number of weekends to consider evidence from those for and against the amendment, to weigh the arguments on either side and reach a conclusion. In the event they came to a very clear view. Of the members of the assembly, 80 per cent were in favour of extending marriage rights to same-sex couples.[2] The referendum followed two years later.

The following year another citizens' assembly, this time consisting of ninety-nine randomly selected individuals (no legislators) was convened to consider an issue that for decades had been in the country's 'too difficult' box.[3] Ireland had some of the most restrictive abortion laws in the world and, to the surprise of many, the assembly recommended by a clear majority that Ireland reform its laws and legalise abortion. Another referendum followed, and this time the specific recommendations of the assembly formed a guide for the parliamentary committee which framed the referendum question. On 25 May 2018 Ireland voted two to one to relax its abortion laws.[4]

As the *Irish Times* recently put it: 'The deliberations of the assemblies were a vital step on the road to generating support for constitutional change on both issues. Politicians had shirked dealing honestly with the abortion issue, in particular, for more than four decades and without the assembly's work it is difficult to see how it would have been resolved.'[5] On the back of these successes, the citizens' assembly has become a seemingly permanent part of Irish politics. It has made recommendations on how to make Ireland a leader on the climate emergency and is now considering how to tackle the barriers to gender equality in Irish society.[6]

Ireland has definitely been a trailblazer when it comes to so-called deliberative democracy, but it is by no means the first place to have employed it. As a child I was a big fan of a series called *Dallas*, much to the bemusement of my Marxist father, and used to sneak into our living room to watch it. (If you're doing a pub quiz and there is a *Dallas* round, you want me on your team.) *Dallas* was the story of the triumphs, trials and tribulations of a family of Texas oil barons, but it turns out oil is no longer the only place Texas gets its energy.

That's because in the late 1990s, Texas governor and future president George W. Bush told his top regulator Pat Wood to 'get smart on wind' as a future source of power. Wood was dubious: wind was 'California, Volvo-driving, Birkenstock-wearing, tree-hugging kind of stuff'.[7] But he happened to meet a young professor at the University of Texas, James Fishkin, an enthusiast about public consultation with randomly selected people, a process he calls deliberative polling. In eight places around the state samples of the local populations were gathered to deliberate for a weekend about the energy choices facing their communities. The groups (ranging in size from 175 to 232) were representative of the communities in terms of both initial opinions and demographic characteristics.[8] The organisers administered detailed questionnaires on first contact and then again at the end of the weekend. What emerged was unexpected – much greater support for renewable energy, even if it meant paying a bit more, support that grew from 52 per cent before people started their deliberations to 84 per cent afterwards. Soon after, the state legislature made additional commitments to renewable energy, setting Texas on course to become America's leader.[9]

James Fishkin also played a part when Mongolia, a relatively new democracy, passed a law in 2017 that prohibited any change to its constitution without a citizens' assembly considering the matter.[10] The former Mongolian minister of foreign affairs and trade had spent some time as a visiting scholar at Stanford University, where Fishkin now teaches, and was so influenced by his work that he got one of the professor's books translated into Mongolian and then persuaded his colleagues that deliberative democracy was a good idea.[11] As a result, 669 Mongolian citizens descended on the capital Ulaanbaatar in April 2017 to discuss a whole range of constitutional questions, including whether there should be a two-chamber legislature and whether presidential elections should be direct or indirect. Going against the country's parliamentarians, the citizens' assembly opted for one chamber and direct presidential elections, and their view was accepted.[12]

This global revival of deliberative democracy all started rather inauspiciously. In 1988, James Fishkin wrote a two-page article in an American monthly magazine called the *Atlantic* entitled 'The Case For a National Caucus', which advocated for bringing together 1,500 representative voters to discuss and deliberate on the main issues at play in the 1988 presidential election.[13] The article did not cause so much as a ripple. Indeed it didn't even feature on the front cover of the magazine, beaten out by a story headlined 'Are We Alone?' about alien-seekers.

He may have been pipped to the cover by the Martians, but Fishkin had actually started something very big. The last three decades have seen a slowly dawning interest and then a massive rise in enthusiasm for the idea of deliberative democracy. Whereas thirty years ago one or two citizens' assemblies took place annually, a recent survey suggests that more than twenty are organised each year, with 177 having taken place worldwide over the last decade.[14] They have been used to consider how to deal with flooding in Gdansk, nuclear reactors in South Korea, a waste dump in South Australia and the climate crisis in the UK.[15] In the US state of Oregon, whenever there is a referendum, a citizens' assembly is convened to issue a factual guide to the matter being decided so that the population can consider its decision on the basis of impartial information.[16] In one part of Belgium, Ostbelgien, there is a permanent citizens' assembly which can decide for itself what to examine.[17]

The fact that deliberative democracy is now very much in vogue is all the more remarkable and thought-provoking when you consider that, to revive democracy today, James Fishkin and his disciples across the world have been turning to a tradition that is in fact 2,500 years old. In ancient Athens the legislative assembly was open to all male citizens. Of Athens' 30,000–60,000 citizens, normally 6,000 chose to attend the assembly, where they voted on laws and appointed top officials. But they also had the Council of Five Hundred, which set the agenda for the assembly and scrutinised proposals before they went there for consideration.[18]

The council was selected by lot, like a criminal jury – a process known as sortition. Assuming an adult lifetime of forty years, every third citizen could expect to serve at least once as a member of the council, and was paid to do so for a year. According to the statesman Pericles, 'ordinary citizens, though occupied with the pursuits of industry, are still fair judges of public matters', and he believed that instead of being a 'stumbling block in the way of action ... [discussion] is an indispensable preliminary to any wise action at all'.[19] Most top officials were also selected in this way – out of 700 paid 'magistrates', only 100 were chosen by election, and the rest by lot.[20]

We certainly shouldn't romanticise the Athenian system, which excluded women, those without property and slaves, but deliberative democracy may have something to offer us. Could the principle implemented on a truly equal basis be a way of reviving our democracy? Aristotle wrote, 'The basis of a democratic state is liberty ... One principle of liberty is for all to rule and be ruled in turn.'[21] We would be hard pressed to say the same is true today.

Sortition never completely died out; it was utilised in the Italian city-states of Venice and Florence and in the Spanish kingdom of Aragon.[22] It even featured in late-imperial China between the sixteenth and early twentieth century.[23] However, absolute monarchical rule was the norm for many hundreds of years, and when notions of democracy were revived in the eighteenth century with the French and American Revolutions, they came in a different form. The mixed model of elections and sortition as used in ancient Greece was discarded in favour of the pursuit of representative democracy. This is hardly surprising: overthrowing the rule of the aristocracy and securing political equality through the vote for all citizens was tough enough, taking the best part of two more centuries to achieve even in countries like ours. Practicality may also have been a factor in the neglect of sortition as most countries (and their populations) were far larger than an ancient Greek city-state.

So why has this idea, which was mostly discarded for centuries, seen a resurgence? In explaining why representative democracy was the right answer in the late eighteenth century, Thomas Jefferson, the father of American independence put it this way: 'There is a natural aristocracy among men. The grounds of this are virtue and talents ... May we not even say that that form of government is the best which provides the most effectually for a pure selection of these natural aristoi into the offices of government?'[24] Given the recent crises we have been through, it is perhaps understandable that many people no longer buy the idea that our current systems, electoral or otherwise, put those of exceptional virtue and talent into positions of power. The Irish example is instructive. The roots of its citizens' assembly lie in the economic crisis of 2008, which hit Ireland very hard. In its immediate aftermath there was a widespread feeling that the country's institutions – including politics and the banking system – had failed the people. This was evident in the Irish election of 2011, when there was much talk of the need for political reform, in particular the fact that the population had little ownership of the country's written constitution, which could only be changed by referendums instigated by the government.

But do citizens' assemblies address the shortcomings of representative democracy? The best case for them is that when they work, they provide a place for informed, thoughtful political conversation rather than shrill, knee-jerk responses. People are given a serious civic responsibility, are paid for it, and all the anecdotal evidence suggests that they take it very seriously – just like jurors in criminal trials do. Like jurors, they answer to no one but themselves and are asked simply to consider what is best, without any regard as to whether it will be popular or not. In the process they bond with each other, and it is striking how positively participants describe their experiences. As one elected parliamentarian who was a member of the original, mixed Irish assembly put it, 'An important ... message which has emanated from the convention is that when a hundred people are put in a room together in the expectation that they will engage in a quality debate, they can be trusted to do just that. Such individuals do not have to be members of political parties or formal groups in order to take part in debates of that nature ... people can follow a debate or a conversation and reach their own conclusions.'[25]

There is also reason to think that citizens' assemblies can speak to one of the biggest challenges of our age. We live in a period of extreme polarisation in politics, but it is ignorance of other people's views, not contact with them, that breeds hatred and anger. If you're in the same room with someone, rather than arguing with them on social media, you are almost bound to achieve a greater understanding of where they are coming from. As a participant in the Belgian citizens' assembly said, 'If we were following the logic of [the reality TV show] *Big Brother*, we'd gradually eliminate the people who got on our nerves. But here, we don't. We have to stick together and we have to show that you can achieve things when you work together.'[26] Nor is there evidence that assemblies are dominated by a vocal minority. When members of the Irish assembly were asked, 70 per cent disagreed with the statement 'Some participants tended to dominate the discussion' and only 14 per cent agreed.[27]

Citizens' assemblies can also potentially lead to better decisions simply because, as a cross-section of the public, they bring with them experience and insights that might not be obvious to politicians. Fishkin cites the example of Mongolia, where a deliberative process on government spending prioritised improved heating for schools and kindergartens not the shiny metro project that politicians favoured.[28] And not all citizens' assemblies deal with the most divisive moral issues, as in Ireland. Some are more practical. In the UK, local authorities are starting to organise their own citizens' assemblies to consider how to tackle climate change in their areas.[29] The advantages to be gained by harnessing the collective intelligence of people are now taken for granted in many walks of life including by many businesses, and yet in the context of our democracy we somehow think it is surprising. It shouldn't be.

What the Irish case also shows is that deliberative democracy can work in conjunction with representative democracy to provide a channel through which decisions on difficult matters can be unblocked. There can be strong interests in the way of change, which sometimes become a barrier to doing what most people want. In Ireland it turned out the public was in a different place from the Catholic church on both same-sex marriage and abortion. It took the citizens' assembly to persuade the politicians to act. The Irish experience also demonstrates that citizens' assemblies provide a way for politicians to test public opinion on tricky issues at relatively low risk to themselves. Often it turns out the public are bolder and more up for change than the politicians assumed.

So citizens' assemblies model a thoughtful form of public discourse, they draw on the knowledge of people and they can unblock tricky issues. They also tackle head on the elephant in the room: lack of trust in politics. By opening politics up to participation by ordinary people, politicians can get public involvement in decisions that might otherwise be dismissed as originating in the partisan interests of politicians. This is particularly relevant to issues like constitutional change, as in Mongolia, or redrawing electoral maps, a very controversial subject in the United States, as has been done in California.[30] And if people are taken seriously – if civic responsibility is given to them – they will respond. Perhaps it is only by asking more of citizens and giving them greater responsibility that we can restore trust in politics. Deliberation exposes people to the trade-offs that are so often a feature of difficult decisions but which are so rarely acknowledged in politics or the media, let alone debated candidly with the public by politicians.

Perhaps it all sounds too good to be true. Before we get too carried away, we need to address the biggest limitation to these experiments in deliberative democracy: the legitimacy of their decisions. It is notable that neither of the Irish assemblies had any legislative authority, and the ultimate decisions were made by referendum. In the case of the French climate assembly, set up in the wake of the *gilets jaunes* (yellow vests) protests at fuel taxes and wider issues of unfairness in French society, relations between some assembly members and President Macron have soured over his failure to implement some of their demands. In the words of the French president: 'Just because 150 citizens have written a document, that doesn't make it the Bible or the Koran.'[31] Macron gets at the key question. The number of people involved in a citizens' assembly is a minute fraction of the electorate, far lower than the turnout at the most obscure election, so how far can their writ run?

The equality and inclusivity of the representative model – with every adult having the right to vote – remain the absolute bedrock of our democracy; we need to do everything we can to strengthen it. But part of doing so requires an acknowledgement of the *limits* of the model in an age of deep doubts about what it delivers, people's desire for more of a say and the very complex problems faced by our society. That is why there is a real need to engage the public. There is a good analogy with the Climate Change Committee set up under the Climate Change Act of 2008, which I piloted through parliament. This committee of experts makes recommendations about what action government should be taking to tackle the climate crisis, including proposing five-year carbon budgets, providing expertise, long-term thinking and non-partisan analysis.[32] This means that even though government makes the final call on what to do, the independent recommendations of the body are hard for them to push aside and strongly shape their decisions. It's possible to imagine a similar role for citizens' assemblies, particularly on issues that cross party lines and have proved consistently intractable. So in which areas might they work?

As we saw in Part II, caring for elderly people is one of the biggest unresolved issues of our time. We have had report after report, commission after commission, under governments of both parties, highlighting the unfairness and inadequacy of our social care provision. No party has succeeded in solving the problem. Two parliamentary select committees did commission a citizens' assembly on social care on a small scale, which did useful work and indeed recommended a rise in taxes to pay for it. As one participant put it, 'It's not a vote loser if people are informed. Don't underestimate the public – once they know they will be willing to pay. The lesson from these two weekends is that when everyone is informed consensus develops.'[33] The problem was the lack of government buy-in. A large-scale citizens' assembly on social care, whatever its conclusions, would be much harder to ignore and might make politicians braver.

An issue which has been around even longer than that of social care is reform of the House of Lords. We are supposed to be a democracy, and yet, as leader of the opposition, I got to choose new Labour peers. Every so often the government would allocate the party a number of peerages, and I had the absolute power to make people legislators. However meritorious the people I chose, and however pleased – or bemused – they were when I called them to make the offer, I always had a nagging sense this was a very odd way to do democracy. Reform of the House of Lords, one of the aims of the original Labour Party, was part of the 1997 Labour manifesto, and the Coalition government tried it in 2010. However, it is bedevilled by serious and important arguments about who should sit in it, what electoral system should be used to appoint them and how to avoid the gridlock that can occur in the US system when the two chambers compete for primacy. And yet there are lots of good ideas out there, such as a chamber of regional and national representatives situated outside London. A government interested in reform could put the various options to an assembly and see whether it could provide a long-term answer, with its deliberations free from partisan constraints and seen to be so.

Finally, we could give a citizens' assembly a permanent role in tackling the climate emergency. Like the permanent Climate Change Committee, a citizens' assembly could monitor progress and make suggestions to government. The key thing about the climate crisis is that it will require everyone to make changes, so all of us need to be part of the journey. I discussed in Chapter 1 the absolute need for fairness to be at the heart of the transition. What better way to get buy-in and find out what can work?

It has to be conceded none of these proposals solves the problem of scale – the fact that any citizens' assembly can only include a tiny fraction of the population – which will inevitably lead some to challenge its legitimacy. James Fishkin concedes that we face a 'trilemma': we want a system based on political equality, deliberation and mass participation, but on the face of it we can have two of them but not all three. Representative democracy gives us mass participation and equality (of a sort), deliberative democracy gives us equality and deliberation but not mass participation.

As a solution, Fishkin and a colleague have suggested deliberation on a much larger scale. The idea is that every Presidential election year but well before the election itself the United States should have a Deliberation Day, when across the country millions of people engage in a large-scale deliberative exercise to consider the major issues of the campaign.[34] Maybe he is on to something. The logistical and financing challenges are obvious, but imagine if we did this on the climate crisis – with clear questions about the issues we wanted citizens to address. It could be very powerful.

It's easy to see the drawbacks of citizens' assemblies, and done badly they could engender even more distrust – for example if their recommendations are ignored. But it's important to remember the burning platform on which we stand. So often representative democracy engages in sham consultation with the public when in reality the decisions have already been taken. Deliberative processes can offer something better than that. The last word goes to Marc from Newcastle, a twenty-year army veteran, on his involvement in the UK Climate Assembly: 'I felt like I'd won the lottery when I got the letter. I'd be daft not to do it – it's amazing to get the chance to have a say and influence what may happen in the future.'[35]

Nobody has ever said to me that voting in an election is like winning the lottery. Marc's words show how distant people feel from power, and how important it is to find new and different ways of bringing them closer. Citizens' assemblies show how we might start to do that, by opening up our democracy and giving people greater control. But this is just the beginning.

CHAPTER 12

The Kids Are All Right

I was a precocious child when it came to politics; my parents encouraged me to have an opinion. It wasn't exactly Karl Marx for breakfast, but even at eleven or twelve I would argue the toss with the slightly nonplussed friends of my parents who came round to dinner. I must have been a pretty irritating child, and at times they would get exasperated and say, 'You won't understand, you're too young.' My dad would invariably step in and tell his friends not to be patronising.

A conversation that took place in Washington DC in February 2019 in the office of eighty-five-year-old California Democratic senator Dianne Feinstein reminded me of that generational gulf. Senator Feinstein was talking to a group of a dozen or so young people, aged ten and upwards, about whether she would support a Green New Deal proposal in the US Senate. It didn't go well. When a child no older than twelve pointed out that scientists are telling us we have only a decade to turn things round, Feinstein said, 'It's not going to get turned round in ten years.' Then the senator asked a vociferous young person who said they had supported her in the election, 'How old are you?' Hearing the response (sixteen) she answered, 'Well you didn't vote for me.'[1]

Every politician has been in that spot where, for whatever reason, they feel they have to say no – and end up doing so in a very clumsy way. I've certainly been there. Feinstein is a

Democrat who really does care about climate change, but she carries the wisdom, and burdens, of age and experience. In the footage of the encounter Feinstein doesn't just look irritated, she looks bewildered; from her perspective, these young people are asking the impossible. In her view, the Green New Deal resolution just won't pass the Senate – a chamber known as the place where good ideas go to die. How will it be paid for? And, she argues, it's hardly a good resolution anyway. Ten-year old Magdalena captures the indignation of the young people best: 'The government is supposed to be of the people, by the people and all for the people.'[2]

As we saw in Chapter 1, the decisions we make now on climate will have massive ramifications long into the future, and it is the young, not the people making those decisions, who will have to live with them. So the gulf in outlook between the senator and her visitors should really worry us. Yet this exchange actually makes me hopeful, because it shows us that young people are actively fighting for their future. We need that urgency, that sense of possibility in our politics. If we want to rebuild our democracy, we should invite the voices of the young into politics, not shut them out. They deserve to be heard and can make a difference. This chapter is about how to ensure that happens.

Currently, we are going in the opposite direction. Rich democracies have a young-people problem: their voice is becoming quieter not louder. An academic paper published in 2014 found that in the UK the average age of the median eligible voter is rising by about a year every decade. It was 44 in 1991, 45 in 2001, 46 in 2010, and forecast to be 47 in 2021 and 49 in 2031.[3] And this ignores how far the old actually outvote the young in elections. It is thought there was a turnout gap of more than 20 percentage points between those aged 18–24 and those over 65 in the 2019 general election.[4] It's not simply that people are more likely to vote as they age; younger generations are significantly less likely to vote than older generations were at the same age. Research conducted in the aftermath of the

2015 general election found that by the age of 30 Generation X (born from the mid-1960s to 1980) and millennials (born in the 1980s and 1990s) are 20 per cent less likely to vote in elections than baby boomers (born in the post-war years) were at the equivalent age.[5]

What explains this disengagement? Polls show young people are less likely to care about the outcome of general elections than previous generations and are less likely to identify with a political party.[6] Youth satisfaction with the performance of democracy is declining across the globe, with the steepest falls in the UK and other developed democracies.[7] Researchers have also found a correlation between on the one hand wealth inequality and youth unemployment, and on the other rising youth dissatisfaction with democracy, suggesting it is partly a result of economic exclusion.[8]

We seem to be in a downward spiral. If young people feel democracy isn't working for them and disengage from it, then politicians have less reason to appeal to them. This further reduces their influence, which makes it less likely that politics will reflect their interests. When only around half of 18- to 24-year-olds vote, as was the case in the 2019 general election, it suggests a profound disconnect between our democracy and a large number of the people it is supposed to represent.[9] As older voters pass away, there is a risk that voting will become a minority sport. We have little hope of rebuilding the social contract if young people aren't engaged in our democratic processes. At the extreme, people may turn elsewhere for political solutions. Young people in the UK, US and Europe are considerably less likely than those born in the post-war years to think that living in a democracy is 'essential' and twice as likely to say democracy is a bad way to run their country.[10] Fully 35 per cent of under-35s in the UK think having the army rule the country is a good idea, against 15 per cent of over-65s. They are more likely to support a 'strongman' leader.[11] British democracy is not on the brink of collapse – and some of this polling was conducted when the UK was going through the tumult of Brexit – but it would be foolish to stick our heads in the sand. Our democracy is like a neglected house in need of refurbishment. It won't necessarily fall down if we don't act soon, but it will become increasingly ramshackle – and it's hard to know who might move in.

So how do we start to hear the voices of young people more clearly in our politics? It might sound counter-intuitive at first, but one way to help break the cycle of disengagement and lack of representation is to lower the voting age to sixteen. I'll come on to why this might help with the practical problem of turnout, but there is a strong case in principle too: because at the moment highly consequential decisions are made about young people without them in the room. Think back to the fate of the Education Maintenance Allowance (EMA) in 2010. First introduced in 2004, EMA gave sixteen- to eighteen-year-olds up to thirty pounds a week for staying in education or training. I was involved with the policy so you may think I'm biased, but independent evaluations say it was a success. It was an educational and financial lifeline for many young people. In particular, it made them far more likely to remain in education.[12] Yet within months of the Coalition government coming to power after the 2010 general election, it was abolished and more than half a million young people lost their entitlement.[13]

EMA was far from the only victim of austerity after 2010, but it's worth noting that the very same spending review that abolished it also set out the 'pension triple lock', which guarantees that pensions rise by a certain amount each year.[14] There are good reasons to think that pensions should be protected; what is striking is that while those who could vote saw their interests safeguarded, those who could not, did not. Imagine a world in which the 1.5 million young people who were sixteen and seventeen at the time were able to vote. Would the EMA have been dispensed with in such a cavalier way? It seems unlikely. There is a reason that men and women fought for the right to vote: if you are a voter, politicians are more likely to take your interests into account.

A reduction in the voting age to sixteen might sound improbable, but the tide of history is running in its favour. In September 2014, for the first time in British history, more than 100,000 sixteen- and seventeen-year-olds were allowed to vote – in the Scottish independence referendum. They grabbed the opportunity with both hands: three quarters of them cast a ballot. Almost all – a staggering 97 per cent – said they would do so again in a general election.[15] Crucially, turnout among this group appears to have been significantly higher than among eighteen- to twenty-four-year-olds.[16]

This experience transformed the debate about young people's role in Scottish politics. In the run-up to the referendum, the Scottish Conservatives had loudly opposed lowering the voting age, but after it even their leader Ruth Davidson described herself as 'a fully paid-up member of the votes-at-sixteen club'.[17] A year after the referendum, every political party in Scotland backed a proposal to lower the voting age for all Scottish and local elections. It passed unanimously in the Scottish Parliament.[18] In November 2019 the Welsh Parliament followed suit. This means UK-wide general elections are now the only major votes in which sixteen- and seventeen-year-olds in Scotland and Wales cannot take part.

In 2007 Austria became the first country in Europe – and one of the first in the world – to lower the voting age to sixteen for all elections.[19] And it works. Austria's sixteen- and seventeen-year-olds are consistently more likely to vote in elections than those a little older – by up to 10 percentage points – and Austria now has the joint highest youth political participation in Europe.[20] Evidence from a string of local elections in Germany and Norway suggests the same: that lowering the voting age can increase youth turnout.[21]

Why might this be? In the UK at the moment people are expected to start voting in their late teens and early twenties (it can be a few years between becoming eligible to vote and a general election), but this often coincides with a time of flux – moving away from home, getting a job, starting further or higher education. Given those distractions, these years can reasonably be described as 'arguably the worst possible years to have one's first vote'.[22] In contrast, those a little younger are more likely to be living at home and have more stability in the rest of their lives, making it easier to register to vote or even engage in the politics of their locality. Voting or non-voting is a habit. You've got to get people voting young for the habit to stick.[23] Think about the contrast we saw between baby boomers and millennials. If younger generations fail to form the habit early, we can't just hope they will pick it up later on in life.

But some question whether sixteen-year-olds are really old enough to be making important decisions about how the country should be run. Those who say they are point out that at sixteen you can pay taxes, get married, leave home and even join the army – fairly consequential life choices. If we trust people to make decisions about their own lives, the argument goes, shouldn't we trust them to make decisions about their society? If people pay taxes, shouldn't they have a say in where the money goes? If they fight for their country, shouldn't they have a say in who determines whether they go to war?

Those on the other side respond by saying that yes, you *can* pay income tax at sixteen, but the vast majority of sixteen-year-olds are not in work and so do not. Yes, you *can* get married or join the army at sixteen, but only with your parents' permission, and sixteen-year-olds are not allowed to serve on the front line. And in some instances where previously you could do something at the age of sixteen – buy fireworks, cigarettes or lottery tickets, for example – we have since increased the threshold to eighteen.

The argument quickly descends into tedious tit for tat. Personally, I think the array of things you can do at sixteen makes a strong case for a lower voting age, but perhaps what is more convincing is the evidence that sixteen-year-olds are perfectly able to make informed choices. Academics investigated how far the voting decisions of this age group in Austria aligned with where they placed themselves on the political spectrum. In other words, did ignorance lead them to vote for parties at odds with their own perceptions of their views and interests? They concluded that they were just as able to choose a party that coincided with their views as voters of any other age.[24]

That chimes with the experience in the UK. When former Scottish Conservative leader Ruth Davidson was asked to explain her change of heart on votes at sixteen, she said, 'I thought sixteen- and seventeen-year-olds were fantastic during the referendum campaign ... there is nothing more terrifying for somebody up on the stage who is trotting off the latest IMF figures to have somebody in the front row with a smartphone googling your answers to make sure that you've got it exactly right.'[25] And let's not forget that in recent years it is young people – sometimes younger than sixteen – who have pricked the conscience of older generations. Greta Thunberg began her campaign of school strikes aged fifteen and inspired people around the world. Not mature enough to vote? Really?

Ultimately, the strongest case for votes at sixteen is that the status quo is not working: young people are losing faith in our democracy and our system needs their voice. But hearing the voice of young people is about much more than the chance to vote. One evening last year I was about to get on the Tube when a couple of sixth-form students came up to me clutching copies of the *Metro* – or rather, a fake *Metro* they had created. The headline declared, BORIS BACKS EMPIRE EDUCATION. It was designed to get people's attention and highlight a campaign they were running to make teaching the history of the British empire compulsory in secondary schools. It turned out they were graduates of the Advocacy Academy, a charity in south London that teaches young people how to channel their frustrations into campaigning for political change.

The Advocacy Academy was set up by former parliamentary researcher Amelia Viney after she saw first hand how young people – particularly those from working-class families and young people of colour – were being ignored in the Westminster debate. It runs a 400-hour 'boot camp' for sixth formers, teaching them how our political system really works and how to lobby, campaign and organise to influence it.[26] Past graduates have helped to persuade Lambeth Council to divest from fossil fuels, set up a community land trust to build affordable homes for young people hit by the housing crisis, and shone a national light on how school exclusions further racial inequality.[27]

Whether leading campaigns on period poverty, LGBT rights or the climate crisis, young people are desperate to have their voices heard. That should mean a genuine opportunity to influence the world around them, not simply voting within our creaking system. What would happen, for example, if a city gave money to young people to spend on whatever they wanted? That's exactly what Boston in the USA has done – $1 million a year, not once, but every year since 2014. Back then Boston's head of youth services Shari Davis was figuring out ways to open up City Hall to young people excluded from local government, when the mayor called her into his office and suggested they give participatory budgeting a try.[28] Participatory budgeting, an idea born in Brazil in the 1980s, involves handing over part of a public budget directly to local people, who develop and vote on ideas for how to spend the money. In Boston everybody between twelve and twenty-five in the city is given a vote each year on how the $1 million is spent. Over the years they've chosen to fund projects such as free WiFi in public places to help those without access at home, an app to help young people find jobs, solar panels on public buildings and water fountains across the city.[29] An evaluation after the first year found that the young people most involved in the project said they were more engaged in their community, more likely to vote in elections and more likely to volunteer in community projects.[30]

It's not just Boston. Each year young people in North Ayrshire in Scotland vote on which youth projects in their area – from sports and dance clubs to children's book festivals – should receive council grants.[31] A similar process takes place in Glasgow.[32] The pioneering UK Climate Assembly that we heard about in the last chapter invited young people to take part.[33] The British Youth Council does a great job at coordinating youth parliaments, youth councils and young mayors at both a local and national level across the country, giving young people a voice on the issues that affect them. These experiments point the way to a different kind of democracy in which the voices of teenagers are taken seriously. Why not scale them up so that every young person in every community across the country has the opportunity to experience democracy in action?

If we want to build a thriving democracy with engaged young people at its heart, we also need to think about what happens in schools. It is complacent to think an appreciation of why voting matters will be automatically passed on from generation to generation; it has to be part of education. When Austria, which has its own historical reasons to know the fragility and importance of democracy, implemented votes at sixteen it realised expanding the franchise would not be enough and so revamped citizenship education at the same time. It launched a campaign to raise awareness about voting both inside and outside school, and a programme of 'democracy workshops' in schools.[34] We too should do a better job of teaching young people about our democracy.

In the late 1990s the Labour government appointed the late Bernard Crick, a political theorist, to lead an inquiry into citizenship education. Then as now, people were worried about disengagement from democracy. Bernard Crick's report led to citizenship becoming a compulsory part of the secondary school curriculum in 2002. 'We aim at no less than a change in the political culture of this country both nationally and locally: for people to think of themselves as active citizens, willing, able and equipped to have an influence in public life and with the critical capacities to weigh evidence before speaking and acting; to build on and to extend radically to young people the best in existing traditions of community involvement and public service.'[35]

Unfortunately, these high hopes have not been met. We know that teaching citizenship properly can improve people's knowledge of politics and increase their likelihood of voting, yet far too few students in the UK get high-quality citizenship education.[36] This isn't the fault of teachers or students, but comes from a failure to take the subject seriously at the very top, where it is seen as a 'soft' subject, with the result that it is not given enough teaching time and lacks specialist teachers.[37] Schools are increasingly judged on student performance in 'core' academic subjects such as maths, science and history; there is little incentive to teach citizenship well. A scathing House of Lords report in 2018 criticised the government for allowing citizenship education to 'degrade to a parlous state'. Just 3 per cent of students take citizenship at GCSE level.[38]

This actually points to a more fundamental question: what is education for? Surely it should set us up to live happy and rounded lives? Accepting this means equipping young people as individuals with the skills, confidence and motivation to learn, build relationships and support themselves in the wider world. But it means something more: learning how to live well together, engage in our communities and shape the world around us – which requires us to teach the values and skills of being an active citizen from a young age. And it needn't be boxed off into a single subject; it could take the form of history lessons about the fight for democracy, from the Chartists through to the suffragettes, or media literacy lessons on how to spot fake news – something they do in Finland.[39] The great thing about votes at sixteen is that all of this would be happening just as people gain the right to vote. Imagine schools and sixth-form colleges buzzing with these initiatives in the run-up to an election day. What better way to build excitement about our democracy among the next generation?

Votes at sixteen, experiments in youth participation, revitalising citizenship education – all of this might not remake the house of democracy as good as new, but it might stop the roof caving in. On so many issues it has taken the voice and perspective of younger people to make older politicians wake up and see what they would otherwise ignore. The past few years haven't been the best for the politics I believe in, but the mobilisation and engagement of young people in politics during this time has been inspiring. And in this there is a lesson for older generations.

Young people definitely tend to greater idealism about what is possible, and there is a tendency to dismiss this as naivety. But maybe it's not that they are naive but that we have become cynical. However old we are, perhaps it's time to think like the young people in Dianne Feinstein's office. They believed we can go big; why shouldn't we?

CHAPTER 13

Westminster Doesn't Know Best

I think this is an important moment in the political life of our country ... The north stands on the brink of being back to where we were in the 1980s – just forgotten and pushed aside. But we won't let that happen and that's why we're taking this stand.

Andy Burnham, 15 October 2020[1]

When Andy Burnham, mayor of Greater Manchester, delivered these words on the steps of Manchester's Central Library, he took a stand which was widely praised across his region. He was protesting against government plans to impose further public health restrictions on Greater Manchester during the Covid crisis without adequate economic compensation. His speech was widely covered in the media and drew attention up and down the country.

Andy served as shadow health secretary when I was Labour leader. I remember talking to him before he made his decision to leave Westminster politics in 2017 to stand for mayor. He was sorry to leave parliament, but Manchester was where he felt he could make most difference. Despite the fact that Sadiq Khan had similarly made the switch from MP to stand as mayor of London just a few years earlier, it was seen as a surprising decision. Why would you leave Westminster, where most power lies?

That question says a lot about the way our country is governed. Britain – and particularly England – is one of the most centralised countries in the world.[2] Power that elsewhere is exercised by local or regional governments is instead held at Westminster. It is occasionally given away, but only sparingly, in a piecemeal fashion and on loan, to be called in at any time. Indeed, when the prime minister doesn't like the leader of a local authority, they can simply abolish it – as Margaret Thatcher did with the Greater London Council in the 1980s.

Why should we be interested in which set of politicians wields power? Because this addresses a far deeper question: whether as citizens of our country we are able to exercise control over what matters to us. The further away decisions that affect our everyday lives are made, the harder it is to hold politicians to account for them. If we are serious about taking back control and restoring our democracy, we need to get serious about giving towns, cities and regions far more control, and central government needs to take a step back.

Let me give an example. Talk to any MP outside London and they will tell you that buses are one of the most neglected elements of our infrastructure. Soon after I was first elected as an MP, I remember going to a polling station during a local council election to check how things were going and being depressed by the fact that, apart from the officials handing out the ballot papers, I was pretty much the only person there. Eventually a voter arrived, and I pounced on him: 'Where is everybody?' 'It's the buses.' He went on to explain that he didn't mean people couldn't get to the polling station, but that whoever they voted for, the buses wouldn't improve, so what was the point?

My experience as an MP tells me he was right. The powers of elected local authorities over bus services are extremely limited. Until recently, buses in Doncaster were governed by a South Yorkshire body with some council representation but very little real power and resources – controlled by Westminster. This might seem a minor point, but it isn't. The availability of good local transport is life-changing. Around three in five public transport journeys are by bus, double the number made by train, but London apart we have a deregulated, unreliable, expensive bus system where 3,000 routes have been altered, reduced or withdrawn in the last decade alone.[3] In Doncaster I see how poor bus services cut people off from decent employment, make it harder for the elderly to do their shopping and prevent young people getting out.

Now let me take you to Dunkirk. The town used to be reliant on heavy industry, but by 2018 the jobs were gone and residents were leaving. A quarter of families didn't have access to a car and public transport was unreliable. For those who did have cars, traffic jams were common, clogging up the streets and polluting the air. The mayor, Patrice Vergriete, concluded Dunkirk needed a 'psychological shock' to improve the lives of its people and change perceptions of the town, and, following the example of Tallinn in Estonia, made travel on the city's buses free for everyone, twenty-four hours a day, seven days a week.[4] Businesses and unions alike were sceptical, but the experiment has been a roaring success. Within a year, bus use was up by 65 per cent during the week and 125 per cent at weekends, with half of the new users switching from their cars. As a result, walking also increased.[5] The €4 million loss in fare income was covered by the payroll tax on local businesses, which had previously paid for 90 per cent of the cost of bus travel anyway.[6] Dunkirk is part of a network of at least thirty-three entirely free public transport networks operating or planned in France.[7] Free bus travel is already a reality in around a hundred towns and cities worldwide, including in Poland, Sweden, Italy, Slovenia and Australia.[8]

I'm telling you all this because local power to innovate as exercised in Dunkirk or Tallinn simply doesn't exist in England. Bus services are a parable for the problems of the way we are governed, even when some positive change is made. It is true that some of England's new elected metro mayors – who cover regions or parts of regions including South Yorkshire – are at long last beginning to gain more powers over bus services, but these are still tightly controlled by Westminster. Mayors are explicitly prohibited by law from running their own municipal bus companies, as they do in Tallinn, and with their limited tax-raising powers and local council budgets slashed by as much as 50 per cent over a decade, they would hardly be able to find the money to follow Dunkirk's example either. They are also required to jump through multiple hoops even to have a London-style system of regulated services.[9] And if you don't live in an area covered by a metro mayor, which is most of the country, your local authority doesn't have London-style powers over buses, but has to apply to central government on a case-by-case basis before it can act.

You may think that free bus travel is a good idea or a bad idea, but that isn't the point. Bus services are a symptom of something bigger. In Britain the powers of local leaders are so constrained that they often lack the ability to experiment, to try new ideas or develop new solutions to the problems their areas face. It's not just public transport. The same is true of the ability to build social housing, regulate private landlords, govern schools, introduce new rules on the energy efficiency of buildings or raise new revenue. Think of an idea to fix a problem and chances are that there will be some restriction on the ability of local leaders to implement it.

This is not how most comparable governments handle things. In the UK just 5 per cent of tax revenue is raised at a sub-national level, compared to 13 per cent in France, 32 per cent in Germany and 35 per cent in Sweden.[10] In Germany, for example, the federal government takes sole responsibility for things that affect the whole country, such as defence, foreign affairs and immigration policy, but most other powers are shared with the regions (known as *Länder*) and local governments. There are whole areas of policy barely touched by national government – from policing to schools, local transport to housing, and culture to economic development.[11] In Germany the idea of ministers micromanaging local government from the capital is preposterous. It isn't alone: Italy, Spain, even comparatively centralised France, all have far more power exercised below the national level.[12]

This isn't just about power over local issues; it is highly relevant to the deep economic inequalities that scar our country. Prosperity, health, life expectancy and wellbeing vary wildly between parts of the UK. Guess how bad the problem is, and I bet you have underestimated the scale of it. Our regional economic divide is one of the worst of any rich country in the world. Researchers recently compared regional inequality in disposable income and productivity per person across members of the OECD – an international organisation of high-income countries, including our European neighbours such as France, Germany, Italy and Spain. The conclusion was unequivocal: the UK has the most severe economic inequality of any country of a similar size and level of development.[13]

We are home to both the richest region in Europe (London) and six of the ten poorest.[14] As a result, median pay is 20–25 per cent lower for residents of the north of England, Midlands and the south-west compared to London.[15] Almost half of new jobs created in England between 2009 and 2019 were in London and south-east England, despite these areas only containing a third of England's population.[16] We also have a bigger divide when it comes to health than any comparable country: mortality rates are significantly higher outside London and the south-east.[17] There is a risk that all of these problems will get worse in the fallout from Covid-19, with some parts of the country much more dependent than others on the parts of the economy that have been hardest hit by the pandemic.[18]

Britain's regional inequality has been driven by the hoarding of political power in Westminster and Whitehall. From London, the Treasury dictates economic policy for the whole of England. Too often it has followed a strategy of maximising growth in certain sectors in London and the south-east in the hope that this will trickle down to the rest of the country.[19] Twice as much is spent per person on transport in London than in the rest of the country. State investment in research and development, a key part of the government's strategic economic spending, is also concentrated in London and the south-east.[20] Trickle-down might be the aim, but the reality is most places have been lucky to see the odd drip. (It's worth noting that trickle-down hasn't worked for the richer regions either – London has the highest poverty rates in the country.[21])

Could the problem simply be about poor economic choices rather than centralisation? Maybe, but studies of rich economies show that decentralised countries tend to be less geographically unequal.[22] Part of the explanation for this is that, while national policymakers are focused on the economic interests of the country as a whole, local and regional leaders are invested in the economic success of their particular area and much better able to tailor strategies to their needs. In the UK, cities, towns and regions lack the tools or resources to challenge or modify national economic strategies when they aren't working for them.

The long-standing argument against devolution – that it risks creating postcode lotteries, meaning the luck of where you live determines the services and resources you have access to – doesn't hold water. Regional inequality in the centralised UK is among the worst in the rich world, and government investment has consistently been concentrated in one corner of the country. There is no guarantee that even with more powers, local and regional leaders would successfully reverse this, but they would have the chance to do so – and would be accountable to their citizens if they failed. Centralisation isn't just bad for democracy; it's a barrier to building a more equal country.

Turning this around won't be easy. Hoarding power runs deep in the veins of the UK government. Perhaps one thing that has slowed our progress is that the UK has been a single political unit for much longer than somewhere like Germany, which was a collection of different states until its unification in 1871; England in particular lacks the tradition of regional power that we see in other countries. This is made worse by the lack of a codified constitution, which means that we have no constitutional constraints on the power of central government. They can hand down responsibilities to other levels of government or take them away at will.

At various points in our history the tendency of central government to hoard power has been challenged. In the second half of the nineteenth century, with national politics dominated by what was widely seen as an out-of-touch aristocracy, local politics emerged as a powerful democratic alternative. In the 1870s Joseph Chamberlain, mayor of Birmingham, presided over its renaissance. The city purchased and began running the local water and gas supply and instigated a world-leading slum clearance programme. The authorities used public money to build schools, libraries, swimming pools and parks. Over the next few years, local authorities across the country created an extraordinary range of public services – from markets to cemeteries, libraries to swimming pools, refuse and sewage disposal services, plus parks, theatres and more. As in Birmingham, many took over the supply of gas, water and electricity.[23] Why do so many cities in the UK have beautiful Victorian and Edwardian town halls in their centres? They are a product of the same history. These buildings were a testament to the wealth, power and civic pride of British municipal governance at the time.

Crucially, this not only improved the lives of ordinary people, but also changed the balance of power across the country. The emergence of a network of powerful municipal authorities in the north, Midlands, and even in London ensured UK politics enjoyed a rare moment of geographical balance. In fact, it was at a municipal level that the twentieth-century social contract started to be built. The NHS was inspired by community activity in Wales in the 1890s and by measures taken by the London County Council in the 1930s.[24]

Yet despite this history, in the post-war years the Left turned to a strong national welfare state as the guarantor of equality, pushing against the municipal politics of the previous century. The attraction of centralisation was that (in theory) it

guaranteed universal standards. Resources could be redistrib-
uted across the country to wherever they were needed most. At
the same time, the Right was also suspicious of local control,
fearing as far back as the nineteenth century that municipal politics might permanently challenge their dominance of
national politics and that local government was a 'hotbed of
socialism'.[25] For most of the last century, both Left and Right
sought to centralise – and Britain's strong state apparatus and
uncodified constitution allowed them to do so.

This all sounds fairly gloomy, yet in the last two decades
something unprecedented has happened. It began in Scotland,
after a long era of Conservative rule from Westminster from
which most Scots felt alienated. This supercharged the long-
standing demand for a Scottish Parliament, culminating in the
1997 referendum and its decisive result, with three quarters
voting for devolution. In Wales devolution passed the same
year but with a much narrower majority.[26] The following year
saw the Good Friday agreement and the establishment of the
Northern Ireland Assembly. These three devolved legislatures
have dramatically changed the way Britain is governed. Just
35 per cent of spending in Scotland is now directed from
Westminster, as against 74 per cent in England. The numbers
for Wales are similar.[27] Decisions about the NHS, education,
home affairs, transport, economic regeneration, as well as substantial law-making powers are devolved. In addition, greater
tax varying powers, including over income tax and stamp duty
have recently been devolved.[28]

Devolution to Scotland, Wales and Northern Ireland represents a breach in the centralising dam, not just because of
the scale of the change, but because it seems unimaginable
that these parliaments could now be abolished. The seemingly
impossible has not just become possible but immovable. And
through the breach have come other forms of devolution.
Shortly after Scottish and Welsh devolution, London's directly
elected mayoralty was established, and a new tier of elected
metro mayors has gradually come into being.

Yet it has been done in an extremely arbitrary and inconsistent way; even when it devolves, Westminster cannot really let go. At the time of writing, nearly two thirds of people in England live in areas still not covered by a devolved metro mayor.[29] Bizarrely, those English metro mayors that do exist have wildly varying powers, depending on the devolution deal that was struck. The terminology rather gives the game away: it is a negotiation between central and local government, where the centre holds all the cards. The result is that, depending on where you live, your metro mayor could have powers over policing or health or transport or all of these or none.[30] Andy Burnham has some of the most comprehensive powers of any mayor outside London but is still very limited in what he controls. He was able to draw attention to the problem of the government's proposed Covid financial support for Greater Manchester, but do little about it himself.

Despite their limited powers, in the few years England has had metro mayors they have pioneered new approaches on everything from tackling homelessness to reducing unemployment to developing local economies.[31] That is what devolution unleashes: the power to try out new solutions to our biggest problems. Bans on smoking in public places, votes at sixteen, taxes on plastic bags, new procedures on organ donation – they all started in the devolved Scottish and Welsh administrations. Devolution allows space for different solutions to emerge and for other parts of the country to learn from them. (In the next chapter I will argue that the state as a whole needs to embrace a culture of experimentation. Local devolution enables that to happen.)

What if we turned Britain's political system on its head? What if, instead of power being held by default at Westminster for the government to give out or withhold on a whim, we started from the assumption that decisions should be made as locally as possible? Here's how we could make it happen.

First, we need a comprehensive plan for devolving power. The recent process has, as we have seen, been based on a piecemeal approach involving backroom deals that have left large areas of the UK out of the picture. Most countries have a set of principles for the distribution of power between central government, regions and local communities. The German constitution, for example, sets out how powers are divided between the federal government and sixteen regional governments, which in turn devolve certain responsibilities to thousands of local municipalities. A new settlement for the country should set out which powers are held by local councils, regions or city-regions such as Greater Manchester, which belong to the nations of England, Scotland, Wales and Northern Ireland and, finally, what is best coordinated at a UK-wide level.

Second, there is no point in undertaking this process unless it gives communities meaningful control, so we should devolve real powers over things that matter – in areas like transport, housing, childcare, education and skills, and employment support – along with the resources to implement decisions. If town, city and regions are to improve their areas they also need much more economic power than they have at the moment, which means looking at additional powers over tax and revenue raising. So much of the devolution that has taken place is of the 'yes but' variety – you can have these powers but subject to not doing the following things. Why shouldn't mayors be able to set up municipal bus companies, for example, if they think that is the right way forward? We need to get away from the 'permission slip' approach.

Third, national decision-making itself should involve a degree of power-sharing between central government and the English regions, as well as with Scotland, Wales and Northern Ireland. This would involve significant reform of our national institutions. While we have the House of Lords, which hugely over-represents the south-east of England, Germany's second chamber is composed of representatives from the regions.[32] We should consider something similar, whether directly elected or comprising nominated representatives from all parts of the country. As we rebalance power between central, regional and local governments, we are also going to need to create new ways for them to coordinate and resolve any disagreements. Throughout the Covid crisis, elected leaders from outside Westminster complained that they were shut out of the decision-making process – indeed that was the reason for Andy's speech from the library steps.[33] A new constitutional settlement should take local and regional leaders seriously as representatives of their areas.

A rebalancing of power that adhered to these principles would give real meaning to taking back control. It would give towns, cities and regions the tools they need to challenge economic neglect. It would give them the opportunity to try out new ways of sorting out the bloody buses. Because that is the lesson to remember from this chapter. Devolution is not about arcane matters of constitutional governance but about the bread-and-butter reality of people's lives.

In that same spirit, we must make sure that we don't simply transfer power from one set of (national) politicians to another set of (local) politicians. As we shall now see, giving real power to citizens is going to require a fundamental change in our mindset about the way the state works.

CHAPTER 14

Constant Gardeners

Unless you're from Doncaster or one of the surrounding villages, you will probably never have heard of Pat Hagan. He works for the council. Not as chief executive or even in one of the most senior management positions. Pat's official title is Head of Localities and Town Centre, but when it comes to floods, he is the fourth emergency service. When a deluge hit my constituency in 2007, he masterminded the response in Toll Bar, the worst-hit village. He won an MBE for his efforts. When floods hit again in 2019 it was time for the council to call on Pat once more.

The picture of Pat I want you to have in your mind is of him in the church in Fishlake, a village where hundreds of houses were under water, a couple of weeks into the crisis. The church is at the centre of relief efforts, providing food, clothing and warmth. People are bustling around. A man approaches me to say that the generator powering everything in the church is running out of fuel. We can get some tonight if we decide quickly, but he's hitting a brick wall getting approval for the spending. I suggest we talk to Pat. Standing in front of the altar, white-haired, slightly stressed-looking, with people queuing up to talk to him, Pat listens. Once he hears the problem, he is decisive and clear. He instructs one of his colleagues to pay for the fuel now on the council credit card so it can be collected.

I could tell you dozens of stories like this about Pat from the floods of 2019, and indeed 2007. There was the family fostering a child who lost their home and had nowhere else to live. They had tried the housing authority multiple times with no luck. I came across them, desperate, in the local pub. Pat made sure they were put up in a hotel and then housed. There were the residents trying to get a pump so they could clear the water from the garden of an immobile elderly couple and stop their house from flooding. Pat sorted it out. There are countless other 'Pat sorted it out' stories that I don't even know about, and millions of other public servants every bit as dedicated and resourceful as he is, but there is something particularly important about Pat – or rather, about something he said in the midst of the crisis. It was, he said, time 'to tear up the rule book'. He recognised that in the face of an emergency, the formal, prescribed way of operating was not just of little help but was actually a massive hindrance.

What the floods also showed is the extraordinary power of local communities to pull together in times of crisis. What was so striking about those days after the floods was people's eagerness to help. Again, the stories are too many to mention, but just to sketch a picture: the people of Fishlake coming to each other's aid, including their heroic efforts at the church; Angie and Scott in the pub continuing to operate and sustain residents; provisions coming in from Stainforth and Moorends. Both these villages suffer from high levels of deprivation, but residents showed extraordinary generosity, providing clothes, food and bedding and ferrying these supplies into the submerged community. Those with the least were helping those who, until the floods, had more.

The people of Bentley Town End, meanwhile, which flooded in 2007 and again in 2019, established their own extraordinary self-help community, led by a local businessman, Shane Miller of Custom Windows and Doors, who turned his premises over to the community. Shane's offices became the food bank, the local authority advice hub, a venue for meetings, the place where food was provided for the soldiers who arrived with sandbags. He worked closely with a council officer, Natasha Mead, and one of the elected local councillors, Jane Nightingale.

Leaving aside for a moment the extraordinary community spirit, one thing really struck me. When the relationships worked, it really became hard to tell who was employed by the state and who was a resident. Hierarchy and position were forgotten, and people worked together as equals. And those relationships, which I saw in action during those weeks, provide a model for the kind of state we need in the future – the subject of this chapter.

People like Pat and Natasha remained accountable for their spending and decisions but walked in the shoes of the people who had lost their homes, seen their village deluged or were helping their elderly neighbours in distress. This empathy was much more powerful and effective than a local authority operating by a rule book. It was the state being flexible and humble, not rigid and hierarchical. Flexible in being willing to adapt to circumstances, and humble in recognising the role of people and communities as partners bringing knowledge and expertise that the state simply may not have. Can such a relationship between citizens and the state only operate in emergencies?[1] I like to think not.

Distributed knowledge is the idea that the wisdom of the many is much greater than the wisdom of the individual. The problem with any rule book is that, by its nature, it only works for situations that have been thought of in advance. In reality, it simply isn't possible to write rules which cater for every circumstance or draw on the knowledge of every front-line service worker, never mind the individual citizen. Of course you need rules, but as soon as something happens that they have not been designed for, the rules become 'Computer says no.' The magic of systems built on distributed rather than centralised knowledge is that they do not need to predict or account for every situation or problem in advance; instead, they empower everyone involved to be a problem-solver themselves.

Wikipedia is a good example of how distributed knowledge can work. It is written and edited by hundreds of thousands of people all across the world, each contributing their own pieces of knowledge and expertise. This has made it as accurate as the expert-written *Encyclopaedia Britannica* and much more widely used, with 269 billion page views each year.[2] Wikipedia would never have got to where it is if one person, or even one organisation, had set out to write the whole thing. And what I saw during the floods in Doncaster was an unleashing of the massive amount of distributed knowledge that exists in that community: Pat's expertise and ability to make decisions, Shane Miller's relationship with the local community, the compassion of neighbours for one another. The emergency tapped into those resources, but they are there all of the time. We do not need to wait for an emergency to use them.

What prevents us from doing so is a mindset – a conception of what the state is and the way it should work. During the floods I got shouted at (rightly) by a woman with three children, including a small baby, because she had been refused temporary accommodation and was getting nowhere being rehoused. Under the rules the housing authority had a duty to make one 'reasonable offer' to her, but the offer was a house nine miles away, and she didn't have a car, making it impossible for her children to attend school. The problem wasn't simply that she felt hard done by or didn't know where to turn; this was a system that could not adapt to her needs – it lacked empathy and imagination. The rules were the rules. The computer had said no. Maybe her piece of luck was to run into me and shout at me. I tried to help and made progress of a sort – ultimately thanks to people in the housing authority who were willing to rip up the rule book – but it shouldn't have been this way.

This will hardly be the only story you have ever heard about the failings of state bureaucracy. A rigid social security system that is unsympathetic to particular needs and seems designed to catch out the claimant and sanction them. A schooling system that can seem unbending and shoves children labelled as difficult from pillar to post. A council housing allocation system that can struggle to take into account the individual's circumstances. To be clear, I'm talking about systems; the public servants involved

usually understand the failings better than anyone and have a
very good idea of how to fix them. When I was an adviser to
the Labour government, I visited those working on the front
line of the benefits and tax credit system on a few occasions.
So often, and this was even before the problems of Universal
Credit, they would have ideas on how to make the process
easier for claimants, more efficient and not necessarily more
expensive, but they were resigned to the fact that those at the
'centre' wouldn't allow it.

People on my side of politics are brilliant at castigating the
failures of the market; we are much less good at being candid
about the shortcomings of the state. Just as the market can
treat people like commodities to be bought and sold, so the
state can treat people like cogs in a machine. Don't get me
wrong – the ideas in this book need a strong and effective
state, whether to build homes, tend to the sick or support businesses – but we need to ask what kind of state we want. If we
preach equality but exclude it when it comes to power and the
operation of government, it makes all the other nice-sounding
ambitions rather meaningless. If we care about having control
over our lives, both when we are served by the institutions
of the state and when we work in them, then tackling these
issues is fundamental.

Now some people might at this point say that conceptions
of what the state is for and its relationship to the public are
all well and good, but isn't the real problem in Doncaster a
shortage of council housing? That's why a 'reasonable offer'
was a property nine miles away. And aren't the shortcomings
of the other services traceable to a lack of resources? In other
words, aren't the deficiencies of the state a result of scarcity?
My answer is an emphatic yes – lack of resources is a very real
problem. The fact that our public services have been starved of
funds for a decade explains so much of the strain. They need
substantial investment. If the aim is to make the state more
flexible and humble in its operation, the means cannot be the
Big Society proposed by David Cameron – which in practice

became an excuse for the abdication of the state's responsibility for properly funding services. But we also need to think about *how* the state operates in order to ensure that the extra investment that is required works in a way that enhances people's control over their lives.

We cannot solve the challenges we now face in the old way – seeing the public services of the state in terms of a one-way mechanism of provision. When Labour was last in government, ministers and advisers were very fond of the term 'delivery' – there was even a Prime Minister's Delivery Unit. Without disparaging the good work done in the unit, there was something problematic about 'delivery'. It conjures up an image of someone waiting at home for their Amazon package, in other words, waiting for something to be done for them. When it comes to, say, inoculating people against Covid, or providing treatments in the NHS, we definitely need delivery. We need our bins collected. We need the trains to run on time. But beyond those specific services that do indeed require a standard package to be delivered, it's hard to see any of the really knotty challenges we face being solved without the engagement and involvement of people.

Before the coronavirus pandemic, so-called long-term health conditions – such as diabetes, cancer or mental illness – accounted for 70 per cent of the costs of the NHS.[3] We are an ageing society, which poses massive challenges of loneliness and a constantly increasing need for care. Worklessness in a world of fast-changing demands for skills, part-time work and the gig economy is a completely different challenge to the one that our systems of unemployment insurance were designed to address after the Second World War. Tackling climate change will require us to be part of significant change, including in how we heat our homes and how we get around.[4] What is striking about all of these challenges is that none of the ways in which public services have been thought about since the war can meet them.

First there was the post-war 'professional knows best' thinking, encapsulated in the words of Douglas Jay cited in the introduction to this section but worth quoting again in full: 'In the case of nutrition and health, just as in the case of education, the gentleman in Whitehall really does know better what is good for people than the people know themselves.'[5] This exemplifies the paternalism and hierarchy that lie at the root of the problem we are trying to address. Then there was the drive, particularly in the 1980s and again in the 2010s, to replace publicly owned services with private provision. A primary driver of private companies is profit, and that can cause real problems in our public services. They will 'seek efficiencies' wherever possible, which can lead to cutting corners and concentrating on the easiest tasks. A notorious example is the disastrous privatisation of probation services. Hundreds of millions of pounds were wasted; nine out of thirteen of the companies involved were rated negatively for their work in reducing re-offending; they 'underinvested in probation services' according to the official spending watchdog; and there was a 22 per cent rise in offences per re-offender.[6] The government has now brought these services back into public hands.

Then there was the approach taken under the Labour government of 1997 to 2010, of which I was a part. Substantial increases in public spending, some of which were financed by higher taxes, were accompanied by a drive to provide clear evidence of improved outcomes. This led to a regime of targets and accountability, mandated from the centre of government, beginning with objectives on basic things like waiting times in accident and emergency units and limits on the time between referrals and hospital operations, which proliferated into a plethora of top-down targets, which were then reproduced at local level. The setting of targets did succeed in diverting money into neglected services like A & E and getting waiting times for operations down, and bodies like the Care Quality Commission, which audits hospitals and care providers, have undoubtedly made a positive difference and saved lives. But as the targets multiplied, much of the discretion, the distributed knowledge, that only front-line producers have, was lost.

These three approaches differ in many ways, but they all embody what Sue Goss calls a 'machine mind'. As she puts it: 'Techniques borrowed from industry turn hospitals and schools into factories while in job centres and benefits offices the "computer says no" without human interaction. The search for private-sector style efficiency has down-graded and diminished human contact.... The cost has been the crushing of autonomy and the removal of judgement from front-line teachers, social workers and nurses.'[7] Goss argues that we need to replace the machine mind with a 'garden mind': 'We need politicians and civil servants, and public service managers to become ... caretakers, guardians and facilitators. Instead of struggling to control and "drive" our economy and our society – we ask them to become "gardeners".'[8]

Full disclosure: I am not a gardener. But there are two reasons why I think this is a powerful idea. Gardeners nurture the growth of living beings but recognise that not everything is under their control. They play a major role by structuring and tending – they plant seeds, provide water and remove weeds – but solutions to the countless daily challenges of growing and surviving come as much from within the plants themselves. Second, gardening involves experimentation: 'Gardeners don't make a perfect garden and leave it alone,' says Goss. 'We try things, we fail, we learn, we move things around.'[9] In other words gardeners need to be flexible and humble.

There are lots of examples of local authorities and public services trying new ways of working, but more than anyone else I know in the UK, social entrepreneur and author Hilary Cottam has experimented with the kind of relationship between citizens and the state that I have in mind. She aims to redesign the public sector around a true relationship of equals. Hilary's book *Radical Help* explains her work, and her insights are invaluable.[10]

In it she tells the story of Ella, a single parent with four children who has had a staggering twenty agencies and seventy-three professionals involved with her and her family – police, tutors, social workers, housing officers, health visitors, counselling officers. The estimated cost of all this was £250,000 a year, but after twenty years none of the problems the state had been attempting to fix had been solved. Ella has experienced 'mind-numbing hours spent navigating the welfare system: queuing to sign on at the Jobcentre; enduring the humiliation of visits from social workers, the police and home tutors; time in Court fighting eviction notices'.[11] Those trying to help have been frustrated by the limitations of their roles and consumed by the administration and monitoring of their own actions in order to justify their work and ensure its continued funding. One social worker Hilary shadowed spent the vast majority of his time recording, tracking, monitoring, referring, assessing and meeting other agencies and just 14 per cent of it with families.

Hilary came to the conclusion that the only way to solve the problems in Ella's life was to build her capability to address them herself, and her answer was to turn the relationship between Ella and the state on its head. Instead of the services being in charge of Ella, what if she was put in charge of them? Ella and Hilary interviewed professionals with expertise in a range of services to assemble a team that could help her. Two rules governed the team's work: 80 per cent of its time would be spent on front-line work not administration, reversing the previous experience, and Ella's family would drive and lead the change. Ella 'hired' eight professionals, who worked with her on building a plan for how she wanted to turn her life around: how she saw her future and that of her kids. Hilary doesn't romanticise or idealise the programme, but it seems to have worked and at a fraction of the previous cost. Ella found her first job and her children re-entered mainstream schooling.[12]

Hilary's other experiments have had similar ideas at their heart. In London she tried taking youth services out of youth centres and mobilising the community to provide opportunities for young people. She took work training and support out of jobcentres and got businesses to help. In Nottingham she got older people to help one another through a support circle and did the same for those with chronic health conditions, recognising that pills and prescribing would never on their own address their problems, including physical conditions like diabetes and mental-health issues like anxiety and depression. What they really needed was someone to listen, to support them and so enhance their ability to help themselves.[13]

In case you think this is just one charismatic revolutionary helping a few individuals, it isn't. Experiments like this are going on all over the country, and are mobilising whole communities. Katie Kelly is the deputy chief executive of East Ayrshire Council in Scotland, which has a population of 120,000. In 2013 the council decided that it would change the way its services were run. Now, twenty-one separate neighbourhoods vote on what they want to see happen in their areas and present this to council officials. As Katie puts it, 'community power really comes into play at these launch events where the community are on the stage ... telling us what it is they want to do, and the council officials, elected members, myself and the director of finance and others are in the audience ... quietly listening'.[14]

An inspiring organisation called New Local driving this kind of change provides lots of other examples of it in action.[15] Cambridgeshire County Council's Neighbourhood Cares programme is empowering front-line professionals to tailor social care for older people to their specific needs, in order to reduce the likelihood of them ending up in hospital.[16] Gateshead Council has found a new way of tackling the thorny problem of Council Tax non-payment, which reduces the need for court orders and repossessions, partly by mobilising the community to support those in difficulty.[17] In both cases the old model was not just unsympathetic but also ineffective, leading to spiralling costs. What all these new approaches have in common is a willingness to empower front-line staff, mobilise the community and experiment – to try things out and sometimes fail.

This last point is fundamental. Indeed, it's a key point in a report commissioned by the government of Finland into its approach to policymaking: 'Humble policymaking departs from … an acknowledgement of the government's fallibility … when dealing with complex problems.' It recommends the replacement of 'top down steering' with a 'continuous and repeated' cycle of feedback and amendment.[18] It's hard to imagine a British government adopting this stance. Imagine the opening line of the Queen's Speech: 'My government will be humble in its approach to policymaking, experiment and learn from its mistakes.' Yikes. I don't think so. But the self-evident truth is that it just isn't possible for Whitehall or even the town hall to get everything right first time. If it was, policy wouldn't be endlessly announced, revised, torn up and abandoned.

If you like the sound of all this, you may wonder how we could achieve it. We have seen some of the solutions: devolution to encourage a culture of experimentation, dealing with the problems of outsourcing and the excesses of target and audit. Above all, we need to take seriously the views of public servants and users in the way services are run and decisions are made, and this will produce change. But how can we make this happen? In my experience there is nothing so powerful as the messages the prime minister and cabinet ministers send out. If a government was brave enough to adopt the kind of approach I have outlined, what I know from my time in government is that public servants would be deeply responsive. The vast majority of them work not for money and certainly not for glamour or gratitude but because they care. Many are wearied by the fads and fashions of central government and politicians. Would this be different? Maybe, since it's about using the creativity and ingenuity of public servants themselves.

The same is true in communities. Think back to the appeal of 'Take back control' and how a shift towards flexible and humble government could address the frustrations and anxieties and desires encapsulated in that slogan. By moving decision-making power away from the centre and placing it in the hands of producers and users, by embracing a culture of experimentation, not rule-following, to solve the most difficult problems we face, by having a state that thinks of itself as tending a living garden rather than fixing an inanimate machine, we could address deep-rooted dissatisfactions with a distant and inflexible state while unleashing the creativity, insights and problem-solving abilities of citizens.

This chapter has been about empowering communities and transforming the way the state operates. But no discussion about taking back control would be complete if I missed out where we spend an enormous amount of our lives – the workplace – which is where I now turn.

CHAPTER 15

The Wrong Trousers

I've got a soft spot for Wallace of Wallace and Gromit, prompted, it is true, by people saying I look like him. But the more I find out, the more I like. It turns out he is kind-hearted, friendly, funny – and a lover of cheese. What's not to admire? But what I also like about Wallace is what he – or rather, his creators – have to tell us about democracy and taking back control in the workplace.

Aardman, the Bristol-based production company that has been so phenomenally successful with stop-motion animations like *The Wrong Trousers* (featuring Wallace and Gromit) and *Shaun the Sheep*, is now majority-owned by its employees. That's because the founders Peter Lord and David Sproxton took the decision two years ago that the best way to secure the future of the company was not to flog it off to the highest bidder. As Sproxton puts it, 'If we sold Aardman [to a big studio] it would just become an asset on the balance sheet to be traded.'[1] Instead, the partners chose to establish what is called an employee ownership trust (EOT), essentially handing most of the company over to its workers. Seventy-five per cent of the firm is collectively owned by its employees, all of whom benefit from annual bonus payments, and a workers' council has been established to contribute to top-level decision-making. What's interesting is that Lord and Sproxton made their decision because they believed that an employee ownership trust was not just the best way to protect the company in the future but for it to succeed in the present: 'The statistics show that employee-owned companies are significantly more successful than conventionally owned companies ... [We] can rest easy that those four decades which have slipped by have paved the way for many more years of great creativity.'[2]

Aardman is part of a still small but growing movement towards this way of organising the ownership of businesses. Less than a year after Aardman's move, Julian Richer, founder of the hi-fi retail chain Richer Sounds, walked into a staff meeting and told his 500 employees that he was transferring 60 per cent of shares in the company he had founded into an employee ownership trust. At the same time Richer also established a 'colleague advisory council' which provides staff with a forum to shape the company's future. For Richer, providing his employees with both a financial stake and a meaningful say in the company he set up as a nineteen-year-old in 1978 was the best way to safeguard its long-term success: 'My hard-working colleagues ... know the business, and especially our rather unusual culture, extremely well, and the business is therefore far more likely to flourish under their own steam because of this.'[3]

Then there's Guy Singh-Watson of veg-box deliverer Riverford Organic, who sold his company to its employees for less than a third of the price he could have got on the open market. He explains his decision colourfully: 'Some people want a super yacht. If you want a super yacht you're going to spend the rest of your life taking Prozac. And if you really think that owning one of those will make you happier, you're an idiot and there's nothing much I can do to persuade that person that coming to work and seeing the sense of agency on people's faces is absolutely priceless.'[4] Riverford's EOT has two employees as trustees on the board running the company.

Estimates suggest there are now 370 employee-owned businesses like these across the country, and what's intriguing is that 60 per cent of these businesses have become worker-owned since

2014.[5] That's partly thanks to a change in the law introduced by the Coalition government that year which established the employee ownership trust model. This enabled owners to sell controlling stakes in their companies to their employees free of capital gains tax and to pay bonuses to individual employees (provided all benefited) free of income tax up to £3,600.[6]

It's really important to underline that selling a company to an employee trust is not an act of charity; it's good business. Between 1992 and 2012, an index of companies owned by employees outperformed their publicly listed peers by 10 per cent a year.[7] Wallace and his friends have shown us that workers can be owners, can have a voice in the way their company is run, and it can be more successful.

We might think of democracy and power as political ideas so irrelevant to our job, but what happens at our place of work is defining for so many of us and can make such a difference to our everyday experiences and quality of life. Why should the ability to control our lives stop at the warehouse gates or office door? And think back to Chapter 5 and how we should foster businesses that concern themselves with interests beyond the short-term profit of their shareholders; where power lies in a company – and the role of workers – has a massive effect on its priorities and direction.

Conventional thinking holds that giving power to employees carries huge risks because the relationship between those who run a firm and those who work for it is inherently adversarial – that unless firms are tightly controlled by those at the top, the workers will obtain unrealistically high wages or unreasonable terms and conditions and the firm will fail. The flip side of this view is that the bosses are constantly trying to maximise profits and do down the workers. Yet as we saw in Chapter 5, neither of these pictures accurately describes the motivation of lots of those who run businesses or their workers. While in all companies there are competing interests, and the trade-offs between them involve conflict, characterising bosses and workers as being continuously at daggers drawn doesn't reflect the way most businesses work – and thrive – day to day. What's more, there is reason to believe that involving workers in the way firms are run, including as owners, makes them much more aware of and therefore understanding of the trade-offs involved.

In the UK we were actually pioneers in this way of doing business. Picture the scene in March 1846 when weaver Eliza Brierley lined up in a queue of male mill workers to pay one pound to join the Rochdale Equitable Pioneers Society. It was a revolutionary act. The twenty-eight Rochdale Pioneers were a group of textile workers responding to desperate times. The transition from hand to powered looms had slashed wages in half and caused widespread hunger, leading to the decade becoming known as the Hungry Forties. The Pioneers set up a shop at 31 Toad Lane in Rochdale where members of the society could buy food and other goods at affordable prices. The shop was owned and run on the principle of one person one vote and an equitable sharing of the profits. Eliza became a member of the cooperative, a full participant in its affairs, more than seventy years before women got the vote.

The Pioneers have an extraordinary legacy. Their principles – of being open to all, treating all members equally, and of members controlling the organisation's capital – still survive as the cornerstone of the cooperative movement across the world today.[8] While the original shop in Toad Lane was a *consumer* cooperative (owned by the customers who used it), it provided the inspiration for *worker* co-operatives all round the world. Worker co-ops are different from employee ownership trusts in that each individual worker owns shares in the company, rather than the shares being collectively owned by the group as a whole.

But while we may pride ourselves on being the original home of the cooperative movement, we now lag behind many other countries. The whole UK cooperative sector – both worker and consumer types – currently accounts for roughly 1 per cent of business turnover, with 7,000 businesses and 241,000 employees, but that includes two businesses accounting for half the turnover: the Co-operative Group and the John Lewis Partnership.[9] On latest estimates, only 500–600 businesses in the UK are worker co-ops.[10] Germany has a cooperative sector four times the size of the UK's as a proportion of GDP, while in France it is six times larger.[11] Spain is home to probably the most famous cooperative. Located in the Basque country, the worker co-op Mondragon has become the fourth-largest employer in Spain, with more than 260 different companies and subsidiaries and over 75,000 workers in 35 countries. In Italy, the 8,000 co-ops of the Emilia-Romagna region produce 40 per cent of the region's GDP.[12]

Global evidence suggests the model creates successful and durable businesses. More than 90 per cent of cooperatives survive their first three years of operation compared with 65 per cent of conventional businesses, and cooperatives, mutuals and employee-owned enterprises with seventy-five employees or fewer outperform conventional businesses of equivalent size, creating higher profits.[13] So why are there so many fewer co-ops in the UK than elsewhere?

The Achilles heel of the cooperative movement, going right back to Rochdale, is the difficulty that co-ops and employee-owned firms face when attempting to raise the capital needed to establish or expand a business. They can't issue new shares to raise money or sell a portion of the company to a big investor because that would dilute each member's stake. The banks, meanwhile, may well be wary of lending to cooperatives because, for example, many members of a new co-op are often unable to provide personal financial guarantees.[14] In Italy they addressed this in 1985 with the introduction of the so-called Marcora Law, named after the finance minister who sponsored it. This gives workers the right to organise a cooperative buyout of a firm if it is under threat and, crucially, makes funds available to provide the capital necessary for the buyout up to the level of that provided by the workers. Since it was introduced, it has enabled over 250 worker buyouts.[15] If we really wanted to supercharge co-ops in the UK we could emulate the Marcora

Law and also do more to incentivise EOTs. By some accounts, if we really put our minds to it, 10 per cent of the economy could be employee-owned within a decade.[16]

Yet even if we achieved this, that still leaves the other 90 per cent of our economy. The low levels of worker ownership are symptomatic of a much wider problem with the way our economy is run and the role of workers in decision-making. Fifty-eight per cent of employees believe they have no influence on workplace decision-making, rising to 70 per cent of part-timers.[17] It's no wonder they feel that way. According to the Taylor review commissioned by the government, which reported in 2017, among companies with fifty employees or more, just one in seven had the most basic form of worker consultation in place – a works council or, as they are also known, a joint consultative committee.[18] This is a mechanism to give employees information on a range of issues, including decisions likely to lead to changes in the way work is organised, and to enable consultation on key issues about the business, from health and safety to the organisation of the working week. Representatives are elected by the workforce. To give a sense of how far behind we are in the UK, out of twenty-eight European countries, we are third from last in the worker participation index, ahead of only Estonia and Latvia.[19]

The coronavirus pandemic brought this home. The evidence is that most businesses did act well, but two in five workers say they had concerns about their safety but did not feel able to raise them, and of those who did bring them up, only one in five said they were fully resolved.[20] As an MP, I had workers appeal to me to get government to make their firms follow the rules. This is exactly the kind of function works councils fulfil, and indeed do in companies that have them. Of course the pandemic was an unprecedented event, but it has brought the problems of today's workplace into sharper focus, as we saw in Chapter 8. How many hours people work, their ability to get time off, the nature of their work, their working environment – so much is out of their hands. If we are concerned about taking back control, this is one of the most meaningful contexts in which we can set about it.

So how do other countries do it? We are in a minority in not requiring a works council for firms beyond a certain size.[21] And in the majority of European countries it is also usual to include workers on company boards at least in state-owned or former state-owned companies. Half, including France, Germany, the Netherlands, the Scandinavian countries, Austria, Croatia, Slovakia, Slovenia and Luxembourg, have laws that require workers to be represented on the boards of *all* larger companies.[22] The system of works councils and board representation is called codetermination and has been a feature of many European economies for most of the last century. In case you're wondering whether the election of employees to boards is taken seriously, in Germany they get turnouts of as much as 77 per cent.[23]

Do the countries that embrace codetermination do better or worse economically than those who don't? On key economic and social measures such as employment, poverty, education and spending on research and development, the answer is simple: they do better.[24] Correlation does not equal causation, but at the very least we can say there is no evidence that worker participation hampers economic performance. In addition, the Covid crisis has shown how companies can benefit from codetermination. There is evidence from Germany, for example, that works councils have played an important role in managing the economic and public heath response to the crisis within firms, on everything from distributing masks to safe shift patterns.[25] A study from the 2008 financial crisis, meanwhile, revealed that many German businesses achieved agreements between bosses and workers on reducing working time to avoid redundancies.[26] The same was true in Scandinavia. Indeed, a recent study of firms in Sweden, Denmark and Norway with workers on their boards showed that these companies were more likely to save jobs by concluding agreements on flexible working, bonuses and work sharing.[27]

Employee representation could also counter the culture of short-termism that scars Britain's economy with its narrow focus on shareholder value, quarterly results and companies' stock market positions. Workers have an interest in their employers' long-term success because their jobs depend on it. And as we saw in Chapter 5, a longer-term view leads to the business investment that is needed for greater productivity. There is also evidence from the UK that where worker consultation does exist, it is associated with higher levels of employee satisfaction and well-being, and we know from numerous studies that greater employee wellbeing is associated with higher productivity, better company profitability and reduced staff turnover.[28]

We have seen how policy – or rather its absence – has hindered the establishment of cooperatives in the UK, while the lack of legal requirements for works councils explains their rarity. So what explains the Curious Case of the Missing Workers from Boards: a British mystery?

Unlike most other countries, we haven't seen much social and political pressure for codetermination. In particular, while in other European countries there was a strong movement on the Left for codetermination after each of the World Wars, trade unions in the UK were more focused on strengthening collective bargaining at work and the Labour Party was focused on nationalising key industries.[29] The thinking of those in charge of the nationalisation programme in the 1945 Labour government was based on the assumption that the relationship between bosses and employees is bound to be adversarial. The nationalised industries needed to be run commercially, and worker representation would therefore be at odds with that. In the gas industry the post-1945 restructuring actually abolished the limited worker representation that had existed.[30] The Conservatives, meanwhile, sometimes talked favourably about treating workers as partners in managing the economy but were lukewarm at best.

Worker participation isn't totally alien to Britain, however. Parts of both the public and private sectors flirted with it throughout the twentieth century, including the steel industry, ports, buses and Royal Mail – even if only briefly.[31] Towards the end of the 1970s, the trade unions were advocating it, and in 1975 Prime Minister Harold Wilson commissioned an inquiry, which ended up proposing that workers at firms with more than 2,000 employees should have the right to equal representation with shareholders on company boards.[32] But the proposals got bogged down in a debate on details and were never going to be implemented once Margaret Thatcher took power. Britain's reluctance to embrace worker representation continued. Even the Labour government of 1997–2010 was timid on this question.

At which point, plot twist. Enter Theresa May during her leadership campaign: 'If I'm prime minister … we're going to have not just consumers represented on company boards, but employees as well.' The problem, as she saw it, was, 'The people who run big businesses are supposed to be accountable to outsiders, to non-executive directors, who are supposed to ask the difficult questions, think about the long term … In practice they are drawn from the same narrow, social and professional circles as the executive team.'[33] In the event, May backed down. The legislation that was passed specified that companies appoint one non-executive director to represent workers' interests, but this doesn't actually need to be a worker, and if they don't want to do this, they can have a panel of workers to provide non-binding advice instead.[34] And if they don't want to do any of that, companies can just explain why they don't intend to do anything at all. Two years after it took effect, indications are that the impact of the act has been extremely limited. Over 30 per cent of relevant firms have done nothing. Of the 70 per cent that have taken action, by far and away the most popular option has been to appoint a non-executive director rather than a worker representative.[35]

So the answer to the mystery is that while all political parties in the UK have at some point advocated workers on boards, none has done so consistently, and it has never been a high-enough priority at the right moment to become a reality. And yet, while there are different ways of giving workers a voice, what seems indisputable is that the status quo isn't working and doing things differently could have a real impact in tackling the challenges that lie ahead for business and our economy – not to mention rebuilding our social contract.

So, what would a meaningful workplace voice in the UK look like? As a first step, we should expand the use of works councils. After recommendations from the Taylor review, the number of employees required to secure a works council has been lowered from 10 to 2 per cent (subject to a minimum of 15 employees).[36] Ultimately, we could consider mandating a works council in firms above a certain size, but in the meantime this represents a real opportunity for unions and others to push for a stronger workers' voice. The second route for employee voice is through workers on boards, as Theresa May originally proposed.

Some people wonder how much difference works councils or workers on boards would make, and they would certainly not remedy all the problems in our workplaces. But they would represent an important change in our culture and point the way to a different way of thinking about the relationship between management and workers. With the shift from mass manufacturing to the service sector, many firms have come to recognise that the model of bosses on one side and workers on the other is outdated. In many sectors, value is produced not by speeding up production lines but by workers using their skills and knowledge to innovate. This is why management is trending towards flat hierarchies and employee engagement, worker autonomy and distributed knowledge.

So the tide is already heading in the right direction. The real question is how to ensure that empowering workers is not a business fad or marketing slogan, but a genuinely different way of running our economy. Ultimately, the argument that could unite workers and business in favour of better worker representation is that our economic model is not the success that we have sometimes pretended. Compared to other countries we are less productive, have more low-wage jobs, and as the Covid crisis has shown, are less resilient in many ways. The case for workers having a stake and a voice, playing a bigger role in companies, is not just a democratic or social one, but an economic one. Us and them is the old model. In this together is the way to go. Now, as we seek to rebuild after Covid, is the time to take this seriously.

Taking back control is about people's right to have a say in the decisions that affect their lives, but it is also the right way for us to set about a project of national renewal. The lesson of history, and the foundation of the final part of this book, is that it is movements of people not individual politicians that create the conditions for the profound changes we need in our society.

PART IV

Changemakers

Over the course of the book I have discussed a range of ideas to rebuild and renew the social contract, protect society from out-of-control markets and give people real power over their lives: the Green New Deal, which tackles inequality, the building of millions of social homes, putting gender equality at the heart of the way we do things, reforming how our companies operate, prioritising care work, taking on the domination of Big Tech, enhancing democratic participation for young people, devolving power and giving a greater voice to working people. Hopefully, you will have been inspired by the notion that a whole raft of better alternatives are available to us, but if everything can be so great, why isn't it that way already? We don't just need a vision of a better society but a strategy to put it into action. Part IV is about how we can all play a part in turning these ideas into reality.

If we're interested in change, then we need to care about how we get the power to make it happen. One answer is to elect the right government to pass the necessary laws. And of course electing a government open to new ideas is absolutely vital. But is that the end of the story? No. Power does not rest with governments alone. Governments are both led and constrained by the wider dynamics of power in society – these shape who gets elected, what they seek to do in office, and whether or not they are ultimately successful. As I noted at the very start of the book, history shows us that changes which at first seem impossible don't occur simply because good politicians come along and decide to make them happen; they begin with groups of people, often at the margins, demanding change, who crucially set out to build the power to force governments to adopt a different course. Such groups may start small but persuade increasing numbers of people of the justness of their cause, building pressure on political parties and governments through their persistence and growing influence.

Even if politicians are open to change, there are always a thousand good reasons to leave things as they are. Change does not come without struggle. One of the biggest barriers to making big ideas a reality is that there are always groups with an interest in the status quo which will put pressure on politicians to maintain it. Unless there is a counterweight to that pressure, change is unlikely. Those who want to see it happen need to work out how to advance their ideas in the face of opposition and be that counterweight.

The other reason electing the right government isn't enough is that our world isn't shaped by the policies and practices of states alone. As we've seen throughout the book, the decisions of businesses, for example, affect their workers, customers and society as a whole. More broadly, the norms and culture of our society have a fundamental impact on the way we all live our lives. So if change is to happen – and I believe it *must* happen – it must take place in all these arenas.

There are three different levels on which people can build and exercise power in order to bring about change.[1] First, groups can try to change individual laws or policies – for example campaigning for a new minimum wage or an environmental regulation, or seeking to persuade a business to pay the living wage or change its practices. Second, groups can try to change where power lies. This might also involve campaigning for a change in the law – for example to make it easier for trade unions to organise or harder for wealthy individuals to fund political campaigns – but by shifting the structure of power, such changes can make it easier to bring about other changes further down the line. Third, groups can focus on changing the national conversation – in other words, on moving the Overton window that I mentioned at the outset of the book. Clearly, laws and policies are shaped by public opinion, so altering the terms of debate can be a route to transformative change.

The first level might produce the most immediately obvious results, and be the most common place for changemakers to focus their efforts, but the other two are also vital and can be underestimated. I started this book by asking how the impossible becomes possible. In the long run, the answer is often that change on these second and third levels is what opens up the space for laws or policies that were once out of the question. Many of the changemakers I will look at in this section try to accomplish change on more than one level.

Those calling for change are often ignored, derided and dismissed. If a change is worth making, it requires effort and struggle to even get it on the agenda, often over years and years. This section of the book addresses the 'how' of social change. How does it come about? Which strategies and methods actually work? I will examine what we can learn from history and from current events, and if there is only one thing you take from this final part of the book, let it be this: we can all be part of making change happen.

CHAPTER 16

You Only Get the Justice You Have the Power to Compel

It's October 2015 and I'm in the William Booth Salvation Army training centre in Denmark Hill in south London. I'm sitting in a circle of about fifty people and a man has just asked us all to say our names and the biggest influence on our lives.

What the hell am I doing here? I ask myself. It's not group therapy, at least it's not intended to be, but a course in what is known as community organising – mobilising for change at the grass roots. I stick out like a sore thumb. The people here are activists of different kinds, many from faith groups, all seeking to learn how community organising can help them with their work in their localities. I'm the recently resigned leader of the Labour Party, with a beard that I trialled on a summer escape to Australia with my family. Somewhat irrationally, I'm hoping the beard might disguise who I am, although the business of saying my name and the major influence on my life is going to give me away. (Resignedly, I shave off the beard that evening.)

Quite why I decided to go on this course eludes me this Monday morning. It was suggested by a friend on the board of Citizens UK, the amazing organisation running the course, which has led campaigns for a living wage, affordable housing, rights for refugees and much else besides.[1] I was reluctant to join, and in the end she shamed me into it by offering to pay the course fee. I declined her kind offer but decided to do it. What did I have to lose?

The truth was also that I was very interested in the idea of community organising. In 2011, shortly after becoming leader of the Labour Party, I had been introduced to an inspirational man called Arnie Graf[2] who had spent fifty years or so in an organisation called the Industrial Areas Foundation, founded by the father of community organising, Saul Alinsky, author of a seminal book called *Rules for Radicals*.[3] The methods outlined in this book were the same ones that trained Barack Obama in his work as a community organiser.

My feelings on meeting Arnie were not so different from the ones I experienced on that day in south London. Arnie was shown into my office; he looked like a kind elderly uncle and had a thick American accent. The person who introduced us promptly disappeared at Arnie's request and left us together. I was in the midst of a sixteen-hour day (like all of them) and had thought to spend twenty minutes with this guy. He asked me all kinds of questions, like how I felt about my job, what motivated me and similar stuff. The answer to the job question was 'Not that good' that day. *What the hell did I agree to meet this guy for?* I wondered for most of the meeting, but by the end a light had come on. Arnie was charming, but that wasn't the thing. His questions to me were not politeness but followed his method. The basis of community organising is to build power not from the top down but through relationships that enable people to act together – by understanding the self-interest of others and thereby forging common interests.[4]

There is something profound about the simple act of talking to someone not in a transactional way but probing deeply into who they are, getting them to reveal their motivations by revealing something about oneself. It sounds so simple, but think for a moment about your meetings with colleagues or co-workers and you will soon realise it's not the way we conduct most of our lives. The act of revelation on both sides gives one insights and a bond that the superficiality of most conversations, even with friends, often don't reveal. Although I didn't know it, Arnie was having what is known as a 'one-to-one' with me.

After that meeting I recruited Arnie to work with the Labour Party. For the young paid organisers working in the constituencies we were trying to win, Arnie became a talisman. He would talk to them, and the light would come on for them too. Too often organising for the Labour Party was about persuading five or ten hardy souls, mainly older, who had worked their hind legs off for decades, to go out and knock on more doors. Arnie taught us a very different method. Make the Labour Party about much more than just knocking on doors for votes. Map where power lies at the grass roots, organise one-to-ones with people there, look for community champions, find out what motivates them, how they want to change their areas. Build local campaigns around these issues with local people, show that a political party is about more than just winning votes, and then maybe come election time it won't be five or ten people knocking on doors, but fifty, a hundred or more. It sounds pretty basic, but believe me it isn't how most political parties work.

In the end Arnie's methods came up against the traditional ways of the Labour Party, and it's fair to say there was a clash of cultures with his ideas squeezed out by the demands of knocking on as many doors as possible.[5] I could see both sides of the argument – the urgent imperative to fight the election but also the longer-term potential of what Arnie offered. One reason I was attending the course was that I hoped by doing the training I would learn why our experiment with Arnie's methods hadn't worked. I could then maybe apply the methods properly to my work with my local Labour Party.

Back at the Salvation Army centre on that Monday morning, I stood up and said who I was and talked about the influence of my father on my life and work. I felt oddly nervous, and the truth was that the first couple of days of the course did not rid me of my 'What am I doing here?' feelings. People were very nice to me, but I wondered if I was going to learn very much. Yet something shifted on day three. Believe it or not, it was a story about Nando's that did it.

One of the organisers of the course, Jonathan Cox, the director of Citizens Cymru Wales, talked about some work he had done with young members of the British-Somali community in Cardiff. Young people in this community had felt stigmatised and alienated for many years. Citizens Cymru had begun by asking them what they wanted to change. It turned out that one of the things that really animated them was that there were three Nando's in Cardiff but none was halal so they couldn't eat there. Nando's had many halal restaurants in the rest of the UK, and even one ten miles away in a part of Wales with few Muslims, but not in Cardiff. In fact, though it has the largest Muslim population in Wales, not a single chain restaurant in the city centre or fashionable Cardiff Bay made any kind of halal provision.

Ali Abdi, a local youth worker, built a team of young people which set about campaigning for a halal Nando's in Cardiff with the support of Citizens Cymru. They wrote letters to the company, which led nowhere, but eventually got them to agree to a meeting after eighty young people – including four who ran, walked, cycled and took the train dressed as chickens – marched to the nearest branch. The Nando's bigwigs came to Cardiff armed with a PowerPoint presentation explaining why it wasn't practical to have a halal restaurant there, but in the event they never got to deliver it.

The locals asked if they could start the meeting by sharing why they loved Nando's so much, gave the visitors Welsh cakes they had baked (which they explained they couldn't themselves eat because they were fasting for Ramadan) and made their case for a halal branch. In response the bigwigs committed Nando's to working with the young people and promised to think about their proposal and come back to them – the kind of thing people in positions of authority say to avoid confrontation. The locals said how pleased they were at this response and that they hoped to celebrate Eid al-Adha (the second festival of Eid, around two months after Eid al-Fitr, which marks the end of Ramadan) at a halal Nando's in Cardiff. But, they said, if that wasn't possible they would recruit the Bishop of Llandaff, the Archbishop of Cardiff and the general secretary of the Muslim Council of Wales to dress up as chickens and do their own 'chicken run' to Nando's on Eid.

The execs went pale. Unbeknown to them, the young people were employing Saul Alinsky's ninth rule of organising: 'The threat is usually more terrifying than the thing itself.' It works. The bigwigs didn't fancy hosting a bishop in a chicken suit; the young people won their campaign, and Nando's now boasts on its website about its halal branch in the Cardiff Old Brewery Quarter.[6]

From this example, we can begin to see why community organising is so powerful. The young people seemed powerless, but it turned out they weren't. Nando's seemed like a powerful organisation a world away from them, but it bent to their demands because of the resources they mobilised, including a coalition spanning churches, local schools and the university. And their success showed them they could get recognition and respect and make change happen. Until they met Citizens Cymru they had felt powerless, but not any more. As the community organising movement would say, 'They took action and got a reaction.' And these young people were empowered by their victory. They got a taste for social change. One is now a professional community organiser, and others have been at the forefront of campaigns for the living wage and to welcome refugees. After completing training with Citizens Cymru, a team pioneered the Community Jobs Compact, which binds major employers into paying the living wage and changing their hiring practices in order to recruit more people from under-represented groups – a campaign which recently won a prestigious award.[7]

I just love this story. For me, the light that came on during that third morning was that this was a different model of leadership from the one in which I had been schooled. While the standard model of political leadership revolves around the charismatic individual, community organising leadership is much more collective and empowering. Train people in methods for making change happen, and anyone, whatever their self-image, can become a leader. That day I wished I had come on the course before meeting Arnie – and indeed before becoming Labour leader. I would have done a better job. I would have understood more about how good leadership can empower others and been a more effective champion of Arnie's methods within the party.

The course also gave me another insight – into why so many progressive campaigns never work out how to achieve their aims. This became apparent during another highlight of proceedings, when we role-played the Melian Dialogue. Described by the ancient Athenian historian Thucydides, these negotiations took place between the citizens of Athens and Melos in 416 BC. During them, the Athenians tell the Melians they intend to conquer their city, so they might as well surrender and spare everyone the trouble of a battle. The Melians are peace-loving people who try to dissuade the Athenians with talk of justice, fairness and high-minded values. The Athenians are ruthless, calculating and strategic, and clear from the very start about what they intend to do and why. Ultimately, as Thucydides' readers would have known, Melos refused, Athens laid siege, and the Melians were enslaved.

No doubt as you read this, unless you have a penchant for invading other countries, you will be feeling sympathetic and warm towards the Melians and pretty hostile to the Athenians, but there is a twist. As the instructors told us part way through the role play, the task of a community organiser is to be an Athenian not a Melian. Not as in laying waste to other countries, but in understanding that nice-sounding values only get you so far. The Melians were undone because they were not clear about their aims or how they would achieve them. As the Athenians say in the Dialogue, 'The standard of justice depends on the equality of power to compel ... the strong do what they have the power to do and the weak accept what they have to accept.'[8] For the community organising movement this is boiled down to an aphorism which has stayed with me more than anything else from the course: 'You only get the justice you have the power to compel.'

To illustrate what this means, let's consider the most famous Citizens UK campaign, its campaign for the living wage. This began in 2003 when Abdul Durrant, a cleaner at HSBC's London offices, confronted the bank's chairman, Sir John Bond, at an AGM to ask why he was being paid £4.50 an hour (then the minimum wage) and Bond earned £2 million per year. Abdul had been trained by Citizens UK, and his question was carefully planned in order to draw attention to the cause of poverty pay – and to shame a powerful person into change.

I can talk about this campaign from personal experience. In 2010 I was drafting the Labour manifesto for Gordon Brown. Matthew Bolton, now director of Citizens UK, asked for a meeting with me to talk about the living wage. The meeting didn't go as I expected. He brought two cleaners with him, one of whom was responsible for the office of Alistair Darling, the chancellor. She explained how hard it was to live on the minimum wage and raise her children. I asked about the tax credit system introduced by Gordon Brown designed to boost the incomes of low-paid workers, which she didn't appear to be receiving. I can't remember her answer, but what I do remember is the realisation that she was talking about something deeper than the money in her purse. As with Abdul and Sir John Bond, she was posing a moral question. Was it right that someone, cleaning the office of a Labour chancellor, was not earning enough to feed her family? There was only one answer. The Labour manifesto I wrote contained the commitment that every government department would pay the living wage.

The living wage campaign has been Athenian in its approach – minus the invasion. It set about gathering power by uniting diverse people and organisations in a common cause, and by building relationships with those who had power. But it found another source of power in shame. It has shamed many corporations, public sector bodies and universities into action, and it has harnessed the power of praise for those who came on board to encourage others to do the same. The result has been that since 2003 the living wage campaign has signed up nearly 7,000 employers, 40 per cent of the FTSE 100 (the largest publicly traded firms in the UK) and won higher wages for more than 250,000 workers.[9] This is an example of the first level of change I talked about in the introduction to this part of the book – changing the policies of businesses – but the living wage movement has also operated at the third level too, by putting the idea of the living wage on the map. This even led a Conservative government to legislate for what it called a national living wage, above the minimum wage, although still below the real living wage.

By the end of the five days' training in 2015, the light that had flashed on when I met Arnie Graf had been illuminated again, and I took away from the course a commitment to campaign with my local Labour Party in Doncaster using community organising methods. I invited those who had recently joined the party as part of the surge in membership under Jeremy Corbyn to come to a meeting. Normally at these meetings I sit at the front and answer questions; this time we all sat in a circle and discussed why we had joined the Labour Party and what we wanted to change locally, facilitated by two Citizens UK staff members, Dan Firth and Sotez Chowdhury, who had given up their spare time to be with us. This was not the way the Labour Party tended to work; it was an exercise in understanding one another's self-interest and building relational power.

After training in methods of community organising, we went out and listened to the community and then came back together and reflected on our priorities. The problem we chose to address was BrightHouse, a company that exploited the poor by selling goods like sofas, cookers, TVs and computers via weekly payments over two or three years, but at interest rates of anywhere up to 99 per cent a year, meaning that their prices were ultimately as much as three times higher than those at a normal high street shop.[10] The principle of thinking like an Athenian kicked in. That meant setting realistic goals that could be achieved and then built on, rather than goals that might be morally right but which couldn't actually be met.

Since BrightHouse was at that point a chain with over 200 stores across the UK, a local campaign in Doncaster was unlikely to shut it down. Parading with placards saying CLOSE DOWN BRIGHTHOUSE would have made us feel good and drawn attention to the issue, but in the community organising view, failing to achieve our aim would only have demonstrated our powerlessness and sapped the energy of campaigners as they questioned what difference we had really made. So instead we set what we saw as a realistic goal: working with a local credit union to sign up 150 members and move them away from BrightHouse.

One Saturday morning we gathered in Mexborough, a town near Doncaster that I represent where the local BrightHouse was located, and handed out leaflets comparing the cost of using BrightHouse finance with buying through the local credit union. It wasn't the kind of thing my local Labour Party normally did – we weren't actually asking anyone to vote for us. What was striking was the trepidation of many members beforehand but also the buzz they felt afterwards. As always after a community organising action, the group reassembled, and the words members used to describe how they felt included 'worthwhile', 'powerful' and 'inspired'. Unlike some political protests, it clearly met Alinsky's sixth rule: 'A good tactic is one that your people enjoy.'

The story does not end here. The campaign succeeded locally in its modest aims but turned out to be one of a chain of events that eventually hastened BrightHouse's demise. It inspired me to make a film for the BBC's *Victoria Derbyshire* programme about BrightHouse. Making that film, I interviewed a local resident, Angela, who had been a BrightHouse customer. Eventually I would bring Andrew Bailey – now the governor of the Bank of

England, but then the head of the Financial Conduct Authority (FCA) – to my constituency to meet Angela to hear her story.

In a meeting room in Mexborough, two worlds – Bailey's and Angela's – came together. She did the talking, not me. She explained the rip-offs, the pressures, the exploitation of BrightHouse. He listened and seemed pretty taken aback. Some months later, and against original indications, the FCA imposed a cap on lending in the sector as had been implemented for payday loans. I received an email from Andrew Bailey at the time of their announcement which mentioned what an impact the conversation with Angela had had on him. Maybe the FCA would have acted without Andrew Bailey's visit to Mexborough, but I know that the meeting with Angela only happened because of the action we took. Once the FCA stopped BrightHouse ripping people off, their business model collapsed. The culmination of this was the company going into receivership, meaning it can't prey on any new customers.

The lessons I draw from that experience are that people have more power collectively than they realise; that rather than waiting for someone else to act – central government, the mayor of Doncaster – it is also possible to make change happen bottom-up; that out of the small, possible actions, the seemingly impossible – in this case the end of BrightHouse – can sometimes be achieved. I also learned about some of the limitations of community organising: it is painstaking; it takes time to build relational power; it hits bumps in the road; campaigns may be slow to produce results. The living wage campaign has been very effective, but it has taken the best part of twenty years to produce the change that it has.

But even though community organising might take time, and even though it would be much easier to have a government do the job for us – pull the levers of powers and introduce a real living wage, deal with the scourge of BrightHouse and all the other injustices – we still need to hold that government to account. We still need ways for people to make their voices heard. As Matthew Bolton puts it, 'the fundamental aim of community organising [is] for people to build and use power, to have control over decision-making and to hold the state and market to account'.[11] Whoever has control of the state, whether they have progressive values or not, needs to be held accountable, and that accountability cannot just come from elections once every few years, as we saw in Part III. Community organising is a vital tool to make change happen and a way to force the powerful to listen.

In his book Matthew Bolton refers to a famous saying of a nineteenth-century politician and thinker: 'Lord Acton is right that absolute and unaccountable power is corrupting, but so is powerlessness. It breeds fear, anger, ill health and apathy.'[12] A major theme of this book has been that fixing our world requires the redistribution not just of income, wealth and opportunity but power as well. The reason for this is practical – it is one of the means to greater fairness and equality. But it is also psychological. Feeling that we have the power to make change happen affects our sense of self-worth. Citizens Cymru saw the effect it had on the young people who got their halal Nando's; Citizens UK have seen it in the countless people who have fought and won a living wage, and I saw it in my party members who acted against BrightHouse and were inspired to do more.

In the Introduction to this book I argued that if we focus on taking small, incremental steps towards the possible, there is a danger that we lose sight of the grander vision, objectives which are not immediately achievable but which we must strive for if we're ever to change things fundamentally. And yet in this chapter it might seem I have argued for a different view: to focus exclusively on what is achievable. So which is it? Without question there are tensions – incremental versus transformational change, arguing for the possible versus the seemingly impossible – but Citizens UK exemplify the possible as the gateway to the seemingly impossible. They are rooted in the principles of community organising, practical, realisable goals, and yet look how they've shifted the terms of debate: twenty years ago, the vision of a living wage certainly looked like the impossible; today it's much more of a reality.

No matter the issue we face, however small or large, community organising means that nobody is completely powerless. That's because there is nothing more powerful than people joining together through their common interests. It's the way political change has always happened – and is happening all around the world today.

CHAPTER 17

Twenty-First-Century Trade Unions

Membership is not our foremost question. Our first concern is winning fifteen dollars and a union.
  Mary Kay Henry, Service Employees International Union[1]

In November 2012, two hundred fast food workers went on strike in New York to demand an increase in their wages from the federal minimum of $7.25 an hour to $15. Pamela Waldron, who had been working for eight years at KFC, explained why: 'I have two kids under six, and I don't earn enough to buy food for them.'[2] Outside branches of McDonald's, Burger King, KFC and Domino's across the city, workers chanted, 'How can we survive on $7.25?'[3]

In a city of eight million workers, their protest was a tiny pebble in a very large pond. It got some media coverage but looked like an attempt to achieve if not the impossible then the highly improbable. Doubling the minimum wage was nowhere near the mainstream political agenda. Trade union membership in the United States, meanwhile, had been in steep decline for decades. Laws protecting workers' rights were weak, and changes to the economy over generations had made union organising far harder.

Yet those 200 workers in New York have spawned a movement that has since won 22 million employees across the United

States more than $68 billion in wage increases.[4] California, Massachusetts, Maryland, New Jersey, Illinois, Connecticut and many other states and cities in the United States have passed laws to raise their minimum wage to $15 an hour, affecting not just fast food workers but employees across the whole economy.[5] The overall boost to workers' income so far is fourteen times larger than that achieved when the federal minimum wage was last increased in 2007.[6] Within five years, 42 per cent of the United States will be covered by $15 an hour wage laws.[7] And President Biden has pledged to seek to raise the federal minimum wage to $15 an hour, which could help over 30 million more workers.[8] The Fight for $15 movement has not only changed the law, it has also profoundly changed the political conversation. Originating in a protest by the marginalised, it is now a mainstream demand involving a union campaign and a movement which has involved people well beyond the workers affected.

This section of the book is about how to make change happen, and that discussion cannot ignore the role of trade unions, which have for two centuries been at the vanguard of winning change for workers. Yet for reasons we will see, the climate for trade unions is now a difficult one, and the Fight for $15 stands out as a success – an example of a new kind of trade unionism.

The New York protest may have begun small but it was not a freelance, spontaneous action; it was mounted by the Service Employees International Union (SEIU) working with community, civil rights and religious organisations and trained union and community organisers. It was followed in 2013 by actions across 100 cities in the United States, doubling in 2015 to 200 cities, when 60,000 childcare workers, supermarket assistants and airport staff joined fast food workers in marches calling for a $15 minimum wage in what became the largest protest of low-paid workers in American history.[9]

The traditional model of trade unionism in the US was to recruit workers into the union, seek recognition for the union from the employer at the level of the firm and then bargain for higher wages and better conditions. Mary Kay Henry, president of SEIU turned this approach on its head.[10] Make the demands first and worry about union membership later. As one organiser put it, 'What Mary Kay Henry was asking the union to do was to make a leap of faith: let's start building a movement of low-wage workers ... around a clear and moral set of demands, and worry about the end game later. Maybe the workers would end up having something like traditional union representation, or maybe a not-so-traditional organization.'[11]

Mary Kay Henry was facing up to the fact that in the US trade union membership in the private sector stood at just 7 per cent. (In the UK it's better, but only 13 per cent.)[12] Fast food workers in particular were almost completely non-unionised. She recognised that if a union waited until it had recruited a significant number of workers in an enterprise before it took action, it would be waiting a long time. She was also responding to the 'fissured' workplace, now common in both the UK and the US and exemplified by McDonald's.[13] The golden arches actually mark the location of franchises: individual business owners rent the brand and the equipment from McDonald's but run their own restaurants, so there is no one central employer. That means the traditional approach of getting a union formally recognised by the business so that it can bargain on its workers' behalf about wages and conditions has become much more complicated.

Fast food outlets are not alone in this. Across the economy, people *working* for a particular organisation are now often not actually *employed* by them; work is increasingly subcontracted or outsourced to other businesses. Apple, for example, employs some 63,000 workers directly, but relies on a global subcontracted workforce of more than 750,000 employed under a variety of relationships to design, manufacture, assemble and sell its products.[14] Companies like Uber and many others in the tech economy go further, not simply outsourcing their employees to others but regarding them as self-employed. This poses a massive challenge to traditional company-level union organising. Bargains struck with the parent company have no effect whatsoever on many of the workers who provide services to it. The old model still works effectively in certain parts of our economy like manufacturing – although here too there is a lot of subcontracted work – but it is much more challenging than it once was.

By targeting the sector not the firm, SEIU was seeking to adapt to this reality and short-circuit the challenges of organising at so many workplaces. And the campaign has mobilised not just workers but in many places the wider population – and electorate. In state after state over the past few years, proposals to legislate for a $15 minimum wage have either been a key promise of candidates for elected office or the subject of a referendum. The Fight for $15 has thus forced its way onto the political agenda and dragged government directly into the fight, challenging the notion that the role of a union is to lobby the employer, with the state acting simply as a mediator, setting the rules of engagement.

The reason for telling the story of the Fight for $15 movement is to show that even the most vulnerable and apparently powerless workers can win. Yet it is not a perfect model, as even its advocates would acknowledge. Its short-cut route to success means that most fast food workers in the US now covered by the $15 minimum wage have remained outside the union, which raises the question of how all the other problems they face, such as disputes over working hours, sick pay and conditions, will be addressed. Mary-Kay Henry's demand was for '$15 *and* a union'. That first need may have been met for millions of workers, but the second hasn't gone away and continues to be at best a work in progress.

Before working out how the lessons of the Fight for $15 might apply here in the UK, it is worth taking a step back to understand why, even today when most of the mass workplace factories have gone, unionisation still really matters. As we have seen so clearly during the pandemic, many workers

– from warehouse staff to carers, delivery drivers to contract cleaners – find themselves in deeply insecure, vulnerable jobs. It is a very basic point but it cannot be taken for granted: a union means that individuals, often with little power, do not have to face their employer alone, but have strength in numbers, organisation and representation. Think back to Chika Reuben from Chapter 7 who worked in social care. She was a member of the GMB union, which fought for PPE equipment and safety standards for care staff. A US study of care homes during the pandemic shows just what a difference trade unions can make: unions were associated with a 30 per cent decrease in the Covid-19 mortality rate and greater access to PPE.[15]

Moreover, it is now a widely accepted argument that unions are a key bulwark against inequality. Between 1980 and 2018, the proportion of all income going to the top 1 per cent of earners in the UK increased from 8.1 to 12.7 per cent.[16] At the same time, workers' share of the country's wealth (known in economics as the labour share) declined: 67 per cent of our national income went to workers in wages in 1975, but this had fallen to 58 per cent by 2018.[17] Until recently there has been some controversy over the causes of this wage squeeze, which has taken place across developed countries. Some have argued that technology has reduced demand for less-skilled labour; others have said it is the result of manufacturing jobs moving to developing countries. But the debate has entirely overlooked the elephant in the room.

In a startling article published in 2015 entitled 'Power from the People' two researchers from the International Monetary Fund concluded, 'we find strong evidence that lower unionisation is associated with an increase in top income shares in advanced economies during the period 1980–2010'.[18] Throughout this period the IMF had been the foremost advocate of policies that weakened the position of workers in the name of 'labour market flexibility', and yet they were now attributing fully half of the rise in income inequality to the weakening of unions.[19] Two years later, the chief economist of the Bank of England gave a speech suggesting that the weakness of Britain's trade unions was preventing wages from growing. He argued, 'there is power in numbers. A workforce that is more easily divided than in the past may find itself more easily conquered.'[20]

Look at the figures, and it is clear that unions are still successful at what they were founded to do: boosting pay and conditions for their members. In Britain union members earn an average of 10 per cent more than non-unionised workers.[21] They have more days of paid holiday and work fewer hours of unpaid overtime. Unionised workplaces are more likely to offer help with childcare and job-sharing provisions – as well as more generous pensions, parental leave and sick pay than required by law.[22]

But strong trade unions can also help the economy as a whole. In the same year that the IMF drew its surprising conclusion, the Organisation of Economic Co-operation and Development (OECD), another pillar of the established economic order, produced a report entitled 'In It Together; why less inequality benefits us all'. Its conclusion was as stark as the IMF's: 'Growing inequality is harmful for long-term economic growth ... the key driver is the growing gap between lower-income households – the bottom 40 per cent of the distribution – and the rest of the population.'[23] So if trade unions help counter inequality, and inequality is bad for economic growth, it makes an economic case for trade unions. What's more, in a more recent report the OECD suggested that having unions negotiate with employers on behalf of employees can, when done in the right way, be good for employment, directly contradicting a long-standing claim made by those who oppose unionisation: 'Collective bargaining, providing that it has a wide coverage and is well co-ordinated, fosters good labour market performance.'[24]

As I also argued in Chapter 15, worker representation can also be an important way to shift a company's focus from short- to long-term goals, something which is crucial to economic growth and continuing prosperity. What's striking to me is that in many workplaces in the UK with a strong union presence the day-to-day activities of the union focus on working with the employer for the overall success of the company. It's not about conflict but cooperation.

Yet if the need for trade unions is as strong as ever, their future looks pretty uncertain. Back in 1979, in the UK trade unions had 13 million members; half of all workers belonged to a union.[25] By 2019 this had dropped to just 6.4 million members – less than a quarter of employees – the majority in the public sector.[26] Over the same period, the proportion of workers covered by a collective bargaining agreement over pay and working conditions has fallen from 70 to just 27 per cent. To be fair, in the last three years we have seen a reversal of the trend, with over 200,000 more joining unions.[27] But union membership today is much older than in the past, and the average age continues to rise. Just 8 per cent of 16–24-year-olds are members of trade unions.[28] Unless trade unions make rapid inroads among young workers, their decline will accelerate as older members retire.[29]

So if we care about tackling inequality and injustice, we can't leave unions out of the account, but the trends are inauspicious. What lessons can we in the UK apply from Fight for $15 and at what levels of power can unions operate? Directly transplanting the Fight for $15 won't work because the structure of our democracy is different: in the US federal system states and even individual cities can set a minimum wage, which is not the case in the UK. Nonetheless, we can broaden the fight for justice for workers whether they are union members or not, use the institutions of the state and focus on the sector not just the firm.

In 2017, the Bakers, Food and Allied Workers' Union organised a strike of McDonald's workers modelled on the Fight for $15 and won a significant pay rise for fast food workers, both those who were union members and those who were not.[30] Smaller, newer unions, meanwhile, such as the Independent

Workers' Union of Great Britain (IWGB) and the United Voices of the World (UVW), are working to recruit and represent outsourced and gig economy workers in precarious, fissured workplaces, building communities across different groups of outsourced workers and encouraging members to lead campaigns themselves.[31] Both unions are still small, with a few thousand members each, but they have won some significant victories. The IWGB helped cleaners and porters at the University of London win a living wage, sick pay and more paid holiday.[32] These are important victories at the first level of power – changing people's day-do-day circumstances.

Trade unions are also learning from the best in digital organising to reach beyond their membership. A hundred years ago employees could discuss their grievances with each other on the factory floor and find common cause, but in a world of Uber drivers and Deliveroo riders, workers are physically far more isolated. The high turnover of staff in many service jobs compounds the challenge of face-to-face organising. In response, a growing number of apps and digital services have been created to help workers connect with each other in online communities that act as virtual factory floors – part of a growing movement dubbed WorkerTech.[33] One example is Organise in the UK. Each week a sample of its 80,000 members are sent a survey about the problems they are facing at work, allowing the team behind the app to identify issues to take action on.[34] This is not a substitute for union membership but might be a gateway to it. The Trade Union Congress has recently launched its WorkSmart app, targeted at young private sector workers, which offers career advice and information on working rights with the aim of providing a path to union membership.[35]

Unions are also using the mechanisms of the state in new ways to counter the isolation of the gig economy. In February 2019 the GMB won a major victory when they came to agreement with German delivery firm Hermes, which agreed to union representation, minimum wage guarantees and holiday pay for its 15,000 UK delivery drivers following a case brought by the union in the courts.[36] What's interesting about this victory, the first of its kind in the gig economy, is that the union used the institutions of the state *and* conventional organising. Early in 2021 the GMB, working alongside the insurgent App Drivers and Couriers Union, scored a famous victory against Uber after a four-year battle to guarantee at least some of its drivers a minimum wage, holiday pay and entitlement to breaks.[37] The power of this approach is recognised by others, with the union Unite having established a dedicated legal unit to tackle exploitation in the gig economy.[38]

What about the question of level – firm or sector? The truth is that both have a role to play. There will always be issues specific to workplaces, especially around the organisation of work, health and safety and terms and conditions. And the battle to recruit and represent workers at the company level is vital. Unions face massive barriers here and not just because of the fissured workplace. They have no legal right to access workplaces in order to recruit. Even a member has no right to be represented by a union on many issues. If grass-roots organising of workers is to happen, these sorts of issues will have to be addressed.

But at the core of the Fight for $15 was the idea of looking across an entire category of employment, not just a single firm. In the UK we actually have a tradition of doing just this – what is known as sectoral bargaining – but while this continues in the public sector, it has all but disappeared in the private. If the nature of the modern economy makes it harder for workers to build power in an individual company, then perhaps this offers a way to change the structural odds that unions face – an example of the second level of change mentioned in the introduction to this section.

Here we have something to learn from a country with economic arrangements similar to ours: New Zealand. There the Labour government of Jacinda Ardern recently commissioned a report from a former National Party prime minister, Jim Bolger. When he was in power in the 1990s he had helped significantly weaken the power of unions, so this might seem an odd choice. However, Bolger had already publicly said he had got it wrong, and his views are interesting, given that they come from a conservatively inclined deregulator. Talking about the so-called neoliberal policies implemented all over the world, he said they had 'failed to produce economic growth and what growth there has been has gone to the few at the top'.[39] His report included a set of radical recommendations for the establishment of bodies comprising representatives of the state, employers and workers. Their job would be to raise pay and improve conditions across sectors where there was a significant employee demand or government belief that it was in the public interest.

It is worth delving further into Bolger's reasoning for what he called fair pay agreements because his description of the problem they were designed to solve is remarkably similar to the situation in the UK: 'New Zealanders work longer hours and produce less per hour ... Wages in New Zealand have grown, but much more slowly for workers on lower incomes than those on high wages ... We have both an inequality and a productivity challenge.'[40] Fair pay agreements, he believed, could offer 'mutual benefits for workers and employers through improved worker engagement, increased productivity and better workplaces' and the opportunity 'for employers to invest and engage without the fear of being undercut by those employers engaged in a "race to the bottom".'[41] These two points are key. First, as the research from the OECD mentioned earlier showed, the UK economy could benefit from such an approach, as it could help us escape the low wage, low productivity trap in which parts of our economy find themselves. Second, by applying agreements across the sector, good employers would be protected against being undercut.

In fact, we don't need to look to the other side of the world to learn this particular lesson; we can simply look to our own past. In 1909 the Liberal government in Britain established something conceptually almost identical. Known as wage boards, these brought together representatives of employers and employees to oversee wage and conditions in specific sectors.[42] At their peak in 1953, the sixty-six wage boards covered about 3.5 million workers, a quarter of all employees.[43] Unfortunately, they were unloved by both Left and Right in the 1960s and 70s. The trade unions, very strong at the time, thought they were a poor substitute for collective bargaining between workers and bosses, and the Right eventually concluded that they conflicted with free market principles. The Conservatives got rid of most in the 1990s, and the Coalition abolished the remaining Agricultural Wages Boards in 2013, though they survive in Scotland, Wales and Northern Ireland.

Of course, today we have what did not exist then: a minimum wage. But a national minimum will always be a blunt instrument and by definition cannot take into account the specific conditions of work in a particular industry, such as whether workers are salaried or self-employed and the precise obstacles they face to raising their pay. As a recent analysis put it, 'Whether it is policing the fuzzy boundary between employment and self-employment, agreeing protocols for the scheduling of insecure hours, setting sectoral wage floors over and above the legal minimum, accrediting new forms of training or countering the growing power of online platforms on labour standards – there is a 21st century hole to be filled.'[44]

Wage boards were far from perfect, and our world is very different from the one for which they were created, but their sector-wide approach – shared by Fight for $15 on the one hand, and by conservative former prime minister Jim Bolger on the other – is absolutely appropriate to tackle the problems that we face, particularly in low-wage parts of the economy. One of those areas is social care, as we saw in Chapter 7, and the Welsh government is actually looking at establishing a sectoral body for social care in which employers, government and unions could work together to raise standards and tackle the issues workers face.[45] For all the reasons previously set out, this is the perfect area to start a new approach.

Transforming the position of weakness in which so many working people find themselves today can seem an impossible task. Millions work in vulnerable, insecure conditions, and the economy has changed in ways that make organising much harder. But there are new (and not so new) ways to make a difference, and together even the most apparently powerless workers have more strength than you might think. Because total success seems unlikely doesn't mean we can't make a difference or that we shouldn't try. If we're asking how we could create a fairer and more equal society, then building the power of workers is a vital part of the answer.

CHAPTER 18

Follow the Money

Follow the money ... just follow the money.
                    Deep Throat, *All the President's Men*

One of my favourite films of all time is *All the President's Men*. Based on a book by Bob Woodward and his fellow journalist Carl Bernstein, it tells the story of how they found out that President Richard Nixon had been funding nefarious deeds against his political opponents, including breaking into Democratic Party headquarters at the Watergate Building in Washington DC. Woodward and Bernstein's investigative journalism ultimately forced Nixon to resign from office. Brilliantly dramatised with Robert Redford as Woodward and Dustin Hoffman as Bernstein, their story briefly made me want to be a journalist. I have even got my kids to watch the film.

If we can't rely on governments alone to bring about change then we would do well to take the advice that Deep Throat, Woodward's anonymous source for his explosive story, gives in the film: follow the money. Just as Woodward and Bernstein did exactly that to bring down a president, a burgeoning movement hopes it can do the same to bring down the fossil fuel industry. This is the improbable story of a group of college students who sparked a movement that in ten years has amassed $14 trillion in assets to support its goal.[1]

Our story starts with Larry Gibson, born in the once idyllic Kayford Mountain area of West Virginia in 1946. His father was a coal miner, as was his grandfather before him. As a child Larry spent his time playing in the trees. The Gibson family had lived in the same spot for 200 years, but when Larry was in fourth grade, his father lost his job, and they were forced to move away. Larry spent the next few decades hundreds of miles away from Kayford Mountain, working in Ohio's automobile industry. When he moved back to the area in the 1980s, what he saw shocked him. The mining companies had taken over the area and begun literally blowing the tops off the hills in order to get to the coal underneath. The once green landscape was increasingly a uniform grey, and the coal firms were buying up the whole mountain.[2]

With memories of the landscape of his childhood at the front of his mind, Larry dedicated himself to resisting the destruction. Over the following years he became known as the keeper of the mountains.[3] Larry refused to sell his own plot to the mining companies – but that wasn't all. He gave talks about mountain top removal (MTR) mining. He mounted protests at government buildings. He invited groups of students, activists and celebrities to tour the area to see the harsh reality of America's dependence on fossil fuels.

In 2010 a handful of students from Swarthmore College in Pennsylvania travelled over 400 miles to Kayford Mountain to see the destruction for themselves. They came home desperate to work out how they could help. Like Woodward and Bernstein they decided to follow the money and discovered that Swarthmore, like many other colleges in the US, had a large endowment fund partially invested in fossil fuel extraction.[4] They recognised that this might give them a small but vital lever. When you own shares in a company, you are effectively lending it your financial support. It seemed imperative to them that Swarthmore withdraw its portion of that support, and the bigger question was: what would happen if everyone else who invested in fossil fuels did the same?

The Swarthmore students started a campaign for their college to sell off the shares it held first in coal companies and later in oil and gas – a process known as divestment and the opposite of investment. They did not succeed in that aim, but their campaign hit the news and helped to spark the biggest divestment campaign in history.[5] It took off in no small part because in 2012 veteran climate activist Bill McKibben published an article in *Rolling Stone* magazine headlined GLOBAL WARMING'S TERRIFYING NEW MATH.[6] The terrifying maths was this. Limiting global warming to 2°Celsius, at that point seen as the tipping point for catastrophic climate change, would require us to cap further emissions of carbon dioxide into the atmosphere at 565 gigatonnes.[7] But according to a report from a London-based organisation called Carbon Tracker, McKibben explained, if all of the coal, oil and gas known to exist at the time of writing were burned, it would lead to CO_2 emissions of 2,795 gigatonnes. In other words, 80 per cent of known fossil fuel reserves need to be kept in the ground. The figures have changed a bit since 2012 – and it is now widely accepted that we should aim for 1.5°C not 2°C warming – but more recent estimates agree that we have to leave about 80 per cent fossil fuel reserves in the ground.[8] As McKibben argued, the big problem is that the fossil fuel industry is unlikely to do that voluntarily.

This article caused the divestment movement to really take off. The terrifying figures, McKibben's argument and the students' campaign appealed to people's conscience: how could it be right for organisations to invest in and profit from the destruction of the planet? Withdrawing financial support for acts of cataclysmic destruction had to be the right thing to do. But divestment also appealed to investors' self-interest. As McKibben pointed out, if governments ever take action to prevent these reserves from being used – spurred on by the pressure of the divestment campaign and as eventually they will have to do if they are to meet their climate commitments – their investments will plummet in value. It will then become clear that the fossil fuel companies are massively overvalued because a significant proportion of their assets is essentially worthless. There is a carbon bubble – a bit like the housing bubble that led to the 2008 financial crisis – which will at some point burst. The Bank of England estimates losses could be as big as $20 trillion.[9] This makes fossil fuels a risky investment, to put it mildly.

There's good reason to believe the fossil fuel companies are not going to change without being forced to. I remember being at a conference a few years back and chatting to a senior European director of one of the major oil companies. He cared about the climate crisis, he worried about the impact on his children and their children, but this was not enough for him to change the direction of the company. Given the shareholder-first model of business in which he operated (discussed in Chapter 5), if he had decided to invest the significant amounts needed to transition his company away from fossil fuels to renewable energy at the pace required, he'd probably be opposed by large numbers of shareholders complaining about the short-term cost. If he went ahead anyway, he might well be out of a job.

That isn't to say there isn't a good business case for change – as well as a planetary one – and there is an example of a fossil fuel company that has made the transition. About the time I was having sleepless nights at the Copenhagen climate summit, DONG [Danish Oil and Natural Gas] Energy was setting out its 85/15 vision – over thirty years it would transform its energy generation from 85 per cent fossil fuels and 15 per cent renewables to 85 per cent renewables and 15 per cent fossil fuels. Today, renamed Ørsted, it is the world leader in offshore wind generation, with 30 per cent of the global market, and it achieved its aim twenty years ahead of schedule. By 2025 green energy will be 99 per cent of the company's output. It now has a higher stock market valuation than BP.[10] Those who ran Ørsted were not just far-sighted, however; the company was 80 per cent owned by the Danish state, which was willing to take a long-term view on investment.[11] Ørsted is unfortunately the exception when it comes to fossil fuel companies, and to turn things around at the speed that is required, we're going to need every tool we can find. That's where the divestment movement comes in.

This isn't the first time divestment has been used to campaign for change. In the 1970s and 80s activists around the world targeted South Africa's apartheid regime with a high-profile campaign. In the US by the end of the 1980s, 155 universities, 200 companies and 26 states had taken action to divest from or sanction companies or banks operating in South Africa.[12] In the UK a student-led campaign pressed individuals, local authorities and charities to stop banking with Barclays until they ended their involvement in South Africa. Barclays' share of the student market halved, and they sold their South African subsidiary in 1986.[13] The divestment campaign was just one of a number which targeted the South African government but is widely considered to have helped delegitimise the apartheid regime.[14] Similar tactics have also been used against the tobacco industry in recent decades.[15]

What distinguishes the fossil fuel divestment movement from previous divestment campaigns is its appeal to both the head – the carbon bubble – and the heart – the sheer wrongness of profiting from planetary destruction. By 2020, more than a thousand institutions worldwide – universities, religious groups, city governments, pension funds – had committed to the movement.[16] Organisations from the British Medical Association to the City of New York have joined. In the 1880s John D. Rockefeller controlled 90 per cent of oil in the US, including the forerunners of contemporary fossil fuel giants Chevron and ExxonMobil. One hundred and thirty years later, even the Rockefeller Family Fund was divesting from the fossil fuel industry.[17]

The ultimate aim is clear, but how do those in the campaign think change will happen? 350.org, a group founded by Bill McKibben which has gone on to be prominent in the divestment movement, says the idea is not to bankrupt the fossil fuel companies, but to attack their 'social licence'.[18] They argue that the companies are so financially powerful, and economies have been so dependent on them, that they often attempt to obstruct governments taking action on the climate crisis. They and others point to research which suggests that the top five publicly traded oil and gas companies spend $200 million a year lobbying to block, limit or delay climate policies.[19] Some fossil fuel companies have also been accused of funding climate deniers while knowing full well the catastrophic impact their businesses have on the planet.[20] The divestment movement is trying to flip this story on its head by using money as a tool for the rest of us to challenge some of the world's most powerful corporations. By persuading institutions we can influence to sever their financial ties with fossil fuels, the argument goes, campaigners can delegitimise the industry and make it easier for governments to act in ways it does not like.

Again, we can think about this in terms of the three levels of political change. We need fossil fuel companies to transform their business models if we're going to tackle the climate crisis. Level-one change would either try to directly persuade the companies to change their practices or put pressure on governments to force them to adapt. This remains the ultimate goal, but economic incentives mean the companies are unlikely to change on their own, while their economic might means they can lobby governments to avoid political intervention. Level-two change would challenge the structural political power of fossil fuel companies, for example by altering campaign finance or lobbying laws to limit the pressure they exert on politicians. That's easier said than done, so the fossil fuel divestment movement is focused on change at level three: shifting the overall conversation. In moving the public debate and changing people's attitudes towards the industry, the aim is to make it easier for politicians to step in. Change at level three makes change at level one possible.

But the question of whether the movement can actually have a meaningful impact is highly contested. Fourteen trillion dollars sounds impressive, but these commitments come from a small proportion of the world's investors overall with most yet to be persuaded, which means a fossil fuel company with a viable economic proposition can always find someone else to stump up the cash. As a result, when an institution divests it neither hits a company's share price nor prevents it investing in further extraction.[21] This problem isn't specific to fossil fuels: a 1999 study found that the anti-apartheid divestment movement had no demonstrable financial impact on the share prices of the South African companies that were targeted, even if it caused damage to the apartheid regime as a whole.[22]

It can also be argued that if a socially responsible institution sells its stake in a fossil fuel company, this may be bought by a less scrupulous investor. Keeping an investment means retaining voting rights at annual general meetings (AGMs), which can be used to put pressure on companies to adopt a more sustainable course – known as shareholder engagement. One investment manager has said, 'divestment isn't a badge of honour; it's a failure of the engagement process'.[23] If you accept this argument, if you want to make a fossil fuel company change course, you're better off keeping your stake and using your votes. Divestment might make you feel good, but at best it is a waste of time and at worst is counter-productive. And a number of large fossil fuel companies are owned by states such as Saudi Arabia rather than being publicly traded, and so are not susceptible to divestment anyway.

There are two main reasons why the critics of divestment are wrong. First and foremost, the divestment campaign has put the future of the fossil fuel industry on the agenda in a way it simply wasn't before. Keep the three levels of change in mind. The divestment movement did not start off seeking to affect the fossil fuel industry itself in order to persuade companies to change their policies directly (level one change); instead, it has focused on shifting the Overton window (level three). Divestment has successfully sparked a debate about whether the behaviour of the fossil fuel industry is compatible with sufficient action on the climate crisis. That debate has had significant knock-on effects.

One of these is Climate Action 100+, an alliance of more than 500 investors, including everyone from the Church of England to Aviva, managing a mind-blowing $52 trillion of financial assets between them.[24] They are committed to using their investments to put pressure on the 100 companies responsible for more than two thirds of greenhouse gas emissions to act on the climate crisis. Many in the coalition, including the Church of England, have said they will divest from companies that do not change.[25] They've won some important victories. Royal Dutch Shell has agreed to link climate targets to executive pay, the world's largest coal exporter Glencore has pledged to cap production at current levels, and BP has been forced to disclose how its company strategy is consistent with the Paris Agreement.[26]

It's hard to believe that all this change in practice would have happened without the divestment movement. In fact, the incompatibility of shareholder engagement with divestment can be overstated. Shareholder engagement can be used to put pressure on companies to transform their business models in line with net zero emissions, as Ørsted has done, and hold companies to account for their climate commitments. But that doesn't rule out the option of divestment from companies that remain resistant to change. Norway's sovereign wealth fund, which manages $1 trillion of assets alone, has combined the two approaches. It has committed itself to selling off shares in coal companies and those that engage in oil and gas exploration, while retaining stakes in fossil fuel companies that are also investing in clean energy.[27] The fund is using its shares in the latter companies to push for greater disclosure about their climate impacts and whether their business models can survive in a zero-carbon world.[28]

Furthermore, when the debate shifts, it has an impact on policymakers. A study by researchers at the University of Oxford in 2013 found that almost every divestment campaign in history, including those mounted against tobacco and South Africa, ultimately managed to persuade policymakers to pass legislation targeting the industry or area. For example, the anti-apartheid divestment movement in the US helped the push for the Comprehensive Anti-Apartheid Act of 1986, which introduced economic sanctions on South Africa.[29] The divestment from fossil fuels campaign may not yet have led to government making the changes in law that it seeks, but the signs are that it could well happen.

The campaign's carbon bubble argument in particular has been noticed by policymakers around the world. Former governor of the Bank of England Mark Carney has led the charge on the massive risks faced by the financial system if we continue to act as if the world's fossil fuel reserves can all be used. He has highlighted the physical danger of climate damage, the risk of carbon-extracting companies being sued down the line, and the chance that their stock market value could suddenly nosedive if governments act.[30] Carney is part of a growing establishment movement demanding that all companies, including fossil fuel firms, outline their climate risks. The UK has now announced that large companies and financial institutions will have to reveal their exposure to climate risks by 2025.[31] This will allow investors to hold companies to account on how they plan to transition to net zero emissions.

Might this shift in the conversation have happened anyway? Perhaps, but the atmosphere and the context created by the divestment movement has undoubtedly helped make the idea of a carbon bubble mainstream in the world of finance. An authoritative study in 2018 found that the divestment movement had 'put questions of finance and climate change on the agenda and played a part in changing discourse around the legitimacy, reputation and viability of the fossil fuel industry'. Crucially, it concluded divestment was helping change attitudes towards the fossil fuel industry among some shareholders, investors and others working in the financial services sector.[32]

The second reason to doubt the critics is that there are some signs that the divestment movement has also had more direct material effects on the fossil fuel industry. It's clear, for example, that certain parts of the industry are more vulnerable to pressure than others. Goldman Sachs says divestment has contributed to the declining value of the coal industry in recent years: 'The fossil fuel divestment movement is gathering pace … a growing number of investors and financial institutions have announced bans or restrictions on coal investments … which have in our view been a driver of the sector de-rating over the past five years.'[33] When Peabody Coal, the world's biggest private-sector coal company, filed for bankruptcy in 2016, it listed divestment as one if its problems because it made it harder to raise capital.[34] There is also evidence that divestment is starting to hit non-coal fossil fuel companies' balance sheets. Shell's 2018 annual report expressed concern about divestment: 'if this were to continue, it could have a material adverse effect on the price of our securities and our ability to access equity capital markets'.[35] This suggests that there are tipping points beyond which divestment can directly hit fossil fuel companies in the pocket.

There is also reason to think the direct effects of divestments could grow. While so far the movement has largely focused on selling shares in fossil fuel companies, that's not the only way to follow the money. Campaigners could have an even bigger impact if the tactic was extended to other parts of the financial system – such as insurance – that provide direct financial support for fossil fuel extraction. That is starting to happen. Campaigners at Insure our Future are pushing for insurance companies to refuse to underwrite fossil fuels extraction, which would make it difficult to carry out exploration projects. In just a few years, twenty-three of the world's biggest insurers have ended or restricted their provision of insurance to the coal sector, leading some to argue that coal is becoming uninsurable.[36] One indication of this is the growing number of insurers refusing to be involved in a highly controversial new coal mine planned in Queensland, Australia.[37]

Other activists are following the money in a different direction. The Rainforest Action Network has discovered that some of the world's largest banks have provided $2.7 trillion in finance for fossil fuel companies since the Paris Agreement was signed. Their analysis shows that finance for the companies most involved in new fossil fuel exploration projects is actually surging.[38] If banks stopped funding new fossil fuel projects and began to phase out all fossil fuel financing this would have a direct material impact on the industry. French bank Credit Agricole has stopped lending to new coal projects and is demanding its clients in the industry disclose their plans for getting out.[39]

Coal is currently the area where victories seem within reach, but it's not hard to see how activists could use the same route – via banking – to push for more ambitious action across the whole fossil fuel sector. Many of the financial institutions underpinning the industry are heavily reliant on individual and business customers. The divestment movement has been successful at encouraging people to use their membership of universities, religious groups and other organisations to exert pressure. A number of campaigns are now emerging which encourage people to use the threat of moving bank accounts, insurance policies or pension pots similarly. Over the last few years, for example, campaigners in the US have been encouraging people to move their bank accounts away from JP Morgan Chase – the biggest bank funder of fossil fuel extraction.[40] There's still a long way to go, but activists heralded a recent announcement from JP Morgan Chase that it would use its financial weight to push for net zero emissions by 2050 as a small victory.[41]

The other side of the coin is that we also actively need to finance the green transition. From wind and solar power to vehicle technology to low carbon manufacturing, sustainable firms need capital to fund the technology and infrastructure of the future. By shifting money from fossil fuels into sustainable investments, individuals and organisations can not only stop funding the problem but also help to fund the solutions. The Climate Change Committee says transitioning to net zero in the UK will require tens of billions of pounds of investment. As we saw in Chapter 1, government will have to fund some of this, but a significant proportion will need to come from the private sector. Again, here we all have the power to make a difference. As the British charity Share Action highlights, our pension pots may include significant fossil fuel investments.[42] By moving to sustainable plans that invest in companies driving the net zero transition, by persuading our employers to move company policies or by putting pressure on our pension providers to change their investment approach, we can redirect the power of the financial system towards good.

For all these reasons, the divestment movement really matters. It has prompted all sorts of actions and campaigns, it has helped put the issue of the carbon bubble on the agenda, pressuring government, and it is spawning a way of thinking which in the perception-driven world of finance can have very significant effects. Is divestment enough on its own? Of course not. We need government to act. But, as we have seen, shifting public opinion can be one of the most effective tools in forcing them to do so. Perhaps the most important lesson of the divestment movement is that using the tools within our reach – and putting pressure on the universities, churches or pension funds that we are part of to do the same – gives everybody some power. We might not have the financial might of the world's biggest corporations, but divestment offers a way for all of us to use what we do have to bring about real change.

CHAPTER 19

The Preston Story

It's time to shift focus from the future of the planet to the history of Preston bus station. Believe it or not, this bus terminus offers a powerful – if unlikely – story about how we can begin to build a better world. It shows that, whoever is in power in central government, there are inspiring people around the country offering a vision of change.

The bus station lies at the northern end of Preston city centre. It is a classic example of twentieth-century brutalism – an imposing concrete building, erected in the late 1960s in the hope and expectation that Preston's population would double, with bays for eighty double-decker buses.[1] It was said to be the largest bus station in Europe.[2] For decades it served the city well, but by 2000 the fortunes of the building had turned. Buses were arriving and leaving empty. A report by Preston City Council argued that not only was it unused but it acted as a barrier to getting around the city centre.[3] Knocking down the bus station became the centrepiece of an ambitious £700 million plan to regenerate the area. Preston was struggling with high unemployment, low wages and higher than average deprivation.[4] But here was a grand plan to transform its city centre and create thousands of new jobs in the process.

For nearly ten years councillors worked hard to get investors on board. They signed up property firms LendLease and Grosvenor to lead the redevelopment of the city and attracted commitments from John Lewis and Marks & Spencer to open flagship department stores.[5] A new transport hub, a spruced-up market and a large new shopping complex were all planned.[6] Then the financial crisis of 2007–08 hit. At first it didn't look like it was going to be too much of a problem; retailers kept signing up to the development even in the wake of the recent crash.[7] But at the end of 2011 John Lewis unexpectedly pulled out, leaving the scheme 'no longer financially viable'. The regeneration plan was promptly dropped altogether.[8] The bus station still stood, and Preston was back to square one.

Looking at the standard playbook, Preston's leaders were out of options. Development plans typically focus on getting investors from outside an area to pump money into it. You try to persuade them to build a new shopping centre, commit to a housing development or perhaps set up a call centre to employ people. But attracting outside investment during a financial crisis is not easy. By 2011 and 2012 the council was already being squeezed by austerity, leaving it little room for manoeuvre. End of story.

Or so the usual story would have gone. However, six months before John Lewis pulled out, a new council leadership had been elected. Long-serving councillor Matthew Brown had joined the leadership team, and was now given the unenviable task of coming up with a new plan for the local economy. Brown refused to accept that Preston City Council was powerless. He brought in some policy experts from an organisation called the Centre for Local Economic Strategies in nearby Manchester to advise him and his colleagues on what their options might be.[9] The experts looked around at what tools Preston had at its disposal and found them in some unlikely places. They dicovered that Preston's public sector institutions, such as the council and police force, were spending £750 million every year on goods and services, but only £1 in £20 was being spent within Preston itself, and just £8 in £20 in the wider area of Lancashire.[10] In other words, while outside investment wasn't coming in, inside investment was flowing out.

Chances are you've never got excited about government procurement – the buying practices of Whitehall departments, local councils, the NHS, the police and others. Now's the moment. Typically, it involves finding the least costly supplier, wherever it might be, and doing a deal. But Preston decided to do something different. The council realised that procurement could be a crucial tool in changing the direction of the local economy and, starting in 2013, began teaming up with local public sector organisations, including the police, a couple of colleges and a housing association. Initially, six organisations committed to buying more from suppliers in the area, often small businesses. Within a few years, instead of £1 in £20, those six organisations were spending nearly £4 in Preston, and in Lancashire the figure doubled from £8 in every £20 to £16. This meant that £200 million that had previously been sucked out of the local economy each year was now staying in the area.[11] Eventually twelve public sector organisations, including hospitals and the University of Central Lancashire, signed up.

Procurement wasn't the only tool the experts found. In 2012 Preston City Council became the first employer in the north of England to be accredited by the Living Wage Foundation and guarantee the living wage to all its staff. It encouraged other large employers to do the same. Within a few years, 4,000 more people in the city were being paid a real living wage.[12] Clearly this was good for them, but it also increased the amount that local people had to spend and, of course, how much they spent locally.

Thinking about how else money generated locally could be kept there, the council redirected £100 million from Lancashire County Council's pension fund.[13] This was used to help finance much-needed student accommodation for the city's expanding university, which was completed in 2018. Preston's iconic Park Hotel, previously converted into uninspiring council offices, is now being returned to its former glory as a hotel, also with investment from the pension fund.[14] The council has adopted other innovative means of promoting the local economy, including assisting the establishment and development of worker-owned co-ops in catering and digital technology, as well as taxi services. The strategy has been not just to buy local, but to do so in a way that spreads wealth within the area.

The result has been a wider renaissance of Preston. Before the pandemic hit, in-work poverty and unemployment were down, social mobility was up.[15] Preston was named the most improved city in the UK by professional services firm PwC in 2018.[16] And the bus station has undergone an award-winning restoration.[17]

There is a reason Preston's story appears in this part of the book: it offers us an important lesson about how change can happen. Too often we feel powerless in the face of large economic forces, but Preston shows that communities have more tools at their disposal than they might think. It is an example of a new economic approach gathering pace in cities across the world, known as community wealth building.[18] This rejects the standard approach to economic development, which is simply to go looking for outside investment. Community wealth building seeks to harness the money already within an area to build a fairer local economy. It also recognises that conventional regeneration too often leaves large parts of the population out. If the original plan for Preston had gone ahead, it might have generated employment, but beyond this there was no guarantee that it would have ensured decent wages or where the profits would have flowed. This is why community wealth building is a big idea. It aspires to build economies where income, wealth and ownership are more fairly spread, economies with justice hard-wired into them.[19]

Community wealth building is centred on organisations like the twelve public sector institutions with which Preston worked. They weren't chosen by accident but are what's known in the jargon as anchor institutions: large local employers with a long-term link to an area so unlikely to move away.[20] Universities and hospitals are the gold standard of anchor institutions because they tend to have large workforces, big budgets and, by their very nature, strong local ties. But other organisations do the job too. Councils, schools, even football clubs are prime candidates. The key thing is they have an interest in local prosperity and the economic power to influence it.

Once you've got your anchors, it's time to put them to work. As we saw in Preston, community wealth building encourages anchors to take action in areas such as the goods and services they buy, the people they employ and the financial assets they hold.[21] It sounds unlikely, but the procurement, human resources and finance departments of these organisations can be the vanguard of progressive change. The idea, as we have seen, is to get anchors both to keep more of their money within the area and to distribute it more evenly among the local population. Changing procurement practices can help create good jobs for local people and support the development of small businesses, cooperatives and community and social enterprises.

For too long the public sector has been indifferent to where its money goes, to the practices and ownership of the companies it buys from and partners with. But an outsourced large multinational, supplying laundry services or school meals to a community at the lowest cost, paying the minimum wage, has a significantly less positive impact on an area than local companies paying the living wage to do the same. Community wealth building enables local people to benefit from higher wages and a greater share of the wealth created. A study for the Federation of Small Businesses backs this up. It found that every pound spent by local authorities with small and medium-sized enterprises (SMEs) generates an additional 63p of benefit for the local economy, compared to just 40p for every pound spent with larger firms.[22]

When it comes to the anchor institutions, they have the power to boost the incomes and job prospects of local people simply by changing their own policies on hiring and pay. That's why Preston's first step was to promote the living wage. They can also offer better in-work training and career development opportunities for their staff or actively employ people from low-income areas or under-represented groups. But the hidden superpower of large institutions lies in their financial assets. Most employers invest in pension funds on behalf of their employees. Moving these assets from generic investments in the global financial system to those that fund local schemes puts money to doubly good use. This could be for investment in infrastructure, as in Preston, or to provide much-needed finance for local businesses. For example, Greater Manchester's pension fund has diverted £50 million to invest in local small businesses.[23]

Community wealth building tells us something else about how change happens. If we rely solely on central government to redistribute income and wealth in order to build a fairer economy, we will always be playing catch-up in the fight against inequality – and losing. To begin with, getting money to people through a benefits system that assesses their income will always be more complex than doing so directly through their wage packets. Universal Credit is an extreme example, but it's true of any system that by definition compensates for the failings of the economy. The scale of intervention needed to achieve a fairer economy is also hard to win political support for, partly because of the power of those who benefit from inequality. And evidence from around the world confirms that it is incredibly difficult to keep inequality from exploding unless you tackle it at source.[24] If you start off with a grossly unfair economy and expect redistribution by government to solve the problem, then it's like running up the down escalator. Community wealth building avoids this by building an economy which is more equal from the start – not just in terms of people's incomes but also the ownership of businesses and other assets.

So that's the case in favour. What are the objections? First, doesn't this risk raising costs for the public sector? Basing procurement decisions not solely on price but on a whole range of factors means you don't necessarily get the cheapest deal. At a time when the public purse is under massive strain, is this affordable or sensible? A recent study has found no conclusive evidence that community wealth building leads to the public sector spending more.[25] And by focusing primarily or solely on the cost of the contract, this argument can obscure or overlook knock-on costs elsewhere.[26]

An obvious example of how low-price contracts can lead to knock-on costs is the need for state subsidies through Universal Credit and housing benefit to compensate for inadequate pay. Every worker with children paid at the minimum wage will have their income topped up by government subsidies, and rightly so, but this cost does not feature in the low-price contract that directly causes it because it's not Preston or its equivalent that pays out but the Department of Work and Pensions. There are longer-term costs too. Low-wage insecure employment without proper training is likely to be less productive and thus generate less overall wealth for the economy, which has knock-on implications for the public purse. Think also of the costs of ill-health and sickness that inevitably accrue in areas dominated by low-paid work, where many workers and their families are in poverty.[27]

A second critique levelled by opponents of community wealth building is that it is protectionism on a local scale.[28] Mainstream economics tells us that, at best, this means any benefit from keeping money in one area comes at a cost to somewhere else. If every area did it, the country as a whole would be no better off. At worst, it means the economy is losing out by not taking advantage of specialised expertise and the fundamental benefits to be had from trade itself and giving contracts to those who will do the best job. However, Preston Council has pointed out that would only be the case if they awarded contracts to 'an inferior local contractor to shield them from competition of better performing and more keenly priced competitors'.[29] Instead, community wealth building actively supports local small businesses, co-ops and others to compete on price, quality and wider value for money with large firms based elsewhere to win public sector contracts. Moreover, the truth is that the odds are generally stacked in favour of large firms because choosing one can so easily seem like the safer, easier option.

Community wealth building helps to overcome that misguided assumption.

The most interesting critique of community wealth building actually relates to something else. How much difference can one local authority or one group of anchor institutions really make? An island of community wealth building in a sea of wealth extraction may not really change much. The approach was pioneered in Cleveland, Ohio, but after a decade of work there are only three successful cooperatives operating as a result.[30] That feels like a long slog to equality.

But that undersells the idea. Community wealth building is not a panacea for all our economic and social ills, but does point the way to something bigger. Good jobs at living wages and locally owned businesses are the building blocks of a fairer national, and global, economy. While community wealth building may not fix the larger structural problems of our economy, it offers a way for local leaders to make a meaningful difference to the lives of people and – most importantly of all – in the process sows the seeds of a different way of organising our economy. By thinking about procurement in terms of social value rather than just price, we bring questions of wellbeing into discussions of public policy and undermine the dominance of GDP. Supporting local co-ops, social enterprises and SMEs promotes the concept of worker ownership and the idea that businesses should be rooted in the community, and undermines the assumption that only shareholders matter. Using the public sector to build a fairer economy reinvigorates local democracy and undermines centralisation and disempowerment. Community Wealth Building fosters a new economic mindset.

What's even more exciting is that we have only just begun to discover what is possible. Preston has inspired a growing network of community wealth builders in towns and cities across the UK. Each version is different, responding and adapting to the specific local challenges and opportunities of its economy. Wirral Council is developing a community bank in order to give its citizens a democratic locally run alternative to the high street banks – just one example of the community banking movement spreading across the country.[31] Islington Council in London has developed a community wealth building approach that focuses less on procurement within its area and more on supporting local cooperatives through affordable workspace programmes.[32] Across the country communities are working together to create fairer local economies.

The next step is to think how the principles of community wealth building might be applied on a national scale, as both the Scottish and Welsh governments are already starting to do.[33] Across the UK, the public sector spends a total of £292 billion on procurement every year – about a third of all public spending.[34] Some have suggested the NHS could become 'the mother of all anchor institutions'.[35] Imagine if hospitals across the UK had an explicit duty to support their regional economies. Given the huge numbers of people employed by the NHS, the size of its pension funds and procurement budget, it could have an extraordinary impact. Indeed, the NHS recognised this power in its long-term plan published in 2019 and has committed to doing more to support local economies.[36]

Community wealth building shows, once again, that change can start today. Not everyone works for an anchor institution; fewer still determine their procurement or employment policies. Yet many of us have links to them – whether it's the hospital we work at, the school we send our children to or the council we elect. Government action is of course vital to building a fairer economy, but we can also put pressure on organisations closer to home. As we strive to make the impossible possible and build a new settlement for the country, there is a tendency to dismiss such ideas as either too trivial to make a difference or too utopian to be achievable.[37] We have to resist this defeatism. The story of Preston and its bus station teaches us something important. By using the tools at our disposal, by pursuing what is possible, we can not only make an immediate difference to people's lives but also open a door to the possibility of more radical change.

CHAPTER 20

It Takes a Movement

Normal politics has failed us. It has brought the whole planet
to the brink of ecological disaster.

Farhana Yamin[1]

I've known Farhana Yamin for more than a decade. An international environmental lawyer, she was at the COP climate
change summit in Copenhagen in 2009, advising highly vulnerable small island states such as the Maldives. Farhana was a
key figure both in Copenhagen and the Paris climate summit six
years later, where she was supporting the Marshall Islands. Her
work was instrumental in getting international agreement on a
global goal of net zero emissions by 2050 and a global warming
target limit of 1.5°Celsius. Farhana worked for countries who
are too often overlooked, fighting for them in the diplomatic
arena as the outsider's insider.

Fast-forward ten years from Copenhagen, and Farhana was
arrested outside Shell's London headquarters. As Extinction
Rebellion protesters gathered on a Tuesday in the middle of
April 2019, Farhana slipped under a line of police tape blocking off the entrance and glued herself to the ground. It took a
number of police officers twenty minutes to get her unstuck.[2]

Farhana was one of more than a thousand protesters arrested
across London over two weeks that April, as activists blocked

bridges, closed roads and even moored a pink boat in the centre of Oxford Circus.[3] Her story echoes many of those in the climate movement. After decades spent talking about the science, writing policy reports and trying to change laws, she concluded that the speed of change was overwhelmingly out of sync with the scale of the problem. We've known about human-created climate change for decades; we've been holding international talks for decades – and still emissions have risen. Farhana and others decided a different kind of action was required. Extinction Rebellion grew out of a conviction that normal politics was failing.

Almost in parallel, a new generation of climate activists burst on to the scene. In August 2018 fifteen-year-old Greta Thunberg sat outside the Swedish parliament with a simple placard: SCHOOL STRIKE FOR CLIMATE. Within a few months, she had inspired thousands of similar school strikes all across the world, as students walked out of their classes in protest at the lack of climate action. The largest strike drew more than four million protestors – both schoolchildren and adults – across the world.[4] In February 2019 I went with my son Daniel to the first organised pupil climate strike in the UK. Claire Perry, the Conservative climate change minister, applauded the children who took time off school to protest.[5] Soon after, Greta Thunberg visited the House of Commons and Michael Gove declared her 'the voice of our conscience'.[6]

Following the school strikes and Extinction Rebellion protests in April 2019, the UK, Scottish and Welsh parliaments passed motions declaring a climate emergency ('telling the truth' was one of Extinction Rebellion's demands).[7] A few weeks later, a UK-wide citizens' assembly on climate was announced (another demand).[8] The week after that, the UK became one of the first countries in the world to enshrine a net zero emissions target into law.[9] All this did not go anywhere near far enough for the movement: Extinction Rebellion had called for a legally binding citizens' assembly and a net zero target of 2025, much more ambitious than the 2050 target announced.[10] But these developments were a sign that the political debate had shifted. Not only that, public opinion had been transformed. Although people were very divided about Extinction Rebellion's tactics, 60 per cent said they supported their aims and just 20 per cent opposed them.[11] In a poll in the middle of 2019 nearly twice as many people named the environment as one of the biggest issues facing the country as had done at the start of the year.[12]

This is the power of social movements: they can transform the political conversation, shifting the Overton window. I remember seeing a climate protestor asked in an interview whether 2025 was an unrealistic and utopian target for net zero. 'Reach for the stars and you might get the sky,' they replied. The protester was right. Whatever our view of Extinction Rebellion's tactics, the climate movement as a whole succeeded in shifting the goal posts. Suddenly, net zero by 2050 – which looked like a radical move just a couple of years earlier – seemed modest, almost conservative.

Climate activists aren't the only ones to have changed the conversation in recent years. Alicia Garza was in a bar with her friends on 13 July 2013 when she learned that George Zimmerman had been acquitted of the murder of Trayvon Martin, an unarmed Black teenager he had shot dead as the young man was walking back from a corner shop. Shocked and angry, Alicia pulled out her phone and posted a stream of updates to Facebook: 'Black people. I love you. I love us. Our lives matter.' 'I continue to be surprised at how little Black lives matter.' One simply read, '#blacklivesmatter'.[13]

This was the birth of Black Lives Matter, which over the last few years has sparked the biggest reckoning on racism for a generation. The protests that followed the killing of George Floyd by a police officer in Minneapolis in May 2020 are thought to be the largest mobilisation of any political movement in US history.[14] These protests rippled across the globe. Hundreds of thousands of people took part in similar actions in towns and cities across the UK.[15] In the wake of the demonstrations across the US, Minneapolis City Council voted to disband the city's police force.[16] In the months that followed, politicians and businesses the world over declared their support for Black Lives Matter. More than a thousand advertisers joined the biggest ad boycott in Facebook's history in protest at its lack of action against racism and hate speech.[17] Books on race, racism and the history of slavery topped the charts as people sought to educate themselves on racial injustice.[18]

Racism is a fundamentally different issue to the climate crisis, but Black Lives Matter also grew out of a frustration with the failure of politics as usual. Six decades since the Civil Rights movement was born, Black people are still three times more likely to be killed by police officers in the US than white people.[19] More than two decades since the Macpherson report that followed the murder of Stephen Lawrence found the Metropolitan Police to be institutionally racist, Black people are nearly ten times as likely to be stopped and searched as white people in Britain.[20] Politicians on both sides of the Atlantic have been far too slow to address these injustices. It's still too early to know how far Black Lives Matter has changed this, but the shift in mood cannot be disputed. More than three quarters of people in the US now think racial discrimination is a big problem, up from just half of people five years ago.[21]

There is still a big partisan divide on the issue in the US, but the political conversation has clearly changed. I remember being in the US in 2016 and hearing scepticism about Black Lives Matter even on the Democratic side. A former Democratic politician told me the problem with the movement was that it didn't have clear demands. During a rally in the 2016 presidential campaign Bernie Sanders responded to being interrupted by Black Lives Matter activists by saying, 'Black lives matter, white lives matter, Hispanic lives matter.' Hillary Clinton similarly declared, 'All lives matter.'[22] Both were criticised for failing to recognise the specific oppression – and the specific threat to their lives – that Black people face.

Few politicians would respond in the same way today. In the wake of the Black Lives Matter protests of 2020 every Democratic politician in Mississippi, along with some Republicans, voted to alter the state flag to omit the saltire associated with the slavery-supporting Confederate side in the American Civil War. Mississippi's Republican governor signed the change into law.[23] During Joe Biden's presidential inaugural address he cited systemic racism as one of the 'cascading crises' that his administration would address.[24] Black Lives Matter has forced politicians to wake up. It has pushed racial injustice up the political agenda.

This returns me to the most important conclusion of Part IV, and indeed the whole book: politics is too important to be left to the politicians. If we really want to make the impossible possible and build a better world, then simply waiting to vote in the right government is nowhere near enough. This chapter is about the importance of social movements which bring together large groups of people to push for change. We've seen social movements again and again throughout the book: the Icelandic women strikers demanding gender equality (Chapter 4), nineteenth-century trade unionists fighting for a shorter working week (Chapter 8), *Stop de Kindermoord* campaigning for safer roads for Duch children (Chapter 10), the climate activists in Senator Feinstein's office (Chapter 12), and the Fight for $15 (Chapter 17) and fossil fuel divestment campaigns (Chapter 18) earlier in Part IV. In all of these cases and more, movements have mobilised people – whether through demonstration, boycotts, signing petitions or a whole host of other tactics – in order to put pressure on those in power to change course. After all, those in power ultimately rely on public consent.

It is true that politicians, including me, can find social movements uncomfortable, frustrating, utopian and sometimes just plain wrong. But they can also help politicians pushing for change who are struggling to make it happen. While I was climate change secretary there was a campaign to end the construction of coal-fired power stations, and I was invited to a 'green carpet' launch of a film called *The Age of Stupid* about the climate crisis starring the late Pete Postlethwaite. I had agreed to an onstage discussion after the film, and during it Pete ambushed me. He said he would give back his OBE if I let a new coal-fired station in Kent called Kingsnorth go ahead. I was fighting internal battles in government to try and shift policy, so I couldn't just say, 'OK, Pete.' I was definitely put on the spot. But actually I'm glad he did it. The campaign helped to change policy, and today new coal-fired power stations in the UK are unthinkable.

I said in the introduction to this part of the book that change can happen on three different levels: groups can seek to shift individual policies, the structure of power or the political conversation. It is on the third level of change that movements really come into their own. Veteran climate activist Bill McKibben, mentioned in Chapter 18, argues that social movements can be a 'bulldozer for reshaping the zeitgeist'.[25] While changing laws and the structure of power can help along the way, movements often focus on trying to shift the national conversation. This can be by demonstrating the scale of existing public support for an issue and so pushing it up the political agenda or, more ambitiously, by changing public opinion itself. By shifting the conversation, movements expand our idea of what change is possible. Indeed, the moral urgency with which movements call out injustices or political failures often makes the case that change *has* to be possible because the current situation is intolerable. Social movements mould the terrain on which 'normal politics' takes place.

That's true of campaigns for equality in the UK throughout history. Perhaps you have heard of Rosa Parks' refusal in 1955 to give up her seat on a bus in the US state of Alabama, leading to the Montgomery bus boycott and eventually the end of segregation on US buses, but you may not have heard of youth worker Paul Stephenson, who in 1963 led the Bristol bus boycott, protesting at the refusal of the Bristol Omnibus Company to employ Black or Asian drivers. The boycott lasted four months, drawing support from local residents as well as national and international attention. Eventually, on 28 August 1963, coincidentally the same day that Martin Luther King delivered his 'I Have a Dream' speech in Washington, the general manager of the Bristol Omnibus Company announced there would be no more racial discrimination in its employment practices. In 1965 the UK government passed the Race Relations Act outlawing 'racial discrimination in public places'; some have cited Stephenson's campaign as critical to the passing of the legislation.[26]

In 1989, Stonewall, now the leading LGBT charity in the UK, was formed to campaign against a pernicious law known as Section 28, which banned schools from 'teaching ... the acceptability of homosexuality'.[27] This was part of the Local Government Act of 1988 introduced by Margaret Thatcher's Conservative government. The age of consent for same-sex couples at that time was twenty-one and equal marriage rights far from the mainstream political agenda. By helping to change social attitudes, the movement of which Stonewall was a part and the activism of brave individuals ultimately forced politicians to act. That movement has led to a panoply of legislative changes: the equal age of consent and equal marriage, repealing the ban on military service, protection from discrimination at work and in the provision of services, laws against hate speech and crimes, the right of same-sex couples to adopt. With each change, more became possible.

This is not to say that every movement brings about big change. For every campaign that has changed the political tide, there are others that have not. One example that sceptics often point to is Occupy, the 2011 protests against inequality and corporate power held outside St Paul's in London, on Wall Street in New York and in other cities around the world. Occupy London had nine demands including 'an end to global tax injustice', 'authentic global equality' and 'a positive, sustainable economic system'.[28] The movement quickly petered out, and these goals clearly haven't been achieved. You could argue that Occupy helped push the issue of inequality up the political agenda – its slogan 'We Are the 99 per cent' has become mainstream – but its legacy is mixed at best.

So how do movements achieve political change? In *This Is an Uprising* social movements experts Mark and Paul Engler, while arguing that Occupy had some impact, say that it did not have 'a shared theory of how they would leverage change', meaning it was 'not well equipped to last beyond a brief cycle of revolt'.[29] In contrast, we've seen throughout this book that the most successful social movements have a theory of change. In other words, they have a reasonably well formed idea of what their goals are, the mechanisms by which their actions can help to achieve them and, crucially, how to persuade others to join them in taking action.

While community organising uses small-scale wins to build long-term power, movements often pursue large, transformational goals through short-term bursts of high-profile activity. This turns the community organising theory of change on its head. If organising thrives on incremental progress, mass mobilisation thrives on disrupting the status quo. Martin Luther King argued that this kind of action 'seeks so to dramatize the issue that it can no longer be ignored'.[30] Think of a demonstration. The aim is to get as many people on the streets at the same time as possible so that it is covered in the news, talked about on social media and noticed by politicians. When Extinction Rebellion protestors blocked roads and glued themselves to the ground, their goal was to disrupt in order to be noticed.

This kind of mobilisation requires lots of people, which are the vital resource that social movements have. Does that mean the way to bring about change is simply to get as many supporters of your cause as you can in one place? If only it was that straightforward. An influential study published in 2011 of 300 social movements across the world during the twentieth century found that every movement that mobilised more than 3.5 per cent of its country's population achieved its goals.[31] On this basis, some of Extinction Rebellion's organisers stated their aim was to get 3.5 per cent of Britain's population out onto the streets, which would have been about two million people. They did not succeed.[32] The appeal of the 3.5 per cent rule is that it provides something clear to aim for, but while numbers are important, they aren't enough. By some estimates around two million people joined the protests against the Iraq War in 2003, but we know that they did not succeed in getting the government to change course.[33] Numbers are a necessary but not sufficient ingredient for success.

Breadth of support also matters. In *This Is an Uprising* the Englers argue that any regime, policy or idea needs 'pillars of support'. These are different sections of society – the media, popular culture, religious organisations, academics, business – whose implicit approval is necessary for the status quo to have legitimacy.[34] So by building support across the range of society, movements can undermine the pillars that hold up the status quo to the point where it will collapse. The success of the divestment movement that we saw in Chapter 18 has been to build a broad coalition across religious groups, universities, city governments and philanthropic institutions to remove the support for continuing to extract fossil fuels.

By definition, building broad support requires activists to reach out beyond their comfort zones. As Alicia Garza, co-founder of Black Lives Matter, says, 'The longer I'm in the practice of building a movement, the more I realize that movement building isn't about finding your tribe – it's about growing your tribe across difference to focus on a common set of goals.'[35] Extinction Rebellion knew their actions would alienate some people, but to attract as broad a spectrum of support as possible they attempted to explain what they were doing by handing out leaflets to passers-by, for example, and after their first protest made an effort to clear up the mess. Perhaps that is one of the reasons why there was initially more public sympathy for them than might have been expected. For the same reason, the ill-judged attempt by a group of Extinction Rebellion protestors to obstruct a commuter train in east London and a protest at the cenotaph on 11 November understandably lost them public sympathy and set the movement back.[36]

I've said that movements often use mass mobilisation rather than small-scale organising to build support and momentum, but that's not the full story. To illustrate why, let's turn to an organisation which you probably won't think of with warmth. The National Rifle Association (NRA) is a body which campaigns for 'the right to bear arms' in the US, a right which they claim is guaranteed by the Second Amendment to the Constitution. When academic Hahrie Han, who grew up in Texas, began studying social movements she wondered why so many of the people she'd known at school ended up joining the NRA.[37] Despite appalling tragedy after tragedy, including mass shootings of children in both primary and secondary schools, the US appears no closer to implementing gun control measures. This is largely because of the successful campaigning of the NRA.

It is true that the NRA has deep pockets. These provide campaign funding for members of Congress who oppose even the most basic gun control legislation. But that's only part of the picture. Gun control advocates on the other side of the debate, such as former New York mayor Michael Bloomberg, also have deep pockets. They have also mobilised millions of people to take to the streets calling for change, so they're not lacking in numbers either.[38] Hahrie Han came to the realisation that all this misses the point. Movements cannot rely on mobilising alone; they also need to develop a base of engaged supporters who will stay involved over the long term. A single mobilisation is rarely enough to win, so movements need their supporters to turn up again and again.

Hahrie Han's friends at school hadn't always been die-hard gun advocates; they just wanted insurance for their guns and a range to shoot them in. The NRA offered both. The ability of the NRA to convert passive gun owners into an organised base of committed supporters is what has made it such a powerful group. New members form friendships with others in the association, build up a sense of community, and for some being a gun owner and NRA member becomes part of their identity. Eventually, members are persuaded to take more overt political action. The NRA is able to cultivate relationships with Republican politicians based on being able to deliver the support of a highly engaged movement, converting its base of supporters into political influence over the Republican Party.[39] Han doesn't argue that the groups on the other side of the debate lack committed supporters, but believes they are more focused on identifying people who agree with them and are already motivated to take action. Gun control groups are typically good at collecting the contact details of supporters and reminding them to go to protests, for example, but less good at converting people who are not already engaged in the issue into committed advocates for the cause.

Organising is often the foundation of a social movement. Alicia Garza and her fellow Black Lives Matter founders started out as activists in the community organising tradition, and this is no coincidence. The Black Lives Matter demonstrations that took place in Ferguson, Missouri in 2014 – among the first protests of the movement – grew out of the work of local community organising groups. The demonstrations didn't just happen spontaneously; they were the result of painstakingly going door to door, building relationships and persuading local residents to turn out for the cause.[40] This shouldn't surprise us. As we saw in Chapter 16, organising is about moving people to take action on the things that affect their lives. These can be individual issues in a community or larger problems which require fundamental changes in how society is run.

So the most successful movements build relationships and use these to transform potential supporters into engaged activists. This makes social media both a blessing and a curse for them. Digital tools make it easier to mobilise people for one-off action, but often at the expense of building those deep relationships. It took Civil Rights leaders more than a decade to organise the famous March on Washington in 1963. Today, thanks to social media, large protests are sometimes organised in a matter of days with hardly any coordination.[41] As a result, one study suggests that while this kind of action has become more common it is also less effective.[42] Organisers can spread the word with ease, but with so much less being invested by those involved there is less likelihood of being able to mobilise the same group again and sustain the movement over the long term. Alicia Garza puts it bluntly: 'I've been asked many times over the years what an ordinary person can do to build a movement from a hashtag. Though I know the question generally comes from an earnest place, I still cringe every time I am asked it. You cannot start a movement from a hashtag. Hashtags do not start movements – people do … . Only organising sustains movements.'[43]

To return to the question I started the whole book with: what have we learned about how to make the impossible possible? In this section we've seen both that incrementalism can be the route to profound change further down the line and that sometimes demands for transforming society can result in rapid shifts in the political debate. More fundamentally, we've seen that the distinction between the two can be overblown, and successful campaigns often involve an element of both. Black Lives Matter has offered a searing critique of racial injustice, without limiting its ambitions to what seems achievable. And yet that movement might never have come about had it not been for the experience of people such as Alicia Garza and the methods of community organising, the painstaking work of making change happen on the ground. Conversely, as we saw in Chapter 16, Citizens UK is rooted in the principles of community organising, and yet look how they've shifted the terms of debate around the living wage.

Change is often more possible than it might appear – and we can't just leave it to others. Take inspiration from the stories you have heard and the changes that have happened. Local campaigns, like those pioneered by the community organising movement and the work of Preston Council, national movements like the Fight for $15, global movements like Black Lives Matter and the divestment campaign: all have shown (in different ways) that they can change laws, change the structures of power and change the conversation and therefore what is possible.

Next time you feel angry about an injustice in our society, don't wait for someone else to fix the problem; start thinking about what you can do and who else you can work with. You might begin with a local campaign. Go door to door in your neighbourhood. Organise others in your workplace. Move your pension fund. Put pressure on your school, university or employer to act. Turn up to a demonstration – or even hold your own. Actions like these have been the roots of profound change throughout history. There is nothing so powerful as people joining with each other to form a movement for change. As the founder of community organising Saul Alinsky put it fifty years ago, 'Together we may find some of what we're looking for – laughter, beauty, love and the chance to create.'[44]

Conclusion

There are moments in history that demand we think big. Big change is hard. It requires ideas, arguments, movements to make it happen. But as we look around us, do we really think we can get away with anything less? We face a decades-long crisis of inequality and insecurity, a fractured society and alarming levels of distrust with our democracy. The coronavirus crisis has starkly exposed the deep inequalities and injustices of our country. Meanwhile, the spectre of the climate emergency looms and demands we reimagine an economy that has run for centuries on fossil fuels.

We must meet the moment by raising the scale of our ambitions for what politics can achieve. There is a new settlement to be built. As we recover from coronavirus, it is the least the British people have a right to expect. We will not achieve this new settlement unless a different guiding spirit animates the way we run our country. As I noted in the Introduction, the crises we face have not come about by accident. If we continue to judge our society by the success of those at the top and continue to believe that the market is our master rather than our servant, we will carry on as we are. We need to recognise a different set of values if we are to tackle the challenges we face.

This book has sketched out what a new order of things could look like. In place of the belief that wealth will trickle down from the top to everyone else, we need a new social contract with greater equality in which everyone has a stake. Rather than believing that market forces produce fair outcomes, we need to put markets in their place so we protect what we value. And we need to underpin these changes with a democratic renewal through which we can give people genuine control over their lives.

The ideas I've discussed are only a start. While important, they are ultimately less significant than how we think. Agree or disagree with different proposals, but let us not lower our ambitions. We need solutions equal to the scale of the injustices we face. Never think that the challenges we confront are too big to be tackled. For too long we have accepted that some things are inevitable, that they can't change, but collectively we created the institutions that we have and collectively we can remake them. Above all, this book has sought to put the case for our collective agency, for our ability, together, to right the world.

Think of the people in this book: Franklin Roosevelt and his New Deal, the Icelandic women strikers, Paul Stephenson and the Bristol bus boycott. All of them looked at the way the world was and said they were not going to accept it. Despite the odds, the obstacles, the forces of inertia, they were going to make the case for change. And then think of the other countries and places we have looked at where change has come about: from the Alaska dividend to the Swedish childcare system to Finnish work flexibility to Austrian votes at sixteen to New Zealand labour rights. People there looked at the way things were and said they could be different.

Let's not pretend it is easy. It isn't. It is far lonelier to make the case for things to be different than to argue they should stay the same. Far easier to accept the status quo. As Niccolò Macchiavelli wrote hundreds of years ago, 'There is nothing more difficult to take in hand, more perilous to conduct, or more uncertain in its success, than to take the lead in the introduction of a new order of things. For the reformer has enemies in all those who profit by the old order, and only lukewarm defenders in all those who would profit by the new order.'

So what can drive us forward? In every walk of life there are people who want something better: pupil climate strikers, B Corps businesspeople, public servants like Pat Hagan, Fight for $15 campaigners, changemakers in Preston. I could tell you many other stories of decent people striving for change, and I am sure you could tell me even more. Look around and you will feel less isolated. Inertia and opposition are overcome through the strength of people coming together. There is nothing as powerful as ordinary people making the case for change. That is indeed the lesson of history.

And what is remarkable is that when change does finally happen, what seemed impossible becomes the norm. For all the obstacles we face, the actual limits to what is possible are set only by our imagination. The NHS was a distant dream a hundred years ago; today it is our most treasured national institution. LGBT rights were unthinkable three decades ago; now they are widely embraced. The national minimum wage was bitterly opposed more than two decades ago; now it is hard to find anyone against it.

I think there is a reason for this. When change speaks to fundamental values of decency and justice, whatever the barriers in its way, it has a chance of success. I have a positive view of human nature. We do care about each other, we do have a deep well of empathy; it is the way our institutions are currently configured that holds us back. The collective response of the last year and more during the pandemic is the ultimate demonstration of what has been called 'the better angels of our nature' and how badly our institutions reflect the best of us. We have come together and looked after each other in all kinds of ways, in every walk of life and every part of our country. Let's now rebuild our country in that spirit.

One last thing. As I write these words, the face of a dear friend, Leo Panitch, dances in front of my eyes. Leo died of Covid at Christmas 2020. For the quarter of a century after the death of my dad, he did a lot to fill the void. It is a terrible loss. Leo and I would often argue about politics, but he used to say something that I believe is important. He would say the struggle that is worth engaging in always extends beyond one's lifetime.

Anyone who fights for progress and justice stands in the footsteps of those who have gone before and prepares the trail for those who come after. This is a struggle that can progress but which will never end. That isn't pessimism but optimism. We take the baton and we pass it on.

There is so much to fight for in the here and now. What happens in the next decade or two will have long-standing consequences. There are good people everywhere who believe in something better for our societies. You are not alone. We are not alone. If we join together we will succeed.

Acknowledgements

I always love reading acknowledgements because I think they say a lot about the author. Now I am feeling the pressure. The debts for this book are numerous and profound, so I will do my best.

First, I want to thank the people who were the founders of the project. That begins with Geoff Lloyd. I met Geoff when he interviewed me in 2015, and if I had gone on to win the election maybe I would not have got to know him any better. One of the upsides of election defeat has been to get to be his friend. He is one of the most generous, kind, patient, sensitive, loving people you will ever meet. As this project took shape, he showed that huge generosity in letting me adapt the RTBC brand for this book. Thank you to him and Sara, his wife, Gene, his son, and Sara's parents, Lynn and Joe Barron, for welcoming me into their lives.

Also, the whole RTBC production, research and back-up team past and present deserves many thanks, in particular Emma Corsham, Alex Feis-Bryce and Joe Kenyon. All of our guests too have played an incredible part in making this book happen.

Then comes Lynsey Tod who has run my office and my life since 2015 and who was the number one believer in this book. It would not have happened without her. My agent Andrew Gordon also deserves huge thanks for sticking with me from 2015, for helping shape the concept of the book and for his encouragement, ideas and input throughout the project. I would also like to express profuse thanks to Will Hammond from The Bodley Head for believing in the book, too – and for his brilliant editing, hugely important insights as well as his great patience and understanding.

Next come the people who made the book possible. Joel Pearce is a hero. This book would simply never have happened without him. His research, his drafting, his advice, his insights, his enormous dedication way beyond the call of duty: I owe him so much and I reflect this in the front of the book. Thanks also go to Claire Cappaert for her research work early on in the process. I also want to mention Guy Shrubsole who first told me to 'go big or go home' some years ago. The phrase stuck with me.

Writing twenty chapters about different subjects turns out to be really hard – much harder than I realised it would be. I am so grateful to the people who actually knew a lot about the subjects for their assistance.

In chapter order, I want to thank: Martin O'Neill for his insights on the social contract; Emily Shuckburgh, Tobias Garnett, Matt Pennycook MP and Alan Whitehead MP for their insights on climate and energy; Mike Amesbury MP, Alastair Harper, Charlie Trew and Chris Wood on social housing; Anthony Painter and Jonathan Reynolds MP on UBI and social security; Halla Gunnarsdóttir on Iceland and gender equality; Sam Smethers on parental leave; and Luke Fletcher, Will Hutton, Paul Lindley, Colin Mayer and Jason Stockwood on purposeful business.

Thank you to Christine Berry and Liz Kendall MP for their thoughts on care and to Karel Williams for his thinking and dialogue on the foundational economy; George Bangham and Will Stronge for such important insights on working time; and Chi Onwurah MP for her thinking and help on technology. Thanks to James Fishkin for reading a key section of the book on deliberative democracy and to Steve Reed MP and Sarah Longlands for commenting on the chapter on devolution. Thank you to Hilary Cottam, Sue Goss and Adam Lent for helping me get to grips with the issues around the role of the state and to Damian Allen for looking over that chapter, Ewan McGaughey for his insights on worker voice and Joe Fortune for his thoughts on the role of co-ops. Profound thanks, too, to Kate Bell and Andy McDonald MP for their insights on the different chapters on workers and trade unions.

Big thanks to Matt Bolton, Jonathan Cox and Dan Firth for reading and commenting on the chapter on community organising; Will Lawrence and Nick Robins for their thoughts on the divestment chapter; Matthew Brown for guiding us through the Preston story and to Hahrie Han for providing feedback on the chapter on social movements.

I am also indebted to Alan Buckle, Charlie Falconer, Daniel Jones, Gavin Kelly and Mathew Lawrence for reading a number of chapters and offering incredibly helpful and intelligent insights.

Thank you profoundly to Juliet Eales, Jonty Leibowitz, Olly Nicholson, Francesca Phillips and Lynsey Tod for their insights and support. Then big thanks to three outside readers who I turned to because of my belief in their wisdom, intelligence and values: Melissa Benn, Marc Stears and Stewart Wood. You more than met your task, your comments were invaluable and I am truly grateful.

Once the book was written, further hard work began, and I am grateful to Hugh Thraves Davies for his masterful copy-editing and to the team at The Bodley Head – Stuart Williams, Alison Davies, Sophie Painter, Rosanna Boscawen and Oli Grant – and also thank you so much to Chris Thompson for producing the audiobook and masterfully helping me through the process of reading it aloud.

Of course, a book does not exist by itself and sits in a context of thinking, ideas and argument developed over a long period. I want to thank those who made possible my visiting fellowship at the Center for European Studies at Harvard University from 2002 to 2004, in particular Trisha Craig and Peter Hall. Things I wrote at the time, and the teaching I did back then, have helped guide some of the thinking of this book, particularly on the role of markets. Thanks also go to Jenny Andersson, with whom I had the pleasure of teaching a class on politics at Sciences Po in Autumn 2018, and the staff and students there.

I also want to thank in particular all my staff who worked for me as Leader of the Opposition from 2010 to 2015 and who supported and sustained me with such great dedication, loyalty and friendship – and taught me so much – as well as all the staff at the Labour party and its members and supporters for their encouragement. Profound thanks also go to my Doncaster office for supporting and teaching me, too, ever since 2005: Chris Taylor, Keir Dawson, Kevin Rodgers, Laura Wigan, Robert Gibbon and the incredible, dedicated Dianne Williams. I also owe enormous thanks to the Labour party members in Doncaster North who have shown such loyalty to me and the voters who have given me the profound honour of electing me to fight for them since 2005.

Then there are all the colleagues and friends who have supported me since 2015. I particularly want to thank Jill Cuthbertson for staying on after the 2015 election, when I wasn't at my most joyful, as well as Simon Alcock, Tom Baldwin, Greg Beales, Torsten Bell, Hilary Benn MP, Karen Buck MP, Sir Stuart Etherington, Paul Greengrass, Ayesha Hazarika, Ros Jones, Jonathan Kestenbaum, Rachel Kinnock, Tim Livesey, Lindsay Mackie, Rosamund McCarthy, Ronnie O'Sullivan, Lucy Powell MP, Rachel Reeves MP, Bob Roberts, Josie Rourke, Alan Rusbridger, Henry Tinsley, Jon Trickett MP and Anna Yearley. I also want to express particular thanks to my constituency neighbour and great friend Rosie Winterton MP and to Charlie Falconer for his amazing and loyal friendship and for always being there throughout the last few years.

Readers, colleagues, friends have all been crucial in the genesis and production of this book but my family and upbringing obviously shaped the person I am and therefore what is in these pages. I want to thank my Mum and Dad for their love and for inspiring me to care about the world, and so too my brother David.

Above all, thanks to Justine, who has been my partner, supporter and friend for more than fifteen years. We have been through so much together, and I love you very much. And then my special boys, Daniel and Sam: you are both unique, lovely people, and I am so proud of you. The good news is that now this book is over, Dad will have more time. This book is dedicated to Justine, Daniel and Sam. Thank you for your love and support. It makes life worth living.

Notes

Introduction

1 www.mutual-aid.co.uk, 'Mutual Aid', https://www.mutual-aid.co.uk/.
2 Míriam Juan-Torres, Tim Dixon and Arisa Kimaram, 'Britain's Choice: Common Ground and Division in 2020s Britain', *More in Common*, 2020, 250, https://www.britainschoice.uk/media/ecrevsbt/0917-mic-uk-britain-s-choice_report_dec01.pdf.
3 Antonio Gramsci, *Selections from the Prison Notebooks of Antonio Gramsci*, ed. Geoffrey Nowell-Smith and Quintin Hoare (London: Lawrence and Wishart, 1971).
4 Neil Prior, 'How World War One Heralded Social Reforms', *BBC News*, 12 November 2018, https://www.bbc.co.uk/news/uk-wales-46118040.
5 William Beveridge, *Social Insurance and Allied Services: Report by Sir William Beveridge* (London: HM Stationery Office, 1942).
6 Margaret Thatcher, *The Downing Street Years* (London: HarperCollins, 1993), 677.
7 For an overview of the history of privatisation, see Institute for Government, 'The Privatisation of British Telecom', 2012, https://www.instituteforgovernment.org.uk/sites/default/files/british_telecom_privatisation.pdf.
8 Jessica Brain, 'The Birth of the NHS', *Historic UK*, 2020, https://www.historic-uk.com/HistoryUK/HistoryofBritain/Birth-of-the-NHS/.
9 Named after a relatively little known think-thank employee, the late Joseph Overton. Mackinac Center for Public Policy, 'The Overton Window', 2021, https://www.mackinac.org/OvertonWindow.

I. A New Social Contract

1 For example, see Conor D'Arcy and Laura Gardiner, 'The Generation of Wealth: Asset Accumulation across and within Cohorts', *Resolution Foundation*, 2017, https://www.resolutionfoundation.org/app/uploads/2017/06/Wealth.pdf.

2   Trussell Trust, 'Mid-Year Stats', 12 November 2020, https://www.trusselltrust.
    org/news-and-blog/latest-stats/mid-year-stats/; Joseph Rowntree Foundation, 'UK
    Poverty 2020/21', 13 January 2021, https://www.jrf.org.uk/report/uk-poverty-
    2020–21.
3   Matthew Taylor, 'The Power to Create (in about 5 Minutes)', *RSA*, 21 July
    2014, https://www.thersa.org/blog/matthew-taylor/2014/07/the-power-to-create-
    in-about-5-minutes.
4   Marii Paskov and Caroline Dewilde, 'Income Inequality and Solidarity in
    Europe', *GINI Discussion Paper* 33, 2012, http://www.gini-research.org/system/
    uploads/379/original/DP_33_-_Paskov_Dewilde.pdf; Richard Wilkinson and Kate
    Pickett, *The Spirit Level: Why Equality Is Better for Everyone* (London: Penguin
    Books, 2010), 49–62.

1. *The End of the World*

1   UNFCCC, 'COP15: Copenhagen Accord – Draft Decision', 2009, 1, https://
    unfccc.int/resource/docs/2009/cop15/eng/l07.pdf.
2   'Copenhagen deal reaction in quotes', *BBC News*, 19 December 2009, https://
    www.https://news.bbc.co.uk/1/hi/sci/tech/8421910.stm.
3   NASA Earth Observatory, 'World of Change: Global Temperatures', https://
    earthobservatory.nasa.gov/world-of-change/global-temperatures.
4   World Meteorological Organization, 'WMO Statement on the State of the Global
    Climate in 2019', 2020, 3, 18–19, 21–22, 25–28, https://library.wmo.int/index.
    php?lvl=notice_display&id=21700#.X7a6T-Vxc2z.
5   UNFCCC, 'Paris Agreement', 2015, https://unfccc.int/sites/default/files/english_
    paris_agreement.pdf.
6   UN News, 'UN Emissions Report: World on Course for More than 3 Degree
    Spike, Even If Climate Commitments Are Met', 26 November 2019, https://news.
    un.org/en/story/2019/11/1052171.
7   IPCC, 'Special Report: Global Warming of 1.5 °C – Summary for Policymakers',
    2018, https://www.ipcc.ch/sr15/chapter/spm/.
8   IPCC, 'Summary for Policymakers of IPCC Special Report on Global Warming
    of 1.5°C Approved by Governments', 8 October 2018, https://www.ipcc.ch/
    2018/10/08/summary-for-policymakers-of-ipcc-special-report-on-global-warming-
    of-1-5c-approved-by-governments/.
9   The White House, 'Statement by President Trump on the Paris Climate Accord',
    1 June 2017, https://trumpwhitehouse.archives.gov/briefings-statements/statement-
    president-trump-paris-climate-accord/.
10 CDP, 'New Report Shows Just 100 Companies Are Source of over 70 per cent
    of Emissions', 10 July 2017, https://www.cdp.net/en/articles/media/new-report-
    shows-just-100-companies-are-source-of-over-70-of-emissions.
11 George Torr, 'Mayor's Fury Over Doncaster Flood Funding Snub', *Doncaster
    Free Press*, 6 August 2020, https://www.doncasterfreepress.co.uk/news/politics/
    council/mayors-fury-over-doncaster-flood-funding-snub-2934483.
12 Phil Holmes et al., 'Doncaster Flood Recovery Report', *Doncaster Council*,
    29 September 2020, 1, https://dmbcwebstolive01.blob.core.windows.net/media/
    Default/Emergencies/Documents/Doncaster%20Flood%20Recovery..pdf; Amanda
    Blanc, 'Independent Review of Flood Insurance in Doncaster', *Department for
    Environment, Food & Rural Affairs*, June 2020, 5, https://assets.publishing.service.

gov.uk/government/uploads/system/uploads/attachment_data/file/932523/review-flood-insurance-doncaster.pdf.

13 Zeke Hausfather, 'Analysis: Why Children Must Emit Eight Times Less CO2 Than Their Grandparents', *Carbon Brief*, 10 April 2019, https://www.carbonbrief.org/analysis-why-children-must-emit-eight-times-less-co2-than-their-grandparents.

14 The Green New Deal Group, 'History of the Green New Deal', https://greennewdealgroup.org/history-of-the-green-new-deal/.

15 Doris Kearns Goodwin, *Leadership In Turbulent Times* (New York: Simon & Schuster, 2018), 275.

16 Franklin D. Roosevelt, 'The Only Thing We Have to Fear Is Fear Itself', *Guardian*, 25 April 2007, https://www.theguardian.com/theguardian/2007/apr/25/greatspeeches.

17 Federal Works Agency, 'Final Report on the WPA Program 1935–43', 1946, 118–50, http://lcweb2.loc.gov/service/gdc/scd0001/2008/20080212001fi/20080212001fi.pdf; New York Times, 'WPA Ups and Quits', *New York Times*, 1 July 1943, https://timesmachine.nytimes.com/timesmachine/1943/07/01/88549554.pdf?pdf_redirect=true&ip=0.

18 History Central, 'The Civilian Conservation Corp,' 2021, https://mail.historycentral.com/DEP/CCC.html.

19 Goodwin, *Leadership In Turbulent Times*, 292.

20 Louise Hall, 'AOC and Squad Members Lobby for Biden to Accept Green New Deal Outside DNC', *Independent*, 20 November 2020, https://www.independent.co.uk/news/world/americas/us-politics/aoc-squad-green-new-deal-rally-dnc-b1759353.html.

21 Terrell Jermaine Starr, 'Meet Rhiana Gunn-Wright, the Black Woman Behind the Green New Deal', *The Root*, 18 December 2019, https://www.theroot.com/meet-the-black-woman-who-is-the-brains-behind-the-green-1840509307.

22 Martina Jackson Haynes, Jacqueline Patterson and Larissa Johnson, 'Coal Blooded Action Toolkit', *NAACP Environmental and Climate Justice Program*, 2013, 6, https://www.naacp.org/wp-content/uploads/2016/04/Coal_Blooded_Action_Toolkit_FINAL_FINAL.pdf.

23 Juan-Torres, Dixon and Kimaram, 'Britain's Choice: Common Ground and Division in 2020s Britain', 227–246.

24 Gemma Holmes et al., 'UK Housing: Fit for the Future?' *Committee on Climate Change*, 2019, 27, https://www.theccc.org.uk/publication/uk-housing-fit-for-the-future/.

25 Climate Change Committee, 'The Sixth Carbon Budget: The UK's Path to Net Zero', 2020, 22, https://www.theccc.org.uk/publication/sixth-carbon-budget/.

26 Matthew Taylor, 'Manchester Theatre Staff Use Skills to Upgrade Homes after Covid Layoffs', *Guardian*, 22 November 2020, https://www.theguardian.com/uk-news/2020/nov/22/manchester-theatre-staff-upgrade-homes-covid-layoffs-retrofitting-scheme.

27 Oil and Gas UK, 'Major Employer', 2021, https://oilandgasuk.co.uk/key-facts/major-employer/.

28 Nathalie Thomas and Chris Tighe, 'Why UK Pledge to Become "Saudi Arabia" of Wind Power Rings Hollow', *Financial Times*, 8 January 2021, https://www.ft.com/content/50cd8a9d-3f2a-461d-9335-08319c5f7626.

29 IndustriALL, 'Spanish Coal Unions Win Landmark Just Transition Deal', 1 November 2018, http://www.industriall-union.org/spanish-coal-unions-win-landmark-just-transition-deal; Teresa Ribera, 'A Just Transition with Climate and Social Ambition,' *Social Europe*, 21 January 2020, https://www.social

europe.eu/a-just-transition-with-climate-and-social-ambition; Arthur Neslen, 'Spain to Close Most Coalmines in €250m Transition Deal', *Guardian*, 26 October 2018, https://www.theguardian.com/environment/2018/oct/26/spain-to-close-most-coal-mines-after-striking-250m-deal.

30 IndustriALL, 'Just Transition for Spanish Thermal Power Plant Workers', 24 April 2020, http://www.industriall-union.org/just-transition-for-spanish-energy-workers.

31 Sarah Young, 'Britain Extends COVID Funding for Railways Ahead of Contract Shake-Up', *Reuters*, 21 September 2020, https://www.reuters.com/article/uk-health-coronavirus-britain-rail/britain-extends-covid-funding-for-railways-ahead-of-contract-shake-up-idUKKCN26C0KB.

32 Climate Change Committee, 'The Sixth Carbon Budget: The UK's Path to Net Zero', 5.

33 Direct Line Group, 'Electric Dreams: Green Vehicles Cheaper Than Petrol', 29 June 2020, https://www.directlinegroup.co.uk/en/news/brand-news/2020/29062020.html.

2. A Housing Revolution

1 Jürgen Czernohorszky, '27. Mind the (Wealth) Gap: a social wealth fund for Britain', *Reasons to be Cheerful with Ed Miliband and Geoff Lloyd*, 26 March 2018, https://podcasts.apple.com/us/podcast/episode-27-mind-wealth-gap-social-wealth-fund-for-britain/id1287081706?i=1000407459295.

2 City of Vienna, 'Municipal Housing in Vienna. History, Facts & Figures', 2018, 22, https://www.wienerwohnen.at/dokumente-downloads.html.

3 URBED Trust and Shelter, 'Learning from International Examples of Affordable Housing', 2018, 1, https://assets.ctfassets.net/6sxvmndnpnos/6mvsDCkpUoz2x LJypI5Wmk/574e0f70d447b24075f89af8c57fb17e/International_examples_of_affordable_housing_-_Shelter_URBED_Trust.pdf.

4 Ibid. 1.

5 City of Vienna, 'Housing in Vienna Annual Report 2018/2019', 2019, 11, https://www.wohnbauforschung.at/index.php?inc=download&id=5923.

6 URBED Trust and Shelter, 'Learning from International Examples of Affordable Housing', 5–7.

7 Shelter, 'A Vision for Social Housing', 2018, 74, https://england.shelter.org.uk/__data/assets/pdf_file/0005/1642613/Shelter_UK_-_A_vision_for_social_housing_full_interactive_report.pdf.

8 MHCLG, 'English Housing Survey: Headline Report', 2020, 6,10, https://assets.publishing.service.gov.uk/government/uploads/system/uploads/attachment_data/file/945013/2019–20_EHS_Headline_Report.pdf; ONS, 'UK Private Rented Sector: 2018', 2018, https://www.ons.gov.uk/economy/inflationandpriceindices/articles/ukprivaterentedsector/2018.

9 ONS, 'UK Private Rented Sector: 2018'.

10 Shelter, 'A Vision for Social Housing', 38.

11 Shelter, 'Shelter Briefing: Urgent Question on the End of the Eviction Moratorium', 1, https://england.shelter.org.uk/__data/assets/pdf_file/0007/1952494/Briefing_-_UQ_End_of_Evictions_Moratorium.pdf.

12 Cecil Sagoe et al., 'Making Renting Fairer for Private Renters', *Shelter*, 2020, 7, https://england.shelter.org.uk/__data/assets/pdf_file/0019/2012239/Time_for_Change_-_Making_Renting_Fairer_for_Private_Renters.pdf.

13 Caroline Rogers et al., 'Touch and Go', *Citizens Advice*, 2018, 2, https://www.citi zensadvice.org.uk/Global/CitizensAdvice/Housing%20Publications/Touch%20 and%20go%20-%20Citizens%20Advice.pdf,'; Shelter, 'A Vision for Social Housing', 13.

14 ONS, 'Living Longer: Changes in Housing Tenure over Time', 2020, 4, https:// www.ons.gov.uk/peoplepopulationandcommunity/birthsdeathsandmarriages/ ageing/articles/livinglonger/changesinhousingtenureovertime#how-has-housing-tenure-for-older-people-changed-over-time.

15 MHCLG, 'Local Authority Housing Statistics 2018/2019, Section C', 2019.

16 B. R. Mitchell, *British Historical Statistics* (Cambridge: Cambridge University Press, 1988), 382–95.

17 John Boughton, *Municipal Dreams – The Rise and Fall of Council Housing* (London: Verso, 2018), 105.

18 MHCLG, 'Live Tables on Housing Supply: Indicators of New Supply, Table 244', 2020, https://www.gov.uk/government/statistical-data-sets/live-tables-on-house-building.

19 Boughton, *Municipal Dreams – The Rise and Fall of Council Housing*, 171.

20 MHCLG, 'Live Tables on Housing Supply: Indicators of New Supply, Table 244'.

21 MHCLG, 'Live Tables on Social Housing Sales, Table 678', 2020, https://www. gov.uk/government/statistical-data-sets/live-tables-on-social-housing-sales.

22 Mark Stephens, Christine Whitehead and Moira Munro, 'Lessons from the Past, Challenges for the Future for Housing Policy – An Evaluation of English Housing Policy 1975–2000', 2005, 6, http://www.ahuri.edu.au/downloads/2005_Events/ Christine_Whitehead/UK_Housing_Policy_1975_2000.pdf; House of Commons Library, 'Welfare-Expenditure-and-Savings-Tool-(WEST)', 2020, https://common slibrary.parliament.uk/research-briefings/cbp-7667/.

23 Shelter, 'A Vision for Social Housing', 110.

24 Crisis and National Housing Federation, 'Housing Supply Requirements across Great Britain: For Low-Income Households and Homeless People', 2018, https:// www.crisis.org.uk/media/239700/crisis_housing_supply_requirements_across_ great_britain_2018.pdf.

25 Pete Jefferys and Toby Lloyd, 'New Civic Housebuilding 2017: Rediscovering Our Tradition of Building Beautiful and Affordable Homes', *Shelter*, 2017, 18, https://england.shelter.org.uk/__data/assets/pdf_file/0005/1348223/2017_03_02_ New_Civic_Housebuilding_Policy_Report.pdf.

26 MHCLG, 'Live Tables on Affordable Housing Supply – Table 1000', 2020, https://www.gov.uk/government/statistical-data-sets/live-tables-on-affordable-housing-supply.

27 Shelter, 'New Data Makes the Case for a New Generation of Social Homes', 29 January 2020, https://blog.shelter.org.uk/2020/01/new-data-makes-the-case-for-a-new-generation-of-social-homes/.

28 Martin Moore-Bick, 'Phase 1 Report Overview – Report of the Public Inquiry into the Fire at Grenfell Tower on 14 June 2017', *Grenfell Tower Inquiry*, 2019, 24, https://assets.grenfelltowerinquiry.org.uk/GTI%20-%20Phase%201% 20report%20Executive%20Summary.pdf.

29 Shelter, 'One in 10 Forced to Report Same Problem with Their Social Home More than 10 Times', 10 June 2019, https://england.shelter.org.uk/media/press_release/one_ in_10_forced_to_report_same_problem_with_their_social_home_more_than_10_ times.

30 Shelter, 'A Vision for Social Housing', 50.

31 Ibid. 59.

32 RIBA, 'Norwich Council Estate Named UK's Best New Building – 2019 RIBA Stirling Prize Winner', 8 October 2019, https://www.architecture.com/knowledge-and-resources/knowledge-landing-page/norwich-council-estate-named-uks-best-new-building-2019-riba-stirling-prize-winner.

33 ONS, 'UK Private Rented Sector: 2018'; Shelter, 'A Vision for Social Housing', 119.

34 Shelter, 'A Vision for Social Housing', 181–184.

35 Ruth Lang, 'Architects Take Command: The LCC Architects' Department', *Volume* 41, 2014, 33, http://volumeproject.org/architects-take-command-the-lcc-architects-department/.

36 John Boughton points out that *Town Planning* by planner Thomas Sharp sold 250,000 copies after it was published in 1940 – the bestselling book ever on town planning. See Boughton, *Municipal Dreams – The Rise and Fall of Council Housing,* 69. .

37 Hansard, 'Housing Bill HC Deb 16 March', 1949, https://api.parliament.uk/historic-hansard/commons/1949/mar/16/housing-bill.

38 Equality Trust, 'A House Divided: How Unaffordable Housing Drives UK Inequality', 2016, 6, https://www.equalitytrust.org.uk/sites/default/files/resource/attachments/A%20House%20Divided%20-%20How%20Unaffordable%20Housing%20Drives%20UK%20Inequality%20.pdf; Shelter, 'A Vision for Social Housing', 43; Social Mobility Commission, 'Social Mobility in Great Britain – State of the Nation 2018 to 2019', 2019, 16–18, https://assets.publishing.service.gov.uk/government/uploads/system/uploads/attachment_data/file/798404/SMC_State_of_the_Nation_Report_2018–19.pdf.

39 Steve Akehurst, 'Six Take Aways From Our Polling in Marginal Seats', *Shelter Blog,* 28 September 2018, https://blog.shelter.org.uk/2018/09/six-take-aways-from-our-polling-in-marginal-seats/.

40 BBC News, 'Meet the Residents of the Riba Stirling Prize-Winning Passivhaus', 9 October 2019, https://www.bbc.co.uk/news/in-pictures-49964986.

3. Free to Choose

1 Thomas Paine, *Agrarian Justice,* 1797, https://en.wikisource.org/wiki/Agrarian_Justice.

2 Mike Dunleavy, 'Alaska PFD Applicants', 2020, https://gov.alaska.gov/dunleavy/alaska-pfd-applicants/.

3 Damon Jones and Ioana Marinescu, 'The Labor Market Impacts of Universal and Permanent Cash Transfers: Evidence from the Alaska Permanent Fund', *National Bureau of Economic Research,* 2020, 1–3, https://www.nber.org/system/files/working_papers/w24312/w24312.pdf.

4 Alaska Permanent Fund Corporation, 'Frequently Asked Questions. Why Did Alaskans Create the Fund?' 2020, https://apfc.org/frequently-asked-questions/#why-did-alaskans-create-the-fund.

5 Economic Security Project, 'Alaska Statewide Telephone Survey of 1004 Voters', 2017, https://www.scribd.com/document/352375996/ESP-Alaska-PFD-Phone-Survey-Graphs-Spring-2017-pdf.

6 Jay Hammond, 'Diapering the Devil: How Alaska Helped Staunch Befouling by Mismanaged Oil Wealth: A Lesson for Other Oil Rich Nations', *The Governor's Solution: How Alaska's Oil Dividend Could Work in Iraq and Other Oil-Rich Countries* (Washington DC: Brookings Institution Press, 2012), 33.

7 Paine, *Agrarian Justice*.

8 Joseph Rowntree Foundation, 'UK Poverty 2020/21 Full Report', 2021, 18, https://www.jrf.org.uk/report/uk-poverty-2020–21.

9 Delphine Strauss, 'Millions of Self-Employed Left out of Latest UK Support Scheme', *Financial Times*, 8 November 2020, https://www.ft.com/content/aa5b8d62-1f16-4ee4-bbbd-aa35b85fa5de.

10 The Trussell Trust, 'UK Food Banks Report Busiest Month Ever, as Coalition Urgently Calls for Funding to Get Money into People's Pockets Quickly during Pandemic', 3 June 2020, https://www.trusselltrust.org/2020/06/03/food-banks-busiest-month/.

11 Money Charity, 'The Money Statistics: September 2020', 2020, 16, https://themoneycharity.org.uk/media/September-2020-Money-Statistics.pdf.

12 G. Bangham, 'In This Coronavirus Crisis, Do Families Have Enough Savings to Make Ends Meet?' *Resolution Foundation*, 3 April 2020, https://www.resolutionfoundation.org/comment/in-this-coronavirus-crisis-do-families-have-enough-savings-to-make-ends-meet/.

13 Joseph Rowntree Foundation, 'UK Poverty 2020/21 Full Report', 4–7.

14 Trust for London, 'Poverty Definitions and Thresholds', 2021, https://www.trustforlondon.org.uk/data/poverty-thresholds/.

15 Andrew Yang, 'The Freedom Dividend', 2020, https://www.yang2020.com/policies/the-freedom-dividend/.

16 Rutger Bregman, 'The Bizarre Tale of President Nixon and His Basic Income Bill', *Correspondent*, 17 May 2016, https://thecorrespondent.com/4503/the-bizarre-tale-of-president-nixon-and-his-basic-income-bill/173117835-c34d6145; Jordan Weissman, 'Martin Luther King's Economic Dream: A Guaranteed Income for All Americans', *Atlantic*, 28 August 2013, https://www.theatlantic.com/business/archive/2013/08/martin-luther-kings-economic-dream-a-guaranteed-income-for-all-americans/279147/; Scotty Hendricks, 'The Right-Wing Case for Basic Income', *Big Think*, 11 June 2019, https://bigthink.com/politics-current-affairs/negative-income-tax?rebelltitem=1#rebelltitem1; Kaitlyn Wang, 'Why Mark Zuckerberg Wants to Give You Free Cash, No Questions Asked', *Inc*, 2018, https://www.inc.com/kaitlyn-wang/mark-zuckerberg-elon-musk-universal-basic-income.html.

17 Dylan Matthews, 'Hillary Clinton Almost Ran for President on a Universal Basic Income', *Vox*, 12 September 2017, https://www.vox.com/policy-and-politics/2017/9/12/16296532/hillary-clinton-universal-basic-income-alaska-for-america-peter-barnes.

18 David Finch and Laura Gardiner, 'Back in Credit? Universal Credit after Budget 2018', *Resolution Foundation*, 2018, 13, https://www.resolutionfoundation.org/app/uploads/2018/11/Back-in-Credit-UC-after-Budget-2018.pdf.

19 Patrick Butler and Sarah Butler, 'Bonus Blow for Greggs Staff Prompts Call for Benefit and Tax Rethink', *Guardian*, 13 January 2020, https://www.theguardian.com/society/2020/jan/13/bonus-blow-for-greggs-staff-prompts-call-for-benefit-and-tax-rethink.

20 The Economist, 'Tax and Benefits – Greggs and the Vegan Sausage Roll Bonus', 18 January 2020, https://www.economist.com/britain/2020/01/18/greggs-and-the-vegan-sausage-roll-bonus.

21 Mike Brewer, David Finch and Daniel Tomlinson, 'Universal Remedy: Ensuring Universal Credit Is Fit for Purpose', *Resolution Foundation*, 2017, 36, https://www.resolutionfoundation.org/app/uploads/2017/10/Universal-Credit.pdf.

22 IFS, 'Current Tax Rates and Past Rates, 1973-2000', 2000, https://www.ifs.org.uk/ff/fiscalfacts2000.xls.

23 Welfare Conditionality Project, 'Final Findings Report', 2018, 4, http://www.welfareconditionality.ac.uk/wp-content/uploads/2018/06/40475_Welfare-Conditionality_Report_complete-v3.pdf.

24 Ioana Marinescu, 'No Strings Attached: The Behavioral Effects of U.S. Unconditional Cash Transfer Programs,' *National Bureau of Economic Research*, 2018, 2, https://www.nber.org/system/files/working_papers/w24337/w24337.pdf.

25 Kela, 'Results of Finland's Basic Income Experiment: Small Employment Effects, Better Perceived Economic Security and Mental Wellbeing,' 6 May 2020, https://www.kela.fi/web/en/news-archive/-/asset_publisher/lNo8GY2nIrZo/content/results-of-the-basic-income-experiment-small-employment-effects-better-perceived-economic-security-and-mental-wellbeing.

26 Economic Security Project, 'Executive Summary of Findings from a Survey of Alaska Voters on the PFD', 2017, https://www.scribd.com/document/352375988/ESP-Alaska-PFD-Phone-Survey-Executive-Summary-Spring-2017.

27 Marinescu, 'No Strings Attached: The Behavioral Effects Of U.S. Unconditional Cash Transfer Programs', 9.

28 Scott Goldsmith, 'The Alaska Permanent Fund Dividend: A Case Study in Implementation of a Basic Income Guarantee', 2010, 12, https://iseralaska.org/publications/?id=1296.

29 Kela, 'Results of Finland's Basic Income Experiment'.

30 Aleksi Neuvonen and Maria Malho, 'Universalism in the Next Era - Moving Beyond Redistribution', *Demos Helsinki*, 2019, 10, https://www.demoshelsinki.fi/julkaisut/universalism-in-the-next-era-moving-beyond-redistribution/.

31 André Gorz, 'On the Difference Between Society and Community, and Why Basic Income Cannot by Itself Confer Full Membership of Either', ed. Philippe Van Parijs, *Arguing for Basic Income: Ethical Foundations for a Radical Reform* (London: Verso, 1992), 184.

32 Luke Martinelli, 'Assessing the Case for a Universal Basic Income in the UK', *IPR Working Paper*, 2017, 43, http://www.bath.ac.uk/publications/assessing-the-case-for-a-universal-basic-income-in-the-uk/attachments/basic_income_policy_brief.pdf.

33 Luke Martinelli, 'The Fiscal and Distributional Implications of Alternative Universal Basic Income Schemes in the UK', *IPR Working Paper*, 2017, 20–21, http://www.mysearch.org.uk/website2/pdf/Analysis-2.pdf

34 Richard Titmuss, *Commitment to Welfare* (London: Allen and Unwin, 1968), 134; Walter Korpi and Joakim Palme, 'The Paradox of Redistribution and Strategies of Equality: Welfare State Institutions, Inequality, and Poverty in the Western Countries', *American Sociological Review* 63:5, 1998, https://doi.org/10.2307/2657333.

35 Korpi and Palme, 'The Paradox of Redistribution and Strategies of Equality', 36.

36 Kevin Peachey, 'Child Trust Funds: Teenagers Get First Chance to Access Cash', *BBC News*, 1 September 2020, https://www.bbc.co.uk/news/business-53935933.

37 HMRC, 'Teenagers to Get Access to Child Trust Funds for First Time', 19 August 2020, https://www.gov.uk/government/news/teenagers-to-get-access-to-child-trust-funds-for-first-time; Gavin Kelly, 'The Child Trust Fund Comes of Age', *Resolution Foundation*, 29 August 2020, https://www.resolutionfoundation.org/comment/the-child-trust-fund-comes-of-age/.

38 Abigail McKnight, 'Estimates of the Asset-Effect: The Search for a Causal Effect of Assets on Adult Health and Employment Outcomes', June 2011, 29–56, http://eprints.lse.ac.uk/43896/1/CASEpaper149.pdf.

39 McKnight, 'Estimates of the Asset-Effect: The Search for a Causal Effect of Assets on Adult Health and Employment Outcomes', 54–55.

40 Gavin Kelly, '156. Bond Baby Bond: Guaranteeing an inheritance for all', *Reasons To Be Cheerful with Ed Miliband and Geoff Lloyd*, 14 September 2020, https://podcasts. apple.com/gb/podcast/156-bond-baby-bond-guaranteeing-an-inheritance-for-all/ id1287081706?i=1000491136273.

41 McKnight, 'Estimates of the Asset-Effect: The Search for a Causal Effect of Assets on Adult Health and Employment Outcomes', 54.

42 Carys Roberts and Mathew Lawrence, 'Our Common Wealth: A Citizens' Wealth Fund for the UK', *IPPR*, 2018, 21, https://www.ippr.org/files/2018-03/cej-our-common-wealth-march2018.pdf.

43 Conor D'Arcy and Laura Gardiner, 'The Generation of Wealth: Asset Accumulation across and within Cohorts', *Resolution Foundation*, 2017, 24, https://www. resolutionfoundation.org/app/uploads/2017/06/Wealth.pdf.

44 Omar Khan, 'The Colour of Money: How Racial Inequalities Obstruct a Fair and Resilient Economy', *Runnymede Trust*, 2020, 12-13, https://www.runnymedetrust. org/uploads/publications/pdfs/2020 reports/The Colour of Money Report.pdf.

45 HM Treasury, 'Child Trust Fund', 2013, 3, https://assets.publishing.service.gov. uk/government/uploads/system/uploads/attachment_data/file/198726/child_trust_ fund_consultation_on_allowing_the_transfer_of_savings_from_a_ctf_to_a_junior_ isa_140513.pdf.

46 Norges Bank, 'The Fund', https://www.nbim.no/en/.

47 Roberts and Lawrence, 'Our Common Wealth: A Citizens' Wealth Fund for the UK', 8.

48 Jillian Ambrose, 'Queen's Property Manager and Treasury to Get Windfarm Windfall of Nearly £9bn', *Guardian*, 8 February 2021, https://www.theguardian. com/business/2021/feb/08/queens-treasury-windfarm-bp-offshore-seabed-rights.

4. *Family Values*

1   Aðalheiður Bjarnfreðsdóttir, quoted in Iris Ellenburger, 'The Day Women Brought Iceland to a Standstill,' *Jacobin*, 24 October 2019, https://www.jacobinmag. com/2019/10/iceland-redstockings-womens-strike-feminism.

2   Max Rennebohm, 'Icelandic Women Strike for Economic and Social Equality, 1975', *Global Nonviolent Action Database*, 15 November 2009, https://nvdatabase. swarthmore.edu/content/icelandic-women-strike-economic-and-social-equality-1975.

3   Ellenburger; Ministry of social affairs, 'Gender Equality in Iceland', 2009, 3, https://www.stjornarradid.is/media/velferdarraduneyti-media/media/acrobat-skjol/ jafnrettisstofa_stepping_stones.pdf.

4   World Bank, 'Labor Force Participation Rate, Female (% of Female Population Ages 15–64) (Modeled ILO Estimate) – Iceland', 2020, https:// data.worldbank.org/indicator/SL.TLF.ACTI.FE.ZS?locations=IS; Government of Iceland, 'Equal Pay Certification,' 2021, https://www.government.is/topics/ human-rights-and-equality/equal-pay-certification/; Ministry of Industries and Innovation, 'Translation of Recent Amendments of Icelandic Public And Private Limited Companies' Legislation (2008–2010) Including Acts 13/2010 (Sex Ratios) and 68/2010 (Minority Protection, Remuneration)', 2018, https://www.government.is/publications/legislation/lex/2018/02/06/ TRANSLATION-OF-RECENT-AMENDMENTS-OF-ICELANDIC-PUBLIC-AND-PRIVATE-LIMITED-COMPANIES-LEGISLATION-2008-2010-including-Acts-13-2010-sex-ratios-and-68-2010-minority-protection-remuneration/; Nordic Co-operation, 'Preschools and In-Home Child Care in Iceland', 2021, https:// www.norden.org/en/info-norden/preschools-and-home-child-care-iceland;

Government of Iceland, ' Iceland remains the top country on the World Economic Forum's gender gap index', 18 December 2019, https://www.government.is/diplomatic-missions/embassy-article/2019/12/18/Iceland-remains-the-top-country-on-the-World-Economic-Forums-index-for-gender-parity/.

5   Guðný Björk Eydal and Ingólfur V. Gíslason, 'Country Reports – Iceland', 2020, 314, https://www.leavenetwork.org/fileadmin/user_upload/k_leavenetwork/country_notes/2020/PMedited.Iceland.withsupplement.31aug2020.pdf; OECD, 'Parental Leave Systems', 2019, 3–9, https://www.oecd.org/els/soc/PF2_1_Parental_leave_systems.pdf; Work in Iceland, 'Maternity and Paternity Leave in Iceland', 2020, https://work.iceland.is/living/maternity-and-paternity-leave; Willem Adema, Chris Clarke, and Olivier Thevenon, 'Background Brief on Fathers' Leave and Its Use', *OECD*, 2016, 11, https://www.oecd.org/els/family/Backgrounder-fathers-use-of-leave.

6   Olof Palme, 'The Emancipation of Man', 1, http://www.olofpalme.org/wp-content/dokument/700608_emancipation_of_man.pdf. .

7   Alison Andrew et al., 'How Are Mothers and Fathers Balancing Work and Family under Lockdown?', *Institute for Fiscal Studies*, 2020, 18, https://www.ifs.org.uk/uploads/BN290-Mothers-and-fathers-balancing-work-and-life-under-lockdown.pdf.

8   Eleanor Attar Taylor and Jacqueline Scott, 'Gender: New Consensus or Continuing Battleground?' *British Social Attitudes* 35, 2018, 1, https://www.bsa.natcen.ac.uk/media/39248/bsa35_gender.pdf.

9   Tracy McVeigh and Isabel Finch, 'Fathers Spend Seven Times More with Their Children than in the 1970s', *Guardian*, 15 June 2014, https://www.theguardian.com/lifeandstyle/2014/jun/15/fathers-spend-more-time-with-children-than-in-1970s.

10 In 2015 the ONS found that men were spending 39 per cent of the time that women spent on childcare. This rose to 64 per cent during lockdown, made possible by many more men working from home. See Fatherhood Institute, 'New Data Shows Men's Childcare Is up 58 per cent during Lockdown', 14 June 2020, http://www.fatherhoodinstitute.org/2020/mens-childcare-up-58-during-lockdown-makes-case-for-father-friendly-jobs/.

11 Fatherhood Institute.

12 Gov.uk, 'Maternity Pay and Leave', https://www.gov.uk/maternity-pay-leave.

13 Robert Bester, 'The Best Workplaces to Start a Family', *Money Guru*, 1 March 2021, https://www.moneyguru.com/insights/the-best-workplaces-to-start-a-family.

14 Gov.uk, 'Paternity Pay and Leave', https://www.gov.uk/paternity-pay-leave.

15 Nikki van der Gaag et al., 'State of the World's Fathers: Unlocking the Power of Men's Care', *MenCare*, 2019, 48, 64, https://s30818.pcdn.co/wp-content/uploads/2019/05/BLS19063_PRO_SOWF_REPORT_015.pdf.

16 BBC News, 'Shared Parental Leave Law Comes into Effect', 5 April 2015, https://www.bbc.co.uk/news/business-32183784.

17 BBC News, 'Shared Parental Leave Take-up May Be as Low as 2 per cent', 12 February 2018, https://www.bbc.co.uk/news/business-43026312; Michaela Lee, 'Honey, I shrunk the Shared Parental Leave take-up figures', *Maternity Action*, 15 February 2021, https://maternityaction.org.uk/2021/02/honey-i-shrunk-the-shared-parental-leave-take-up-figures/.

18 Alexandra Topping, 'Want gender equality? Then fight for fathers' rights to shared parental leave', *Guardian*, 11 February 2020, https://www.theguardian.com/commentisfree/2020/feb/11/gender-pay-gap-shared-parental-leave-finland.

19 Women and Equalities Select Committee, 'Fathers and the Workplace', *House of Commons*, 2018, 23, https://publications.parliament.uk/pa/cm201719/cmselect/cmwomeq/358/358.pdf.

20 Richard H. Tawney, *Equality* (London: Allen & Unwin, 1983), 267.

21 Anders Chronholm, 'Fathers' Experience of Shared Parental Leave in Sweden', *Recherches Sociologiques et Anthropologiques* 38–2, 15 December 2007, 9–25, https://doi.org/10.4000/RSA.456.

22 Katrin Bennhold, 'The Father of Sweden's Fathers' Leave', *New York Times*, 9 June 2010, https://www.nytimes.com/2010/06/10/world/europe/10iht-swedenside. html.

23 Swedish Social Insurance Agency, 'Social Insurance in Figures 2019', 2019, 20, https://www.forsakringskassan.se/wps/wcm/connect/cec4cea8-1d6c-4895-b442-bc3b64735b09/socialforsakringen-i-siffror-2019-engelsk.pdf?MOD= AJPERES&CVID=.

24 Anita Haataja, 'Fathers' use of paternity and parental leave in the Nordic countries', *The Social Insurance Institution of Finland (Kela)*, 2009, 8, 17, https:// core.ac.uk/download/pdf/14905616.pdf.

25 Carl Cederström, 'State of Nordic Fathers', *Nordic Council of Ministers*, 2019, 7, https://doi.org/10.6027/no2019-044.

26 Laurie DeRose, 'Gender Equality at Home Takes a Hit When Children Arrive', *The Conversation*, 8 August 2019, https://theconversation.com/ gender-equality-at-home-takes-a-hit-when-children-arrive-118420.

27 Maria C Huerta et al., 'Fathers' Leave and Fathers' Involvement: Evidence from Four OECD Countries', *European Journal of Social Security*, 2014, 329, https:// doi.org/10.1177/138826271401600403.

28 Nathaniel Popper, 'Paternity Leave Has Long-Lasting Benefits. So Why Don't More American Men Take It?', *New York Times*, 17 April 2020, https://www. nytimes.com/2020/04/17/parenting/paternity-leave.html.

29 Yekaterina Chzhen, Anna Gromada and Gwyther Rees, 'Are the World's Richest Countries Family-Friendly? Policy in the OECD and EU', *UNICEF*, 2019, 6, https://www.unicef-irc.org/publications/pdf/Family-Friendly-Policies-Research_ UNICEF_ 2019.pdf.

30 Ingela Naumann, '"Universal childcare" and Maternal Employment: the British and the Swedish Story', *Social Policy Association*, 80, http://www.social-policy. org.uk/wordpress/wp-content/uploads/2015/04/22_naumann.pdf.

31 *The Economist*, 'The Early Years Are Getting Increasing Attention', 3 January 2019, https://www.economist.com/special-report/2019/01/03/the-early-years-are-getting-increasing-attention.

32 OECD, 'Is the Last Mile the Longest? Economic Gains from Gender Equality in Nordic Countries', 14 May 2018, 12, https://doi.org/10.1787/9789264300040-en.

33 Ibid. 38; M. E. de Looze et al., 'The Happiest Kids on Earth. Gender Equality and Adolescent Life Satisfaction in Europe and North America', *Journal of Youth and Adolescence* 47:5, 2018, 1073–85, https://doi.org/10.1007/s10964-017-0756-7.

34 Pamela Duncan and Mattha Busby, 'UK Elects Record Number of Female MPs', *Guardian*, 13 December 2019, https://www.theguardian.com/politics/2019/ dec/13/uk-elects-record-number-of-female-mps.

35 World Bank, 'Proportion of Seats Held by Women in National Parliaments (%) – Sweden, Denmark, Finland, Norway', *World Bank*, 2021, https://data.worldbank. org/indicator/SG.GEN.PARL.ZS?end=2000&locations=SE&start=1997.

36 Inter-Parliamentary Union, 'Sweden: Historical Archive of Parliamentary Election Results', 2008, http://archive.ipu.org/parline-e/reports/2303_arc.htm; Colin Rallings and Michael Thrasher, *British Electoral Facts 1832–2006* (London: Routledge, 2007), 132.

37   Thushyanthan Baskaran and Zohal Hessami, 'Competitively Elected Women as Policy Makers', *CESifo Working Papers*, 2019, 22, https://ideas.repec.org/p/ces/ceswps/_8005.html.

38   Aviva, 'Equal Parental Leave Programme', 2020, https://www.avivainvestors.com/en-gb/about/our-culture/equal-parental-leave-programme/.

39   Aviva, 'Equal Parental Leave Shows Men Are Eager to Share Childcare', 20 November 2018, https://www.aviva.com/newsroom/news-releases/2018/11/avivas-paid-parental-leave-shows-men-are-eager-to-share-childcare-duties/.

40   Aviva, 'Equal Parental Leave: Why It's Good for Employers Too', 4 February 2019, https://www.aviva.co.uk/business/business-perspectives/featured-articles-hub/equal-parental-leave/.

41   Sam White, '64. Sharing and Caring: the case for paternity leave', *Reasons to be Cheerful with Ed Miliband and Geoff Lloyd,* 10 December 2018, https://podcasts.apple.com/us/podcast/64-sharing-and-caring-the-case-for-paternity-leave/id12870 81706?i=1000425464505.

42   Gréta Sigríður Einarsdóttir, 'Twelve-Month Parental Leave Approved', *Iceland Review*, 20 November 2020, https://www.icelandreview.com/news/twelve-month-parental-leave-approved/.

43   Ministry of Social Affairs and Health, 'Family Leave Reform Aims to Improve the Wellbeing of Families and to Increase Gender Equality,' *Finnish Government*, 5 February 2020, https://valtioneuvosto.fi/en/-/1271139/perhevapaauudistus-tahtaa-perheiden-hyvinvointiin-ja-tasa-arvon-lisaamiseen.

5. Everybody's Business

1   Milton Friedman, 'The Social Responsibility of Business Is to Increase Its Profits', *New York Times*, 13 September 1970, https://www.nytimes.com/1970/09/13/archives/a-friedman-doctrine-the-social-responsibility-of-business-is-to.html.

2   David Gelles, 'Patagonia v. Trump,' *New York Times*, 5 May 2018, https://www.nytimes.com/2018/05/05/business/patagonia-trump-bears-ears.html; Cassie Werber, 'How Patagonia Became the B Corps Poster Child,' *Quartz at Work*, 17 February 2020, https://qz.com/work/1795975/how-patagonia-became-the-b-corps-poster-child/.

3   Bcorporation.uk, 'Certified B Corporation', 2021, https://bcorporation.uk/.

4   Living Wage Foundation, 'What Is the Real Living Wage?', 2020, https://www.livingwage.org.uk/what-real-living-wage.

5   Rosie Brown, 'What's the Value in a Values-Oriented Workplace?', *Medium*, 4 September 2020, https://medium.com/reinventing-business/whats-the-value-in-a-values-oriented-workplace-6bfb386002b3.

6   Post Reporters, 'Former Unilever Boss Polman Backs Legislation on Company Purpose to "Upgrade Capitalist System"', *Pioneers Post*, 4 December 2019; https://www.pioneerspost.com/news-views/20191204/former-unilever-boss-polman-backs-legislation-on-company-purpose-upgrade.

7   These are businesses that make a profit but reinvest or donate a sizeable portion of it to serve a social or environmental purpose. Arguably social enterprises are a more established idea: there are 100,000 in the UK with combined turnover estimated at £60 billion. See Dan Gregory and Charlie Wigglesworth, 'Hidden Revolution: Size and Scale of Social Enterprise in 2018', *Social Enterprise UK*, 2018, 11-12, https://sewfonline.com/wp-content/uploads/2018/09/The-Hidden-Revolution-FINAL-1.pdf.

8   Colin Mayer, *Prosperity: Better Business Makes the Greater Good* (Oxford: OUP, 2018), 228.

9   Friedman, 'The Social Responsibility of Business Is to Increase Its Profits'.

10   Andrew G Haldane, 'Who Owns a Company? (speech)', *University of Edinburgh Corporate Finance Conference*, 22 May 2015, 11–12, https://www.bankofengland.co.uk/speech/2015/who-owns-a-company.

11   British Academy, 'Principles for Purposeful Business – How to Deliver the Framework for the Future of the Corporation', 2019, 27, https://www.thebritishacademy.ac.uk/documents/224/future-of-the-corporation-principles-purposeful-business.pdf.

12   Schroders, 'Three Reasons Why the UK Stock Market Looks Compelling', 21 May 2019, https://www.schroders.com/id/uk/adviser/insights/markets/three-reasons-why-the-uk-stock-market-looks-compelling/.

13   Lenore Palladino, 'The Lost Opportunity in Buyback Spending', *Roosevelt Institute*, 1 April 2020, https://rooseveltinstitute.org/2020/04/01/the-lost-opportunity-in-buyback-spending/.

14   Kristen McGachey, 'Will Covid Prompt Even More UK Companies to Get the "Buyback Bug"?' *Portfolio Adviser*, 5 May 2020, https://portfolio-adviser.com/will-covid-prompt-even-more-uk-companies-to-get-the-buyback-bug/.

15   IPPR Commission on Economic Justice, 'Prosperity and Justice: A Plan for the New Economy', 2018, 130,https://www.ippr.org/files/2018-08/1535639099_prosperity-and-justice-ippr-2018.pdf.

16   Certified B Corporation, 'System Upgrade: Press Release', 21 July 2020, https://bcorporation.uk/news/system-upgrade-press-release.

17   Deloitte, '2018 Deloitte Millennial Survey', 2018, 5, https://www2.deloitte.com/content/dam/Deloitte/global/Documents/About-Deloitte/gx-2018-millennial-survey-report.pdf.

18   Business Roundtable, 'Business Roundtable Redefines the Purpose of a Corporation to Promote "An Economy That Serves All Americans"', 19 August 2019, https://www.businessroundtable.org/business-roundtable-redefines-the-purpose-of-a-corporation-to-promote-an-economy-that-serves-all-americans.

19   Lillian Ortiz, 'Using Business as a Force for Good', *Shelterforce*, 20 October 2016, https://shelterforce.org/2016/10/20/using-business-as-a-force-for-good-2/.

20   Cassie Werber, 'What Are B Corps, and Can They Fix Capitalism?' *Quartz at Work*, 17 February 2020, https://qz.com/work/1802794/what-are-b-corps-and-can-they-fix-capitalism/.

21   Frederick Alexander et al., 'From Shareholder Primacy to Stakeholder Capitalism', 2020, 3, https://theshareholdercommons.com/wp-content/uploads/2020/09/From-Shareholder-Primacy-to-Stakeholder-Capitalism-TSC-and-B-Lab-White-Paper.pdf.

22   Marco Rubio, 'Rubio Releases Report on Domestic Investment – Press Releases', 15 May 2019, https://www.rubio.senate.gov/public/index.cfm/2019/5/rubio-releases-report-on-domestic-investment.

23   Legislation.gov.uk, 'Companies Act 2006', 2006, https://www.legislation.gov.uk/ukpga/2006/46/section/172.

24   Haldane, 'Who Owns a Company? (speech)', 9.

25   Financial Reporting Council, 'A UK Corporate Governance Code That is Fit for the Future', 16 July 2018, https://www.frc.org.uk/news/july-2018/a-uk-corporate-governance-code-that-is-fit-for-the.

26   B Lab UK, 'System Upgrade', https://bcorporation.uk/system-upgrade; Imperative 21, 'Imperative 21', https://www.imperative21.co/.

27 Haldane, 'Who Owns a Company? (speech)', 14–15.
28 Tomorrow's Company, 'UK Business What's Wrong? What's Next?', 2016, 11, http://www.tomorrowscompany.com/wp-content/uploads/2016/05/UK-Business-Whats-wrong-Whats-next.pdf.
29 Sunny Sidhu, 'International Comparisons of UK Productivity (ICP), Final Estimates', *Office for National Statistics*, 6 April 2018, https://www.ons.gov.uk/economy/economicoutputandproductivity/productivitymeasures/bulletins/internationalcomparisonsofproductivityfinalestimates/2016.
30 Cornelis A. de Kluyver, 'Corporate Governance Elsewhere in the World', *A Primer on Corporate Governance* (New York: Business Expert Press, 2009), 17.
31 Mariana Mazzucato, *The Entrepreneurial State: Debunking Public vs. Private Sector Myths* (London: Anthem, 2013), 100.
32 Ibid. 12.
33 Ibid. 6.

II. Life Beyond the Market

1 Karl Polanyi, *The Great Transformation: The Political and Economic Origins of Our Time* (Boston: Beacon Press, [1944] 2001), 76.
2 Margaret Thatcher Foundation, 'Interview for Sunday Times', 3 May 1981, https://www.margaretthatcher.org/document/104475.
3 Adam Smith, *An Inquiry into the Nature and Causes of the Wealth of Nations* (Hertfordshire: Wordsworth Classics, [1776] 2012), 19.
4 Michael Sandel, *What Money Can't Buy: The Moral Limits of Markets* (London: Penguin Books, 2012), 10.
5 Polanyi, *The Great Transformation,* 76.
6 Margaret Thatcher Foundation, 'Interview for Sunday Times'.

6. That Which Makes Life Worthwhile

1 Robert F. Kennedy, 'Remarks at the University of Kansas, March 18, 1968', 2020, https://www.jfklibrary.org/learn/about-jfk/the-kennedy-family/robert-f-kennedy/robert-f-kennedy-speeches/remarks-at-the-university-of-kansas-march-18-1968.
2 GDP rather than GNP is the measure now commonly used. The difference is that GNP measures what is produced by a country's citizens, both at home and abroad, while GDP measures what is produced within a country's borders, by citizens and non-citizens alike. Shobhit Seth, 'Understanding GDP vs GNP', *Investopedia*, 24 March 2020, https://www.investopedia.com/ask/answers/030415/what-functional-difference-between-gdp-and-gnp.asp.
3 Bank of England, 'What Is GDP?', https://www.bankofengland.co.uk/knowledgebank/what-is-gdp.
4 Drew DeSilver, 'For Most Americans, Real Wages Have Barely Budged for Decades', *Pew Research Center*, 7 August 2018, https://www.pewresearch.org/fact-tank/2018/08/07/for-most-us-workers-real-wages-have-barely-budged-for-decades/.
5 FRED Economic data, 'Real Gross Domestic Product', *Federal Reserve Bank of St. Louis*, 22 December 2020, https://fred.stlouisfed.org/series/GDPC1.

6   Matthew Whittaker, 'Follow the Money: Exploring the link between UK growth and workers' pay packets', *Resolution Foundation*, 2019, 17-18, https://www.resolutionfoundation.org/app/uploads/2019/09/Follow-the-money-report.pdf.

7   Torsten Bell, 'For Labour, It's All about What You Say', *Resolution Foundation*, 23 September 2017, https://www.resolutionfoundation.org/comment/for-labour-its-all-about-what-you-say/.

8   Quoted in Ida Kubiszewski, 'Beyond GDP: Are There Better Ways to Measure Well-Being?', *The Conversation*, 1 December 2014, https://theconversation.com/beyond-gdp-are-there-better-ways-to-measure-well-being-33414.

9   Sarah O'Connor, 'Drugs and Prostitution Add £10bn to UK Economy', *Financial Times*, 29 May 2014, https://www.ft.com/content/65704ba0-e730-11e3-88be-00144feabdco.

10   Chris S. Payne and Gueorguie Vassilev, 'Household Satellite Account, UK', *Office for National Statistics*, 2 October 2018, https://www.ons.gov.uk/economy/national accounts/satelliteaccounts/articles/householdsatelliteaccounts/2015and2016estim ates.

11   Jon Gertner, 'The Rise and Fall of the G.D.P.', *New York Times*, 13 May 2010, https://www.nytimes.com/2010/05/16/magazine/16GDP-t.html.

12   Ben Hall, 'France to Count Happiness in GDP', *Financial Times*, 15 September 2009, https://www.ft.com/content/1af2194c-a12f-11de-a88d-00144feabdco.

13   J. F. Helliwell et al., 'World Happiness Report 2020', *World Happiness Report*, 20 March 2020, https://worldhappiness.report/.

14   Ansuya Harjani, 'This Will Be the "Rockstar" Economy of 2014', *CNBC*, 5 Jan 2014, https://www.cnbc.com/2014/01/05/rockstar_economy_2014.html.

15   Jenée Tibshraeny, 'The NZ Economy May Have Been Coined the "Rockstar" Economy in 2014, but Not Everyone Benefited from This Growth, Says the Finance Minister as He Explains How His "Wellbeing Budget" Aims to Change This', *Interest*, 15 May 2019, https://www.interest.co.nz/news/99693/nz-economy-may-have-been-coined-rockstar-economy-2014-not-everyone-benefited-growth-says.

16   New Zealand Treasury, 'The Wellbeing Budget 2019', 2019, https://www.treasury.govt.nz/sites/default/files/2019-05/b19-wellbeing-budget.pdf.

17   Government of Iceland, 'Indicators for Measuring Well-Being', 2019, https://www.government.is/lisalib/getfile.aspx?itemid=fc981010-da09-11e9-944d-005056bc4d74.

18   Future Generations Commissioner for Wales, 'Well-Being of Future Generations (Wales) Act 2015', 2020, https://www.futuregenerations.wales/about-us/future generations-act/.

19   BBC News, 'M4 relief road: Newport Motorway Plans Scrapped', 4 June 2019, https://www.bbc.co.uk/news/uk-wales-48512697.

20   Sarah Coates, 'Personal Well-Being in the UK', *Office for National Statistics*, 30 July 2020, https://www.ons.gov.uk/peoplepopulationandcommunity/wellbeing/bulletins/measuringnationalwellbeing/april2019tomarch2020.

21   OECD, 'Beyond GDP', in *Beyond GDP: Measuring What Counts for Economic and Social Performance*, 2018, https://www.oecd-ilibrary.org/sites/9789264307292-7-en/index.html?itemId=/content/component/9789264307292-7-en.

22   Office for National Statistics, 'Measures of National Well-Being Dashboard', 23 October 2019, https://www.ons.gov.uk/peoplepopulationandcommunity/wellbeing/articles/measuresofnationalwellbeingdashboard/2018-04-25.

23   Gavin Jackson, 'England's Life Expectancy Gap between Rich and Poor Areas Widens', *Financial Times*, 27 March 2019, https://www.ft.com/content/5726b82c-5085-11e9-9c76-bf4a0ce37d49.

24 I would commend the work of Annie Quick, which helped me to unpack some of my vague intuitions on this issue. Annie Quick, 'Does New Economics Need Wellbeing?' *New Economics Foundation*, 20 March 2019, https://neweconomics. org/2019/03/does-new-economics-need-wellbeing.

25 Kate Raworth, *Doughnut Economics: Seven Ways to Think Like a 21st-Century Economist* (London: Random House, 2017), 44.

26 Doughnut Economics Action Lab, 'About Doughnut Economics', https://doughnut economics.org/about-doughnut-economics.

7. *Jobs of the Future*

1 Skills for Care, 'The Size and Structure of the Adult Social Care Sector and Workforce in England, 2020', 2020, 6, https://www.skillsforcare.org.uk/adult-social-care-workforce-data/Workforce-intelligence/documents/Size-of-the-adult-social-care-sector/Size-and-Structure-2020.pdf.

2 Nye Cominetti, Laura Gardiner and Gavin Kelly, 'What Happens after the Clapping Finishes?', *Resolution Foundation*, 2020, 3, https://www.resolution foundation.org/app/uploads/2020/04/Care-workers-spotlight.pdf; Skills for Care, 'The State of the Adult Social Care Sector and Workforce in England', 2020, 9, https://www.skillsforcare.org.uk/adult-social-care-workforce-data/ Workforce-intelligence/documents/State-of-the-adult-social-care-sector/The-state-of-the-adult-social-care-sector-and-workforce-2020.pdf.

3 Chika Reuben, '157. Why Did It Take a Pandemic?: valuing the everyday economy', *Reasons to Be Cheerful with Ed Miliband and Geoff Lloyd*, 21 September 2020, https://podcasts.apple.com/mt/podcast/157-why-did-it-take-a-pandemic-valuing-the-everyday-economy/id1287081706?i=1000491912845.

4 Office for National Statistics, 'Coronavirus (COVID-19) Related Deaths by Occupation, England and Wales', 25 January 2021, https://www.ons. gov.uk/peoplepopulationandcommunity/healthandsocialcare/causesofdeath/ bulletins/coronaviruscovid19relateddeathsbyoccupationenglandandwales/ deathsregisteredbetween9marchand28december2020.

5 Social Mobility Commission, 'The Stability of the Early Years Workforce in England', 5 August 2020, https://www.gov.uk/government/publications/ the-stability-of-the-early-years-workforce-in-england; Sally Weale, 'One in Eight Childcare Workers in England Earn Less than £5 an Hour', *Guardian*, 5 August 2020, https://www.theguardian.com/money/2020/aug/05/one-in-eight-childcare-workers-in-england-earn-less-than-5-an-hour.

6 Sara Bonetti, 'The Early Years Workforce in England', *Education Policy Institute*, 2019, 6, https://epi.org.uk/wp-content/uploads/2019/01/The-early-years-workforce-in-England_EPI.pdf.

7 Early Years Alliance, 'A Quarter of Childcare Providers Fear Closure within a Year', 4 May 2020, https://www.eyalliance.org.uk/news/2020/05/quarter-childcare-providers-fear-closure-within-year.

8 Social Mobility Commission, 'The Stability of the Early Years Workforce in England', 3.

9 National Day Nurseries Association, 'NDNA 2018/19 Workforce Survey: England', 2019, 11, https://www.ndna.org.uk/NDNA/News/Reports_and_ surveys/Workforce_survey/nursery_workforce_survey_2019.aspx; Skills for Care, 'The State of the Adult Social Care Sector and Workforce in England,' 9.

10 Ibid. 12; Skills for Care, 'The State of the Adult Social Care Sector and Workforce in England', 66.

11 Laura Gardiner and Shereen Hussein, 'As If We Cared', *Resolution Foundation*, 2015, 7, https://www.resolutionfoundation.org/app/uploads/2015/03/As-if-we-cared.pdf.

12 Katrín Jakobsdóttir, 'Building an Inclusive Economy', *Finance & Development* 56:1, 2019, 12, https://www.imf.org/external/pubs/ft/fandd/2019/03/gender-equality-in-Iceland-inclusive-economy-jakobsdottir.htm.

13 Skills for Care, 'The State of the Adult Social Care Sector and Workforce in England', 106.

14 Jerome De Henau and Susan Himmelweit, 'Stimulating OECD Economies Post-Covid by Investing in Care', *Open University IKD Working Paper*, 2020, 5, http://www.open.ac.uk/ikd/publications/working-papers/85.

15 Department for Business, Energy & Industrial Strategy, 'Industrial Strategy: Building a Britain Fit for the Future', 2017, 4, https://assets.publishing.service.gov.uk/government/uploads/system/uploads/attachment_data/file/664563/industrial-strategy-white-paper-web-ready-version.pdf.

16 Steve Fothergill, Tony Gore and Peter Wells, 'Industrial Strategy and the Regions: The Shortcomings of a Narrow Sectoral Focus', *Sheffield Hallam: Centre for Regional Economic and Social Research*, 2017, 2, https://www4.shu.ac.uk/research/cresr/sites/shu.ac.uk/files/cresr30th-industrial-strategy-regions.pdf.

17 Isaac Stanley, 'Love's Labours Found: Industrial Strategy for Social Care and the Everyday Economy', *Nesta*, 14 February 2020, https://www.nesta.org.uk/report/loves-labours-found/.

18 Age UK, 'Why Call It Care When Nobody Cares?', 2018, 2–7, https://www.ageuk.org.uk/globalassets/age-uk/documents/reports-and-publications/reports-and-briefings/care–support/RB_mar18_social_care_campaignreport.pdf .

19 Richard Heys, 'Learning the Lessons from the Atkinson Review', *ESCOE*, 29 July 2019, https://www.escoe.ac.uk/learning-the-lessons-from-the-atkinson-review/.

20 Adam Smith, *An Inquiry into the Nature and Causes of the Wealth of Nations* (Hertfordshire: Wordsworth Classics, [1776] 2012), 19.

21 Katrine Marçal, *Who Cooked Adam Smith's Dinner?* (London: Portobello Books, 2015), 16.

22 Skills for Care, 'The State of the Adult Social Care Sector and Workforce in England', 70; Social Mobility Commission, 'The Stability of the Early Years Workforce in England', 12.

23 Skills for Care, 'The State of the Adult Social Care Sector and Workforce in England', 74.

24 Helen Hester, 'Care under Capitalism: The Crisis of "Women's Work"', *IPPR Progressive Review* 24:4, 2018, 347, https://onlinelibrary.wiley.com/doi/epdf/10.1111/newe.12074.

25 Sunder Katwala, 'The NHS Beat Monarchy and Olympics as Main Source of British Pride', *British Future*, 22 January 2013, https://www.britishfuture.org/commitment-to-nhs-founding-principles-remain-high-in-uk/.

26 Lars Gunnarsson, Barbara Martin Korpi and Ulla Nordenstam, 'Early Childhood Education and Care Policy in Sweden', *Ministry of Education and Science*, 1999, 22–23, http://www.oecd.org/education/school/2479039.pdf.

27 European Commission, 'Eurydice: Sweden', 1 December 2020, https://eacea.ec.europa.eu/national-policies/eurydice/content/organisation-programmes-pre-primary-education-1_en.

28 Susanne Garvis, 'Quality of Employment in Childcare: Country Report: Sweden', *HIVA*, 2018, 3, https://www.epsu.org/sites/default/files/article/files/Country%20 report%20Sweden%20childcare.pdf; National Day Nurseries Association, 'NDNA 2018/19 Workforce Survey: England', 7.

29 Statistics Sweden, 'Salary Search – How Much Do They Earn?', *Statistics Sweden*, 2021, https://www.scb.se/en/finding-statistics/sverige-i-siffror/salary-search.

30 Working Families, 'Free Childcare for Children Aged Two, Three and Four', 2020, https://workingfamilies.org.uk/articles/free-childcare-for-children-aged-two-three-and-four/#two15.

31 Lester Coleman, Mohammed Dali-chaouch and Claire Harding, 'Childcare Survey 2020', *Coram*, 2020, 4, https://www.familyandchildcaretrust.org/sites/default/files/Resource%20Library/Coram%20Childcare%20Survey%202020_240220.pdf.

32 Rachel Lawler, 'Government Reveals Local Authority Funding Rates for 2020/21', *Early Years Alliance*, 31 October 2019, https://www.eyalliance.org.uk/news/2019/10/government-reveals-local-authority-funding-rates-202021.

33 Social Mobility Commission, 'The Stability of the Early Years Workforce in England', 8.

34 The Economist, 'The Early Years Are Getting Increasing Attention', 5 January 2019, https://www.economist.com/special-report/2019/01/03/the-early-years-are-getting-increasing-attention; Social Mobility Commission, 'The Stability of the Early Years Workforce in England', 8.

35 Rebecca Johnes and Jo Hutchinson, 'Widening the Gap? The Impact of the 30-Hour Entitlement on Early Years Education and Childcare', *Education Policy Institute*, 2016, 21–23, https://epi.org.uk/publications-and-research/widening-gap-impact-30-hour-entitlement-early-years-education-childcare/.

36 James J. Heckman, 'Invest in early childhood development: Reduce deficits, strengthen the economy', *Heckman Equation*, 2013, 1–2, https://heckmanequation.org/www/assets/2013/07/F_HeckmanDeficitPieceCUSTOM-Generic_052714-3-1.pdf.

37 Kate Barker, 'A New Settlement for Health and Social Care', *King's Fund*, 2014, 1–2, https://www.kingsfund.org.uk/sites/default/files/field/field_publication_file/Commission%20Final%20%20interactive.pdf.

38 Community Health and Social Care Directorate, 'Free Personal and Nursing Care: Questions and Answers', *Scottish Government*, 28 March 2019, https://www.gov.scot/publications/free-personal-nursing-care-qa/.

39 Commission on Funding of Care and Support, 'Fairer Care Funding: The Report of the Commission on Funding of Care and Support', 2011, 5, https://webarchive.nationalarchives.gov.uk/20120713201059/http://www.dilnotcommission.dh.gov.uk/files/2011/07/Fairer-Care-Funding-Report.pdf.

40 Stanley, 'Love's Labours Found', 13.

41 Isaac Stanley, Adrienne Buller and Mathew Lawrence, 'Caring for the Earth, Caring for Each Other: A Radical Industrial Strategy for Adult Social Care', *CLES/Common Wealth*, 2020, 26, https://cles.org.uk/wp-content/uploads/2020/11/CW_GND-Social-Care11.pdf.

42 Gill Plimmer, 'Private Equity and Britain's Care Home Crisis', *Financial Times*, 9 February 2020, https://www.ft.com/content/952317a6-36c1-11ea-a6d3-9a26f8c-3cba4; Tim Jarrett, 'Four Seasons Health Care Group – Financial Difficulties and Safeguards for Clients', *House of Commons Library*, 2019, 11, https://commonslibrary.parliament.uk/research-briefings/cbp-8004/; Gill Plimmer, 'Britain's Biggest Care Homes Rack up Debts of £40,000 a Bed', *Financial*

Times, 14 July 2019, https://www.ft.com/content/17c353c8-91b9-11e9-aea1-2b1d33ac3271.

43 Stanley, Buller and Lawrence, 'Caring for the Earth, Caring for Each Other', 19–24.

8. The Time of Our Lives

1 Football Stadiums, 'First Ever English League Football Matches & Goals', 2021, https://www.football-stadiums.co.uk/articles/first-ever-football-matches/.

2 Live Football on TV, 'Football TV Blackout Rule – Why Aren't 3pm Football Matches On TV?', 2021, https://www.live-footballontv.com/football-tv-blackout-rule-uk.html.

3 B. Hutchins and A. Harisson, *A History Of Factory Legislation* (London: P. S. King Son, 1911), 105.

4 QI Elves, *Funny You Should Ask …: Your Questions Answered by the QI Elves* (London: Faber & Faber, 2020), 110.

5 George Bangham, 'The Times They Aren't a-Changin'', *Resolution Foundation*, 2020, 29, https://www.resolutionfoundation.org/app/uploads/2020/01/The-times-they-arent-a-changin.pdf; Trade Union Congress, 'A Future That Works for Working People', 2018, 22-24, https://www.tuc.org.uk/sites/default/files/FutureofWorkReport1.pdf.

6 Kate Bell, 'A four-day week with decent pay for all? It's the future', *TUC*, 30 July 2019, https://www.tuc.org.uk/blogs/four-day-week-decent-pay-all-its-future.

7 Ibid.

8 United Kingdom Encyclopedia of Law, 'History of Working Time', 2013, https://lawi.org.uk/History-of-Working-Time/.

9 Lord Skidelsky and Rachel Kay, 'How to Achieve Shorter Working Hours', *Progressive Economy Forum*, 2019, 15, https://progressiveeconomyforum.com/publications/how-to-achieve-shorter-working-hours/.

10 Ibid. 10.

11 Trades Union Congress, 'A Future That Works for Working People', 22-23.

12 Jonny Gifford, 'UK Working Lives Survey Report 2018', *CIPD*, 2018, 35, https://www.cipd.co.uk/Images/UK-working-lives-2_tcm18-40225.pdf.

13 Health and Safety Executive, 'Work-Related Stress, Anxiety or Depression Statistics in Great Britain', 2020, 3, https://www.hse.gov.uk/statistics/causdis/stress.pdf.

14 Bangham, 'The Times They Aren't a-Changin'', 37–39.

15 Olesya Dmitracova, 'UK Working Hours Would Be Shorter If Pre-1980 Trend Had Not Been Derailed, New Study Says', *Independent*, 9 December 2019, https://www.independent.co.uk/news/business/news/uk-working-hours-productivity-pay-new-economics-foundation-a9102446.html.

16 D. Clark, 'Number of People on a Zero Hours Contract in the United Kingdom (UK) from 2000 to 2020', *Statista*, 2020, https://www.statista.com/statistics/414896/employees-with-zero-hours-contracts-number/.

17 Daniel Wheatley and Jonny Gifford, 'UK Working Lives Executive Summary', 2019, 5, https://www.cipd.co.uk/Images/uk-working-lives-summary-2019-v1_tcm18-58584.pdf.

18 CIPD, 'Flexible Working in the UK', 2019, 3, https://www.cipd.co.uk/Images/flexible-working_tcm18-58746.pdf; Wheatley and Gifford, 'UK Working Lives Executive Summary,' 4.

19 Andrew Barnes and Stephanie Jones, *The Four Day Week* (London: Piatkus, 2020), 1-3.

20 Ministry of Employment and the Economy, 'Working Hours Act', 1996, 5, https://www.finlex.fi/en/laki/kaannokset/1996/en19960605_20100991.pdf.

21 Ministry of Economic Affairs and Employment, 'New Working Time Act in a Nutshell', 2020, https://tem.fi/en/new-working-time-act-in-a-nutshell.

22 Maddy Savage, 'Why Finland Leads the World in Flexible Work', *BBC Worklife*, 8 August 2019, https://www.bbc.com/worklife/article/20190807-why-finland-leads-the-world-in-flexible-work.

23 Ryland Thomas and Samuel H. Williamson, 'What Was the U.K. GDP Then?', *MeasuringWorth*, 2021, http://www.measuringworth.com/ukgdp/.

24 Skidelsky and Kay, 'How to Achieve Shorter Working Hours', 13.

25 Barnes and Jones, *The Four Day Week*, 8.

26 Department for Business, Energy & Industrial Strategy, 'Trade Union Membership 2019: Statistical Bulletin', 2020, 5, https://www.gov.uk/government/statistics/trade-union-statistics-2019.

27 Skidelsky and Kay, 'How to Achieve Shorter Working Hours', 21-22; Doug Pyper, 'Trade Union Legislation 1979–2010', *House of Commons Library*, January 2017, 4–6, https://commonslibrary.parliament.uk/research-briefings/cbp-7882/.

28 Bangham, 'The Times They Aren't a-Changin'', 57.

29 Ibid. 36-38. For the average worker, the statistic is more than one in three.

30 Ibid. 24.

31 Trades Union Congress, 'A Future That Works for Working People', 29.

32 Henley Business School, 'Four-Day Week Pays Off For UK Business', 2019, https://www.henley.ac.uk/fourdayweek.

33 Bangham, 'The Times They Aren't a-Changin'', 16.

34 Brendan Duke, 'To Raise Productivity, Let's Raise Wages', *Center for American Progress*, 2 September 2016, https://www.americanprogress.org/issues/economy/reports/2016/09/02/142040/to-raise-productivity-lets-raise-wages/.

35 'The UK has a much lower level of investment in machinery, robots and ICT than other countries such as France, Germany or Italy: in 2017 we had just 33 robot units for every 10,000 employees, compared with 93 in the US, 170 in Germany and 154 in Sweden.' Will Stronge and Aidan Harper, 'The Shorter Working Week: A Radical And Pragmatic Proposal', *Autonomy*, 2019, 30, http://autonomy.work/wp-content/uploads/2019/03/Shorter-working-week-docV6.pdf.

36 Henley Business School, 'Four-Day Week Pays Off For UK Business', 1.

37 Kari Paul, 'Microsoft Japan Tested a Four-Day Work Week and Productivity Jumped by 40 per cent', *Guardian*, 4 November 2019, https://www.theguardian.com/technology/2019/nov/04/microsoft-japan-four-day-work-week-productivity.

38 Rebecca Greenfield, 'How the Six-Hour Workday Actually Saves Money', *Bloomberg*, 17 April 2017, https://www.bloomberg.com/news/articles/2017-04-17/how-the-six-hour-workday-actually-saves-money?sref=eJNaMUgQ.

39 Working Families, 'COVID-19 and Flexible Working: The Perspective from Working Parents and Carers', 2020, 7, https://workingfamilies.org.uk/wp-content/uploads/2020/06/June-2020-FlextheUK-survey-briefing-Covid-19-and-flexible-working.pdf.

40 Ibid. 8.

41 CIPD, 'Embedding new ways of working: implications for the post-pandemic workplace', 2020, 9, https://www.cipd.co.uk/Images/embedding-new-ways-working-post-pandemic_tcm18-83907.pdf.

42 Martha, Crawford, 'Living Hours', *Living Wage Foundation*, 2019, 12, https://www.livingwage.org.uk/sites/default/files/Living Hours Final Report 110619_1.pdf.

43 Frances O'Grady, 'Everyone Deserves the Right to Work Flexibly – It's Time for Flex for All', *TUC*, 2 September 2019, https://www.tuc.org.uk/blogs/everyone-deserves-right-work-flexibly-its-time-flex-all.

9. Lina and Goliath

1   Rana Foroohar, 'Lina Khan: "This Isn't Just about Antitrust. It's about Values"', *Financial Times*, 29 March 2019, https://www.ft.com/content/7945c568-4fe7-11e9-9c76-bf4a0ce37d49.

2   ABC News, 'Mark Zuckerberg Founds Social Network', *YouTube*, 4 February 2015, https://www.youtube.com/watch?v=actqKMgK7gs.

3   Lina M. Khan, 'Amazon's Antitrust Paradox', *Yale Law Journal*, 126:3, 2017, 716, https://www.yalelawjournal.org/note/amazons-antitrust-paradox.

4   Ibid.

5   David Streitfeld, 'Amazon's Antitrust Antagonist Has a Breakthrough Idea', *New York Times*, 7 September 2018, https://www.nytimes.com/2018/09/07/technology/monopoly-antitrust-lina-khan-amazon.html.

6   Robinson Meyer, 'Lina Khan and the "Hipster Antitrust" Movement', *The Atlantic*, July 2018, https://www.theatlantic.com/magazine/archive/2018/07/lina-khan-antitrust/561743/.

7   Office for National Statistics, 'Internet Access – Table 1: Households with internet access, 1998 to 2020', 7 August 2020, https://www.ons.gov.uk/peoplepopulationand community/householdcharacteristics/homeinternetandsocialmediausage/datasets/internetaccesshouseholdsandindividualsreferencetables.

8   TNS opinion and social at the request of the European Commission, 'Special Eurobarometer 447 Report: Online Platforms', 2016, 8, 11, https://ec.europa.eu/information_society/newsroom/image/document/2016-24/ebs_447_en_16136.pdf.

9   Tech Nation, 'UK Tech for a Changing World', 2020, https://technation.io/report2020/#33-work-and-tech.

10 Micah L. Sifry, 'Essembly.Com: Finally, a Friendster for Politics', *Personal Democracy Forum*, 13 March 2006, https://personaldemocracy.com/content/essemblycom-finally-friendster-politics.

11 At the start of 2020, the six most valuable publicly traded companies in the world were Saudi Aramco, Apple, Microsoft, Alphabet, Amazon and Facebook. See PricewaterhouseCoopers, 'Global Top 100 Companies by Market Capitalisation', 2020, 26, https://www.pwc.com/gx/en/audit-services/publications/assets/global-top-100-companies-2020.pdf.

12 Financial Times, 'Prospering in the Pandemic: The Top 100 Companies', 19 June 2020, https://www.ft.com/content/844ed28c-8074-4856-bdeo-20f3bf4cd8fo.

13 Chuck Collins, 'Updates: Billionaire Wealth, U.S. Job Losses and Pandemic Profiteers', *Inequality.org*, 9 December 2020, https://inequality.org/great-divide/updates-billionaire-pandemic/.

14 Rupert Neate, 'Wealth of US Billionaires Rises by Nearly a Third during Pandemic', *Guardian*, 17 September 2020, https://www.theguardian.com/business/2020/sep/17/wealth-of-us-billionaires-rises-by-nearly-a-third-during-pandemic.

15 For example, see Will Evans, 'Amazon's Internal Records Show Its Worker Safety Deception', *Reveal*, 29 September 2020, https://revealnews.org/article/how-amazon-hid-its-safety-crisis/.

16 For an example of the relationship between market dominance and inequality, see Lina Khan and Sandeep Vaheesan, 'Market Power and Inequality: The Antitrust Counterrevolution and Its Discontents', *Harvard Law & Policy Review* 11, 2017, 235–94, https://papers.ssrn.com/sol3/papers.cfm?abstract_id=2769132.

17 StatCounter Global Stats, 'Search Engine Market Share UK', December 2020, https://gs.statcounter.com/search-engine-market-share/all/united-kingdom/#monthly-201912-202012.

18 Competition and Markets Authority, 'Online Platforms and Digital Advertising: Market Study Final Report', 2020, 9, https://www.gov.uk/cma-cases/online-platforms-and-digital-advertising-market-study.

19 Lauren Fruncillo, 'UK Ecommerce Market Dominated by Amazon', *Tamebay*, 11 December 2019, https://tamebay.com/2019/12/uk-ecommerce-market-dominated-by-amazon.html.

20 StatCounter Global Stats, 'Mobile Operating System Market Share UK'.

21 Digital Competition Expert Panel, 'Unlocking Digital Competition', 2019, 91, https://assets.publishing.service.gov.uk/government/uploads/system/uploads/attachment_data/file/785547/unlocking_digital_competition_furman_review_web.pdf.

22 IG UK, 'Acquisitive Tech: Publicly-Known Tech Acquisitions since 1991', 2021, https://www.ig.com/uk/cfd-trading/research/acquisitive-tech#/acquisitions.

23 The Economist, 'Into the Danger Zone – American Tech Giants Are Making Life Tough for Startups', 2 June 2018, https://www.economist.com/business/2018/06/02/american-tech-giants-are-making-life-tough-for-startups.

24 Khan, 'Amazon's Antitrust Paradox', 756–68.

25 European Commission, 'Antitrust: Commission Fines Google €2.42 Billion', 27 June 2017, https://ec.europa.eu/commission/presscorner/detail/en/IP_17_1784.

26 Shoshana Zuboff, *The Age of Surveillance Capitalism: The Fight for a Human Future at the New Frontier of Power* (New York: Public Affairs, 2019).

27 Competition and Markets Authority, 'Online Platforms and Digital Advertising: Market Study Final Report', 5.

28 Digital Competition Expert Panel, 'Unlocking Digital Competition', 42–50.

29 Competition and Markets Authority, 'Online Platforms and Digital Advertising: Market Study Final Report', 214.

30 Ibid. 5–9.

31 Ibid. 215.

32 Ibid. 320.

33 Ibid. 318–20.

34 Khan, 'Amazon's Antitrust Paradox', 768.

35 Rana Foroohar, 'Release Big Tech's Grip on Power', *Financial Times*, 18 June 2017, https://www.ft.com/content/173a9ed8-52b0-11e7-a1f2-db19572361bb; Open Secrets, 'Federal Lobbying – Top Industries', 2021, https://www.opensecrets.org/federal-lobbying/industries?cycle=2020; Open Secrets, 'Federal Lobbying – Top Spenders', 2021, https://www.opensecrets.org/federal-lobbying/top-spenders.

36 Olivia Solon and Sabrina Siddiqui, 'Forget Wall Street – Silicon Valley Is the New Political Power in Washington', *Guardian*, 3 September 2017, https://www.theguardian.com/technology/2017/sep/03/silicon-valley-politics-lobbying-washington.

37 Adam Satariano and Matina Stevis-Gridneff, 'Big Tech Turns Its Lobbyists Loose on Europe, Alarming Regulators', *New York Times*, 14 December 2020, https://www.nytimes.com/2020/12/14/technology/big-tech-lobbying-europe.html.

38 Khan, 'Amazon's Antitrust Paradox', 717–22.

39 Ibid. 719–20.

40 Digital Competition Expert Panel, 'Unlocking Digital Competition', 5.

41 Khan, 'Amazon's Antitrust Paradox', 737.

42 Digital Markets Taskforce, 'A New Pro-Competition Regime for Digital Markets Advice of the Digital Markets Taskforce', 16 December 2020, 22, https://www.gov.uk/cma-cases/digital-markets-taskforce.

43 Andrew Glass, 'Theodore Roosevelt Assails Monopolies, Dec. 3, 1901', *Politico*, 3 December 2018, https://www.politico.com/story/2018/12/03/this-day-in-politics-december-3-1027800.

44 Andrew Pollack, 'Bell System Breakup Opens Era of Great Expectations and Great Concern', *New York Times*, 1 January 1984, https://www.nytimes.com/1984/01/01/us/bell-system-breakup-opens-era-of-great-expectations-and-great-concern.html.

45 Kari Paul, '"This Is Big": US Lawmakers Take Aim at Once-Untouchable Big Tech', *Guardian*, 19 December 2020, https://www.theguardian.com/technology/2020/dec/18/google-facebook-antitrust-lawsuits-big-tech.

46 European Commission, 'The Digital Markets Act: Ensuring Fair and Open Digital Markets', 15 December 2020, https://ec.europa.eu/info/strategy/priorities-2019-2024/europe-fit-digital-age/digital-markets-act-ensuring-fair-and-open-digital-markets_en.

47 Department for Business, Energy and Industrial Strategy, 'New Competition Regime for Tech Giants to Give Consumers More Choice and Control over Their Data, and Ensure Businesses Are Fairly Treated', 27 November 2020, https://www.gov.uk/government/news/new-competition-regime-for-tech-giants-to-give-consumers-more-choice-and-control-over-their-data-and-ensure-businesses-are-fairly-treated.

48 Andrea Coscelli, 'Ahead of the Curve – Bannerman Competition Lecture', *Competition and Markets Authority*, 9 February 2021, https://www.gov.uk/government/speeches/andrea-coscelli-ahead-of-the-curve-bannerman-competition-lecture.

49 Digital Competition Expert Panel, 'Unlocking Digital Competition', 93.

50 Digital Markets Taskforce, 'A New Pro-Competition Regime for Digital Markets Advice of the Digital Markets Taskforce', 55, https://www.gov.uk/cma-cases/digital-markets-taskforce.

51 Digital Competition Expert Panel, 'Unlocking Digital Competition', 67–68.

52 For a discussion of how pro-competition tools such as data mobility and interoperability could work in the technology industry, see Digital Competition Expert Panel, 'Unlocking Digital Competition', 65–74; Digital Markets Taskforce, 'A New Pro-Competition Regime for Digital Markets Advice of the Digital Markets Taskforce', 41–46.

53 HM Treasury, 'Bank Account Switching Service Set to Launch,' 10 September 2013, https://www.gov.uk/government/news/bank-account-switching-service-set-to-launch.

54 Digital Competition Expert Panel, 'Unlocking Digital Competition', 67–68.

55 The Economist, 'What If Large Tech Firms Were Regulated like Sewage Companies?' 23 September 2017, https://www.economist.com/business/2017/09/23/what-if-large-tech-firms-were-regulated-like-sewage-companies.

10. *On Your Bike – and Your Feet*

1　Daniel Susskind, *A World Without Work: Technology, Automation, and How We Should Respond* (London: Allen Lane, 2020), 1; Elizabeth Kolbert, 'Hosed: Is There a Quick Fix for the Climate?', *New Yorker*, 9 November 2009, https://www.newyorker.com/magazine/2009/11/16/hosed.

2　Kolbert, 'Hosed: Is There a Quick Fix for the Climate?'

3　Brian Groom, 'The Wisdom of Horse Manure', *Financial Times*, 2 September 2013, https://www.ft.com/content/238b1038-13bb-11e3-9289-00144feabdco.

4　For an example of how some of the details of the Great Manure Crisis have been disputed, see Rose Wild, 'We Were Buried in Fake News as Long Ago as 1894', *The Times*, 13 January 2018, https://www.thetimes.co.uk/article/we-were-buried-in-fake-news-as-long-ago-as-1894-ntr23ljd5.

5　Susskind, *A World Without Work*, 2; Groom, 'The Wisdom of Horse Manure'; Kolbert, 'Hosed: Is There a Quick Fix for the Climate?'

6　Simon Gunn, 'People and the Car: The Expansion of Automobility in Urban Britain, c.1955–70', *Social History* 38:2, 2013, 233–35, https://doi.org/10.1080/03071022.2013.790139.

7　Regina Guthold et al., 'Worldwide Trends in Insufficient Physical Activity from 2001 to 2016: A Pooled Analysis of 358 Population-Based Surveys with 1·9 Million Participants', *Lancet Global Health* 6:10, 2018, Appendix 5, https://doi.org/10.1016/S2214-109X(18)30357-7.

8　Justin Varney, Mike Brannan and Gaynor Aaltonen, 'Everybody Active, Every Day: An Evidence-Based Approach to Physical Activity', *Public Health England*, 2014, 6, https://assets.publishing.service.gov.uk/government/uploads/system/uploads/attachment_data/file/374914/Framework_13.pdf.

9　WHO, 'Physical Activity: Factsheet', 26 November 2020, https://www.who.int/en/news-room/fact-sheets/detail/physical-activity.

10　Blue Zones, 'Blue Zones Project', https://www.bluezones.com/services/blue-zones-project/.

11　Dan Buettner, '9 Lessons from the World's Blue Zones on Living a Long, Healthy Life', *World Economic Forum*, 26 June 2017, https://www.weforum.org/agenda/2017/06/changing-the-way-america-eats-moves-and-connects-one-town-at-a-time/.

12　Department for Transport, 'Reported Road Casualties in Great Britain: Provisional Estimates Year Ending June 2020', 2020, 2, https://assets.publishing.service.gov.uk/government/uploads/system/uploads/attachment_data/file/956524/road-casualties-year-ending-june-2020.pdf.

13　Royal College of Physicians, 'Every Breath We Take: The Lifelong Impact of Air Pollution', 2016, 4, https://www.rcplondon.ac.uk/projects/outputs/every-breath-we-take-lifelong-impact-air-pollution.

14　Rosie Brook and Katie King, 'Updated Analysis of Air Pollution Exposure in London', *Aethner*, 2017, 3–4, https://www.london.gov.uk/sites/default/files/aether_updated_london_air_pollution_exposure_final_20-2-17.pdf.

15　Transport for London, 'Segregated Cycling Infrastructure: Understanding Cycling Levels, Traffic Impacts, and Public and Business Attitudes', 2018, 17, http://content.tfl.gov.uk/segregated-cycling-infrastructure-evidence-pack.pdf.

16　Lisa Hopkinson and Lynn Sloman, 'Planning for Less Car Use', *Transport for Quality of Life/Friends of the Earth*, 2019, 4, https://www.transportforqualityoflife.com/u/files/3%20Planning%20for%20less%20car%20use%20briefing.pdf.

17　Joel Pett, 'What If It's a Big Hoax and We Create a Better World for Nothing?' *GoComics*, 13 December, 2009, https://www.gocomics.com/joelpett/2009/12/13.

18 Climate Change Committee, 'The Sixth Carbon Budget: Surface Transport', 2020, 5–6, https://www.theccc.org.uk/publication/sixth-carbon-budget/.

19 Climate Change Committee, 'The Sixth Carbon Budget: The UK's Path to Net Zero', 2020, 97, https://www.theccc.org.uk/publication/sixth-carbon-budget/.

20 Climate Change Committee, 'The Sixth Carbon Budget: Surface Transport', 23.

21 Ibid. 18–20.

22 The average UK household spends £21.20 a week on 'Transport Services' – £6.90 of this is on international air fares, which have been excluded from the figure cited. See Office for National Statistics, 'Family Spending in the UK: April 2018 to March 2019', 19 March 2020, https://www.ons.gov.uk/people populationandcommunity/personalandhouseholdfinances/expenditure/bulletins/ familyspendingintheuk/april2018tomarch2019.

23 European Cyclists' Federation, 'Cycling Data Map', 2020, https://ecf.com/ cycling-data.

24 Department for Transport, 'National Travel Survey: 2019, Table NTS0308a', 5 August 2020, https://www.gov.uk/government/statistics/national-travel-survey-2019.

25 Simon Gunn, 'The Buchanan Report, Environment and the Problem of Traffic in 1960s Britain', *Twentieth Century British History* 22:4, 25 January 2011, 523, https://doi.org/10.1093/tcbh/hwq063.

26 Ibid. 527–28.

27 Ibid. 524.

28 Ibid. 528–33.

29 Ibid. 533–34; Gunn, 'People and the Car: The Expansion of Automobility in Urban Britain, c.1955–70', 225.

30 Department for Transport, 'Transport Statistics Great Britain: Modal Comparisons, Table TSGB0101', 2020, https://www.gov.uk/government/statistical-data-sets/ tsgb01-modal-comparisons.

31 Carlton Reid, 'Why Is Cycling Popular in the Netherlands: Infrastructure or 100+ Years of History?', *Roads Were Not Built For Cars*, 8 December 2012, https:// roadswerenotbuiltforcars.com/netherlands/.

32 Malcolm J. Wardlaw, 'History, Risk, Infrastructure: Perspectives on Bicycling in the Netherlands and the UK', *Journal of Transport and Health* 1:4, 2014, 245, https://doi.org/10.1016/j.jth.2014.09.015.

33 Peter Walker, *Bike Nation: How Cycling Can Save the World* (London: Yellow Jersey Press, 2017), 37–38.

34 Ibid. 39–40.

35 Wardlaw, 'History, Risk, Infrastructure: Perspectives on Bicycling in the Netherlands and the UK', 245.

36 David Roberts, 'No Helmets, No Problem: How the Dutch Created a Casual Biking Culture', *Vox*, 26 December 2018, https://www.vox. com/science-and-health/2018/8/28/17789510/bike-cycling-netherlands-dutch-infrastructure.

37 EMTA, 'EMTA Barometer 2020 – Based on 2018 Data', 2020, 31, https://www. emta.com/spip.php?article267.

38 Murray Goulden, Tim Ryley and Robert Dingwall, 'Beyond "Predict and Provide": UK Transport, the Growth Paradigm and Climate Change', *Transport Policy* 32, 2014, 139–47, https://doi.org/10.1016/j.tranpol.2014.01.006.

39 Lisa Hopkinson and Lynn Sloman, 'More than Electric Cars', *Transport for Quality of Life/Friends of the Earth*, 1 February 2019, https://policy.friendsoftheearth. uk/insight/more-electric-cars.

40 Miguel Anxo Fernández Lores, quoted in Stephen Burgen, '"For Me, This Is Paradise": Life in the Spanish City That Banned Cars', *Guardian*, 8 September 2018, https://www.theguardian.com/cities/2018/sep/18/paradise-life-spanish-city-banned-cars-pontevedra?

41 Burgen, '"For Me, This Is Paradise"'.

42 Concello de Pontevedra, 'Alternative Mobility', 2020, http://ok.pontevedra.gal/mobilidade-alternativa/.

43 Burgen, '"For Me, This Is Paradise"'.

44 Concello de Pontevedra, 'City Award', 2020, http://ok.pontevedra.gal/cidade-de-premio/.

45 R. Marqués et al., 'How Infrastructure Can Promote Cycling in Cities: Lessons from Seville', *Research in Transportation Economics* 53, 2015, 38, https://doi.org/10.1016/j.retrec.2015.10.017.

46 Ibid. 32.

47 Ibid. 37–38; R. Marqués, M. Calvo-Salazar and J. A. García-Cebrián, 'Seville: How a Small Spanish City Became a Cycling Hub for All', *Euronews*, 12 October 2018, https://www.euronews.com/2018/10/12/seville-how-a-small-spanish-city-became-a-cycling-hub-for-all-view.

48 Transport for Greater Manchester, 'Beelines: Greater Manchester's Cycling and Walking Infrastructure Proposal', 2018, 3, https://tfgm.com/made-to-move/publications.

49 Chris Boardman, '149. We Built This City on Bikes and Strolls', *Reasons to Be Cheerful with Ed Miliband and Geoff Lloyd*, 27 July 2020, https://podcasts.apple.com/us/podcast/149-we-built-this-city-on-bikes-and-strolls/id1287081706?i=1000486203737.

50 Transport for Greater Manchester, 'Greater Manchester to Deliver 24 Miles of Cycling and Walking Routes Using National Government's Active Travel Fund', 15 December 2020, https://news.tfgm.com/news/greater-manchester-to-deliver-24-miles-of-cycling-and-walking-routes-using-national-governments-active-travel-fund.

51 Feargus O'Sullivan and Laura Bliss, 'Paris's 15-Minute City Could Be Coming to an Urban Area Near You', *Bloomberg Businessweek*, 12 November 2020, https://www.bloomberg.com/news/features/2020-11-12/paris-s-15-minute-city-could-be-coming-to-an-urban-area-near-you.

52 Adele Peters, 'Paris's Mayor, Anne Hidalgo, Wants to Build a "15-Minute City"', *Fast Company*, 29 January 2020, https://www.fastcompany.com/90456312/pariss-mayor-has-a-dream-for-a-15-minute-city; Kim Willsher, 'Paris Mayor Unveils"15-Minute City" Plan in Re-Election Campaign', *Guardian*, 7 February 2020, https://www.theguardian.com/world/2020/feb/07/paris-mayor-unveils-15-minute-city-plan-in-re-election-campaign.

53 State Government of Victoria, 'Plan Melbourne 2017–2050: 20-Minute Neighbourhoods', accessed 9 February 2021, https://www.planning.vic.gov.au/policy-and-strategy/planning-for-melbourne/plan-melbourne/20-minute-neighbourhoods.

54 Carlos Moreno et al., 'Introducing the "15-Minute City": Sustainability, Resilience and Place Identity in Future Post-Pandemic Cities', *Smart Cities* 4:1, 2021, 93–111, https://doi.org/10.3390/smartcities4010006; Natalie Whittle, 'Welcome to the 15-Minute City', *Financial Times*, 17 July 2020, https://www.ft.com/content/c1a53744-90d5-4560-9e3f-17ce06aba69a.

55 Peters, 'Paris's Mayor, Anne Hidalgo, Wants to Build a "15-Minute City"'.

56 Transport for New Homes, 'Project Summary and Recommendations', 2018, 7, https://www.transportfornewhomes.org.uk/wp-content/uploads/2018/07/transport-for-new-homes-summary-web.pdf.

57 Department for Transport, 'Transport Use during the Coronavirus (COVID-19) Pandemic', 3 March 2021, https://www.gov.uk/government/statistics/transport-use-during-the-coronavirus-covid-19-pandemic.

58 Greater London Authority, 'Car-Free Zones in London as Congestion Charge and ULEZ Reinstated', 15 May 2020, https://www.london.gov.uk/press-releases/mayoral/car-free-zones-in-london-as-cc-and-ulez-reinstated; Laura Laker, 'Milan Announces Ambitious Scheme to Reduce Car Use after Lockdown', *Guardian*, 21 April 2020, https://www.theguardian.com/world/2020/apr/21/milan-seeks-to-prevent-post-crisis-return-of-traffic-pollution; Francesca Perry, 'How Cities Are Clamping down on Cars', *BBC*, 30 April 2020, https://www.bbc.com/future/article/20200429-are-we-witnessing-the-death-of-the-car.

59 Department for Transport, 'Transport Use during the Coronavirus (COVID-19) Pandemic'.

60 Bike Is Best, 'Public Backs Greener, Safer Streets, Research Shows', 23 July 2020, https://www.bikeisbest.com/press-release-yougov-study-shows-public-support-cycling-investment.

III. Take Back Control

1 Lukas Audickas, Richard Cracknell and Philip Loft, 'UK Election Statistics: 1918-2019: A Century of Elections', *House of Commons Library*, 27 February 2020, 25, https://commonslibrary.parliament.uk/research-briefings/cbp-7529/.

2 Roberto S. Foa et al., 'The Global Satisfaction with Democracy Report 2020', *Centre for the Future of Democracy*, 2020, 2, https://www.bennettinstitute.cam.ac.uk/media/uploads/files/DemocracyReport2020_nYqqWio.pdf.

3 Alison Park et al., 'British Social Attitudes: The 30th Report', *NatCen Social Research*, 2013, 71–72, https://www.bsa.natcen.ac.uk/latest-report/british-social-attitudes-30/politics/the-younger-electorate-what-s-the-future.aspx.

4 Sung Min Han and Eric C. C. Chang, 'Economic Inequality, Winner–Loser Gap, and Satisfaction with Democracy', *Electoral Studies* 44, 2016, 85–97, https://doi.org/10.1016/j.electstud.2016.08.006.

5 Foa et al., 'The Global Satisfaction with Democracy Report 2020', 2.

6 Douglas Jay, *The Socialist Case* (London: Faber & Faber, 1937), 317.

11. Jury Service

1 Henry McDonald, 'Ireland Becomes First Country to Legalise Gay Marriage by Popular Vote', *Guardian*, 2015, https://www.theguardian.com/world/2015/may/23/gay-marriage-ireland-yes-vote.

2 Convention on the Constitution, 'Third Report of the Convention on the Constitution Amending the Constitution to Provide for Same-Sex Marriage', 2013, 6, 43, http://www.constitutionalconvention.ie/AttachmentDownload.ashx?mid=c90ab08b-ece2-e211-a5a0-005056a32ee4.

3 Citizens' Assembly, 'Establishment of the Assembly', 2021, https://2016-2018.citizensassembly.ie/en/About-the-Citizens-Assembly/Background/.

4   BBC News, 'Irish Abortion Referendum: Ireland Overturns Abortion Ban', 26 May 2018, https://www.bbc.co.uk/news/world-europe-44256152.

5   Irish Times, 'The Irish Times View on Citizens' Assemblies: Out-Sourcing Political Decisions', *Irish Times*, 14 June 2019, https://www.irishtimes.com/opinion/editorial/the-irish-times-view-on-citizens-assemblies-out-sourcing-political-decisions-1.3924889.

6   Ronan McGreevy, 'Citizens' Assembly Vote for Comprehensive Climate Change Regime', *Irish Times*, 5 November 2017, https://www.irishtimes.com/news/ireland/irish-news/citizens-assembly-vote-for-comprehensive-climate-change-regime-1.3280848; Laura Fletcher, 'Citizens' Assembly Begins Hearings on Gender Equality', *Raidió Teilifís Éireann*, 15 February 2020, https://www.rte.ie/news/ireland/2020/0215/1115491-citizens-assembly/.

7   Kate Galbraith, 'Book Excerpt: How the Public Got Behind Texas Wind Power', *Texas Tribune*, 17 September 2013, https://www.texastribune.org/2013/09/17/book-excerpt-how-public-got-behind-tx-wind-power/.

8   Rui Wang, James Fishkin and Robert Luskin, 'Does Deliberation Increase Public-Spiritedness?', *Social Science Quarterly*, 2020, 7, https://cdd.stanford.edu/mm/2020/09/wang-ssq-public-spiritedness.pdf.

9   James Fishkin, *Democracy When the People Are Thinking: Revitalizing Our Politics Through Public Deliberation* (Oxford: Oxford University Press, 2018), 160.

10   Law of Mongolia, 'About the Consultative Poll', 9 February 2017, https://legalinfo.mn/law/details/12492?lawid=12492.

11   Milenko Martinovich, 'Collaboration at Stanford Leads to Mongolian Parliament Passing Law on Public Opinion Polling', *Stanford News*, 2 May 2017, https://news.stanford.edu/press-releases/2017/05/02/collaboration-st-opinion-polling/.

12   James Fishkin and Gombojav Zandanshatar, 'Deliberative Polling for Constitutional Change in Mongolia: An Unprecedented Experiment', *ConstitutionNet*, 20 September 2017, https://constitutionnet.org/news/deliberative-polling-constitutional-change-mongolia-unprecedented-experiment.

13   James Fishkin, 'The Case for a National Caucus', *The Atlantic Monthly*, no. August 1988 (1988), 16–17, https://www.unz.com/print/AtlanticMonthly-1988aug-00016/.

14   OECD, *Innovative Citizen Participation and New Democratic Institutions: Catching the Deliberative Wave* (Paris: OECD Publishing, 2020), https://doi.org/10.1787/339306da-en.

15   Tin Gazivoda, 'Solutions: How the Poles Are Making Democracy Work Again in Gdansk', *BlogActiv*, 20 November 2017, https://guests.blogactiv.eu/2017/11/20/solutions-how-the-poles-are-making-democracy-work-again-in-gdansk/; Sonal Patel, 'Citizens' Jury Recommends Resuming Nuclear Construction in South Korea', *Power*, 20 October 2017, https://www.powermag.com/citizens-jury-recommends-resuming-reactor-construction-in-south-korea/; South Australia's Citizens' Jury, 'South Australia's Citizens' Jury on Nuclear Waste: Final Report', 2016, http://assets.yoursay.sa.gov.au/production/2016/11/06/07/20/56/26b5d85c-5e33-48a9-8eea-4c860386024f/final jury report.pdf; Climate Assembly UK, 'About', https://www.climateassembly.uk/about/index.html.

16   Participedia, 'Oregon Citizens' Initiative Review', 2021, https://participedia.net/method/592.

17   The Economist, 'Tiny Democracy – A Belgian Experiment That Aristotle Would Have Approved Of', 3 October 2019, https://www.economist.com/europe/2019/10/03/a-belgian-experiment-that-aristotle-would-have-approved-of.

18 The Economist, 'Amateurs to the Rescue – Politicians Should Take Citizens' Assemblies Seriously', 19 September 2020, https://www.economist.com/leaders/2020/09/17/politicians-should-take-citizens-assemblies-seriously; Fishkin, *Democracy When the People Are Thinking: Revitalizing Our Politics Through Public Deliberation*, 51-54.

19 Quoted in Claudia Chwalisz, 'A New Wave of Deliberative Democracy', *Carnegie Europe*, 26 November 2019, https://carnegieeurope.eu/2019/11/26/new-wave-of-deliberative-democracy-pub-80422.

20 David Van Reybrouck, *Against Elections: The Case for Democracy,* Trans. Liz Waters, (London: Bodley Head, 2016) 65.

21 Ibid. 66.

22 Ibid. 68–69.

23 Pierre-Étienne Will, 'Appointing Officials by Drawing Lots in Late Imperial China (1594–1911)', *Participations*, 2019, 303–42, https://www.cairn-int.info/journal-participations-2019-0-page-303.htm?contenu=resume.

24 Thomas Jefferson, 'Letter to John Adams, 28 October 1813' in *The Adams-Jefferson Letters: The Complete Correspondence between Thomas Jefferson and Abigail and John Adams*, ed. Lester J, Cappon, (Chapel Hill: University of North Carolina Press, 1959), https://press-pubs.uchicago.edu/founders/documents/v1ch15s61.html.

25 Catherine Murphy, 'Report of the Convention on the Constitution: Statements – Dáil Éireann (31st Dáil)', *Houses of the Oireachtas*, 2013, https://www.oireachtas.ie/en/debates/debate/dail/2013-07-18/23/.

26 Anne Dänner et al., 'Citizens Assemblies – How and Why They Work', 2020, 7, https://www.buergerrat.de/english/citizens-assemblies-how-and-why-they-work/.

27 David M. Farrell et al., 'The Effects of Mixed Membership in a Deliberative Forum: The Irish Constitutional Convention of 2012–2014', *Political Studies* 68:1, 2020, 61, https://doi.org/10.1177/0032321719830936.

28 Fishkin, *Democracy When the People Are Thinking: Revitalizing Our Politics Through Public Deliberation*, 95.

29 For example, Leeds Climate Commission, 'Leeds Climate Change Citizens' Jury', 2019, https://www.leedsclimate.org.uk/leeds-climate-change-citizens-jury; Involve, 'Camden Citizens' Assembly on the Climate Crisis: Recommendations for Tackling the Climate Crisis in Camden', 2019, https://www.camden.gov.uk/documents/20142/0/Camden+Citizens%27+Assembly+on+the+Climate+Crisis+-+Report.pdf/947eb4e5-5623-17a1-9964-46f351446548.

30 Archon Fung, 'Putting the Public Back into Governance: The Challenges of Citizen Participation and Its Future', *Public Administration Review* 75:4, 2015, 516, https://doi.org/10.1111/puar.12361.

31 Yahoo News, 'Temperatures Rise as Climate Debate Divides French Citizens' Assembly, MPs', 8 December 2020, https://uk.news.yahoo.com/temperatures-rise-climate-debate-divides-133218946.html.

32 Climate Change Committee, 'About the Climate Change Committee', https://www.theccc.org.uk/about/.

33 Citizens' Assembly on Social Care, 'Recommendations for Funding Adult Social Care', 2018, 21, https://publications.parliament.uk/pa/cm201719/cmselect/cmcomloc/citizens-assembly-report.pdf.

34 Fishkin, *Democracy When the People Are Thinking: Revitalizing Our Politics Through Public Deliberation*, 175, 205–7.

35 Climate Assembly UK, 'The Assembly Members', 2020, https://www.climateassembly.uk/about/assembly-members/.

12. The Kids Are All Right

1   NowThis News, 'Sen. Feinstein VS. Child Activists on Green New Deal', *YouTube*, 2019, https://www.youtube.com/watch?v=2EfHOAZg3xc.

2   Democracy Now, 'Meet the Kids Who Confronted Sen. Feinstein: We're the Ones Who Will Have to Live with It', 1 March 2019, https://www.democracynow.org/2019/3/1/meet_the_kids_who_confronted_sen.

3   Craig Berry, 'Young People and the Ageing Electorate: Breaking the Unwritten Rule of Representative Democracy', *Parliamentary Affairs* 67:3, 2014, 710–13, https://doi.org/10.1093/pa/gss056.

4   British Election Study, 'Age and Voting Behaviour at the 2019 General Election', 27 January 2021, https://www.britishelectionstudy.com/bes-findings/age-and-voting-behaviour-at-the-2019-general-election/#.YCu-gTJxeUk; Ipsos MORI, 'How Britain Voted in the 2019 Election', December 2019, 10–11, https://www.ipsos.com/ipsos-mori/en-uk/how-britain-voted-2019-election.

5   Laura Gardiner, 'Votey McVoteface: Understanding the Growing Turnout Gap between the Generations', *Resolution Foundation*, September 2016, 7, https://www.resolutionfoundation.org/publications/votey-mcvoteface-understanding-the-growing-turnout-gap-between-the-generations/.

6   Ibid. 16–17.

7   Roberto Stefan Foa et al., 'Youth and Satisfaction with Democracy', *Centre for the Future of Democracy*, October 2020, https://www.cam.ac.uk/system/files/youth_and_satisfaction_with_democracy.pdf.

8   Ibid. 2.

9   British Election Study Team, 'Age and Voting Behaviour at the 2019 General Election'.

10 Roberto Stefan Foa and Yascha Mounk, 'The Signs of Deconsolidation', *Journal of Democracy* 28:1, 2017, 6, https://www.journalofdemocracy.org/articles/the-signs-of-deconsolidation/; Roberto Stefan Foa and Yascha Mounk, 'The Danger of Deconsolidation', *Journal of Democracy* 27:3, 2016, 9, https://www.journalofdemocracy.org/articles/the-danger-of-deconsolidation-the-democratic-disconnect/.

11 Onward, 'The Politics of Belonging', 2019, 4, 22, https://www.ukonward.com/wp-content/uploads/2019/10/Politics-of-Belonging-FINAL.pdf.

12 S. Middleton et al., 'Evaluation of Education Allowance Pilots: Young People Aged 16 to 19 Years', 2005, 25–28, https://repository.lboro.ac.uk/articles/online_resource/Evaluation_of_Education_Allowance_Pilots_young_people_aged_16_to_19_years/9598373.

13 BBC News, 'Q&A: EMA Grants', 28 March 2011, https://www.bbc.co.uk/news/uk-wales-politics-50561883.

14 HM Treasury, 'Spending Review 2010', 2010, 41, 67, https://assets.publishing.service.gov.uk/government/uploads/system/uploads/attachment_data/file/203826/Spending_review_2010.pdf.

15 Electoral Commission, 'Scottish Independence Referendum: Report on the Referendum Held on 18 September 2014', December 2014, 1, http://www.electoralcommission.org.uk/__data/assets/pdf_file/0010/179812/Scottish-independence-referendum-report.pdf.

16 UK in a changing Europe, 'Votes at 16: What Effect Would It Have?', 18 November 2015, https://ukandeu.ac.uk/votes-at-16-what-effect-would-it-have/.

17 Decca Aitkenhead, 'Ruth Davidson, Scottish Conservative Leader: "Up Here, You Have to Make More of an Effort"', *Guardian*, 12 June 2015, https://www.theguardian.com/politics/2015/jun/12/ruth-davidson-scottish-conservative-leader-interview.

18 BBC News, 'Cut in Scottish Voting Age Passed Unanimously', 18 June 2015, https://www.bbc.co.uk/news/uk-scotland-scotland-politics-33173488.

19 Republik Osterreich, 'Parliamentary Correspondence No. 439 Dated June 5, 2007', 5 June 2007, https://www.parlament.gv.at/PAKT/PR/JAHR_2007/PK0439/index.shtml; Mette Kirstine Schmidt, 'A Vote for the Young People,' *The Danish Youth Council*, 2007, 4, http://www.cje.org/descargas/cje4965.pdf.

20 Eva Zeglovits and Julian Aichholzer, 'Are People More Inclined to Vote at 16 than at 18? Evidence for the First-Time Voting Boost Among 16- to 25-Year-Olds in Austria', *Journal of Elections, Public Opinion and Parties* 24:3, 2014, 358, https://doi.org/10.1080/17457289.2013.872652; Eurobarometer, 'Flash Eurobarometer 455 – September 2017 European Youth', *Eurobarometer*, vol. 455, 2018, 15, https://ec.europa.eu/commfrontoffice/publicopinion/index.cfm/survey/getsurveydetail/instruments/flash/surveyky/2163.

21 Eva Zeglovits, 'Voting at 16? Youth suffrage is up for debate', European View 12:2, 1 December 2013, https://journals.sagepub.com/doi/full/10.1007/s12290-013-0273-3; Robert Vehrkamp, Niklas Im Winkel and Laura Konzelmann, 'Wählen ab 16', Bertelsmann Stiftung, 2015, 90-91, https://www.bertelsmann-stiftung.de/fileadmin/files/BSt/Publikationen/GrauePublikationen/ZD_Studie_Waehlen_ab_16_2015.pdf.

22 APPG on Votes at 16, 'Campaign Report 2019', April 2019, 14, https://www.byc.org.uk/wp-content/uploads/2019/04/Votes-at-16-APPG-Campaign-Report-2019.pdf.

23 Sarah Birch, Glenn Gottfried and Guy Lodge, 'Divided Democracy: Political Inequality in the UK and Why It Matters', *IPPR*, 2013, 7, https://www.ippr.org/publications/divided-democracy-political-inequality-in-the-uk-and-why-it-matters.

24 Markus Wagner, David Johann and Sylvia Kritzinger, 'Voting at 16: Turnout and the Quality of Vote Choice', *Electoral Studies* 31:2, 2012, 372–83, https://doi.org/10.1016/j.electstud.2012.01.007.

25 Aitkenhead, 'Ruth Davidson, Scottish Conservative Leader: "Up Here, You Have to Make More of an Effort"'.

26 The Advocacy Academy, 'About', https://www.theadvocacyacademy.com/.

27 Marie-Claire Chappet, 'Inside Advocacy Academy: The Radical Programme Turning Angry Young People into Activists', *The Face*, 31 July 2019, https://theface.com/society/inside-south-londons-advocacy-academy-with-the-social-activists.

28 Sandra Larson, 'Come for the Pizza, Stay for the Power: Why Boston Let Teenagers Set Its Budget', *Guardian*, 2016, https://www.theguardian.com/cities/2016/mar/31/boston-pizza-teenagers-budget-youth-lead-change.

29 City of Boston, 'Youth Lead the Change', https://www.boston.gov/departments/youth-engagement-and-employment/youth-lead-change.

30 Tara Grillos, 'Youth Lead the Change: The City of Boston's Youth-Focused Participatory Budgeting Process: Pilot Year Evaluation', August 2014, 25, https://scholar.harvard.edu/files/grillos/files/pb_boston_year_1_eval_0.pdf.

31 Young Scot, 'North Ayrshire Youth Participatory Budgeting', 2021, https://young.scot/campaigns/north-ayrshire/north-ayrshire-youth-participatory-budgeting.

32 PB Scotland, 'South Glasgow Youthbank Big Grant Giveaway', 8 February 2018, https://pbscotland.scot/blog/2018/2/2/south-glasgow-youth-bank-jan-2018.

33 Climate Assembly UK, 'Who Took Part?', 2020, https://www.climateassembly.uk/detail/recruitment/.

34 Zeglovits and Aichholzer, 'Are People More Inclined to Vote at 16 than at 18? Evidence for the First-Time Voting Boost Among 16- to 25-Year-Olds in Austria', 354.

35 Advisory Group on Citizenship, 'Education for Citizenship and the Teaching of Democracy in Schools', 1998, 7, https://dera.ioe.ac.uk/4385/1/crickreport1998.pdf.

36 Jon Tonge, Andrew Mycock and Bob Jeffery, 'Does Citizenship Education Make Young People Better-Engaged Citizens?', *Political Studies* 60:3, 2012, 596–99, https://doi.org/10.1111/j.1467-9248.2011.00931.x; Ana Isabel Pontes, Matt Henn and Mark D. Griffiths, 'Youth Political (Dis)Engagement and the Need for Citizenship Education: Encouraging Young People's Civic and Political Participation through the Curriculum', *Education, Citizenship and Social Justice* 14:1, 2019, 16–17, https://doi.org/10.1177/1746197917734542; Avril Keating and Jan Germen Janmaat, 'Education Through Citizenship at School: Do School Activities Have a Lasting Impact on Youth Political Engagement?' *Parliamentary Affairs* 69, 2016, 424, https://doi.org/10.1093/pa/gsv017.

37 David Kerr, 'We Need Renewed Political Commitment to Citizenship Education and Ongoing Monitoring of Its Provision in Schools', *Democratic Audit*, 19 June 2014, https://www.democraticaudit.com/2014/06/19/enhancing-the-political-literacy-of-young-people-is-a-shared-responsibility/.

38 House of Lords Select Committee on Citizenship and Civic Engagement, 'The Ties That Bind: Citizenship and Civic Engagement in the 21st Century', 2018, 43, 31, https://publications.parliament.uk/pa/ld201719/ldselect/ldcitizen/118/118.pdf.

39 Jon Henley, 'How Finland Starts Its Fight against Fake News in Primary Schools', *Guardian*, 29 January 2020, https://www.theguardian.com/world/2020/jan/28/fact-from-fiction-finlands-new-lessons-in-combating-fake-news.

13. Westminster Doesn't Know Best

1 Andy Burnham, 'Greater Manchester's Covid Press Conference: Manchester Central Library Steps', *YouTube*, 2020, https://www.youtube.com/watch?app=desktop&v=eDUs1a3_O4g.

2 Luke Raikes, Arianna Giovannini and Bianca Getzel, 'State of the North 2019 – Divided and Connected: Regional Inequalities in the North, the UK and the Developed World', *IPPR*, November 2019, 23, https://www.ippr.org/research/publications/state-of-the-north-2019.

3 House of Commons Transport Committee, 'Bus Services in England Outside London: Ninth Report of Session 2017–19', May 2019, 3-14, https://publications.parliament.uk/pa/cm201719/cmselect/cmtrans/1425/1425.pdf.

4 Michiel Modijefsky, 'Free Public Transport Launched Successfully in Dunkirk', *Eltis*, 19 September 2018, https://www.eltis.org/discover/news/free-public-transport-launched-successfully-dunkirk; Emilie Boyer King, 'Want a Free Ride? French Cities Opt for Free Public Transport', *France 24*, 9 November 9, 2017, https://www.france24.com/en/20171109-france-french-cities-public-transport-free-dunkirk-compiegne.

5 Michiel Modijefsky, 'Free Public Transport in Dunkirk, One Year Later', *Eltis*, 10 October 2019, https://www.eltis.org/in-brief/news/free-public-transport-dunkirk-one-year-later.

6 Henri Briche, Maxime Huré and Oliver Waine, 'Dunkirk as a New "Laboratory" for Free Transit – Metropolitics', *Metro Politics*, 2018, 7, https://metropolitiques.eu/Dunkirk-as-a-New-Laboratory-for-Free-Transit.html; Lynn Sloman et al., 'We Need Fare-Free Buses! It's Time to Raise Our Sights', *Transport for Quality of*

Life, 2018, 2, http://www.transportforqualityoflife.com/u/files/180317 Fare-free buses_ time to raise our sights.pdf.

7   Briche, Huré and Waine, 'Dunkirk as a New "Laboratory" for Free Transit – Metropolitics', 4.

8   Sloman et al., 'We Need Fare-Free Buses! It's Time to Raise Our Sights', 1.

9   Legislation.gov.uk, 'Bus Services Act 2017', 2017, https://www.legislation.gov.uk/ukpga/2017/21/contents/enacted; National Audit Office, 'Financial Sustainability of Local Authorities 2018', National Audit Office, March 8, 2018, https://www.nao.org.uk/press-release/financial-sustainability-of-local-authorities-2018/.

10 OECD, 'OECD Fiscal Decentralisation Database', 2019, http://www.oecd.org/tax/federalism/fiscal-decentralisation-database/.

11 OECD, 'Germany Regional Policy', 2016, 1–2, https://www.oecd.org/regional/regional-policy/profile-Germany.pdf.

12 Luke Raikes, 'The Devolution Parliament: Devolving Power to England's Regions, Towns And Cities', *IPPR*, 2020, 28, https://www.ippr.org/files/2020-02/the-devolution-parliament-feb20.pdf.

13 Raikes, Giovannini and Getzel, 'State of the North 2019 – Divided and Connected: Regional Inequalities in the North, the UK and the Developed World', 11; Philip McCann, 'Perceptions of Regional Inequality and the Geography of Discontent: Insights from the UK', *Regional Studies* 54:2, 2020, 14, https://doi.org/10.1080/00343404.2019.1619928.

14 UK2070 Commission, 'Make No Little Plans – Acting At Scale For A Fairer And Stronger Future', 2020, 9, http://uk2070.org.uk/wp-content/uploads/2020/02/UK2070-FINAL-REPORT.pdf.

15 Raikes, 'The Devolution Parliament: Devolving Power to England's Regions, Towns And Cities', 11.

16 Ibid. 9.

17 Raikes, Giovannini and Getzel, 'State of the North 2019 – Divided and Connected: Regional Inequalities in the North, the UK and the Developed World', 13.

18 ICAEW, 'Coronavirus Economic Outlook: Differences between regions', 2020, https://www.icaew.com/technical/economy/economic-insight/coronavirus-uk-economic-outlook-differences-across-regions.

19 Raikes, 'The Devolution Parliament: Devolving Power to England's Regions, Towns And Cities', 16.

20 Ibid. 17.

21 Raikes, Giovannini and Getzel, 'State of the North 2019 – Divided and Connected: Regional Inequalities in the North, the UK and the Developed World', 8.

22 Andres Rodriguez-Pose and Roberto Ezcurra, 'Does Decentralization Matter for Regional Disparities? A Cross-Country Analysis', *Spatial Economic Research Centre*, 2009, 34–37, https://ideas.repec.org/p/cep/sercdp/0025.html; Hansjörg Blöchliger, David Bartolini and Sibylle Stossberg, 'Does Fiscal Decentralisation Foster Regional Convergence', *OECD Economic Policy Paper*, 2016, 5, https://doi.org/10.1787/5jlr3c1vcqmr-en; David Bartolini, Sibylle Stossberg and Hansjörg Blöchliger, 'Fiscal Decentralisation and Regional Disparities', *OECD*, 2016, 7, https://doi.org/10.1787/5jlpq7v3j237-en.

23 Ellen Leopold and David A. McDonald, 'Municipal Socialism Then and Now: Some Lessons for the Global South', *Third World Quarterly*, 33:10, 2012, 1837–53, https://doi.org/10.1080/01436597.2012.728321.

24 Owen Hatherley, 'The Government of London', *New Left Review*, Mar–Apr 2020, 89, https://newleftreview.org/issues/ii122/articles/owen-hatherley-the-government-of-london.pdf.

25 J. A. Chandler, 'Accounting for the Evolution of Local Government in Britain', *Explaining Local Government* (Manchester: Manchester University Press, 2007), 314-317, https://doi.org/10.7765/9781847792099.00018.

26 Richard Dewdney, 'Results of Devolution Referendums', *House of Commons Library*, 97, 1997, 9-10, https://commonslibrary.parliament.uk/research-briefings/rp97-113/.

27 Aron Cheung, Akash Paun and Lucy Valsamidis, 'Devolution at 20', *Institute for Government*, 2019, 50, https://www.instituteforgovernment.org.uk/sites/default/files/publications/Devolution%20at%2020.pdf.

28 Delivering for Scotland, 'Devolution in Scotland – UK and Scottish Governments Working Together', 2021, https://www.deliveringforscotland.gov.uk/scotland-in-the-uk/devolution/.

29 Including Greater London, just over 20 million people, 37 per cent of England's population, have a devolved metro mayor. Note that these are different to directly elected city mayors, who cover a single local authority and essentially act as leader of the local council. Akash Paun, James Wilson and Elspeth Nicholson, 'English Devolution: Combined Authorities and Metro Mayors', *Institute for Government*, 2020, 1, https://www.instituteforgovernment.org.uk/explainers/english-devolution-combined-authorities-metro-mayors.

30 Neil McInroy & Tom Lloyd Goodwin, 'Levelling up takes genuine devolution', *CLASS*, 2020, 26–27, http://classonline.org.uk/pubs/item/what-will-it-really-take-to-level-up.

31 Raikes, Giovannini and Getzel, 'State of the North 2019 – Divided and Connected: Regional Inequalities in the North, the UK and the Developed World', 26–27.

32 Raikes, 'The Devolution Parliament: Devolving Power to England's Regions, Towns And Cities', 20.

33 Steven Morris and Libby Brooks, 'Welsh and Scottish Leaders: Johnson Hasn't Talked to Us for Months', *Guardian*, 18 September 2020, https://www.theguardian.com/politics/2020/sep/18/welsh-and-scottish-leaders-johnson-hasnt-talked-to-us-for-months.

14. *Constant Gardeners*

1 It's worth pointing out that the same experience as we saw in the floods has been seen across the country during Covid. Simon Kaye and Luca Tiratelli, 'Communities vs. Coronavirus: The Rise of Mutual Aid', *New Local*, 2020, https://www.newlocal.org.uk/publications/communities-vs-coronavirus-the-rise-of-mutual-aid/.

2 Natalie Wolchover, 'How Accurate Is Wikipedia?', *Live Science*, 24 January 2011, https://www.livescience.com/32950-how-accurate-is-wikipedia.html; Wikimedia Statistics, 'Total Page Views', 2021, https://stats.wikimedia.org/#/all-projects/reading/total-page-views/normal%7Cbar%7C1-year%7C~total%7Cmonthly.

3 Department of Health, 'Long Term Conditions Compendium of Information: Third Edition', 2012, https://www.gov.uk/government/publications/long-term-conditions-compendium-of-information-third-edition.

4 Climate Change Committee, 'The Sixth Carbon Budget: The UK's Path to Net Zero', 2020, 70, https://www.theccc.org.uk/publication/sixth-carbon-budget/.

5 Jay, *The Socialist Case*, 317.

6 Comptroller and Auditor General, 'Transforming Rehabilitation: Progress Review', *National Audit Office*, March 2019, 6–10, https://www.nao.org.uk/wp-content/uploads/2019/02/Transforming-Rehabilitation-Progress-review.pdf.

7   Sue Goss, 'Garden Mind', *Compass*, 2020, 8, https://www.compassonline.org.uk/
    wp-content/uploads/2020/07/GardenMind_SG_FINAL.pdf.
8   Ibid. 7
9   Ibid.
10 Hilary Cottam, *Radical Help* (London: Little, Brown Book Group, 2018).
11 Ibid. 47.
12 Ibid. 70.
13 Ibid. 91.
14 Katie Kelly, 'Community Power and Me: Katie Kelly, East Ayrshire', *New Local*,
    7 December 2020, https://www.newlocal.org.uk/video/community-power-and-
    me-katie-kelly-east-ayrshire/.
15 Adam Lent and Jessica Studdert, 'The Community Paradigm', *New Local*, 2010,
    https://www.newlocal.org.uk/wp-content/uploads/2019/03/The-Community-Paradigm_
    New-Local.pdf.
16 Cambridgeshire County Council, 'Neighbourhood Cares', 2021, https://www.
    cambridgeshire.gov.uk/residents/adults/organising-care-and-support/types-of-
    support/neighbourhood-cares.
17 Lent and Studdert, 'The Community Paradigm', 70–71.
18 Mikko Annala et al., 'Humble Government: How to Realize Ambitious Reforms
    Prudently', 2020, 5–7, https://tietokayttoon.fi/en/-/review-addressing-the-most-
    complex-problems-of-the-21st-century-demands-a-humble-approach-to-policy-
    making.

15. The Wrong Trousers

1   Sarah Butler, 'Wallace & Gromit Producers Hand Stake in Business to Staff',
    Guardian, 10 November 2018, https://www.theguardian.com/film/2018/nov/10/
    wallace-gromit-producers-hand-stake-in-business-to-staff.
2   Aardman, 'Oscar Winning Studio Aardman Determines Its Own Future Through
    Employee Ownership', 10 November 2018, https://www.aardman.com/oscar-
    winning-studio-aardman-determines-its-own-future-through-employee-ownership/.
3   Zoe Wood, 'Richer Sounds Founder Hands over Control of Hi-Fi and TV Firm
    to Staff', *Guardian*, 14 May 2019, https://www.theguardian.com/business/2019/
    may/14/richer-sounds-staff-julian-richer.
4   Hazel Sheffield, 'How a Switch to Employee Ownership Is Bearing Fruit',
    Financial Times, 18 July 2019, https://www.ft.com/content/b5481020-a4bf-11e9-
    a282-2df48f366f7d.
5   Ibid.
6   HM Treasury, 'Supporting the Employee-Ownership Sector', 2013, 5–6, https://
    assets.publishing.service.gov.uk/government/uploads/system/uploads/attachment_
    data/file/264504/PU1588_Employee_ownership_response_to_consultation.pdf.
7   EOA, 'Employee Ownership Impact Report', 2012, 8, https://employeeownership.
    co.uk/wp-content/uploads/The-Impact-Report.pdf.
8   Mervyn Wilson, Linda Shaw and Gillian Lonergan, 'Our Story', Rochdale Pioneers
    Museum, 2012, 1–29, http://coop.eco.ku.ac.th/newdesign/document/Our-Story-
    rochdale.pdf; Dame Pauline Green, 'Co-operatives Are Building a Better World for
    Women', *Co-operative News*, 8 March 2012, https://www.thenews.coop/37434/
    topic/equality/co-operatives-are-building-better-world-women/.
9   Mathew Lawrence, Andrew Pendleton and Sara Mahmoud, 'Co-operatives
    Unleashed: Doubling the Size of the UK's Co-operative Sector', *New Economics*

Foundation, 2018, 4, https://neweconomics.org/uploads/files/co-ops-unleashed. pdf; Co-operatives UK, 'The Co-op Economy 2020', 2020, 3, https://www. uk.coop/sites/default/files/uploads/attachments/co-op_economy_2020_0.pdf.

10 Virginie Pérotin, 'What Do We Really Know about Workers' Co-operatives?' *Cooperation: A Business Model for the 21st Century* (Manchester University Press, 2015), 3, https://doi.org/10.7765/9781526100993.00019.

11 Lawrence, Pendleton and Mahmoud, 'Co-operatives Unleashed: Doubling the Size of the UK's Co-operative Sector', 17.

12 Ibid. 23–24.

13 Ibid. 12.

14 Co-operatives UK, 'Simply Finance', 2011, 33, https://www.uk.coop/sites/default/ files/2020-10/simplyfinance_webdownload_0_0.pdf.

15 Marcelo Vieta, 'The Italian Road to Creating Worker Cooperatives from Worker Buyouts: Italy's Worker-Recuperated Enterprises and the Legge Marcora Framework', *Euricse Working Papers*, 2015, 3, 8–11, https://doi.org/10.2139/ ssrn.2641057.

16 Lawrence, Pendleton and Mahmoud, 'Co-operatives Unleashed: Doubling the Size of the UK's Co-operative Sector', 30–32.

17 Co-operatives UK, 'The Co-operative Option: Public Perceptions of Co-operatives in Our Communities, Workplaces and Economy', 2015, 5, ttps://www.uk.coop/ sites/default/files/2020-11/the_co-operative_option_report.pdf.

18 Matthew Taylor et al., 'Good Work: The Taylor Review of Modern Working Practices', *Department for Business, Energy & Industrial Strategy*, 2017, 52, https://www.gov.uk/government/publications/good-work-the-taylor-review-of- modern-working-practices.

19 S. De Spiegelaere and S. Vitols, 'A Better World with More Democracy at Work', European Trade Union Institute, 2020, https://europeanparticipationindex. eu/#EPI_vs_Indicators?democracy.

20 Lindsay Judge and Hannah Slaughter, 'Failed Safe? Enforcing Workplace Health and Safety in the Age of Covid-19', 2020, 13–15, https://www.resolutionfoundation. org/app/uploads/2020/11/Failed-safe.pdf.

21 Worker-Participation.eu, 'Compare Countries', 2021, http://www.worker- participation.eu/National-Industrial-Relations/Compare-Countries?countries%2 55B%255D=250&countries%255B%255D=157&countries%255B%255D=65 4&countries%255B%255D=5337&countries%255B%255D=514&countries% 255B%255D=290&countries%255B%255D=262&countries%255B%255D=5 80&countries%255.

22 Worker-Participation.eu, 'Across Europe', 2021, https://www.worker-participation. eu/National-Industrial-Relations/Across-Europe.

23 Sandra Vogel, 'Germany: Survey on Works Council Elections in 1,600 Companies', 2015, 1, https://www.iwkoeln.de/fileadmin/publikationen/2015/263866/Works_ councilc_Expertise_IW.pdf.

24 Worker-Participation.eu, 'The European Participation Index: Measuring Worker Participation and Europe 2020 Targets', 2020, https://www.worker-participation. eu/About-WP/European-Participation-Index-EPI/The-European-Participation- Index-measuring-worker-participation-and-Europe-2020-targets.

25 Sarah Lawton, 'Three-Quarters of German Workers Satisfied with Employers' Response to COVID-19, Survey Finds', Euractiv.de, 14 September 2020, https://

www.euractiv.com/section/economy-jobs/news/three-quarters-of-german-workers-satisfied-with-employers-response-to-covid-19-survey-finds/.

26 Böckler Impuls, 'Strong Codetermination – Solid Companies. An Interview with Prof. Dr. Michael Wolff', Euractiv.de, 5 September 2019, https://www.euractiv.com/section/economy-jobs/opinion/strong-codetermination-solid-companies-an-interview-with-prof-dr-michael-wolff/.

27 Aleksandra Gregorič and Marc Steffen Rapp, 'Board-Level Employee Representation (BLER) and Firms' Responses to Crisis', *Industrial Relations* 58:3, 2019, 384–385, https://doi.org/10.1111/irel.12241.

28 Rafael Gomez et al., 'The "Good Workplace"', *Journal of Participation and Employee Ownership*, 2:1, 2019, 82, https://doi.org/10.1108/jpeo-09-2018-0024; George Ward, 'Happy Employees and Their Impact on Firm Performance', *LSE Business Review*, 15 July 2019, https://blogs.lse.ac.uk/businessreview/2019/07/15/happy-employees-and-their-impact-on-firm-performance/.

29 Ewan McGaughey, 'Votes at Work in Britain: Shareholder Monopolisation and the "Single Channel"', *Centre for Business Research, University of Cambridge*, March 2017, 10–16, https://www.cbr.cam.ac.uk/fileadmin/user_upload/centre-for-business-research/downloads/working-papers/wp487.pdf; Ewan McGaughey, 'The Codetermination Bargains: The History of German Corporate and Labour Law', *LSE Law, Society and Economy Working Papers*, 2015, 3, https://doi.org/10.2139/ssrn.2579932.

30 Ibid. 12.

31 Ibid. 1.

32 Roy Lewis and Jon Clark, 'The Bullock Report', *Modern Law Review* 40:3, 1977, 324–31, https://www.jstor.org/stable/1095416.

33 Stefan Stern, 'New PM Spells Big Change for Boards', *Financial Times*, 21 July 2016, https://www.ft.com/content/0d2170ae-49ae-11e6-8d68-72e9211e86ab.

34 Ewan McGaughey, 'Corporate Governance Reform: The End of Shareholder Monopoly with Votes at Work', *Oxford Business Law Blog*, 8 December 2017, https://www.law.ox.ac.uk/business-law-blog/blog/2017/12/corporate-governance-reform-end-shareholder-monopoly-votes-work.

35 Financial Reporting Council, 'Review of Corporate Governance Reporting', November 2020, 30, https://www.frc.org.uk/getattachment/c22f7296-0839-420e-ae03-bdce3e157702/Governance-Report-2020-2611.pdf.

36 Georgia Roberts, 'Reduced Percentage for Requesting an Information and Consultation Agreement in the Workplace', Clarkslegal, 28 January 2020, https://www.clarkslegal.com/Blog/Post/Reduced_percentage_for_requesting_an_information_and_consultation_agreement_in_the_workplace.

IV. *Changemakers*

1 I owe this way of thinking to a highly original and thought-provoking essay by Archon Fung. See Archon Fung, 'Four Levels of Power: A Conception to Enable Liberation', *Journal of Political Philosophy* 28:2, 2020, 131–57, https://doi.org/10.1111/jopp.12196.

16. You Only Get the Justice You Have the Power to Compel

1   See Citizens UK, 'Campaigns', https://www.citizensuk.org/campaigns/.
2   Through Maurice Glasman.
3   Saul D. Alinsky, *Rules for Radicals: A Pragmatic Primer for Realistic Radicals* (New York: Random House, 1971).
4   For a brilliant primer, see Matthew Bolton, *How to Resist* (London: Bloomsbury, 2017).
5   This work was eventually built on under the Corbyn leadership, with a community organising unit in the Labour Party.
6   Nando's, 'Halal Chicken Restaurants', https://www.nandos.co.uk/halal.
7   Sheila McKechnie Foundation, 'Community Jobs Compact', https://smk.org.uk/awards_nominations/community-jobs-compact/.
8   Thucydides Trans. Rex Warner, *History of the Peloponnesian War* (London: Penguin Books, 1954), 412.
9   Living Wage Foundation, 'What Is the Real Living Wage?', https://www.livingwage.org.uk/what-real-living-wage.
10 Zoe Wood, 'BrightHouse Admits Affordability Checks Are Hurting Business Model', *Guardian*, 4 October 2016, https://www.theguardian.com/money/2016/oct/04/brighthouse-admits-affordability-checks-are-hurting-business-model; Lex, 'BrightHouse: Dark Outlook,' *Financial Times*, 1 June 2018, https://www.ft.com/content/22efae32-64cd-11e8-90c2-9563a0613e56.
11 Bolton, *How to Resist*, 8.
12 Ibid. 27.

17. Twenty-First-Century Trade Unions

1   Quoted in David Rolf, *The Fight for Fifteen: The Right Wage for a Working America* (New York: New Press, 2016), 93.
2   Quoted ibid. 91.
3   Steven Greenhouse, 'Fast-Food Workers in New York City Rally for Higher Wages', *New York Times*, 28 November 2012, https://www.nytimes.com/2012/11/30/nyregion/fast-food-workers-in-new-york-city-rally-for-higher-wages.html.
4   Yannet Lathrop, 'Impact of the Fight for $15: $68 Billion in Raises, 22 Million Workers', *NELP*, 29 November 2018, https://www.nelp.org/publication/impact-fight-for-15-2018/.
5   Alexia Fernández Campbell, 'Maryland Minimum Wage: State Passes $15 Minimum Wage Bill', *Vox*, 28 March 2019, https://www.vox.com/2019/3/28/18285346/maryland-passes-15-minimum-wage.
6   Lathrop, 'Impact of the Fight for $15: $68 Billion in Raises, 22 Million Workers.'
7   Yannet Lathrop, 'Raises From Coast to Coast in 2021', *NELP*, 2020, 2, https://www.nelp.org/publication/raises-from-coast-to-coast-in-2021/.
8   Gillian Friedman, 'Once a Fringe Idea, the $15 Minimum Wage Is Making Big Gains', *New York Times*, 31 December 2020, https://www.nytimes.com/2020/12/31/business/economy/minimum-wage-15-dollar-hour.html.
9   Steven Greenhouse and Jana Kasperkevic, 'Fight for $15 Swells into Largest Protest by Low-Wage Workers in US History', *Guardian*, 15 April 2015, https://

www.theguardian.com/us-news/2015/apr/15/fight-for-15-minimum-wage-protests-new-york-los-angeles-atlanta-boston.

10 For a definitive account of the theory here, see Kate Andrias, 'The New Labor Law', *Yale Law Journal* 126:1, 2016, 2–100, https://repository.law.umich.edu/articles/1816.

11 Rolf, *The Fight for Fifteen: The Right Wage for a Working America*, 93.

12 Quoctrung Bui, '50 Years Of Shrinking Union Membership, In One Map', *NPR*, 23 February 2015, https://www.npr.org/sections/money/2015/02/23/385843576/50-years-of-shrinking-union-membership-in-one-map?t=1615495228053; Department for Business, Energy & Industrial Strategy, 'Trade Union Membership 2019: Statistical Bulletin', 2020, 14, https://www.gov.uk/government/statistics/trade-union-statistics-2019.

13 David Weil, *The Fissured Workplace* (Massachusetts: Harvard University Press, 2014).

14 Ibid. 7.

15 Adam Dean, Atheendar Venkataramani and Simeon Kimmel, 'Mortality Rates From COVID-19 Are Lower In Unionized Nursing Homes', *Health Affairs* 39:11, 2020, 1993–2001, https://doi.org/10.1377/hlthaff.2020.01011.

16 World Inequality Database, 'Top 1% National Income Share, United Kingdom, 1918–2019', 2021, https://wid.world/country/united-kingdom/.

17 Joe Dromey, 'Power to the People', *IPPR*, 2018, 6, https://www.ippr.org/files/2018-06/cej-trade-unions-may18-.pdf.

18 Florence Jaumotte and Carolina Osorio Buitron, 'Power from the People', *Finance & Development* 52:1, 2015, 30, https://www.imf.org/external/pubs/ft/fandd/2015/03/jaumotte.htm.

19 Ibid. 31.

20 Andrew G Haldane, 'Work, Wages and Monetary Policy', *Bank of England*, 20 June 2017, 5, https://www.bankofengland.co.uk/speech/2017/work-wages-and-monetary-policy.

21 Department for Business, Energy & Industrial Strategy, 'Table 1.9: Trade Union Membership Statistics 2019: Tables', 2019, https://www.gov.uk/government/statistics/trade-union-statistics-2019.

22 Alex Bryson and John Forth, 'The Added Value of Trade Unions', *TUC*, 2017, 5–6, https://www.niesr.ac.uk/sites/default/files/publications/Bryson and Forth 2017 lit review.pdf.

23 OECD, 'In It Together: Why Less Inequality Benefits All', 2015, 15, https://doi.org/10.1787/9789264235120-en.

24 OECD, 'Negotiating Our Way Up: Collective Bargaining in a Changing World of Work', 2019, 14, https://doi.org/10.1787/1fd2da34-en.

25 Department for Business, Energy & Industrial Strategy, 'Trade Union Membership 2019: Statistical Bulletin', 5; Stephen Machin, 'Union Decline in Britain', *British Journal of Industrial Relations* 38:4, 2000, 631, https://doi.org/10.1111/1467-8543.00183.

26 Department for Business, Energy & Industrial Strategy, 'Trade Union Membership 2019: Statistical Bulletin', 5.

27 Ibid. 15; Dromey, 'Power to the People', 19.

28 Department for Business, Energy & Industrial Strategy, 'Table 1.4: Trade Union Membership Statistics 2019: Tables', 2019.

29 Gavin Kelly and Dan Tomlinson, 'Inexorable Decline or Moment of Opportunity?', *Resolution Trust*, April 2018, http://resolutiontrust.org/wp-content/uploads/2018/04/Generational_challenge_unions.pdf.

30 Bakcrs Food and Allied Workers Union, 'BFAWU McDonalds Strike Press Release', 18 August 2017, https://www.bfawu.org/bfawu_mcdonalds_strike_press_release; Ashleigh Webber, 'McDonald's to Increase Pay Following Strike', *Personnel Today*, 4 January 2018, https://www.personneltoday.com/hr/mcdonalds-increase-pay-employees-following-strike/.

31 Independent Workers Union of Great Britain, 'Who We Are', https://iwgb.org.uk/page/about-us; United Voices of the World, 'About', https://www.uvwunion.org.uk/en/about/; Bethan Staton, 'The Upstart Unions Taking on the Gig Economy and Outsourcing', *Financial Times*, 19 January 2020, https://www.ft.com/content/576c68ea-3784-11ea-a6d3-9a26f8c3cba4; Yvonne Roberts, 'The Tiny Union Beating the Gig Economy Giants', *Guardian*, 1 July 2018, https://www.theguardian.com/politics/2018/jul/01/union-beating-gig-economy-giants-iwgb-zero-hours-workers.

32 Robert Booth, 'University of London Cleaners Win 10-Year Outsourcing Battle', *Guardian*, 3 November 2020, https://www.theguardian.com/education/2020/nov/03/university-of-london-cleaners-win-10-year-outsourcing-battle.

33 Resolution Trust, 'Workertech', http://resolutiontrust.org/worker-tech.

34 Organise, 'About Us', https://www.organise.org.uk/about.

35 Antonia Bance, 'Introducing WorkSmart: A New Trade Union Offer for UK 21–30s from the TUC', *Medium*, 4 June 2018, https://medium.com/@abance/introducing-worksmart-a-new-trade-union-offer-for-uk-21-30s-from-the-tuc-9f922e01a94b.

36 GMB Union, 'Hermes and GMB in Groundbreaking Gig Economy Deal', 4 February 2019, https://www.gmb.org.uk/news/hermes-gmb-groundbreaking-gig-economy-deal; Haroon Siddique, 'Hermes Couriers Are Workers, Not Self-Employed, Tribunal Rules', *Guardian*, 25 June 2018, https://www.theguardian.com/business/2018/jun/25/hermes-couriers-are-workers-not-self-employed-tribunal-rules.

37 GMB Union, 'Historic Workers' Rights Win: Supreme Court Rules in Uber Drivers' Favour', 19 February 2021, https://gmb.org.uk/news/uber-workers-rights-historic-gmb-supreme-court-drivers-legal-battle.

38 Ryan Fletcher, 'Gig economy doubles', *UniteLive,* 1 July 2019, https://unitelive.org/gig-economy-doubles/.

39 Guyon Espiner, 'The Negotiator – Jim Bolger', *RNZ*, 21 April 2017, https://www.rnz.co.nz/programmes/the-9th-floor/story/201840999/the-negotiator-jim-bolger.

40 Fair Pay Agreements Working Group, 'Fair Pay Agreements Supporting Workers and Firms to Drive Productivity Growth and Share the Benefits', 2018, 2, https://www.mbie.govt.nz/assets/695e21c9c3/working-group-report.pdf.

41 Ibid. 9.

42 Gavin Kelly, 'Churchill, the Crisis and a Better Deal for Britain's Low Paid', *Medium*, 6 May 2020, https://gavinkellyblog.com/churchill-the-crisis-and-a-better-deal-for-britains-low-paid-d83f3daca6cc.

43 Julia Lourie, 'A Minimum Wage', *House of Commons Library*, 1995, 4, https://researchbriefings.files.parliament.uk/documents/RP95-7/RP95-7.pdf.

44 Kelly, 'Churchill, the Crisis and a Better Deal for Britain's Low Paid'.

45 Welsh Government, 'Terms of Reference and Membership: Social Care Fair Work Forum', 2021, https://gov.wales/social-care-fair-work-forum/terms-of-reference.

18. Follow the Money

1   Fossil Free, 'Divestment Commitments', accessed 27 February 2021, https://gofossilfree.org/divestment/commitments/.

2 Matt Schudel, 'Larry Gibson, W. Va. activist who fought mountain mining, dies at 66', *Washington Post*, 13 September 2012, https://www.washingtonpost.com/local/obituaries/larry-gibson-w-va-activist-who-fought-mountain-mining-dies-at-66/2012/09/13/93af1cf6-fdbe-11e1-a31e-804fccb658f9_story.html; Suzanne Goldenberg, 'West Virginia Anti-Mining Crusader Larry Gibson Dead at 66', *Guardian*, 10 September 2012, https://www.theguardian.com/world/2012/sep/10/west-virginia-antimining-larry-gibson.

3 James B Stewart, 'A Clash of Ideals and Investments at Swarthmore', *New York Times*, 16 May 2014, https://www.nytimes.com/2014/05/17/business/a-clash-of-ideals-and-investments-at-swarthmore.html.

4 Swarthmore Mountain Justice, 'Our Campaign', https://swatmountainjustice.wordpress.com/ourcampaign/.

5 Joanna Walters, 'Swarthmore College Says It Will Not Pursue Fossil Fuel Divestment', *Guardian*, 2 May 2015, https://www.theguardian.com/us-news/2015/may/02/swarthmore-college-fossil-fuel-divestment-decision.

6 Bill McKibben, 'Global Warming's Terrifying New Math', *Rolling Stone*, 19 July 2012, https://www.rollingstone.com/politics/politics-news/global-warmings-terrifying-new-math-188550/.

7 Carbon Tracker, 'Unburnable Carbon – Are the World's Financial Markets Carrying a Carbon Bubble?', 13 July 2011, https://carbontracker.org/reports/carbon-bubble/.

8 Alan Livsey, 'Lex in Depth: The $900bn Cost of "Stranded Energy Assets"', *Financial Times*, 4 February 2020, https://www.ft.com/content/95efca74-4299-11ea-a43a-c4b328d9061c.

9 Sarah Breeden, 'Avoiding the Storm: Climate Change and the Financial System', *Bank of England*, 15 April 2019, https://www.bankofengland.co.uk/-/media/boe/files/speech/2019/avoiding-the-storm-climate-change-and-the-financial-system-speech-by-sarah-breeden.pdf; Richard Partington, 'Mark Carney Tells Global Banks They Cannot Ignore Climate Change Dangers', *Guardian*, 17 April 2019, https://www.theguardian.com/environment/2019/apr/17/mark-carney-tells-global-banks-they-cannot-ignore-climate-change-dangers.

10 David Wighton, 'Short-Termism May Be Here for the Long Run – but That's Not All Bad', *The Times*, 27 October 2020, https://www.thetimes.co.uk/article/sometimes-investors-are-wise-to-put-short-term-interests-first-pc3olxwos.

11 Nicolas Maennling, 'Lessons Learned From an Energy Company's Green Transformation', *Columbia Center on Sustainable Investment*, 15 April 2019, http://ccsi.columbia.edu/2019/04/15/lessons-learned-from-an-energy-companys-green-transformation/; Eric Reguly, 'A Tale of Transformation: The Danish Company That Went from Black to Green Energy', *Corporate Knights*, 16 April 2019, https://www.corporateknights.com/channels/climate-and-carbon/black-green-energy-15554049/.

12 Richard Knight, 'Sanctions, Disinvestment, and U.S. Corporations in South Africa', in *Sanctioning Apartheid*, ed. Robert Edgar (Trenton: Africa World Press, 1990), http://richardknight.homestead.com/files/uscorporations.htm.

13 Ryan Leitner, 'British Students Force End of Barclays Bank's Investments in South African Apartheid 1969–1987', *Global Nonviolent Action Database*, 8 February 2014, https://nvdatabase.swarthmore.edu/content/british-students-force-end-barclays-bank-s-investments-south-african-apartheid-1969-1987#case-study-detail.

14 For example see Belinda Gan, 'Divestment – Does It Drive Real Change?', *Schroders*, 2019, 7, https://www.schroders.com/getfunddocument/?oid=1.9.3338808.

15 Atif Ansar, Ben Caldecott and James Tilbury, 'Stranded Assets and the Fossil Fuel Divestment Campaign: What Does Divestment Mean for the Valuation of Fossil

Fuel Assets?', 2013, 12, 65–66, https://www.smithschool.ox.ac.uk/publications/reports/SAP-divestment-report-final.pdf.

16 Fossil Free, 'Divestment Commitments'.

17 Rubert Neate, 'Rockefeller Family Charity to Withdraw All Investments in Fossil Fuel Companies', *Guardian*, 23 March 2016, https://www.theguardian.com/environment/2016/mar/23/rockefeller-fund-divestment-fossil-fuel-companies-oil-coal-climate-change.

18 Fossil Free UK, 'Why Divestment?', https://gofossilfree.org/uk/why-divestment/.

19 InfluenceMap, 'Big Oil's Real Agenda on Climate Change', 2019, 2–3, https://influencemap.org/report/How-Big-Oil-Continues-to-Oppose-the-Paris-Agreement-38212275958aa21196dae3b76220bddc.

20 Felicity Lawrence, David Pegg and Rob Evans, 'How Vested Interests Tried to Turn the World against Climate Science', *Guardian*, 10 October 2019, https://www.theguardian.com/environment/2019/oct/10/vested-interests-public-against-climate-science-fossil-fuel-lobby.

21 C. J. Polychroniou, 'Are Fossil Fuel Divestment Campaigns Working? A Conversation With Economist Robert Pollin', *Global Policy Journal*, 29 May 2018, https://www.globalpolicyjournal.com/blog/29/05/2018/are-fossil-fuel-divestment-campaigns-working-conversation-economist-robert-pollin.

22 Siew Hong Teoh, Ivo Welch and C. Paul Wazzan, 'The Effect of Socially Activist Investment Policies on the Financial Markets: Evidence from the South African Boycott', *Journal of Business* 72:1, 1999, https://doi.org/10.1086/209602.

23 Martin Wright, '"Divestment Isn't a Badge of Honour; It's a Failure of Engagement"', *Reuters Events*, 26 February 2019, https://www.reutersevents.com/sustainability/divestment-isnt-badge-honour-its-failure-engagement.

24 Climate Action 100+, 'About Climate Action 100+', accessed 27 February 2021, https://www.climateaction100.org/about/.

25 The Church of England, 'Church of England Restricts Investment in Companies That Don't Meet Its Climate Standards', 15 December 2020, https://www.churchofengland.org/news-and-media/news-and-statements/church-england-restricts-investment-companies-dont-meet-its.

26 Climate Action 100+, '2019 Progress Report', 2019, 7, https://www.climateaction100.org/wp-content/uploads/2020/10/English-Progress-Report-2019.pdf; Anjli Raval, 'BP Shareholders Vote in Favour of Greater Climate Disclosure', *Financial Times*, 21 May 2019, https://www.ft.com/content/fcb14d66-7bcd-11e9-81d2-f785092ab560.

27 Jillian Ambrose, 'World's Biggest Sovereign Wealth Fund to Ditch Fossil Fuels', *Guardian*, 12 June 2019, https://www.theguardian.com/business/2019/jun/12/worlds-biggest-sovereign-wealth-fund-to-ditch-fossil-fuels.

28 Gwladys Fouché, 'Norway Wealth Fund to Test Business Model of Biggest CO_2 Emitters', *Reuters*, 3 September 2020, https://www.reuters.com/article/us-norway-swf/norway-wealth-fund-to-test-business-model-of-biggest-co2-emitters-idUKKBN25U1MN?edition-redirect=uk.

29 Ansar, Caldecott and Tilbury, 'Stranded Assets and the Fossil Fuel Divestment Campaign: What Does Divestment Mean for the Valuation of Fossil Fuel Assets?', 10–14.

30 Mark Carney, 'Breaking the Tragedy of the Horizon – Climate Change and Financial Stability', *Bank of England*, 29 September 2015, https://www.bankofengland.co.uk/speech/2015/breaking-the-tragedy-of-the-horizon-climate-change-and-financial-stability.

31 HM Treasury, 'Chancellor statement to the House – Financial Services', 9 November 2020, https://www.gov.uk/government/speeches/chancellor-statement-to-the-house-financial-services.

32 Noam Bergman, 'Impacts of the Fossil Fuel Divestment Movement: Effects on Finance, Policy and Public Discourse', *Sustainability*, 2018, 1,9, https://doi.org/10.3390/su10072529.

33 Michele Della Vigna et al., 'Re-Imagining Big Oils: How Energy Companies Can Successfully Adapt to Climate Change', *Goldman Sachs*, 2018, 40, https://www.goldmansachs.com/insights/pages/reports/re-imagining-big-oils-f/re-imagining-big-oils-report-pdf.pdf.

34 Bill McKibben, 'At Last, Divestment Is Hitting the Fossil Fuel Industry Where It Hurts', *Guardian*, 16 December 2018, https://www.theguardian.com/commentisfree/2018/dec/16/divestment-fossil-fuel-industry-trillions-dollars-investments-carbon.

35 Shell, 'Shell Annual Report and Form 20-F 2017', 2017, 13, https://reports.shell.com/annual-report/2017/servicepages/downloads/files/strategic_report_shell_ar17.pdf.

36 David Mason and Peter Bosshard, 'Insuring Our Future', *Insure Our Future*, 2020, 5, https://insureourfuture.co/2020scorecard/.

37 Graham Readfearn, 'Adani Mine: Three Major Insurers to Have No Further Involvement in Coal Project', *Guardian*, 11 June 2020, https://www.theguardian.com/environment/2020/jun/12/adani-mine-three-major-insurers-to-have-no-further-involvement-in-coal-project.

38 Rainforest Action Network, 'Banking on Climate Change – Fossil Fuel Finance Report 2020', 2020, 3–4, https://www.ran.org/bankingonclimatechange2020/; Patrick Greenfield and Kalyeena Makortoff, 'Study: Global Banks 'Failing Miserably' on Climate Crisis by Funelling Trillions into Fossil Fuels', *Guardian*, 18 March 2020, https://www.theguardian.com/environment/2020/mar/18/global-banks-climate-crisis-finance-fossil-fuels.

39 Bill McKibben, 'Money Is the Oxygen on Which the Fire of Global Warming Burns', *New Yorker*, 17 September 2019, https://www.newyorker.com/news/daily-comment/money-is-the-oxygen-on-which-the-fire-of-global-warming-burns.

40 Stop the Money Pipeline, 'Chase Funds Climate Chaos', https://stopthemoneypipeline.com/chase/.

41 Jessica Corbett, 'Chase Climate Pledge "Shows the Power of Relentless Environmental Activism" But "Not Aggressive Enough"', *Common Dreams*, 6 October 2020, https://www.commondreams.org/news/2020/10/06/chase-climate-pledge-shows-power-relentless-environmental-activism-not-aggressive.

42 Share Action, 'What World Could Your Money Build?', https://shareaction.org/pensions/i-want-to-learn/.

19. The Preston Story

1 Christina Malathouni, 'Preston Bus Station', *Twentieth Century Society*, 24 February 2013, https://c20society.org.uk/casework/preston-bus-station; Rowan Moore, 'Preston Bus Station Review – a Glorious Reprieve', *Guardian*, 9 June 2018, https://www.theguardian.com/artanddesign/2018/jun/09/preston-bus-station-renovation-ove-arup-glorious-reprieve-john-puttick.

2   Cassidy & Ashton, 'Preston Bus Station Scoops Three RIBA Awards', *Cassidy + Ashton*, 21 May 2019, https://www.cassidyashton.co.uk/preston-bus-station-scoops-three-riba-awards/.

3   Preston Borough Council, 'Preston Town Centre Analysis Precis Document', 2000, 11, https://web.archive.org/web/20070929092445/http://www.preston.gov.uk/Documents/General/Public Relations/summary.pdf.

4   Department of the Environment Transport and the Regions, 'English Indices of Deprivation 2000: District Indices', 10 December 2020, https://www.gov.uk/government/collections/english-indices-of-deprivation.

5   Place North West, 'Lend Lease and Grosvenor Formalise Tithebarn Agreement', 8 October 2007, https://www.placenorthwest.co.uk/news/lend-lease-and-grosvenor-formalise-tithebarn-agreement/; Lancashire Telegraph, 'Marks & Spencer Plan Massive New Store in Preston', 8 September 2008, https://www.lancashiretelegraph.co.uk/news/3653822.marks-spencer-plan-massive-new-store-in-preston/.

6   Preston Tithebarn, 'Frequently Asked Questions', 2008, https://web.archive.org/web/20100521064120/http://www.prestontithebarn.com/questions.htm#.

7   Place North West, 'Grosvenor/Lend Lease Agree Cineworld Deal at Tithebarn', 19 December 2008, https://www.placenorthwest.co.uk/news/grosvenorlend-lease-agree-cineworld-deal-at-tithebarn/.

8   BBC News, 'Preston Tithebarn Scheme Abandoned after John Lewis Withdraws', 3 November 2011, https://www.bbc.co.uk/news/uk-england-lancashire-15571764.

9   Hazel Sheffield, '"Poverty Was Entrenched in Preston. So We Became More Self-Sufficient"', *Guardian*, 14 February 2017, https://www.theguardian.com/society/2017/feb/14/poverty-was-entrenched-in-preston-so-we-became-more-self-sufficient; Clifford Singer, 'The Preston Model', *Next System Project*, 9 September 2016, https://thenextsystem.org/the-preston-model.

10   CLES and Preston City Council, 'How We Built Community Wealth in Preston: Achievements and Lessons', 2019, 11, https://cles.org.uk/wp-content/uploads/2019/07/CLES_Preston-Document_WEB-AW.pdf.

11   Ibid. 12–13.

12   Ibid. 10, 20.

13   Ibid. 15.

14   Lancashire Evening Post, 'Park Hotel to Be Returned to Former Glory', 22 June 2016, https://www.lep.co.uk/business/park-hotel-be-returned-former-glory-774799.

15   CLES and Preston City Council, 'How We Built Community Wealth in Preston: Achievements and Lessons', 20–21.

16   Richard Partington, 'Preston Named as Most Improved City in UK', *Guardian*, 1 November 2018, https://www.theguardian.com/politics/2018/nov/01/preston-named-as-most-most-improved-city-in-uk.

17   Lancashire Post, 'Preston Bus Station's Grand Reopening after a £19m Facelift', 10 July 2018, https://www.lep.co.uk/news/traffic-and-travel/preston-bus-stations-grand-reopening-after-aps19m-facelift-1015241.

18   CLES, 'What Is Community Wealth Building?', https://cles.org.uk/community-wealth-building/what-is-community-wealth-building/.

19   Joe Guinan and Martin O'Neill, *The Case for Community Wealth Building* (Cambridge: Polity Press, 2020), 5–9.

20   Ted Howard, 'Owning Your Own Job Is a Beautiful Thing', *Investing in What Works for America's Communities* (San Francisco: San Francisco Federal Reserve, 2012), 205–7, https://community-wealth.org/content/owning-your-own-job-beautiful-thing-community-wealth-building-cleveland-ohio.

21   CLES, 'What Is Community Wealth Building?'

22 Federation of Small Businesses, 'Local Procurement: Making the Most of Small Business, One Year On', 2013, 4, https://cles.org.uk/wp-content/uploads/2016/10/FSB-procurement-2013.pdf.

23 Greater Manchester Pension Fund, 'Annual Report & Accounts 2016', 2016, 5, https://www.gmpf.org.uk/getmedia/61e7866b-58fe-4503-aa62-7dd990d6a9f2/AnnualReport2016.pdf.

24 For example, see Antoine Bozio et al., 'Pre-Distribution Versus Redistribution: Evidence from France and the US', *VOX,CEPR Policy Portal*, 18 November 2020, https://voxeu.org/article/pre-distribution-versus-redistribution.

25 Alan Lockey and Ben Glover, 'The Wealth Within The "Preston Model" and the New Municipalism', 2019, 31, https://demos.co.uk/project/the-wealth-within-the-preston-model-and-the-new-municipalism/.

26 Foundational Economy Collective, *Foundational Economy: The Infrastructure of Everyday Life* (Manchester: Manchester University Press, 2018), 44.

27 British Medical Association, 'Health at a Price: Reducing the Impact of Poverty', 2017, https://www.bma.org.uk/media/2084/health-at-a-price-2017.pdf.

28 The Economist, 'Labour's Plans – Preston, Jeremy Corbyn's Model Town', 19 October 2017, https://www.economist.com/britain/2017/10/19/preston-jeremy-corbyns-model-town.

29 Preston City Council, 'What Is Preston Model?', https://www.preston.gov.uk/article/1339/What-is-Preston-Model-.

30 See Evergreen Cooperatives, 'About Us', http://www.evgoh.com/about-us/.

31 LabourList, 'Wirral Launches "Ethical Economics" Community Wealth Building Strategy', 25 February 2020, https://labourlist.org/2020/02/wirral-launches-ethical-economics-community-wealth-building-strategy/.

32 CLES, 'Community Wealth Building 2019', 2019, 13, https://cles.org.uk/wp-content/uploads/2019/09/CWB2019FINAL-web.pdf.

33 Scottish Government, 'Cities and Regions: Community Wealth Building', accessed 1 March 2021, https://www.gov.scot/policies/cities-regions/community-wealth-building/; Welsh Government, 'Progress towards the Development of a New Procurement Landscape in Wales', 18 March 2020, https://gov.wales/progress-towards-the-development-of-a-new-procurement-landscape-in-wales-html.

34 Cabinet Office, 'New Plans Set out to Transform Procurement, Providing More Value for Money and Benefitting Small Business', 15 December 2020, https://www.gov.uk/government/news/new-plans-set-out-to-transform-procurement-providing-more-value-for-money-and-benefitting-small-business.

35 Guinan and O'Neill, *The Case for Community Wealth Building*, 15.

36 NHS, 'The NHS Long Term Plan', 2019, 120, https://www.longtermplan.nhs.uk/publication/nhs-long-term-plan/.

37 I am grateful to Roberto Mangabeira Unger for this insight. See 'The Boutwood Lectures', 2002, https://www.robertounger.com/2017/01/18/the-boutwood-lectures-the-second-way/.

20. It Takes a Movement

1 Farhana Yamin, 'Die, Survive or Thrive?' in *This Is Not a Drill: An Extinction Rebellion Handbook*, ed. Clare Farrell et al. (London: Penguin Books, 2019), 22.

2 Andrew Anthony, 'Farhana Yamin: "It Took 20 Minutes to Unglue Me from Shell's Office. It Was a Bit Painful"', *Guardian*, 19 May 2019, https://www.theguardian.com/environment/2019/may/19/farhana-yamin-extinction-rebellion-unglue-shell.

3   Ella Wills and Olivia Tobin, 'Extinction Rebellion Activists Gather in Hyde Park to Mark End of Disruptive Protests with "Closing Ceremony"', *Evening Standard*, 25 April 2019, https://www.standard.co.uk/news/london/extinction-rebellion-protesters-gather-in-london-to-mark-end-of-demonstrations-with-closing-ceremony-a4126796.html.

4   Eliza Barclay and Brian Resnick, 'How Big Was the Global Climate Strike? 4 Million People, Activists Estimate', *Vox*, 22 September 2019, https://www.vox.com/energy-and-environment/2019/9/20/20876143/climate-strike-2019-september-20-crowd-estimate.

5   BBC News, 'Climate strike: Schoolchildren protest over climate change', 15 February 2019, https://www.bbc.co.uk/news/uk-47250424.

6   Elina Couria, 'After Greta Thunberg, All Eyes Are on Michael Gove', *New Statesman*, 23 April 2019, https://www.newstatesman.com/politics/staggers/2019/04/after-greta-thunberg-all-eyes-are-michael-gove.

7   BBC News, 'UK Parliament Declares Climate Change Emergency', 1 May 2019, https://www.bbc.co.uk/news/uk-politics-48126677.

8   UK Parliament, 'Select Committees Announce Plans for Citizens' Assembly', 20 June 2019, https://committees.parliament.uk/committee/365/business-energy-and-industrial-strategy-committee/news/96965/select-committees-announce-plans-for-citizens-assembly/.

9   Department for Business, Energy & Industrial Strategy, 'UK Becomes First Major Economy to Pass Net Zero Emissions Law', 27 June 2019, https://www.gov.uk/government/news/uk-becomes-first-major-economy-to-pass-net-zero-emissions-law.

10   Exctinction Rebellion, 'Our Demands', 2021, https://extinctionrebellion.uk/the-truth/demands/.

11   Sky Data, 'Extinction Rebellion Poll', 23 April 2019, https://interactive.news.sky.com/XR_TABS_230419.pdf.

12   Matthew Smith, 'Concern for the Environment at Record Highs', *YouGov*, 5 June 2019, https://yougov.co.uk/topics/politics/articles-reports/2019/06/05/concern-environment-record-highs.

13   Alicia Garza, *The Purpose of Power* (London: Transworld, 2020), 110–11.

14   Larry Buchanan, Quoctrung Bui and Jugal K. Patel, 'Black Lives Matter May Be the Largest Movement in U.S. History', *New York Times*, 3 July 2020, https://www.nytimes.com/interactive/2020/07/03/us/george-floyd-protests-crowd-size.html.

15   Aamna Mohdin, Glenn Swann and Caroline Bannock, 'How George Floyd's Death Sparked a Wave of UK Anti-Racism Protests', *Guardian*, 29 July 2020, https://www.theguardian.com/uk-news/2020/jul/29/george-floyd-death-fuelled-anti-racism-protests-britain.

16   Sam Levin, 'Minneapolis Lawmakers Vow to Disband Police Department in Historic Move', *Guardian*, 8 June 2020, https://www.theguardian.com/us-news/2020/jun/07/minneapolis-city-council-defund-police-george-floyd.

17   Tiffany Hsu and Eleanor Lutz, 'More Than 1,000 Companies Boycotted Facebook. Did It Work?', *New York Times*, 1 August 2020, https://www.nytimes.com/2020/08/01/business/media/facebook-boycott.html; Stop Hate for Profit, 'Participating Businesses', 2020, https://www.stophateforprofit.org/participating-businesses.

18   Alison Flood, 'Black British Authors Top UK Book Charts in Wake of BLM Protests', *Guardian*, 10 June 2020, https://www.theguardian.com/books/2020/jun/10/black-british-authors-uk-book-charts-blm-bernardine-evaristo-reni-eddo-lodge-waterstones.

19 Mappingpoliceviolence.org, 'Mapping Police Violence', 16 February 2021, https://mappingpoliceviolence.org/.

20 Home Office, 'Ethnicity Facts and Figures: Stop and Search', 22 February 2021, https://www.ethnicity-facts-figures.service.gov.uk/crime-justice-and-the-law/policing/stop-and-search/latest#by-ethnicity.

21 Monmouth University, 'Protestors' Anger Justified Even If Actions May Not Be', 2 June 2020, https://www.monmouth.edu/polling-institute/reports/monmouthpoll_us_060220.

22 Tamara Keith, 'Democratic Candidates Stumble Over Black Lives Matter Movement', *NPR*, 31 July 2015, https://www.npr.org/sections/itsallpolitics/2015/07/31/427851451/democratic-candidates-stumble-over-black-lives-matter-movement.

23 Christopher A. Cooper et al., 'Southern Democrats' Split with Republicans over Confederate Symbols Is More Recent than You Might Think', *LSE US Centre*, 10 July 2020, https://blogs.lse.ac.uk/usappblog/2020/07/10/southern-democrats-split-with-republicans-over-confederate-symbols-is-more-recent-than-you-might-think/.

24 White House, 'Inaugural Address by President Joseph R. Biden, Jr.', 20 January 2021, https://www.whitehouse.gov/briefing-room/speeches-remarks/2021/01/20/inaugural-address-by-president-joseph-r-biden-jr/.

25 Bill McKibben, *Falter: Has the Human Game Begun to Play Itself Out?* (London: Wildfire, 2019), 217.

26 Elizabeth Jones, 'The Bristol Bus Boycott of 1963', *Black History Month 2021*, 7 October 2018, https://www.blackhistorymonth.org.uk/article/section/bhm-heroes/the-bristol-bus-boycott-of-1963/.

27 National Archives, 'Local Government Act 1988: Section 28', 1988, https://www.legislation.gov.uk/ukpga/1988/9/section/28/1991-02-01.

28 Bolton, *How to Resist*.

29 Mark Engler and Paul Engler, *This Is an Uprising: How Nonviolent Revolt Is Shaping the Twenty-First Century* (New York: Bold Type Books, 2016), 162.

30 Martin Luther King Jr., 'Letter from Birmingham Jail', 1963.

31 Erica Chenoweth and Maria J. Stephan, *Why Civil Resistance Works: The Strategic Logic of Nonviolent Conflict* (New York: Columbia University Press, 2011); Erica Chenoweth, 'Questions, Answers, and Some Cautionary Updates Regarding the 3.5% Rule', *Carr Center Discussion Paper*, 2020, https://carrcenter.hks.harvard.edu/files/cchr/files/CCDP_005.pdf.

32 Jonathan Leake, Shanti Das and Shingi Mararike, 'We'll Win Fight with Maths, Vow Extinction Rebellion Protesters', *Sunday Times*, 21 April 2019, https://www.thetimes.co.uk/article/well-win-fight-with-maths-vow-extinction-rebellion-protesters-hxjx29bqf.

33 BBC News, '"Million" March against Iraq War', 16 February 2003, http://news.bbc.co.uk/1/hi/2765041.stm.

34 Engler and Engler, *This Is an Uprising: How Nonviolent Revolt Is Shaping the Twenty-First Century*, 91–92.

35 Garza, *The Purpose of Power*, 136.

36 Mark Townsend, 'Tube Protest Was a Mistake, Admit Leading Extinction Rebellion Members', *Guardian*, accessed 19 February 2021, https://www.theguardian.com/environment/2019/oct/20/extinction-rebellion-tube-protest-was-a-mistake.

37 Hahrie Han, 'Want Gun Control? Learn From the N.R.A.', *New York Times*, 4 October 2017, https://www.nytimes.com/2017/10/04/opinion/gun-control-nra-vegas.html.

38 Ibid.

39 Hahrie Han and Carina Barnett-Loro, 'To Support a Stronger Climate Movement, Focus Research on Building Collective Power', *Frontiers in Communication* 3:55, 2018, 1–2, https://doi.org/10.3389/fcomm.2018.00055.

40 Garza, *The Purpose of Power*, 127–29.

41 Zeynep Tufekci, 'Do Protests Even Work?', *The Atlantic*, 24 June 2020, https://www.theatlantic.com/technology/archive/2020/06/why-protests-work/613420/.

42 Erica Chenoweth, 'The Future of Nonviolent Resistance', *Journal of Democracy* 31:3, 2020, 70, https://www.journalofdemocracy.org/articles/the-future-of-nonviolent-resistance-2/.

43 Garza, *The Purpose of Power*, xiii–xiv.

44 Alinsky, *Rules for Radicals: A Pragmatic Primer for Realistic Radicals*, xxvi.

INDEX

Note: EM indicates Ed Miliband.

Aardman 196–7, 198
Abdi, Ali 215
Advocacy Academy 168–9
Age of Stupid (film) 261–2
Agricultural Wages Board 234
air pollution 28, 33, 89, 135, 175
Alaska Permanent Fund Dividend
    (PFD) 45–6, 48, 51, 52, 53, 57,
    272
Alinsky, Saul: *Rules for Radicals* 213,
    216, 220, 269
All the President's Men (Woodward/
    Bernstein) 236
Alphabet (Google's parent company)
    121
Amazon (online retailer) 189
    'Amazon's Antitrust Paradox'
    (Khan) 119–20, 126, 127
    corporate lobbying 125
    Covid-19 and value of 121–2
    e-book prices and 122, 125
    market dominance of 119–20,
    121–2, 125, 128
    Marketplace platform 128
    takeovers of smaller firms 122, 128
anchor institutions 251–3, 255, 256
Angela (BrightHouse customer) 220–1
App Drivers and Couriers Union 232

Apple (technology company) 80, 119,
    121, 122, 128, 226
Ardern, Jacinda 94, 232–3
Aristotle 154
AT&T 127
Athens, ancient
    Council of Five Hundred/delibera-
    tive democracy in 153–4
    Melian Dialogue/community organ-
    ising and 217–19
Atlantic 152
austerity policies, UK government 3,
    4, 165, 249
Austria
    housing in 35–6, 38, 40, 44
    voting age in 166, 167–8, 170, 272
    worker representation in 202
automation 6, 50, 115
Aviva 68, 243

Bailey, Andrew 220–1
Bakers, Food and Allied Workers'
    Union 230
Bank of England 74, 77, 90, 220–1,
    228–9, 239, 244
banks/banking system
    community bank 255–6
    cooperatives and 200

divestment and 240, 246
financial crisis (2007–8) and 3, 155
Barclays Bank 240
Barnes, Andrew 112, 115
B Corporation (B Corp) 70–1, 75–6,
    77, 273
Bee Network, Greater Manchester
    140–1
Belu water 71
benefits system 20, 58
    bureaucracy and 50, 188, 191, 192
    childcare workers and 99
    Covid-19 and 5, 37, 58
    freedom dividend and 53, 57
    housing benefit 37, 38, 39, 43, 254
    means testing and 49, 50, 53, 54
    'poverty trap' and 49
    sanctions applied in 49–50
    social inheritance and 57
    tax rate on payments 49
    Universal Credit 47, 49–50, 54,
        188, 253, 254
Betts, Pete 22
Bevan, Aneurin 43–4
Beveridge Report (*Social Insurance
    and Allied Services: Report by Sir
    William Beveridge*) (1942) 8
Bezos, Jeff 121–2
Biden, Joe 225, 261
BiFab 32
Big Society 188–9
Big Tech, domination of 2, 119–30,
    209 *see also* technology
Bismarck, Otto von 9
Bjarnfreðsdóttir, Aðalheiður 59
Black Friday 70
Black Lives Matter 259–61, 265, 267,
    268, 269
Blair, Tony 17
Bloomberg, Michael 266
blue zones (longevity hotspots) 134
Boardman, Chris 140–1
Bolger, Jim 232–3, 234
Bolton, Matthew 218, 221–2
Bond, Sir John 218
Boston, US, participatory budgeting
    in 169
Brexit 1, 3, 4, 19, 91, 148, 165
Brierley, Eliza 199

BrightHouse 219–22
Bristol Omnibus Company 262–3
British Social Attitudes 62
British Youth Council 170
Brown, Gordon 22–3, 111, 218
Brown, Matthew 249
Buchanan Report (1963) 137
bureaucracy, state 50, 187–95
Burnham, Andy 140, 141, 173–4, 181,
    183
Bush, George W. 151, 152
business 70–81
    B Corporations (B Corp) 70–1,
        75–6, 77
    Corporate Governance Code
        changes (2018) 77
    Covid-19 pandemic, response to
        73, 81
    deregulation of finance (1980s) 74
    divestment and *see* divestment
    Friedman model of capitalism and
        70–1, 72–3, 74–5, 76, 79, 81
    'industrial strategy', government
        and 79–81, 100–2
    market economics and *see* market
        economics
    ownership models 79, 196–201
    patient capital and 74, 79, 80
    productivity and 78, 90, 112–16,
        118, 177, 203, 233
    share buybacks 74
    shareholder value 71–9, 198, 203,
        239, 255 *see also* shareholder
    UK Companies Act (2006) Section
        172 and 77–9
    worker power/participation and
        196–206 *see also* workplace
    working hours and 109–18 *see also*
        working hours
Business Roundtable 75
bus services 33, 136, 174–6, 183, 204,
    248, 249, 251, 256, 262–3, 272

Café Direct 71
Cambridgeshire County Council:
    Neighbourhood Cares pro-
    gramme 193
Cameron, David 11, 41, 91, 94–5,
    188–9

carbon emissions 94
  budgets 27, 158
  carbon bubble 239, 240, 243, 244, 246, 247
  carbon footprint figures, GDP and 96–7
  fossil fuel reserves and 238
  housing and 28, 30, 31, 42, 43, 189
  jobs and 31, 102
  net zero emissions target 11, 243, 244, 246, 247, 257, 258–9
  structural injustice and 23, 25
  transport and 33, 135, 136, 139 *see also* climate change *and* greenhouse gas emissions
Carbon Tracker 238
Care Quality Commission 190–1
care work *see* social care
Carney, Mark 244
cars 33, 34, 102, 131–2, 135–40, 142, 143, 175, 187
  electric cars 33, 34, 98, 135–6
Centre for Local Economic Strategies 249
Chamberlain, Joseph 179
Chartered Institute of Personnel and Development 112
childcare 20, 59, 60
  B Corps and 70
  Covid-19 and 61, 62, 117
  investing in/Swedish system 104–6, 272
  parental leave and 65, 66, 67
  workers 99–100, 101, 102, 104–6, 225
child poverty 17, 94
Child Trust Fund 55–7, 58
Chowdhury, Sotez 219
Church of England 243
cities
  climate change and 24, 139–42
  community wealth building and *see* community wealth building
  housing/cost of living in 35–7, 44
  inequality in 18, 35–7
  sortition and 154
  transport and 131, 134, 137, 138, 139–43, 175
  wages and 225, 230

citizens' assemblies 97, 150–61, 258
  climate emergency and 157–8, 159–60
  drawbacks of 157–9, 160
  French climate assembly 157–8
  House of Lords reform and 159
  Mongolian constitution and 152, 156, 157
  origins of 151–4, 156, 160
  renewable energy in Texas and 151–2
  representative democracy shortcomings and 154–8
  same-sex marriage legalisation in Ireland and 150–1, 155, 156–7
  social care and 158–9
  sortition and 153–4
  UK Climate Assembly 160–1, 170
Citizens Cymru Wales 215–16, 222
citizenship education 170–1
Citizens UK 212–13, 218, 219, 222, 268
Civilian Conservation Corps 29
Civil Rights movement, US 48, 260, 267
class stratification 15–16, 19
Clegg, Nick 63, 64
Climate Action 100+ 243
climate change 2, 6, 18, 21, 22–34, 159–60, 271
  carbon emissions and *see* carbon emissions
  citizens' assemblies and 156, 157–8, 159–60, 170, 258
  Climate Change Act (2008) 158
  Climate Change Committee (CCC) 34, 158, 159, 247
  Copenhagen climate summit (2009) 22–4, 25, 29, 239, 257
  democratic public ownership and 33–4
  divestment and 237–41, 243, 244, 245–7
  Extinction Rebellion 257–9, 264–5
  fairness of transition to renewable energy/fossil fuel economy workers and 26–7, 32–3
  generational gap and 27, 162–3, 172, 261

Green New Deal 28–9, 34, 43,
   162–3, 209
home heating and 28, 30, 31, 189
industrial policy and 32, 100–1
net zero greenhouse gas emissions
   target 11, 243, 244, 246, 247,
   257, 258–9
Paris Climate Accord (2015) 11, 24,
   26, 246, 257
renewable energy 31–2, 57, 79, 80,
   150, 151–2, 239
school climate strikes 168, 258, 273
social contract and 25–34
social movements and 168, 257–9,
   261–2, 264–5, 273
temperature rises/warming targets,
   1.5°C/2°C 22–4, 238, 257
transport and 33, 34, 98, 102,
   131–43, 175, 187
UK enshrines net zero emissions
   target into law 258
UK, Scottish and Welsh parliaments
   pass motions declaring a climate
   emergency 258
young people and 27, 162–3, 168,
   169, 170, 172, 258, 261, 273
Clinton, Hillary 48, 53, 260
Coalition government, UK (2010–15)
   10, 55, 159, 165, 198
codetermination 202–4
colleague advisory council 197
collective bargaining 203, 229, 230,
   234
community banks 255–6
Community Jobs Compact 216
community organising 212–23
   Alinsky: *Rules for Radicals* and
      213, 216, 220, 269
   BrightHouse campaign 219–21
   Citizens Cymru Wales and 215–16,
      222
   Citizens UK and 212–13, 218, 219,
      222, 268
   Community Jobs Compact 216
   EM attends course on 212–17
   incremental versus transformational
      change and 222–3, 264, 268
   living wage campaigns 212, 216,
      218–19, 221, 222–3, 268

Melian Dialogue and 217–18
Nando's, campaign for halal branch
   in Cardiff 215–16
shame, power in 219
social movements and 264, 267,
   268–9
community wealth building 248–56
   anchor institutions 251–3, 255, 256
   cooperatives and 251, 252, 255,
      256
   defined 251
   economic mindset, fosters new 255
   inequality, tackles 253
   Islington Council approach to 256
   living wage and 250–1, 252
   low-price contracts, knock-on costs
      of 254
   redirection of funds in generic
      investments in global financial
      system to funding local schemes
      250–3
   national scale, principles of com-
      munity applied on a 256
   network of community wealth
      builders, Preston inspires 255–6
   objections to 253–5
   Preston City Council and 248–53,
      254, 255, 256, 268–9, 273
   procurement and 249–50, 252
   Wirral Council community bank
      255–6
Companies Act (2006), UK, Section
   172 77–9
Competition and Markets Authority
   (CMA) 123–4, 127, 128, 129
   Digital Market Unit proposal 128
Comprehensive Anti-Apartheid Act,
   US (1986) 244
Conservative Party 9, 38, 41, 44,
   66–7, 133, 166, 168, 180, 203,
   219, 258, 263
consumer welfare 126–7
Cook (B Corp) 71
Co-operative Group 200
cooperatives 31, 79, 199–201, 203,
   251, 252, 255, 256
Copenhagen climate summit (2009)
   22–4, 25, 29, 239, 257
Corbyn, Jeremy 219

Corporate Governance Code 77
Cottam, Hilary: *Radical Help* 191–3
council housing 15, 17, 38–9, 40, 41, 42, 43, 187, 188
Council of Five Hundred, ancient Athens 153–4
Covid-19 pandemic 4–5, 59, 81, 201, 202, 206
  best and worst in society exposed by 4–5, 271
  big change, case for and 9–10
  Big Tech and 121–2
  business response to 73, 81
  care sector and 99, 101, 106, 108, 228
  climate change and 30
  family and gender roles and 61, 62
  flexible working and 116–17
  furlough scheme 54
  GDP and 90
  housing and 37
  inequality and 4–6, 8, 54, 271
  poverty and 47
  PPE equipment and 228
  public finances and 57
  regional inequality and 178
  safety at work and 201–2
  social contract and 18, 30
  transport and 33, 142–3
  unions and 228
  welfare system, and 47–8
  working hours and 116–17
Cox, Jonathan 215
Credit Agricole 246
Crick, Bernard 170
cycling 43, 131–43
  cycle lanes 133, 135, 138, 140, 141
  EM and 132–4
Czernohorszky, Jürgen 35

Dallas (television series) 151
Daly, Herman 92
Darling, Alistair 218
data, sale/value of 123–6, 129, 130
Davidson, Ruth 166, 168
Davis, Shari 169
deliberative democracy 150–61
  climate change and 157–8, 159–60
  Deliberation Day proposal 160
  deliberative polling 151–2

  drawbacks of/legitimacy of decisions 157–9, 160
  French climate assembly 157–8
  House of Lords reform and 159
  Mongolian constitution and 152, 156, 157
  origins of 151–5, 156, 160
  renewable energy in Texas and 151–2
  representative democracy and 154–8
  same-sex marriage legalisation in Ireland and 150–1, 155, 156–7
  social care and 158–9
  sortition and 153–4 *see also* citizens' assemblies
'delivery', Labour government fondness for term 189
democracy 28, 119, 124, 127, 145–206
  business/workplace, democratizing 196–206 *see also* workplace
  citizens' assemblies/deliberative democracy 150–61 *see also* citizens' assemblies *and* deliberative democracy
  dissatisfaction with 147–8
  fight for representative 147
  local communities, empowering 184–95 *see also* local communities, empowering
  local politics/devolution and 173–83 *see also* devolution
  promise of 147
  rebooting 147–206
  'take back control' political slogan 148–9, 194–5, 206
  young people and 162–72 *see also* young people
Democratic Party, US 29, 162–3, 236, 260, 261
Denmark 32, 67, 93, 102, 136, 148, 202, 212
Department of Defense, US 80
deregulation of finance (1980s) 74
devolution 173–83, 194, 209
  arguments against 178–9
  centralised nature of UK and 173–4, 178–9

English regions, power-sharing
between central government and
173–80, 181–3
House of Lords and 182
innovation and 174–7
mayors and 173–4, 175–6, 179,
181–2, 183
municipal authorities and 179–80
national, Labour government introduces 180–2
NHS and 180
public transport, lack of local authority over 174–6
regional inequalities and 177–9
tax and revenue raising powers 175,
176, 180–2
tradition of regional power, UK and
178–9
Di-Aping, Lumumba 23
digital advertising 122, 124–5
distributed knowledge 186–8, 190,
205
divestment 236–47, 261, 265, 269
banks and 240, 246
broad coalition, building a 243, 265
carbon bubble and 239, 240, 244,
247
Climate Action 100+ 243
critics of/problems with 241–5
fossil fuel companies climate risks,
push for disclosure of 244
green transition financed with
divested funds 246–7
insurance companies and 245–6
lobbying and 241
McKibben and 238–9
Norwegian sovereign wealth fund
and 243
Ørsted and 239–40
policymakers, impact on 243–4
Rockefeller Family Fund and 240
Royal Dutch Shell and 243
shareholder engagement and 243
'social licence' of fossil fuel companies, attacking 240–1
South African apartheid regime and
240, 242
Swarthmore College, Pennsylvania
and growth of 237–8

three levels of political change and
241, 242–3
dividend pay-outs to shareholders 74,
78–9
Divine Chocolate 71
Doncaster, EM's constituency in
Brexit and 4
buses in 174–5
floods in 27, 184–6, 187, 188
Labour Party in 219
mining in 16
Dunkirk, France, public transport in
175, 176
Dunleavy, Michael J. 45
Durrant, Abdul 218

East Ayrshire Council 193
e-book prices 122, 125
economics, market *see* market economics
education
childcare and 105–6
citizenship education 170–1
devolution and 180, 182, 190
Education Maintenance Allowance
(EMA) 165
purpose of 171–2
schools *see* schools
see also young people
electric cars 33, 34, 98, 135–6
Ella (single parent) 192
employee ownership trust (EOT) 79,
196–8, 199, 200–1
Equal Pay Act (1970) 21
Etsy 75
European Union (EU) 4, 122–3, 127,
130, 148
Extinction Rebellion 257–9, 264–6

Facebook 133
corporate lobbying 125
market dominance 119–21, 122,
123, 124, 125, 126, 127, 128,
129
social movements and 259, 260
takeovers of smaller firms 122, 128
Factory Acts, UK
(1850) 109–10
(1874) 110

families, gender equality and 59–69
  Covid-19 pandemic and 59, 61, 62
  flexible working 62, 66
  gender pay gap 62–3, 64
  Iceland and 59–60, 65, 67, 69
  Nordic countries' approach to
    59–60, 64–6, 67–8, 69
  Palme 'The Emancipation of Man'
    61, 64, 69
  parental leave 20, 60–9, 104, 229
  political representation, equal 66–7
  ranking of family-friendly policies,
    UNICEF 66
  second shift (unpaid work in the
    home) 65
Federation of Small Businesses 252
Feinstein, Dianne 162–3, 172, 261
Fight for $15 movement, US 224–6, 227,
  230–1, 232, 234, 251, 261, 269, 273
Financial Conduct Authority (FCA)
  220–1
financial crisis, global (2007–8) 3, 4,
  6, 18, 19, 28, 29, 74, 202, 239, 249
Finland 51, 52, 67, 69, 93, 112–13,
  116, 118, 171, 194, 272
Firth, Dan 219
Fishkin, James 151–3, 156, 160
  'The Case For a National Caucus'
    152–3
'fissured' workplace 226–7, 231, 232
flexible and humble government/
  policymaking ('garden mind' approach) 184–95
flexible working 62, 66, 112, 112–18,
  202
Floyd, George 259
foodbanks 19, 47, 185
fossil fuels 31, 80, 86, 92, 265
  divestment campaigns and 169,
    236–47, 261
  economy 26–7, 271
four-day week 112, 114–16
Four Seasons 107
freedom dividend 48–54, 57
France
  citizen climate assembly in 157–8
  cooperative movement in 200
  gilets jaunes (yellow vests) protests
    157

local power in 177
  public transport in 175, 176
  worker representation in 202
Friedman, Milton 48, 70–1, 72, 73,
  74–5, 76, 81
Friendster 121
furlough scheme 54

'garden mind' (humble and flexible
  government) 184–95
Garza, Alicia 259, 265, 267, 268
Gateshead Council 193
GDP *see* gross domestic product
  (GDP)
Gender Equality Index 60
gender pay gap 62–4 *see also* women
general elections, UK
  (2010) 165, 218
  (2015) 1, 11, 163–4
  (2019) 4, 66–7, 163, 164
  voter turnout 147–8, 163–4, 165,
    166–7
  voting age and 165–70
Germany 78, 80, 114, 136, 166,
  176–7, 178, 182, 200, 202
Gibson, Larry 237
gig economy 125, 189, 226–7, 231–2
gilets jaunes (yellow vests) protests
  157
Gini coefficient 56
Glencore 243
GMB union 228, 231, 232
go big, why we need to 3–12
Goldman Sachs 245
Goldsmith Street development, Norwich 42, 43–4
Good Friday agreement (1998) 180
Google
  corporate lobbying 125
  Maps 128
  market dominance 120, 121, 122–5,
    126, 127, 128
  Search 124, 126, 128
  Shopping 122–3, 128
  takeovers of smaller firms 128
Gorz, André 52
Goss, Sue 191
Gove, Michael 258
GPS technology 80

Graf, Arnie 213–14, 217, 219
Gramsci, Antonio 6
Great Depression 28, 90
Greater London Council 174
Great Manure Crisis 131
greenhouse gas emissions 11, 31, 243, 244, 246, 247, 257, 258–9 *see also* carbon emissions
Green, Joe 121, 129
Green New Deal 28–9, 34, 43, 162–3, 209
green transition, divestment and 246–7
Greggs 49
Grenfell Tower disaster (2017) 41
gross domestic product (GDP) 89–97, 103, 200, 255
  damage to society of measuring success with 90
  dashboard of success, devising an alternative 95–7
  decision-making/government policy and 92–3
  Human Development Index and 93
  Kennedy on inadequacies of 89–90, 91
  partial and misleading nature of measurement 90–2
  'wellbeing' measurements 93–6, 97
  World Happiness Report and 93
Grosvenor 248
G77 bloc of developing countries 23
Gunn-Wright, Rhiana 29–30

Hagan, Pat 184–5, 186, 187, 273
Haldane, Andy 77
Han, Hahrie 266, 267
heating, home 28, 30, 31, 189
Henley Business School 115–16
Henry, Mary Kay 224, 226, 227
Hermes 231–2
Hidalgo, Anne 141–2
'hipster anti-trust' movement 120
House of Lords 159, 171, 182
housing 35–44
  affordable homes 18, 19, 35, 38, 39, 40, 42, 86, 169
  car use and 142
  council housing 15, 17, 38–9, 40, 41, 42, 43, 187, 188

  crisis in UK 25, 35, 36, 38
  divestment and 169
  Goldsmith Street development 42, 43–4
  Green New Deal and 43
  housing associations 36, 39, 40, 41, 43, 250
  housing benefit 37, 38, 39, 43, 254
  Housing Bill (1949) 43
  market economics and 86
  mixed communities, Bevan's vision of 43–4
  poverty and 47
  private sector and 35–40
  renting costs 35–6, 37, 38, 39, 40, 42
  Right to Buy scheme 38–9
  Shelter commission on 41–3, 44
  social contract and 15, 16, 36, 44
  social housing 20, 36–9, 40–2, 44, 176
  town planners and 43
  Vienna and 35–6, 38, 40, 44
Howe, Sophie 94

Iceland 67, 94
  parental leave in 60, 65, 69
  women strike demanding gender equality (1975) 59–60, 67, 261, 272
  World Happiness Report and 93
income inequality 52, 56, 95–6, 228
incremental change, transformational change and 10, 11, 222–3, 264, 268
Independent Workers' Union of Great Britain (IWGB) 231
Industrial Areas Foundation 213
industrial policy/strategy 32, 79–81, 100–2
Industrial Strategy Challenge fund 102
inequality 2, 3, 5, 6, 7, 8, 17, 18, 21, 271, 272
  Big Tech and *see* technology
  climate and 25, 27, 28, 30, 33, 34
  community wealth building and 253
  democracy and 158, 160

financial crisis (2007–8) and 18
freedom dividend and 47, 52, 54,
  56–7, 58
GDP and 90, 94, 95–6
gender and 59–69, 96, 104, 151,
  209, 261, 263–4
Gini coefficient measurement of 56
housing and 36, 42
New Labour and 17
power and 148
racial *see* race
regional 18, 173–83
social mobility and 18–19, 99, 251
unions and 228–9, 230, 235
insecurity, housing and employment
  16, 17, 18, 19–20, 271
Instagram 122
Insure our Future 245–6
Intergovernmental Panel on Climate
  Change (IPCC) 24
International Monetary Fund (IMF)
  168, 228, 229
internet 80, 120, 126
iPhone 80
Ireland
  citizens assembly and same-sex
    marriage legalisation in (2015)
    150–1, 155, 156, 157
  general election (2011) 155
Islington Council 256

Jakobsdóttir, Katrín 94, 101–2
Japan 78, 116, 134
Jay, Douglas 148, 189–90
Jefferson, Thomas 154–5
jobs 98–108
  automation and 6, 50
  childcare 99–100, 104–6
  climate change and 27, 28, 31–2, 34
  Community Jobs Compact 216
  community wealth building and
    248, 252, 255
  furlough scheme 54
  GDP and 103
  hierarchy of work and 104
  industrial policy and 100–3
  key workers 4–5, 99
  NHS and 104
  parental leave and *see* parental leave

regional inequalities and 177
social care 98–104, 106–8
social contract and 15–16, 18, 19,
  20
technology and 120
transport and 132
unions and *see* unions
wages and *see* wages
workplace and *see* workplace
zero-hours contracts 73, 99,
  111–12, 117
John Lewis Partnership 200, 249
Joseph Rowntree Foundation 47
JP Morgan Chase 246

Kayford Mountain, US 237
Kelly, Gavin 55
Kelly, Katie 193
Kennedy, Robert Fitzgerald 89, 91
key workers 4–5, 99
KFC 224
Khan, Lina 119
  'Amazon's Antitrust Paradox'
    119–20, 126, 127
Khan, Sadiq 173
King, Martin Luther 34, 48, 263,
  264
Kingsnorth coal-fired power station
  261–2
Kuznets, Simon 90

Labour Party 1, 9
  Child Trust Fund and 55–7
  citizenship education and 170
  community organising and 214,
    219–21
  'delivery', Labour government fond-
    ness for term 189
  devolution, introduces national
    180–2
  Doncaster North constituency, EM's
    214, 219–21
  House of Lords reform and 159
  housing and 38, 43, 44
  living wage and 218
  manifesto (1997) 159
  manifesto (2010) 218
  nationalises key industries (1945–50)
    203

New Labour 17, 55–7, 77, 159, 170, 189, 190–1, 204, 218
  targets and accountability, regime of 189, 190–1
  social contract and 17
  worker representation and 170, 204
Lambeth Council 169
Lancashire County Council 250–1
Langenhoff, Simone 137–8
Langenhoff, Vic 138
Lawrence, Stephen 260
LendLease 248
LGBT rights 9, 16, 17, 169, 263, 273
living wage 73, 210
  B Corp and 70, 71, 75
  care sector and 98, 99, 106–7
  community organising and 212, 216, 218–19, 221, 222–3, 268
  community wealth building and 250, 252–3, 255
  parental leave and 63
  trade unions and 231
Living Wage Foundation 250
Lloyd, Geoff 1, 133
lobbying 125, 140, 169, 227, 241
local communities, empowering 184–95
  Big Society concept and 188–9
  distributed knowledge and 186–8, 190, 205
  Doncaster floods as example of flexible relationship between citizens and state 184–8
  'garden mind' approach (humble and flexible government/policy-making) 191–5
  'machine mind' approach (state bureaucracy techniques borrowed from industry) 188–90
  New Labour government and 189, 190–1
Local Government Act (1988) 263
local mutual aid groups 5
local politics, empowering *see* devolution
London County Council 43, 179
London mayoralty 173, 180, 181
Lord, Peter 196–7
Lores, Miguel Anxo Fernández 139

low-price contracts, knock-on costs of 254

'machine mind' (state bureaucracy techniques borrowed from industry) 188–90
Macron, Emmanuel 157–8
Major, John 19
Manchester, Greater
  Bee Network 140–1
  cooperatives in 31
  Covid-19 and 173, 181
  pension fund diverts £50 million to invest in local small businesses 253
Marçal, Katrine 103
Marcha Negra (Black March), Spain (2012) 32
Marcora Law, Italy (1985) 200–1
market economics 3, 6, 7, 12, 67, 73, 80, 83–143, 188, 209, 222, 234, 271, 272
  Big Tech dominance/anti-trust and 119–30 *see also* technology
  commodities, treating people as 87
  defined 85
  'embedded' in social and democratic choices, need for markets to be 87
  Friedman model of 70–1, 72–3, 74–5, 76, 79, 81
  gross national product (GDP) and measuring performance of 89–97, 103
  jobs and 98–108 *see also* jobs
  market failures 86–7, 123
  Thatcher and 85, 87–8
  transport/public space and 131–43 *see also* transport/public space
  trickle-down economics 7, 17, 178, 271
  wellbeing measurements and change in view of 93–7
  working hours and 109–18 *see also* working hours
  see also business
Marks & Spencer 249
Marshall Islands 257
Martin, Trayvon 259

Mayer, Colin 71
mayors 2, 139, 140–1, 169, 170,
    173–4, 175–6, 179, 180–1, 182,
    221, 266
May, Theresa 204, 205
Mazzucato, Mariana 80
McDonald's 224, 226, 230
McKibben, Bill 238–9, 262
Mead, Natasha 185, 186
means testing 49, 50, 53, 54
Melbourne, Australia 141–2
Melian Dialogue 217–19
metro mayors 175–6, 180–1
Metropolitan Police 260
Microsoft 116, 120, 121, 128
Miliband, Daniel 111, 258
Miliband, Justine 62
Miliband, Sam 62, 111
Miller, Shane 185, 187
minimum wage 9, 210
    care sector and 98, 99
    community organising and 218,
        219
    community wealth building and
        252, 254
    New Labour government and 17
    opposition to 273
    trade unions and 224, 225, 227,
        230, 231, 232, 234
    working hours and 115
mining 16–17, 32, 70, 237
Minneapolis City Council 259–60
Mondragon 200
Mongolia 150, 152, 156, 157
monopolies 86, 119, 120, 122, 123,
    125, 126, 127, 130
mountain top removal (MTR) mining
    237
municipal authorities, emergence of
    179–80
Musk, Elon 48, 80

Nando's, Cardiff 215–17, 222
National Rifle Association (NRA)
    266–7
National Science Foundation 80
nationalisation programme, Labour
    government (1945–50) 203
neoliberal policies 233

net zero greenhouse gas emissions
    target 11, 243, 244, 246, 247,
    257, 258–9
Netherlands 136, 137–8, 140, 202
network effects 125–6, 129
New Deal, US 28–9, 30, 272
New Labour 17, 55–6, 77, 159, 170,
    189, 190–1, 204, 218
New Local 193
news publishers 124–5
New Zealand
    Bolger report/labour rights in
        232–3, 234, 272
    'wellbeing' budget 94, 97
NHS 25, 46, 73, 188, 250, 273
    anchor institutions and 256
    community activity/local power
        inspires creation of 179
    creation of 8, 10, 13, 15, 43, 46, 179
    devolution of powers over 180
    means testing and 54
    social care and 104, 106
Nicoya, Costa Rica 134
Nightingale, Jane 185
Nixon, Richard 48, 236
Nordic nations 59–69, 102, 104–5 *see
    also individual nation name*
North Ayrshire, Scotland, youth vot-
    ing on youth projects in 169–70
North Sea oil revenues 32, 57
Norway 67, 93, 148, 166, 202
    sovereign wealth fund 57, 243

Obama, Barack 1, 48, 213
Ocasio-Cortez, Alexandria 29
Occupy movement 263–4
Office of National Statistics: wellbeing
    measurements 94–5
Okinawa, Japan 134
100–80-100 rule (working hours) 115
O'Neill, Lord Jim 41
Organisation of Economic Co-oper-
    ation and Development (OECD)
    177
    'In It Together; why less inequality
        benefits us all' report 229, 233
Ørsted 239–40, 243
Osborne, George 11, 91, 101
outsourcing 194, 226, 231, 252

Overton window 10–11, 211, 242, 259
overwork, crisis of 111–12
Owen, Robert 110

Paine, Thomas: *Agrarian Justice* 45, 46–7, 54–5
Palme, Olof: 'The Emancipation of Man' 61, 64, 69
Panitch, Leo 273–4
parental leave 20, 60–9, 104, 229
Paris Climate Accord (2015) 11, 24, 26, 246, 257
Paris, France: *ville du quart d'heure* (fifteen-minute city) 141, 142
Parks, Rosa 262
participatory budgeting 169
Patagonia 70–1
patient capital 74, 79, 80
payday loans 220–1
Peabody Coal 245
Pence, Mike 76
pensions 15, 20, 31, 54, 56, 72, 73, 165, 229, 246, 247
   pension funds 74, 240, 247, 250, 253, 256, 269
Pericles 153–4
Permanent Fund Dividend (PFD), Alaska 45–6, 48, 51, 52, 53, 57, 272
'permission slip' approach 182
Perpetual Guardian 112, 115
Perry, Claire 258
Perry, James 71
Polanyi, Karl: *The Great Transformation* 85, 87–8
political change, three levels of 241, 242–3
political representation, equal 66–7
Pontevedra, Spain 139–40
Postlethwaite, Pete 262
poverty 17, 19, 47, 48, 49, 50, 53, 72, 90, 94, 96, 169, 178, 202, 218, 251, 254
   'poverty trap' 49
'Power from the People' (article, 2015) 228–9
'predict and provide', principle of 139
Preston City Council 248–53, 254, 255, 256, 268–9, 273 *see also* community wealth building

privatisation 10, 17, 190
probation services, privatisation of 190
procurement 107, 249–56
productivity 78, 90, 112–16, 118, 177, 203, 233
'professional knows best' thinking 189–90
protectionism 254–5
public transport 28, 33, 34, 43, 132, 133, 135, 136, 141, 174–6, 182, 204, 248, 249, 251, 256, 262–3, 272 *see also* transport

race 16, 21
   air pollution and 135
   Black Lives Matter 259–61, 265, 267, 268, 269
   Bristol bus boycott (1963) 262–3
   care work and 104
   Civil Rights movement, US 48, 260, 267
   Macpherson report (1999) 260
   Race Relations Act (1965) 263
   school exclusions and 169
   social contract and 21
   wealth gap and 56
Rainforest Action Network 246
Raworth, Kate: *Doughnut Economics* 96
Reagan, Ronald 72
Reasons to be Cheerful podcast 1–3, 9, 55
regional inequalities 18, 173–83 *see also* devolution
renewable energy 31–2, 57, 79, 80, 150, 151–2, 239
renting costs 35–6, 37, 38, 39, 40, 42
Republican Party, US 45, 76, 261, 267
Resolution Foundation 91
Retrofit Get In 31
Reuben, Chika 98–9, 228
Richer, Julian 197
Richer Sounds 197
Right to Buy scheme 39
Riverford Organic 197
Robertson, Grant 94
Rochdale Equitable Pioneers Society 199
Rockefeller Family Fund 240

Roosevelt, Franklin Delano (FDR)
  28–9, 30, 31, 127, 272
Royal Dutch Shell 243, 245, 257
Royal Mail 10, 204
Rubio, Marco 76

Saint Monday 110
Sandel, Michael 86
Sardinia 134
Sarkozy, Nicolas 93, 95
schools 8, 37
  childcare and 105–6
  citizenship education 170–1
  climate strikes 168, 258, 273
  Covid-19 and 61, 73
  freedom dividend and 51–2
  local politics and 176, 179
  state bureaucracy and 187–8, 191,
    192
  transport and 137–8, 142
  voting age and 168, 169, 170–1
Scotland 32, 42, 234, 256
  devolution 180, 181, 182, 193
  independence referendum (2014)
    166, 168
  Scottish Parliament 42, 166, 180, 258
  social care and 106
  young people in 169–70
Scottish Conservatives 166
second shift (unpaid work in the
  home) 65
Second World War (1939–45) 8, 10,
  13, 15, 38, 43, 87, 104, 110, 111,
  189
Section 28, Local Government Act
  (1988) 263
sectoral bargaining 232–4
self-employment 47, 226–7, 234
Sen, Amartya 93
Service Employees International Union (SEIU) 224, 225–6, 227
Seville, Spain 139, 140
share buybacks 74
shareholder
  dividend pay-outs to 74, 78–9
  engagement 242, 243
  value 71–9, 114, 198, 203, 204,
    239, 255
Shelter 41–3, 44

short-termism 203
Singapore 37
Singh-Watson, Guy 197
Siri 80
six-hour working day 116
Smith, Adam 85
  The Wealth of Nations 103
social care 20, 98–104, 106–8, 158–9,
  193, 228, 234
social contract 11–12, 15–81, 105,
  148, 164, 179, 205, 209
  Brexit and 19
  broken contract, sense of 18–19
  business and 70–81 *see also* busi-
    ness
  climate change and 22–34 *see also*
    climate change
  Covid-19 pandemic and 18
  defined 11, 15
  dismantling of, post-war 16–17, 19
  families and 59–69 *see also* families
  financial crisis (2007–8) and 18, 19
  housing and 35–44 *see also* housing
  inequality and 18–19, 21
  minimum standard of living, guar-
    anteed 19–20
  New Labour and 17–18
  origins of 15–16
  'power to create' and 20
  redrawing 19–21
  risk protection and 20–1
  second post-war social contract
    16–19
  social inheritance and 45–58 *see*
    also social inheritance
  stake in society/social solidarity and
    15, 16, 19, 21, 46, 72
social housing 20, 36–9, 40–2, 44,
  176
social infrastructure 42, 101–2
social inheritance 45–58
  Alaska Permanent Fund Dividend
    (PFD) 45–6, 48, 51, 52, 53, 57
  annual income versus one-off lump
    sum 46–58
  Child Trust Fund 55–7, 58
  destitution in UK and 47–8
  freedom dividend/universal basic
    income (UBI) 48–54, 57

furlough scheme 54
Norway sovereign wealth fund 57
Paine and concept of 45, 46–7,
  54–5
welfare benefits system and 47–8,
  49–50, 53–4, 57
'social licence' 240–1
Social Mobility Commission 99
social movements 138, 257–69
  Black Lives Matter 259–61, 265,
    267, 268, 269
  breadth of support, importance of
    265–7
  Bristol bus boycott (1963) 262–3
  as 'bulldozer for reshaping the
    zeitgeist' 262
  Civil Rights movement, US 48, 260,
    267
  climate school strikes 168, 258, 273
  community organising and 264,
    267, 268–9
  Extinction Rebellion 257–9, 264–6
  Feinstein, young climate activists
    meet 251
  Fight for $15 movement 224–6,
    227, 230–1, 232, 234, 251, 261,
    269, 273
  fossil fuel divestment campaigns
    and 251
  goals, importance of clear 263–4
  Icelandic women strikers demand
    gender equality 59–60, 67, 261,
    272
  National Rifle Association (NRA)
    266–7
  Occupy movement 263–4
  Overton window and 257–8
  Postlethwaite ambushes EM over
    Kingsnorth coal-fired power sta-
    tion 261–2
  Section 28, Stonewall and 263
  social media and 264, 267–8
  Stop Der Kindermoord 137–8, 261
  3.5 per cent rule (numbers of people
    mobilised and effectiveness of)
    264–5
  working week, nineteenth-century
    trade unionists fight for shorter
    109–12, 261

social security *see* welfare benefits
Sókn trade union 59
solar panels 79, 98, 169
sortition 153–4
South Africa, apartheid regime in 240,
  242, 244
Sproxton, David 196–7
Stephenson, Paul 262–3, 272
Stern, Todd 24
Stonewall 263
Stop de Kindermoord (Stop the Child
  Murders) 137–8, 261
surveillance capitalism 123–4
Swarthmore College, Pennsylvania
  237–8
Sweden 64, 65, 67, 102, 104–5, 116,
  175, 176, 202

'take back control' political slogan
  148, 194–5
takeovers, anti-competitive 122,
  128–9
Tallinn, Estonia 175, 176
targets and accountability, New Labour regime of 190–1
Tawney, R. H. 64
tax credits 17, 99, 188, 218
taxes 17, 43, 49, 79, 157, 158–9, 167,
  175, 176, 177, 180, 181, 182,
  190, 193, 198, 263
Taylor review (2017) 201, 205
technology 2, 6, 20, 48, 80, 90, 110,
  113, 118, 119–30, 209, 226, 228,
  246–7, 251
  Big Tech concentration of power
    119–23
  Competition and Markets Author-
    ity (CMA) and 123–4, 127, 128,
    129
  consumer welfare and 126–7
  Covid crisis and 120, 121–2
  digital advertising spending 122,
    124–5
  e-book prices 122, 125
  as force for good 121
  government failure to tackle Big
    Tech concentration of power
    126–7
  'hipster anti-trust' movement and 120

inequality and 121–2
Khan 'Amazon's Antitrust Paradox' treatise 119–20, 126, 127
lobbying and 125
monopolies and 119, 120, 122, 123, 125, 126, 127, 130
network effects and the value of data 125–6, 129
news publishers and 124–5
surveillance capitalism business model 123–4
switching platforms 130
takeovers within sector 122, 128–9
trust busting and 127–8
utilities, regulating tech companies as 130
Tesla 80
Texas, renewable energy in 151–2
Thatcher, Margaret 10, 17, 38–9, 67, 72, 85, 87–8, 174, 204, 263
350.org 240
3.5 per cent rule (social movement campaign effectiveness ratio) 264–5
This Is an Uprising (Mark and Paul Engler) 264, 265
Thucydides 217
Thunberg, Greta 168, 258
Titmuss, Richard 53–4
town planners 43
trade unions 9, 16, 17, 59, 110, 113–14, 116–17, 203, 204, 210–11, 224–35, 261
  collective bargaining 203, 229, 230, 234
  economic growth and 229–30, 233
  Fight for $15 movement and 224–6, 227, 230–1, 232, 234, 269
  'fissured' workplace and 226–7, 230–2
  future of 230
  gig economy, uses mechanisms of state to counter isolation of 230–2
  importance of 227–30
  inequality and 228–9, 233
  New Zealand and 232–3, 234
  Organisation of Economic Co-operation and Development

(OECD) 'In It Together; why less inequality benefits us all' report and 229
  pay and conditions for members, boosts 229
  'Power from the People' article (2015) and 228–9
  reach beyond membership/WorkerTech 231–2
  sectoral bargaining 232–4
  Service Employees International Union (SEIU) overturns traditional US trade union model 224, 225–6, 227
  wage boards and 233–4
  WorkSmart app, Trade Union Congress 231
Trans-Alaska Pipeline 46
transport/public space 131–43, 174–5, 251, 256, 262–3, 272
  air pollution 28, 135, 175
  Bee Network, Greater Manchester 140–1
  blue zones and 134
  Buchanan Report (1963) 137
  bus services 33, 136, 174–6, 182, 204, 248, 249, 251, 256, 262–3, 272
  car use *see* cars
  climate change and 33, 34, 98, 102, 131–43, 175, 187
  Covid crisis and 141–2
  cycling *see* cycling
  free public transport networks 174–5
  Great Manure Crisis 131
  inactivity and 134
  Melbourne twenty-minute city initiative 141–2
  Paris *ville du quart d'heure* (fifteen-minute city) initiative 141, 142
  Pontevedra pedestrianisation 139–40
  'predict and provide', principle of 139
  public transport 28, 33, 34, 43, 132, 133, 135, 136, 141, 174–6, 182, 204, 248, 249, 251, 256, 262–3, 272
  Seville cycle lanes 139, 140
  walking *see* walking

trickle-down economics 7, 17, 178, 271

Trump, Donald 1, 6–7, 26, 70, 76, 91

trust busting 127–8

Twitter 2, 29, 133

2°C climate warming target 22–4, 238

Uber 125, 226–7, 231, 232

UK Climate Assembly 160–1, 170

United Nations (UN)
  Copenhagen climate summit (2009) 22–4, 25, 29, 239, 257
  Human Development Index 93
  Paris Climate Accord (2015) 11, 24, 26, 246, 257
  World Happiness Report 93

United Voices of the World (UVW) 231

universal basic income (UBI) 48–54, 57

Universal Credit 47, 49–50, 54, 188, 253, 254

University of Central Lancashire 250

University of London 231

Vergriete, Patrice 175

Victoria Derbyshire programme, BBC 220–1

Vienna, Austria 35–6, 38, 40, 44

Viney, Amelia 168–9

voting
  age/votes at sixteen 165–71, 181, 272
  turnout 147, 148, 158, 163–7, 202

wages 3, 4, 5, 25, 32, 39, 47, 54, 55, 56, 73, 86, 91, 92, 114, 115, 116, 198, 199, 206, 248, 251, 253
  living *see* living wage
  minimum *see* minimum wage
  wage boards 233–4
  working hours and 114, 115, 116

Waldron, Pamela 224

Wales 94, 166, 182, 215, 216, 234
  community wealth building in 256
  devolution of political power to 166, 180, 181, 182, 258
  Wellbeing of Future Generations Act (2015) 94

Welsh Parliament 166, 258

walking 43, 134, 135, 136, 139, 140, 141, 142, 143, 175, 215

Warsi, Baroness Sayeeda 41

Waze 122

wealth gap 56

welfare-state 8, 20, 47–9, 179

Westerberg, Bengt 64–5

White, Sam 68

Whole Foods 122

Wikipedia 186–7

William Booth Salvation Army training centre, London 212–13, 214–15

Wilson, Harold 204

wind energy 31–2, 34, 57, 79, 151, 239, 246

Wirral Council 255–6

women
  care work and 103–4
  Covid-19 pandemic and 59
  employment discrimination 8, 15–16
  family rights, gender equality and 59–69
  flexible working and 62
  GDP and 92
  Gender Equality Index 60
  gender pay gap 62–3, 64
  Icelandic women strike demanding gender equality (1975) 59–60, 67, 261, 272
  New Labour and 17
  parental leave and 20, 60–9, 104, 229
  second shift (unpaid work in the home) 65, 92
  social contract and 21
  voting rights 199

Wood, Pat 151–2

WorkerTech 231–2

working hours 109–18
  Covid-19 pandemic and 116–17
  crisis of overwork 111–12
  EM and 111
  Factory Act (1850) 109–10
  Factory Act (1874) 110
  Finland and 112–13, 116, 118
  flexible working 62, 66, 112, 112–18, 202
  four-day week 112, 114–16